A Cultural History
of the Chinese Language

ALSO BY SHARRON GU

Language and Culture in the Growth of Imperialism
(McFarland, 2012)

A Cultural History of the Chinese Language

SHARRON GU

McFarland & Company, Inc., Publishers
Jefferson, North Carolina, and London

LIBRARY OF CONGRESS CATALOGUING-IN-PUBLICATION DATA

Gu, Sharron.
    A cultural history of the Chinese language / Sharron Gu.
        p.   cm.
    Includes bibliographical references and index.

    ISBN 978-0-7864-6649-8
    softcover : acid free paper ∞

    1. Chinese language — History.   2. Language and culture —
China.   I. Title.
    PL1075.G44 2012
    495.1'09 — dc23   2011047290

BRITISH LIBRARY CATALOGUING DATA ARE AVAILABLE

On the cover: Portrait of Li Qingzhao (Palace Museum, Beijing)

Manufactured in the United States of America

McFarland & Company, Inc., Publishers
  Box 611, Jefferson, North Carolina 28640
  www.mcfarlandpub.com

Table of Contents

Preface

This book is a general history of the Chinese language from the ancient to early modern period. It is written in the familiar terms of English speakers. It attempts to show that the way in which Chinese literature grew and reacted to its music and visual expression is essentially the same as contemporary English and other Western languages. The only difference is timing. The longer a language lives, the richer, more diverse and refined it becomes. What happened to Chinese will take place in younger languages in their own time and in their unique and native forms.

An understanding of the history of Chinese language and its impact upon the Chinese mind can be helpful for the students of Western culture because it illustrates an experience beyond the horizon of contemporary speakers of Western languages whose literatures have evolved for only a few hundred years. One might see a future of a mature literary language that is overly inflated with law, and a political system that is maintained by increasingly sophisticated media rhetoric. Western scholars of social science and humanities might also benefit from this study. Within Chinese cultural history, they can find explanations for many major issues that have been haunting historians and cultural theorists for decades. How does language relate to worldview? What would happen to law after its language loses absolute boundary and binding power? How do music, visual, and theatrical images influence literature, especially a mature literature? How does an established language and ideology penetrate and cultivate the collective consciousness and unconsciousness by creating endless repetition of seemingly varied images and tones?

This historic revision provides an alternative to the linguistic history that is constructed by established cultural theories and in linguistic jargons such as semantic system, universal grammar, phonology, or morphology. These "scientific" theories ignore or deny the restrictions of their own language. To play god in the field of cultural studies is an attempt to counteract gravity

1

by pulling one's hair or fly as a bird soaring, swooping, and changing direction instinctively. Contemporary cultural theories have produced as little penetrating or valid worldview as the bold claim of a teenager who announces that he knows everything about life before he has lived it. The only way to fly beyond the limitation of one's own language is to study the history of other (preferably older) cultures.

This book traces the emergence of Chinese language from its concrete interaction with various sub-verbal idioms, music, theatre, and visual imageries, and investigates how these idioms contributed to particular literary repertoire at a given time. It sees no fixed boundaries and barriers between the variety of cultural expressions that interacted with literature differently according to the maturity of literary language. Without a universal or psychological shape, the meanings and connotations of literary language always fluctuate and transform with the flow of communication in various idioms at various times.

Focusing on diversity and non-linear development, this history sees the interaction and exchange among various forms of expression (tones, images, words, and gestures) as the main dynamic of Chinese cultural development. Its language grew and transformed through an accumulation of sub-literary, literary, and post-literary expression. Chinese imagination and reasoning were constantly inspired by and evolved through the expansion of its literary repertoire.

I would like to express my deepest gratitude to my editor, Norman Christie, who has been supporting my research and writing for the past ten years. His inspiration and insight have contributed to the form and content of this work. His poetic instinct and commitment to correct translation of Chinese texts into ear-pleasing English have made this work a better read.

Introduction

This is an introduction to Chinese cultural history, and it is written for people whose first language is not Chinese. Chinese, as used here, refers to cultural rather than ethnic characteristics. By this definition, the shape and capacity of the Chinese mind do not include a biological inheritance. To understand the Chinese mind, one has to speak, read, and to understand the tone, rhythm, imagery, and gestures of the language and see the world through the Chinese imagination, which is expressed in a diverse multi-media spectrum, crowded with images and connotations that have accumulated and refined for over five thousand years.

Cultural identity is not determined by the origin of one's ancestors, although this factor can provide easy entrance to a culture. It is, rather, a way of life that is defined and cultivated by a unique world of idioms, rhythms, gestures, attitudes, and wisdom. It is reflected in the way that one sees, feels, listens and speaks, and how one sings, dances, laughs, cries, and dreams. It also includes the ways that one communicates and relates to others and how one thinks of oneself and the world.

Language often sets the horizon of vision. As it ages, it provides more and varied images, expands the scope of imagination, and stimulates deeper thoughts. Cultural history tells the story of a community as it constantly reaches for its horizons, shifts perspectives and sets sail into the unknown and foreign. As they accumulate new expression and connotation, speakers and readers find a higher level of consciousness and a deeper awareness of their potential as well as their limitations.

This book illustrates the evolution of the Chinese repertoire of expression as it accumulated and transformed. It depicts how Chinese, as a language and culture, acquired its unique characteristics as it continuously reinvented itself.

The initial inspiration for this book is my son. He was born in North America and considers Chinese, my first language, to be gibberish. Like many

3

Chinese parents in North America, I failed to keep him in a language school to read Chinese literature. It seemed irrelevant and had little to do with his life here. He thought and still thinks that learning Chinese is very difficult and extremely boring. He has become one of those people who everyone thinks is Chinese, yet he knows practically nothing about his heritage. He is Chinese in appearance only. Even after three trips to China, his impressions remain a collection of scattered images: exotic food, the babble of a foreign tongue, and busy streets with an ocean of people on bicycles.

The first time that I encountered a person like my son was thirty years ago, shortly after I arrived in America to study in a graduate school. I had no family in Philadelphia and I spent most of my weekends at the home of my friend, Dr. Yang, a math-professor-turned-businessman. To become a successful American, he gave up university teaching and opened a restaurant. He made a fortune and bought a huge house in an exclusive suburban neighborhood. He was very proud to be a member of the affluent middle class. In order to emulate the American lifestyle (which he believed would open doors for his three children), he became a Christian and a loyal churchgoer. He was also spending a fortune on schooling for his children.

Yang had an American born sixteen-year-old daughter. Grace spoke, gestured, thought, and behaved like any American teenager. Before long, I realized that she had no consciousness of her own face.

One Sunday in 1981, Yang was hosting a house party. I arrived at his elegantly decorated mansion just as Grace was returning from the church.

Grace loved Sundays because she got to wear her designer dresses and hats and sing in the choir. She greeted me at the door with American hugs and kisses, a warm and emotional expression that a native Chinese rarely displays. She seemed very happy, and why not? She possessed everything that her imagination could conceive. Yes, this was America. With her father's money she could have everything, including the dream that she was someone else.

My conversation with her on that day concerned one of her teachers, whom she greatly adored. "He told me that I am the best and brightest student that he has ever taught in his twenty-year career." This flattering comment obviously had a great impact on her. She was so excited that her eyes were sparkling and her voice began to tremble. "Guess what?" she whispered in my ear. "I did not tell him I am a Chinese! He has yet to see my parents.... To tell you the truth, I did not tell him because I was afraid that he would change his mind about me." As she averted her beautiful brown eyes, and looked down, I could see her long lashes trembling as they struggled to hold back her tears. Her Chinese roots seemed to be a burden that was too heavy for her fragile soul to carry.

Looking at her pretty, yet mindful face, I could feel her pain. I really wanted to cry for her. O, God! She had no idea that her face had already revealed all of her secrets! She really wished that she was someone else.

On that day I promised myself that if I had a child, I would let him know what it meant to be Chinese. I probably would not mind if he decided to ignore his heritage, but he must at least hear the story of the real China from a real Chinese.

From my son's sixteenth birthday, I began to search for a book about Chinese cultural history written for English readers. After years of research in my field (cultural history), and checking all the books published on the subject, I have yet to find a single one that portrays the essence of Chinese culture. This was, perhaps, the same reason that I chose to stay away from Chinese studies in my graduate school. I studied the history of America, Germany, Italy, England, and Egypt. English publications about China at the time definitely did not present the China that I know.

Later on in my life, I married a Canadian poet and literary writer. As a boy he spent hours and hours in his back yard digging holes and dreaming that he could reach China. As we were planning our first China trip together, I searched for a book of cultural history of China to prepare him for the journey.

Once again, I was disappointed. Most books about China are too superficial for my husband's taste. The academic books, mainly written by Chinese scholars, are written in such poor prose that educated English readers hardly have the patience to follow them. A few American Sinologists write well, but their knowledge and comprehension of China are fragmentary. The high degree of difficulty of the Chinese language and the monumental size of its literature forced them into increasingly narrow fields. In a rigidly structured academic system, they spend their entire lives researching textual details and footnotes rather than dealing with more general and interesting issues. They are representative of the fundamental difference between Chinese culture and those of the West, and clearly exhibit the reasons that Chinese language and the social and political institutions that it has spawned have acquired unprecedented sustaining power.

The limitation of Sinologists, Chinese or otherwise, is a language and methodology that is derived from Western theories of social science and humanities. Most of these theories were originally formulated by German philosophers. German is the most competent language in philosophy among the modern European languages, but it is the least sensitive, refined and poetic. To apply German philosophy to Chinese literature is an attempt to measure the volume of the ocean with a soup bowl, an impossible task. Chinese experience and reasoning as cultivated by its ancient literary language is many times more rich, subtle, and more diverse than the expressive capacity of contemporary cultural theories. Compared to German, English and Spanish have a higher degree of poetic fluidity and suggestiveness; however, they lack the German logical clarity that can elevate poetic ambiguity to philosophical precision.

Weary of my search, I have decided to write the book myself.

I was born in Beijing and spent my formative years (during the nineteen fifties, sixties and a part of the seventies) in China. I am part of a multi-generational family of intellectuals who have held prominent positions in Chinese politics, military, law, media and education. My great-grandparents, grandparents and parents were members of the high societies of the Manchu Imperial, Nationalist and Communist regimes. Chinese history, especially that of the modern period, is also the history of my family.

I was among the youngest of the educated generation of the Cultural Revolution. I witnessed both the madness and profoundness of social change and understood the impact of Chinese language and culture upon its ideology and its social and political institutions. To enhance the intellectual portfolio of many generations of my family, I experienced, first hand, life at the bottom of Chinese society. During my teens, I lived as a peasant in a remote village at the cradle of Mao's revolution where he built his military base. As I toiled, starved, and suffered, I developed not only empathy for the peasants who had sacrificed everything for the Revolution (yet were left in the same poverty afterwards), but also a deeper understanding of how and why the Chinese system has survived for thousands of years.

I left China in the 1970s and since then have traveled the world extensively and been away long enough to acquire a non–Chinese perspective of the world. It took me almost ten years to learn how to think (not just speak) in English, and about twenty years to feel and express emotions in the English sense. During the past thirty years I have been to four continents, thirty countries, and learned many non–Chinese languages. I have written several books on legal philosophy and global cultural history. Each time that I read and write in a different language I compare it with my native tongue and my Chinese frame of mind, seeking similarities and differences. I find a slice of Chinese in each and every language, be it English, Latin, Greek, German, French, Italian, Spanish, Hebrew, and Arabic. But, there are always some things missing. This book is about the things that are uniquely Chinese.

Long and uninterrupted literary tradition sets Chinese culture apart from the rest of the world. Like English today (the youngest international language), the written language of China, however pronounced regionally, has been one of the great unifying and stabilizing factors in Chinese civilization.

Chinese is not the only civilization whose history goes back five thousand years, but it is the longest surviving and continuing literary tradition in the world. Writing was used in Greece and Crete during the Bronze Age, but the written material surviving from that period appears to consist of inventories and other administrative records, rather than literature. Greek was a rich oral language (more precisely a collection of regional dialects) until the eighth century BC, when it successfully adopted the Phoenician alphabet. At that time, written Chinese was nearly a thousand years old and possessed a large vocabulary. All other ancient languages that had developed their own scripts and phonic systems and were contemporary to ancient Chinese either died or were replaced, completely or partially, by other languages. Sumerian, ancient Egyptian, Babylonian, and Latin now exist only as reference material to solve scholarly puzzles. Ancient Semitic languages were reoriented many times and replaced by several modern languages. Sanskrit, Latin, and ancient Hebrew became so abstract that they uprooted from their original oral form and adopted various vernaculars.

The continuing literary tradition channeled Chinese history along a unique path: a unified empire (with periodic political instability and war), sustained by a combination of a secular morality and legal institution, administrated by a lasting monarchy (including Mao's Communist kingdom). China would have died (as did ancient Egypt and Rome) as an empire of God or law if its written language had not been revitalized by its poetry, rooted in songs and oral expression. China might have turned into a Christian or Buddhist country if its worship of high God and elaborate religious rites had not been transformed into secular philosophies and complex ethics through centuries of literary cultivation. China would have become a diverse and fragmented India if its increasingly refined literary language had been completely uprooted from its everyday speech as Sanskrit had. Chinese civilization survived because its literary tradition lived and was nourished by a rich soil of oral, regional, and artistic idioms.

Chinese literature absorbed and assimilated the expression of music, visual imagery, and dramatic gestures. This historical accumulation of idioms substantially expanded the horizon of Chinese imagination and elevated its reasoning. The Chinese mind became able to see and hear; it could imagine and suggest sound and imageries that other languages were unable to do in words alone until the twentieth century. Chinese evolved into a language as abstract and analytic as German, as fluid as Arabic, and as suggestive and flexible as English and Spanish. Most important of all, Chinese had become a language of all of these capacities at the same time.

Part I: Music, Dance and the Sound of Poetry, describes how Chinese language emerged with music, dance, and visual images. Chapter 1, "Music, Dance and Words," is a history of formative Chinese poetry. Like ancient Greek, ancient Chinese was born and grew up intact with its music and dance. The oldest musical instrument dated back to 8000 BC and the earliest depiction of dance is dated about 3500 BC. The legends about the pre-history life of music and dance were handed down by word of mouth, recorded on oracle bones and isolated pictographs, and accompanied by musical instruments that have been unearthed by archaeologists.

The formal connection between words, music, and dance was rhythm. Percussion instruments, which had remained in the background of the Western music composition until the twentieth century, were the most important music instrument in the early Chinese antiquity. Like the ancient Greek epic, the tone and rhythm of Chinese poetry was fundamentally shaped, transformed, and refined by music through singing, chanting, and recitation.

Chapter 2, "From Pictures and Graphs to Words," illustrates the birth of the Chinese writing system. Although the exact date of the beginning of the Chinese written language remains uncertain, scholars have agreed that the Shang oracle bones inscription (1766–1122 BC) exhibit a well-developed system of writing. This system is compared here with Egyptian, Sumerian and Akkadian writings. It focuses on when and how these systems emerged from graphic signs and visual arts and gradually distilled into symbols of meanings and ideas. By the beginning of the first millennium BC, Chinese words, although pictographic in appearance, were no longer pictographs in function. They were words representing concepts rather than symbols representing things or objects.

Chapter 3, The "Music of Poetry," is a history of the formation of Chinese literary poetry. Unlike the Medieval Latin text that dominated the sound of church music and produced an increasingly perfected unison between words and melody, Chinese poetry allowed music, both native and foreign, to provide original and innovative rhythm and tone for its poetic form. Every type of Chinese poetry originated from song, which provided the basic rhythmic and verbal structure of the poetic composition. Since Han dynasty (202 BC–AD 220), the grammatical structure of Chinese has not changed, yet its poetry has accumulated increasingly sophisticated forms. Initially, music that carried poetic rhyme with four, five, and seven character lines was established as the predominant poetic form until the Tang dynasty (618–907). Ci (literally lyrics of a song) in the Song dynasty (960–1279) inspired new forms of poetry. This broke the monopoly of quantitative poetic structure and led to the emergence of poetry of uneven lines. This innovation allowed poets more creative freedom while maintaining a highly complex form.

Part II: Painting, Theatre and the Imagery of Poetry, depicts the development of literary poetry in the context of the evolution of artistic imagery of Chinese painting and theatre.

Chapter 4, "History of Painting," traces this art form from its beginning as ornamental design, such as Stone Age pottery painted with spirals, zigzags, dots, or animals. The artists from Han to Tang dynasties mainly painted human figures. Many examples have been found in burial sites, where paintings were preserved on silk banners, lacquered objects, and tomb walls. However, landscape is considered the highest form of Chinese visual art. The Five Dynasties period (907–960) and the Northern Song period (907–1127) are known as the great age of Chinese landscape.

Chapter 5, "Imagery and Narrative of Nature," focuses on the poetic nature of Chinese landscape and its contribution to literary refinement. Chinese landscape painting projects a personal vision of nature on the canvas rather than its imitation. On this canvas, the painter expresses particular emotion and momentary mood in various shapes, colors, and shades, and in distinct degrees of contrast, movement, and harmony. Painting does not intend only to be seen, but also to be felt. It is poetry for one's eyes. This visual poetry contributed a great deal to refocusing and refining verbal imagery, which gradually became as sharp and precise as painting. It inspired poets to use words as line and color to paint mental pictures into the minds of readers.

Poetry is the topic of Chapter 6, "Rhythm and Imagery of Feeling." Chinese lyric poetry could be called romantic, but only in the sense of the English poetry of the twentieth century. The natural images in Chinese poetry were much more enriched compared to those in English Romantic poetry of the eighteenth and nineteenth centuries. Chinese poetry never had to make a general choice between nature and man. Chinese believed that nature was neither divine in origin nor universal in its structure. Mountains, rivers, trees, and flowers as isolated objects described a specific vision of a single literary mind and portrayed the pulse of his emotion.

Chapter 7, "Poetry on Stage," describes the influence of theatrical performance upon Chinese literature. Unlike Greek, Roman and English Renaissance theatre, Chinese theatre, which emerged and flourished from the 8th to 17th century, was a post-literary theatre, comparable to Italian opera and the modern theatres of Europe and North America during the twentieth century. It was concerned less with story (plot) and concentrated on the theatrical display and performance as words were heard, seen and acted out. It equipped words with music and dramatic effect that was not possible to be perceived by silent reading alone. After being saturated in theatre for centuries, Chinese words now, like modern English, provoke various sound (music), imagery (scenery and gesture), and meaning.

Chapter 8, "A Few Final Words," addresses the most distinct characteristic of Chinese culture: its exceptional diversity and fluidity. The boundaries between words, literary genres, literature and philosophy, reality and fiction, have leveled out and intermingled during a timeless literary evolution. A literary mind that is trained in its entire repertoire acquires a much larger and multi-dimensional vision compared to one that emerges from younger culture. The Chinese mind can simultaneously reach for the most analytical and the most sensual expression without losing its literary and logical coherence. However, only a small minority of Chinese speakers is adequately educated in its literature because everyday spoken Chinese only includes a small fraction (perhaps one or two percent) of its known written vocabulary, and a functional literacy requires knowledge of only about up to five percent of Chinese words.

PART I

MUSIC, DANCE AND
THE SOUND OF POETRY

As it did in ancient Mesopotamia and Greece, poetry in China emerged in songs that were performed with music and dance.[1] The earliest Chinese word for dance [*wu*] was a pictorial symbol depicting a dancing man with an ox tail in each of his hands. As ancient Chinese dance took place during religious rituals, the dancer was often the shaman who led the ritualistic performance. There were different pictographs referring to different types of dance for various rituals. Rain dance [*yǔ wǔ*] depicted a dancing shaman with raindrops on his head; devil dance [*qi wu*] was a pictograph of a dancer with a mask of a devil. Sometimes the dancing mask was made of bearskin. *Zhou li (Xia gong)* [Rites of Zhou] (2nd century BC) described the face of the devil as having a pointed head, four golden eyes and erect ears adorned with long earrings. This image was exactly the pictograph that portrayed a strange looking man dancing with a sword and shell. *Zou wu* was a man who was dancing while playing music.

The Chinese word for music [*yinyue*] consisted of two characters: *yin* and *yue*. If written and used separately (in isolation or combination), they each have an array of meanings. *Yin* appeared earlier in pre–Qin (221–206 BC) historic documents such as *Yijing. Yu* [Book of Changes] and *Shujing. Shundian, Lunyu. yanghuo* [Book of History]. It literally meant sound, a rather general term. In these documents, *yue*, a much narrower term, was also used when referring to an activity that combined music, dance, and chanting. As in pre-classical Greek, the interchangeable use of the two characters reflected a stage of linguistic evolution wherein nature (sound) and art (music) were not yet clearly defined. As music increased in its forms and diversity, the two characters for *yin* and *yue* originally distanced from each other, but later combined to form a new word that carries a meaning that is similar to the modern concept of music.

This long conceptual evolution recorded the growth and maturity of a

11

musical culture in ancient China. An orchestra that played at a great archery tournament of Zhou (1046–256 BC) was described in *Yili* [Rites and ceremonies], a document from the third century BC:

> On the east of the eastern steps [of the Palace], musicians set up their instruments. The sonorous stones associated with the mouth-organs are facing west; south of these are the bells [*zhong*] associated with the mouth-organs, and further south are other bells [*bo*]. West of the eastern steps a drum is set up; it is beaten from the south. The answering drum is to the east of this; it is struck from the south. To the west of the western steps are the sonorous stones associated with laudatory declamation; they face east. To the south of these are bells and to the south of these are other bells; these are all arranged in order towards the south. To the south of all these a drum is set up; it is struck from the east. To the north of this is the starting drum [*bi*]. A drum is set up to the east of the western steps, it faces south. In the space between the set-up drums are the bamboos [flutes and mouth organs, presumably]. The hand-drum, *taur* [struck by two buttons on two strings] rests on the western cords supporting the sonorous stones associated with laudatory declamation.[2]

Chinese practiced heterophony in which a single melody was played and sung by a variety of instruments and voices. Each of these components played the melody differently, either in a different rhythm or tempo, pitch, or with various embellishments and elaboration. Heterophony was not introduced in Western music until the early modern period.[3]

According to historic records the Zhou melodies were played by *di* [flute], *hu* [Chinese violin], and *zheng* [Chinese zither]. The second instrument that accompanied the first was usually of the same type but it played a variation on the melody of the first in different key. At this time, the interests of the Chinese hear for this combination of sounds was to experience simultaneous presentation of theme and variant (early Latin music experimented in this *fusio*) rather than in their interaction and incidental clashes.[4]

Unlike the West, where instruments of percussion did not play an important role in music until the modern period, percussion was among the first types of music to flourish in ancient China. This characteristic derived from the simultaneous development of music and poetry, as musical accompaniment provided poetry with its basic rhythmic pattern. As poetry was composed and set to music, the clarity and precision of scale and rhythm were important. Chinese music took its initial form in the company of words as it began to evolve from simple chanting to sophisticated tonal organization.

The increasingly varied and sophisticated sound of music and dancing rhythm contributed a great deal in the formation of Chinese poetry and its sound, rhythm and imagery. After many centuries of assimilation of musical forms, Chinese classical poetry cultivated repetitive rhythm, as did Homeric Greek and ancient Arabic.

1

Music, Dance and Words

The history of Chinese music is as old as that of ancient Greece and Mesopotamia. The oldest type of Chinese instrument that has survived is a wind instrument, constructed first in clay, then bone, and finally wood. The oldest of these that have been excavated are a set of bone transverse flutes found at the early Neolithic site of Jiahu, in Henan Province, and is dated to about 6000 BC. They are twenty centimeters long and have seven holes. They are believed to be the oldest complete, playable multi-note musical instruments in existence. There is another later discovery of one hundred and sixty long flutes made of bird bone from Zhejiang Province. Many of them remain playable and are dated to about 5000 BC.[1]

These well-crafted flutes are made from the ulnae, or wing bones, of the red-crowned crane and they have five, six, seven or eight holes. They are well-preserved and have been played, tested, and tonally analyzed by the Music School of the Art Institute of China. This sound from thousands of years ago is recorded and can be heard by historians of music. The analysis reveals that the seven holes correspond to a tone scale remarkably similar to the Western eight-note scale. This carefully selected tone scale suggests that the Neolithic musicians could play not only single notes, but also simple melodies. However, it took Chinese musicians many more centuries to develop and establish a heptatonic scale (a musical scale with seven pitches per octave). It was not completed until late Shang dynasty (1766–1122 BC).[2]

During Shang, Chinese musicians developed a system (scale) of tones along with the stone chime to produce its sound. These chimes were sets of L-shaped marble slabs called *qing*, suspended in wooden frames and struck with mallets. During the late Shang, stone chimes were used to play music in parts of the middle Yellow River Valley.[3] Many Shang tombs contain sets of stone chimes and hand bells. The largest known qing (36 inches long × 24 inches wide × 1½ inches high) was excavated in Lajia, Qinghai province, in

2000. It was shaped as an ancient stone knife and pierced with small holes to hang it from a frame. Many Shang qing in various shapes and sizes have also been discovered in other locations. They were organized into sets (or groups)[*bian qing*] and each was inscribed with a specific name that denoted the specific pitch that it could produce. Some of these *qing* were exquisitely made with smooth, level surfaces and contained additional engravings of inscriptions and animal figures.[4]

From the period of the Western Zhou dynasty (1046–771 BC), the form of the qing was standardized. Its body was made uniformly flat, and it was shaped like an irregular chevron but with a curved rather than angular bottom edge. Each set had 8 to 24 pieces. The set unearthed at the tomb of Zenghouyi had as many as 32 pieces (plus nine spare pieces). Each piece was engraved with the name of the tone it produced. The additional pieces were used as needed to sound tones that were in between those of the main set.

The Chinese armory of musical instruments expanded during the Zhou dynasty (1046–249 BC). Zhou musicians played more than seventy different types of instruments which were classified into eight categories. There were those made of metal, stone, clay, hide, silk, wood, reed, and bamboo.[5] The music that these instruments made was called *ba yin* [eight sounds]. Among these instruments, hide and bamboo instruments accounted for more than half of those used. The most complex and one of the oldest wind instrument was *sheng* [mouth organ]. By virtue of its construction, this was the only Chinese musical instrument in the orchestra that could play up to six notes simultaneously. Sheng was also the first musical instrument in the world that utilized a coupled acoustical system between an air column and a free reed. Sheng consisted of 13 to 17 bamboo pipes with different lengths mounted together onto a base. The base was traditionally a gourd-shaped, wooden wind-chest. Each bamboo pipe had a free reed made of brass. Players produced music by blowing and sucking the air through a metal tube connected to the base. From the base the air rushed through the other pipes. A player determined the notes to play by allowing the air to rush through selected pipes while pressing on selected keys near the base. By covering two or more holes on various pipes, Chinese players defined chords. With exceptional clarity of tone, sheng was used as both a solo and accompaniment instrument.

There were two half-tube zithers, *qin* and *se*, which later survived as *guzheng* (ancient zither) with various numbers of silk or brass strings. New aerophones included cross flutes, a double pipe, *guan*, and panpipes, *xiao*. Scrapers (idiophones) dated back to the earliest Neolithic times. Zhou musical scenes were described in an early poetry that depicted songs and the playing of music to welcome a noble lady guest.[6]

Bronze instruments exhibited the highest degree of craftsmanship among the ancient instruments. By the Zhou dynasty, bronze bells [*zhong*] were hung downward, usually in sets of 8 or 16, and tuned chromatically. A *bianzhong* [set of bells] from the Han dynasty (206 BC–AD 220) contained bells in which different pitches could be produced by striking marked spots on the lip of each bell. Bell chimes were part of court and temple ensembles. Each ruler recalibrated the sound of his bell set by tuning, as the Chinese believed that accurate sound of music would keep China in harmony with the universe.

The most impressive bell set unearthed was a complete ceremonial set of 65 zhong bells in the tomb of Marquis Yi, the ruler of Zeng, one of the Warring States (475–221 BC). The largest bell within the set was as tall as a man and weighed over 200 kg. On the body of each bell, inscriptions were engraved and inlaid with gold. The total range of its sound covered five octaves, close to that of a modern piano. The set of bells was mellow in tone and beautiful in color, featuring a whole set of high, medium and low tunings along with inflexion in some modes of ancient Chinese music. It could also play 12 semitones as well as melodies of pentatonic and diatonic scale. The bells were fully playable after almost 2500 years and capable of producing the complete scale tone, as each bell could make two distinct sounds by being struck at different locations on its body.

The *guqin* [zither] without bridges, like the harp in the ancient West, was another old instrument. It originally had five strings and later increased to seven. One of its more sophisticated versions was *se* that had twenty-six strings of silk-gut and a movable bridge. Contrary to wind and bronze instruments that produced high and clear tones, guqin was a very quiet instrument with a range of about four octaves and its open strings were tuned in the bass register. Its lowest pitch was about two octaves below middle C, or the lowest note on the cello. Sounds were produced by plucking open strings, stopped strings, and harmonics. The use of glissando (sliding tones) gave it a sound reminiscent of a pizzicato cello, fretless double bass or a slide guitar. The *qin* was also capable of many harmonics, of which 91 were most commonly used. These various harmonic melodies were recorded in a special kind of notation transmitted from player to player for thousands of years. The guqin was often referred to as the instrument of sages not only because Confucius was a master of it but also because it was an important part of self-cultivation of high culture and functioned as did the piano in the West.[7]

Rich historical records suggest that a well-established musical culture had developed in ancient China. Contrary to general assumption that Chinese culture had evolved in isolation, cultural interaction between China and the world around it was, in fact, recorded during the early Zhou dynasty when exchange of music culture was quite common. Emperor Zhou Mu (977–922 BC) visited the countries of mid-western Asia in 964 BC. He took with him a heavy load of gifts and a large orchestra. During the trip (that covered eighteen thousand kilometers) the Chinese delegation held concerts and musical and dance performances wherever they went. On his way home and before he crossed the Chinese border, Zhou Mu encountered a Western puppet maker and his performing puppets. One of the puppets could walk rapidly while moving its head up and down. It could sing and dance in perfect time. The emperor mistook the puppet for a real dancer and called his wives and concubines to join him for the performance. Before the show ended, the puppet began to flirt with the royal ladies. The Chinese emperor was offended and ordered his guards to execute the puppet maker. Afraid for his life, the puppet maker opened the puppet for the emperor. The emperor examined it carefully and found all the internal organs complete: liver, gall, heart, lungs, spleen, kidneys, stomach and intestines. Encasing these were muscles, bones and limbs with their joints, skin, teeth and hair. All parts were made of colored leather, wood, fur, glue and paint. The emperor was delighted and impressed with the craftsmanship and decided to take the artist with him to China.[8]

From about 2100 BC, Chinese imperial courts frequently held large-scale musical performances for ceremonies and celebrations. In accordance with their functions, the court music was classified into two major kinds: court ritual (ceremonial) music and music for entertainment. The former was played at different religious ceremonies, such as sacrificial rites, mourning practice at temples and at honor guard parades; the latter included banquet performance (entertainment), the music played for the emperor's inspection tours, pipe, and drum music.[9]

Zhou ceremonial music had various categories of compositions: *yayue* [fine music] (comparable to chamber music in Western tradition), lyric music and the Six Dynasty music that referred to different historic compositions relevant to different dynasties. The Six Dynasty music amalgamated all sorts of performing arts such as poetry recitation, singing, dancing and instrument playing. The dance movements were slow and extending. The tunes of the songs were soft and harmonious, producing an atmosphere of majesty, harmony and serenity. The choreography included paying tribute to heaven, earth, mountains and rivers, or complimenting certain monarchs on the prosperity and liberal-mindedness of their reigns. Chamber music, here, refers to the musical performance given inside the court, with the major part made up of folk songs accompanied solely with *qin* and *se* (lute and zither). It was often performed by imperial concubines for the double purpose of entertaining the emperor and informing him of the situation of the nation under his reign. As for lyrical music, it was mainly composed of lyrics accompanied by music that was revised and edited by professional musicians using folk ballads as a base reference.

As nonverbal musical notation did not exist, the sound of ritual music could only be imagined from the descriptions of orchestras and the names of songs associated with a particular ritual or particular occasion. In general (like the Latin Christian music), early Chinese music was mainly composed to prolong, phrase, and emphasize the recitation of poetry. Poetry expressed will; song prolonged expression; music carried the prolongation. In their minds, words and music were conveyed in one and the same voice to communicate with spirits: "Quei [the director of music] said, when the sonorous stones are struck lightly or heavily, when *qin* and *se* are struck lightly or heavily, and their sounds alternate with human voices, the spirits of the ancestors come; the guest of Yu [the (ancient) emperor Shuen] takes his place, the crowd of princes display their virtue in mutual courtesy. Down below, the flutes [double vertical flutes] and the small drums play together as soon as the signal is given by the wooden trough and cease as soon as the signal is given by the tiger-scraper. The mouth organs and the bells play in the intervals."[10]

During the Spring and Autumn Period (770–476 BC) and the Warring States Period (the time of Confucius) larger-scale bands were established in addition to the soloists and some small-sized instrumental ensembles. The most conventional ensemble mode was played with chimes and drums. Chamber music was only occasionally played, with *guqin* [seven-string zither] and *se* [zither with 16 to 25 strings] as the most representative musical instruments.

At Hubei Province, 124 musical instruments were unearthed from the Tomb of Marquis Yi, also dated to the Spring and Autumn period. The instruments include *bian zhong* [set of bells], *bian qing* [set of stone tablets that were hung by ropes and struck using a mallet], ten-stringed *qin* [zither], five-stringed *qin, se, sheng* [wind instrument with 17–36 pipes], *xiao* [panpipes], and small drums. The excavated *bian zhong* consist of sixty-four bells, the largest set of bells in the world with a total weight of approximately 2,500 kilograms. The smallest bell is 20.4 centimeters long and 2.4 kilograms in weight, while the biggest one is 153.4 centimeters high and weighs 203.4 kilograms. The set of bells covers roughly five octaves and twelve scales and can produce all semitones in three octaves, which meant that the chimes could make melodies in seven musical scales with modulation. This indicates the completed musical systems and complicated modes of note composition at that time. In addition, gold inscriptions (of 2,828 words) are carved on the body of the chime bells to indicate the scale, octave or musical pitch of each bell. It was confirmed through tests that each bell was capable of producing two tones, usually a major or a minor, when struck on the front or the flank sides. This illustrates that the ancient Chinese had mastered the musical principle of round-shaped objects. The whole set of bells is extremely elaborate and finely cast, and indicates how advanced musical skill and bronze production were in ancient China.

There were other musical instruments in the central chamber (the ceremonial hall) of Marquis Yi's tomb, such as drums and shengs of different sizes and shapes. Beneath the east wall in the central chamber lay some drinking vessels positioned opposite the musical instruments. It is assumed that this hall was where the marquis entertained his guests. In the east chamber of the tomb (the master bedroom) were found instruments like qin and se, mainly for playing chamber music at the imperial court. From the arrangement of the musical instruments in the central and east chambers it appears that a variety of instruments were used to produce the increased range of musical styles of the Spring and Autumn Period.[11]

But with the development of musical instruments and increasingly complex composition of orchestration, the way in which music related to words did not change much until the Tang period. This practice of musical composition remained in Chinese ritual music for many centuries. For example, the "Hymn for Sacrifice to Confucius" played in the sixteenth century maintained much of the character of the corresponding hymn performed in Tang times. The hymn illustrated not only transposition into five keys other than the initial key (each key being one tone higher than the preceding key) but also the constant distance of the fourth key between the accompanying orchestra and the voices. The difference that two thousand years of practice had made was that inherited musical composition and phrasing became formula. It was described in detail as: the instruments play in F, the chant is in A sharp … for the sacrifice to the celestial spirits. For the sacrifice to the terrestrial spirits the instruments play in G, the chant is in C.... This practice has been found similar to one type of medieval organum in the Latin composition of church music: the organum (originally an instrument) accompanied the cantus at the fourth or fifth key below.[12]

The most important evolution of musical accompaniment of poetry during the later centuries was elucidation of the ancient practice of prolonging a note. Instead, the prolonged notes now were replaced by plucked stringed instruments (such as qin and se whose sound quickly decay) by means of a rapidly executed figuration. It was believed that the vestiges of the old *caoman* was used by performers to tune their instruments. In it, the intervals of the octave and the fifth (the keys on the fifth line of the staff) were played in succession to words meaning "the moon is bright, the wind is soft." As result, the song (for example the opening line of the second stanza of the "Hymn from the Temple of the Ancestors") changed its sound. The string figuration differs in minor details and the mouth-organ part has been converted into chords of octave and scales on the fifth or fourth lines. The pitch of the mouth-organ may well be an octave lower than that at which it is written.[13]

The Han Dynasty (202 BC–AD 220) witnessed another peak in the development of imperial court music. *Yuefu*, an administrative institution, was established in court. It was responsible for collecting and editing folk songs and ballads, composing and revising musical pieces, and giving performances and concerts. Yuefu had a court appointed director who supervised the court orchestra, which was comprised of four different sections and employed more than 800 musicians.[14]

During Han, regional music and musical theatre began to evolve distinctively from court music. These musical performances led finally to the development of Chinese opera in later centuries. As in the evolution of Greek drama, a performance originally of religious or even magical significance, Chinese ritual performance evolved and transformed into a form of entertainment. These musical performances were called *baixi* [hundred theatre and episodic music (variety show)]. They combined folk music, poetry, dance, and magic shows, elaborate staging and costumes.[15] As early as the Zhou times a ceremony of exorcism was performed by a wizard. His show consisted of dances and songs executed by a troupe of performers masked as animals. This ritualistic performance took place every year on two occasions: in the annual *nuo*, a ceremony for driving away disease, and at funerals to drive away the ghost.

During Han, the same performance continued but transformed into a show of entertainment. It consisted of an orchestra of strings, flutes, and hand bells. The strings included *qin, se, pipa, zheng,* and vertical flute [*xiao*]. This band was also used for military and general purposes in the court. The *xiao* and handbells were absent from the popular orchestra, but it did include the mouth-organ and the cross-flute [*di*]. It seems probable that in the transformation of the performance from an exorcistic ceremony to an entertainment of songs, dances, and music there was also a change in the status of its music from that of the court to that of the common people.

The first musical theory in China appeared in the writings of Lü Buwei (291?–235 BC) and contained an account of emerging music and the establishment of its tonal standard. It said: "Yellow King ordered Ling Lun to create pitch-standard. Ling Lun went to the shady slope of Kunlun Mountain after passing through the western regions of Daxia. He selected bamboo, taking those grown of uniform bore and thickness. He cut the bamboo, into pieces of three inches and nine tenths between two nodes. He blew onto the piece and fixed its sound as *gong* on the yellow bell pitch standard [the fundamental of the Chinese system]."[16]

Chinese music initially set up a pentatonic scale (without semitones), which was calculated based on mathematical ratios such as 2:3. It consisted of three whole tones and two minor thirds, the thirds being separated by one or two whole tones. The scale had the form *do re mi sol la*, which was similar to the construction of modes in modern Western music. However, as Chinese define scale verbally rather than in mathematical or graphical terms (staff), they called the five notes within the scale *gong, shang, jue, zhi,* and *yu.* As verbal scaling did not convey an equal tempered tuning (tuning according to a precise measurement), a melody that was played beginning from the note [lù] nearest to A would not necessarily sound the same as when playing it starting from some other note since the wolf interval would occupy a different point in the scale. In musical tuning, when the twelve notes within the octave are tuned using meantone temperament, one of the fifths will be much wider than the rest. This interval is known as a diminished sixth, which is meant to be the enharmonic equivalent to a fifth; however, the interval did not sound the same as the other fifths; it was severely wide and dissonant, and seemed to howl like a wolf because of the beating. By extension, any interval which is regarded as howling in like manner may be called a wolf. The effect of changing the starting point of a song can be rather like the effect of shifting from a major to a minor key in Western music.

These five-note melodies existed as early as Zhou, when they were referred to as the "five degrees" and compiled in the third or fourth centuries BC. However, Zhou also knew seven sounds or the seven "beginnings" of music, which indicated that a seven-note scale with two semitones was sometimes played. The process by which the lowest note (Yellow Bell) engendered the rest of the notes in the Chinese system was also described in the writings of Lü Buwei. "To the three parts of the generator add one part, making the superior generation. From the three parts of the generator reject one part, making the lower generation."[17] This explained the way in which the complete note-series (six notes [liu lü]) was obtained by cutting bamboo tubes of the same diameter to lengths calculated by alternately subtracting and adding one-third of the length of the preceding tube according to the ratio of the length of any pipe to that of the next in the series. In addition, the Chinese method of classifying and defining musical notes did not stop at mathematical terms. The notes given by pipes in the series was, in fact, a double six tone system that was further classified into distinct sub-series: *ying* series and *yang* series.

When the words *ying* and *yang* were used during the third century BC, they represented a primal (non-absolute) distinction similar to the distinction of day/night, man/god, sun/earth and male/female (as in the pre-classical Greek). The *ying* notes were said to belong to the inferior generation, the six female notes [lü], made according to legend from the singing of the female *roc,* a gigantic mythical bird. The six remaining notes, *yang* notes were said to belong to the superior generation, the six male lü made according to legend from the singing of the male roc. Theoretically this procedure yielded a chain of ascending fifths and descending fourths and, if arranged in ascending order, a note sequence of F, F#, G, G#, A, A#, B, C, C#, D, D#, E.[18]

Lü Buwei's *Liu Lü* [the complete note-series] was not a "chromatic scale" in an English sense, but an array of all the notes in the Chinese musical firmament of the third century BC. To include twelve-tone (or be able to make the sound of these notes) was one thing and to be able to compose music in a chromatic scale was quite another. This formal difference reveals different degrees of maturity of a given musical language.[19]

In Western musical tradition the transition from diatonic to chromatic scale was a natural progression after music distanced itself from word and became an independent art. Then it took only a few centuries for musical composition to grow beyond the established scale of classical music and only a handful of decades for theorists to catch up. In Chinese tradition, chromatic scale was initially used to define the starting tone rather than a complete superstructure of composition. Therefore, although bell sets had been able to define twelve tones by a fairly early time, China did not cultivate an absolutely-defined musical system during the following three thousand years. This limitation derived from both musical and non-musical circumstances.

Technically, Chinese musicians did not have a single instrument that could produce a musical scale as wide as that of an organ or piano. Bell sets gradually declined in favor after string instruments replaced them for tone definition. As a result, like many older musical traditions in the world, Chinese melodies transmitted and recreated concretely as pieces or modes of music rather than an abstract superstructure. The same music could be played (or arranged, in the modern sense of the word) very differently as it changed its key and instrument. This variant approach to musical language demonstrated itself in several ways in which music was written and composed.

Unlike Western music that evolved within a measurable structure manifested in the keyboard, Chinese music evolved within a relative system of tone and was written in words. Melody could start from any given key without specific reference to the universal scale (keys for the piano, for example). In other words, music was composed, played, and listened to without a universally understood scale. Chinese musical notation was verbal rather than spatial; it was called *Gōngchě* notation.[20]

Gongche notation or *gongchepu* was a traditional musical notation method once popular in ancient China. It used Chinese characters to represent musical notes. Sheet music written in this notation is still used for traditional Chinese musical instruments such as *guzheng* [ancient zither] and Chinese traditional operas. This notation usually used a movable "do" system. There were variations of the character set used for musical notes.

To represent other notes in different octaves, each type of opera (there were more than several dozen in China) and each of its traditions (according to different types of characters) had different notations.[21] Imagine each genre of modern music with its own script. Pop, country, jazz, and classical musicians could not read each other's music!

Gongche notation, invented during the Tang period and flourishing in Song, was a system of mode [*diao*] closer to a wide range of musical phenomena such as the Arabic *maqam*, Indian *raga*, Persian *dastgah*, and Javanese *pathet*. Within the realm of Chinese music, *diao* was no less problematic because the parameters used to define it tended to vary from one historical period to another and from one genre and regional music tradition to another. For example, in modal theories from the Song and Ming dynasties, absolute pitch, scale and hierarchy of pitches seem to be the main determining factors of diao.[22] In qin [zither] music, in addition to these three factors, ornamentation, melodic motifs, range, tessitura, register, and kinesthetic and timbral aspects are the parameters that are significant in mode identification and differentiation.[23] In Guangdong *xiaoqu*, the *sizhu* [string and wind instrument] tradition native to the Pearl River delta area, the tuning of the open strings of bowed instruments play an important role in defining mode along with scale, hierarchy of pitches, melodic contour and recurring melodic motifs.[24]

Gongche was written in the same format as Chinese written in traditional style, from top to bottom and then from right to left. The rhythm marks were written to the right of the note characters. Using this method, only the number of notes within a beat could be specified. The actual length of each note was determined by tradition and the interpretation of the artist.

This notation was not accurate in a modern sense. It provided a musical skeleton that allowed musicians to improvise. The detailed variations and creative sound imagery usually were passed on orally or by example. However, once lost, it is very difficult to reconstruct how the music was supposed to sound. Variations among different traditions increased the difficulty of mastering the notation.

The best example for how the notation for a specific instrument worked is the *pipa* music. Pipa, a four-stringed lute with 30 frets, was brought to the central plains of China from India. By the time of Tang, pipa had become a major instrument during all sorts of musical occasions and played an important role in the development of singing and dancing. Its popularity was clearly shown in the impressive Tang poems, many of which give vivid descriptions of the origin, construction, playing techniques and repertoires of pipa music. The following is from the well-known poem "Pipa Song" by Bai Juyi (772–846):

> Thick strings rattled like splatters of sudden rain,
> Fine strings hummed like lovers' whispers.
> Chattering and pattering, pattering and chattering,
> Like pearls, large and small, fall on a jade plate.
> Sweet melody recalls oriole singing among flowers,
> Sobbing music brings gushing spring from glacier.
> As strings ceased vibration, it froze the spring.
> It stopped water flowing and silence set in.
> A spell of deep feeling emerges in heart,
> Silence tells more in this magical moment.
> Suddenly a strain of notes burst out
> Like water splattering out of a fallen vase
> Or horsemen riding among a forest of spears.
> She struck the four strings all at once
> As if the silk curtains were ripped by great force.
> With her plectrum sweeping over the string,
> The music came to an end with a crystal snap.
> And tranquil overwhelmed in the boats far and near,
> Only the autumn moon shining in the river so pale.[25]

Tang was an era of extensive intercourse between China and central Asia. Many new instruments were introduced and many types of orchestras were assembled, most performing with their unique troupes of dancers, jugglers, or acrobats, characteristically costumed. The size and composition of these orchestras was recorded in historic documents and represented in the frescoes in the Thousand Buddha Caves at Duenhwang. The cave paintings illustrated *yueqin,* a four-stringed flat lute whose strings were said to be tuned in pairs a fifth apart as well as *sanxian,* a three-stringed flat lute played with a jade plectrum, the strings tuned *do fa do* or *do re la.*[26]

Other musical instruments were also imported. A bowed zither, related to the *zheng,* was recorded as played in Chinese court about AD 900. Bowed lutes and fiddles were introduced at a slightly later date. All of these varieties were collectively given the Chinese name huqin [barbarian lute], suggesting that the instrument came to China from central Asia. *Erhu* became the most commonly used type of *huqin.* It has a hexagonal tubular wooden body a few inches long, one end of which is covered with snakeskin while the other end is open. The whole acts as a resonator. The handle is inserted into the body at right angles to its long axis. There are two strings of silk-gut tuned a fifth apart, stopped by the fleshy part of the fingers, and the hair of the bow passes between the strings. The instrument is played with constant vibrato and glissandi, producing a mellow and beautiful veiled tone.

Sui and Tang dynasties witnessed musical performance of the largest scale. This performance was organized and managed by an army of government institutions: *Dayue Shu* [great music bureau], *Guchui Shu* [the piping and drumming instrument bureau], *Jiaofang* [the conservatory] and *Liyuan* [the Pear Garden Musical Academy]. Dayue Shu was in charge of *yayue* [elegant music] and *yanyue* [music and dance for banquet entertainment]. The responsibility of Guchui Shu was to manage all ceremonial musical performances, while the Pear Garden Musical Academy taught students folk music and ritual music for Buddhist and Taoist practices. These institutions cultivated strict disciplines with regulations for training and testing. According to "History of Rites and Music" of The *New Tang Annals*, when the Tang Dynasty was at its zenith, the number of music performers reached tens of thousands. These musicians, singers, dancers and their apprentices were all under the administration of the court sectors named Taichang Temple and Guchui Shu.

During Tang, Chinese secular music [*suyue*] reached its peak. Emperor Tai Zong (597–649) had ten different orchestras, eight of which were made up of members of various non–Chinese tribes. Foreign orchestras included those from India, Bokhara, East Turkestan, Cambodia, Burma, Annam, Tibet, and Mongolia. All of the court performers and dancers appeared in their native costume. The imperial court also had a large outdoor band of nearly 1400 performers. Portions of Tang music were preserved in Japanese court music, or *gagaku*.[27]

Influential foreign music also began to be incorporated into the imperial court music during the Sui and Tang dynasties. In Sui, the so-called "Nine-part Music" was established with nine constituent parts: *Kangguo* Music from Samarkand of Uzbekistan and *Anguo* Music from Bukhara of Uzbekistan, both from the west of Congling Mountain, *Shule* Music from Kashgar and *Quici* Music from Kucha at the northern part of the Silk Road; *Xiliang* Music of Gansu Province, *Qingshang* Music, *Tianzhu* Music of India, *Gaoli* Music of Korea, and *Libi* Music, the music marking the ending of a certain ceremony. On the basis of the Nine-part Music, yanyue and Gaochang Music were added while Libi Music was removed to form the Ten-part Music in the Tang Dynasty. It is clear from these musical pieces that music from outside China played an influential role in imperial court music, the most popular being Qingshang Music, Xiliang Music and Quici Music, representing three distinctive styles. Qingshang was the traditional court music of the Han nationality and dominated the musical performances of the court. Xiliang was a combination of the music from the Western regions and the Central Plains, while Quici was typical of the Western regions.

The only specimen of Tang music that was supposedly transcribed from a contemporary document and claimed to be authentic is the melody for the first song in the *Book of Songs*, printed by Prince Qiu Zaiyu in 1596. According to Qiu the melody was taken from the edition of the classics engraved on stone in an ancient city of Tang. However, the stone, which was truly engraved during Tang period, contains no musical notation. Qiu's melody, which had to be recorded at a post–Tang time, was for drum, clapper, se, sonorous stones, and voice. Another score is for voice, qin, se, two kinds of bells, sonorous stones of two kinds, clapper, mortar, tiger drum, and small drum. The tune is remarkable in that it constantly avoids re but makes frequent use of both of the auxiliary notes, fe and si. The chords supplied by Qiu use only notes in the mode. Each four-syllable line of the lyrics is separated from the next by two bars of percussion and there are 3½ bars of percussion at the end of each of the five stanzas. The first stanza is quoted here:

> By riverside are cooing
> A pair of turtledoves;
> A good young man is wooing
> A fair maid he loves.

The single indisputably authentic relic of Tang music survives in the manuscript from the Thousand Buddha Caves at Duenhwang. It includes "Emptying-   the-cup Music" and is apparently written in a tonal notation. The name of this tune was known and documented in Tang historic record as belonging to the category of *daqu*. It was said to consist of at least ten movements.[28]

Daqu had its origin in Han *xianghe Daqu*, which took its initial form from *tuge*, an improvised solo folk song.[29] *Tuge* as a song type was historically recorded in name only. However, *dange*, another genre that grew out of tuge was described in detail as a group song. *Dange* was performed by four singers (still without musical a instrument), one lead singer and three others added to the leading voice harmoniously. Over time, *dange* further evolved into *xianghege* [literally harmoniously blending song]. *Xianghege* was characterized by harmoniously blending [*xianghe*] voices, the *si* [silk/string] and *zhu* [bamboo/wind] instruments. A percussionist played a wooden clapper and sang.[30]

Although no music of the Han *daqu* has survived, its structure could be reconstructed by reading its lyrics that were recorded in classical texts. It appears that *daqu* had four sections, each of which had different musical characteristics. The first section, called *yan*, was performed without meter as an optional prelude rather than a part of the *daqu* proper. Two-thirds of the surviving *daqu* had no *yan*; those *daqu* that had a *yan* could be either voice, dance, and instrument or instrument alone. *Yan* (literally means beautiful) music was relaxing but captivating, as the word *yan* implies. *Qu* [means song] was the second and longest section of Han *daqu*. It often contained between three and eight subsections called *jie*. This sequence of *jie* was alternatively arranged sections of slower and more relaxing vocal music and vigorous dance subsections, contrasting strongly to the more static yan prelude.[31] The third section, *qū*, was substantially faster, as the word *qū* means quicker. The *qū* often contained instrumental and dance music. On rare occasions, this section was also named *luan* [chaos]. As it was believed that only chaotic music could excite and entertain an audience, this exciting finale was more enchanting than the regular quick music.[32]

Tang dynasty was the golden age of *daqu*, which became an important part of Tang *yanyue*, or court banquet music. Emperor Xuanzong was a well-known music lover and its strongest supporter. He personally selected three hundred musicians to form his string division and watched them practice. Whenever a musician made a mistake in a performance, the emperor always recognized the imperfection and suggested a way to correct it. This musical emperor even composed *daqu* himself. A piece called *Yulinling* was credited to Xuanzong. With the wealth of the Tang court and personal involvement of the emperor, Tang *daqu* had a much more elaborate structure than the Han *daqu*.[33]

Tang daqu retained the three-part structure of the Han daqu, but each major section of the Tang daqu was expanded and further divided into many subsections. It became a highly complex form. Bai Juyi described the characteristics of each section of a Tang daqu in his poem *Nichang Yuyi Ge*. According to Bai, the three sections of a Tang daqu were called *sanxu*, *zhongxu*, and *po*. *Sanxu* [loose introduction] was simply a slow and unmetered prelude of *daqu*. Bai, in a remark on the *Nichang* poem, explains how the instruments were presented in the *sanxu*.

At the beginning, musical instruments did not play together and they came one after another. The instruments made of metal (bells and tuned slabs), stone (*qing*, tablets that are hung by ropes from a wooden frame and struck by a mallet), silk (strings such as guqin, se, pipa, and harp) and bamboo (winds such as sheng and flute) were played separately and in sequence. As there was no common meter in the section, there was neither dance nor song. The *sanxu*, as a prelude of *daqu* was a short or very long section of instrumental music.[34]

Zhongxu [middle prelude] was a metered section. It was a very long movement that was further divided into three subsections, known as *paibian*, *dian*, and *zhengdian*. Both characters of *pai* and *bian* could mean to arrange various elements of music. *Bian* could also mean change and suggest that different sub-subsections were probably composed by music portraying different movements and rhythm.

The first sub-subsection of *paibian* was *getou* [song head]. It initiated the *zhongxu* [middle prelude] as a section of singing. The slow song in the *zhongxu* section connected the beginning [*getou*] and the *po*, which was much faster dancing music. This arrangement of slow singing maintained a fluid flow of music in the piece of *daqu*. It is not certain whether dancing was included in the *zhongxu*. Bai Juyi's poem *Nichang* has suggested to historians that dancing might have been as important as singing in this middle prelude. However, the structure of other pieces of music suggests otherwise. Dancers might not have entered the performance until the po section of the *daqu*.[35]

The inner structure of the *po* section was the most complex among the three sections of *daqu*. There were seven subsections of *po*: *rupo, xucui, qiangun, shicui, zhonggun, xiepai* and *shagun*. *Rupo* [entering the *po* section] was the first and it distinguished itself from the preceding *zhongxu* by incorporating string and wind instruments. The rhythm of the music became faster. As various types of drums jammed with string and wind instruments, the music of *rupo* sounded more energetic and rhythmic than the preceding *zhongxu*. The second subsection was *xucui* [false hastening], to distinguish from the *shicui* [real hastening]. The main difference between *xucui* and *shicui* was the speed of tempo through different applications of the drums. In the *xucui*, drums were played only as an accompaniment and did not press on the tempo, but in *shicui*, the tempo became faster as a result of the faster drum beat. This is why the former *cui* was called a "false" *cui* whereas the latter was a "real" *cui*.

In between the false and real *cuis* was the *qiangun*, and later in the *po* section, there was also a *zhonggun* and *shagun*. As the word *gun* referred to the rapidly-repeated notes of the pipa or the rapidly-repeated strokes of the drums, it was used in the names of these three subsections to describe figuratively the extremely fast tempo of the music in these parts. In between *zhonggun* and *shagun*, there was *xiepai*, in which the music stopped momentarily so that the tension of the music built up in *po* could be slightly relaxed before the end of the *daqu*. *Zhonggun* was the section that carried the fastest tempo in the entire *daqu*.[37]

Eventually, the structure of Tang *daqu* became so extensive that it would accumulate 20, 30 or even 50 movements. The classic form of this *daqu* was divided into three major parts and each consisted of a defined number of sections. The first part was the *sanxu* [random sequence], which utilized a rhythm of free accented beats. The word *xu* means sequence. The arrangement of this sequence was in random accented beats and random associations. *Sanxu* was purely instrumental, either solo, alternating or ensemble. The next part, *zhongxu* [middle sequence] had a fixed rhythm which could be dictated by clappers, and so it was also called "clapper sequence." It was also known as the first song, as singing, sometimes accompanied by dancing, was the centerpiece. Most of the middle sequence consisted of slow accented beats. The final part was the *po* which contained dance, sometimes accompanied by singing, and it was also called *wupian* [dance piece]. The rhythm became increasingly more quick in this section until it reached a crescendo.

Like its poetry, post Tang music became increasingly personalized and lyricalized. Away from *daqu*, a Chinese version of symphonic form, solo instrumental pieces became more prominent. In traditional China most of the well-educated people and monks could play classical music as a means of self-cultivation, meditation, spiritual elevation, union with nature, identification with the values of sages and divine beings, and communication with friends and lovers. They would never perform in public or for commercial purposes, as they would never allow themselves to be considered professional musicians, mainly to distance themselves from the entertainment industry, where performing artists were among the lowest in social status. Masters of classical music clearly had their own professions as scholars and officers and would consider it shameful if they had to make their living from music. They played music for themselves, or for their friends and students, and they discovered friends or lovers through music appreciation.

This partially explains why the classical music of the literati was intimately linked with poetry and to various forms of drama, and became, more or less, poetry without words. In the same manner as poetry, music set out to express human feelings, soothe suffering and bring spiritual elevation. In solo performance, instruments demanded not only a mastery of technique but a high degree of sensitivity (and power) to evoke the subtle sonorities and deep emotional expression that relies on left hand techniques such as sliding, bending, pushing or crossing of the strings to produce typical singing effects and extreme dynamic ranges. Synchronized ensemble playing was virtually impossible without losing a certain amount of subtlety that the educated Chinese ear demanded.

This type of music has come down to us as an oral tradition from masters to students, although written scores that combine numbers and symbols representing pitch and finger techniques have been in use for nearly two thousand years. For instance, the earliest discovered scores for guqin are from the third century. However, it is almost impossible to play directly from the score without first being taught by a master.

Printed musical scores from the Song dynasty (960–1279) are the earliest that survive. The famous Song Confucian philosopher Zhu Xi (1130–1200) collected twelve melodies for twelve songs from the *Book of Songs*. One of the complete melodies that has survived in this collection is the following[37]:

> The cress short and tender,
> Water flows left and right.
> For the beautiful maiden,
> The youth yearns day and night
>
> He can't fall asleep,
> As his desire grow strong.
> He loves and suffers so deep,
> He tosses all night long.
>
> Cress long, short and tender,
> To gather them left and right.
> To the bride sweet and slender,
> O lute, play music bright!
>
> The cress long, short and tender,
> Feast friends at left and right.
> To the bride is so sweet and slender,
> O bells and drums, perform delight
> The bride so sweet and slender!

This is one of the twelve Tang melodies of the reign of Emperor Xuanzong (713–741). As a whole, the melody was heptatonic, but the first stanza is entirely pentatonic and the last stanza is pentatonic except for the last line. The mode was stated to be *re* on D sharp but was in fact a mixture of this and *do* on F.

Jiang Gui, a Daoist poet and composer, wrote *Nine Songs for Yue* state (Yue is the ancient name for Zhejiang and Jiangxi Provinces) written in Liulu notation; a song with zither accompaniment and interlude and a number of tunes in pipa notation.

The first six of the nine songs utilized only the seven notes of the diatonic scale, the mode of *do* or *re* in various keys. The song described the singer awaiting the goddess of the Wuchang Gulf, pouring a libation and riding the waves. The bar-lines mark the end of the lines, determined from the sense and from the verse-form; the comma indicates the caesura; the double bar marks the ends of the stanzas. The mode is *re* on G sharp. In these tunes, many lengthened notes were specified so their rhythmic organization was virtually explicit.[38]

Jiang's song with zither accompaniment was prefaced with explicit directions for tuning the seven strings to the scale F G A B d e g. The song was entitled "Old Regrets." In it a woman sings in bitterness as she realizes that her beauty has slipped away. After the first stanza there is an interlude in harmonics for zither alone; at the end of this the normal position is resumed and the voice re-enters. The bar-lines mark the end of the lines (determined from the sense); the double bar marks the end of the stanzas (explicit in the layout of the text); and the comma marks a caesura. The tablature does not indicate the duration of the notes; the minimum values are supplied on the principle that a note at the end of a line is likely to be prolonged for at least two beats of the basic note-value. A change in the direction of the stems of successive notes at the same pitch, but played in different positions, indicates that the timbre is changed. Though the finger technique is rudimentary compared with later zither technique, the variety of positions in which the same note is taken, and hence variety of timbre, is considerable. If the example is played on the piano, the sustaining pedal and *una corda* would be depressed until the end of each bar, and as much variety in touch as possible would be given to notes at the same pitch. The voice presumably reduced the zither part to the range of one octave.

From various sources it is known that the street performance in Song times were accompanied by music known as *qingyue*. *Qingyue* was the term used by Sui and Tang writers to refer to the old-style (non-ritual) music of Han and Wei times; the term persisted until Song times and was used in contrast to *huyue* (foreign music).[39]

The *qingyue* orchestra included several instruments absent from the Song imperial band, such as the *fangsheang* (a chime of sixteen pieces of iron), *sheng*, and *di*. *Qingyue* was also adopted by many songs that were originally composed as the *yan* (banquet) music within the repertoire of secular entertainment in the palace. In *qingyue*, the cross-flute [*di*] was the chief melodic instrument supporting the voice. The same melodies survived as *nanqu* [Southern Songs]. *Beiqu* was other type melody that survived, using the words and music of *yanyue* songs. Its chief instrument supporting the voice was the pipa. This was the origin of the *Beiqu* [Northern Songs]. Both Southern song and Northern song later became a part of the repertoire of classical opera. The difference between the two genres are notable since the Northern Songs were strongly influenced by foreign music reaching China from the north, while the Southern Songs reflected the musical atmosphere of the more conservative south.

The music of entertainment survived but underwent constant revision at the hands of successive generations of performers. The lyrics of Beiqu were written in a special verse form, the *ci*, in which the lines are of irregular length and the syllables succeed each other in an ordered pattern of tones. The Chinese language was essentially monosyllabic, and since there are no double or triple initial consonants and only two finals in the northern dialect (for example), the sound equipment was poor. The number of different monosyllables was increased to something less than 1,400 by pronouncing each syllable with four different varieties of melodic accent: the four tones. The origin, history and consequences of accompaniment of music with poetry will be analyzed in detail in Chapter 3.

In the Song Dynasty, imperial court music was divided into three types: fine music [*yayue*] pipe and drum music, and music played for entertainment at banquets. The Song yayue [elegant music] was played at ceremonies and festivals such as sacrificial rites and court audiences, grand feasts at gatherings in local areas, and banquets to honor those who passed the highest imperial examination. There was a set of strict performing rules covering pitches, scales, ranges, tunes, instruments and performance forms. Louder music (played by pipes and drums) was also used as martial music and as part of the music played during court audiences. The music played for entertainment at banquets covered the miscellaneous forms of dramas, songs, dances, instrumental performances and variety shows [*baixi*].

The music in the Ming and Qing dynasties was similar to that of the preceding dynasties, although it became increasingly diversified into court and popular music. The best example of this diversification was the emergence of regional operas which derived from various local tunes and popular performance. The oldest Chinese opera was *Canjun* opera (*Chuanju*) that originally emerged from the Three Kingdoms period (220–280).[40] Chinese opera in a more organized form began during the Tang Dynasty with Emperor Xuanzong founding the "Pear Garden" [*líyuán*], the first known opera troupe in China. The troupe mostly performed for the emperor's personal pleasure. To this day operatic professionals are still referred to as "Disciples of the Pear Garden" [*liyuan dizi*].

In the Yuan Dynasty (1279–1368), *Zaju* [variety plays] became a dominant form of theatre. In Yuan theatre, forms of music became more characteristic and personalized. They were sung, gestured and acted based on the characters' specialized roles of *dan* [female], *sheng* [male], *hua* [character with painted-face] and *chou* [clown]. As the melodies became more stereotyped according to theatrical role, the language in both singing and recitation changed on stage. Although actors in theatrical performances of the Song

Dynasty (960–1279) strictly adhered to speaking in Classical Chinese, during the Yuan Dynasty actors speaking in the vernacular tongue gained popularity on stage.[41]

The dominant form of musical theatre in the Ming (1368–1644) and early Qing (1644–1912) dynasties was *kunqu,* which originated in the Wu cultural area. It later evolved into a longer form of play called *chuanxi,* which became one of the 5 melodies that made up *Sichuan* opera. Currently Chinese operas continue to exist in 368 different forms, the best known being Peking opera, which assumed its present form in the mid–19th century and was extremely popular in the latter part of Qing.[42] Chapter 7 will provide a more detailed history of the development of Chinese theatre, especially musical theatre.

The development of musical theatre as well as a national opera was only a part of the history of Chinese music. Hundreds of types of folk music and musical theatre flourished simultaneously in different provinces. These melodies and operas were sung and recited in regional dialects and developed distinct forms of music and lyrics.[43] *Chaozhou xianshi* music is one example. *Xianshi* is a string ensemble music tradition indigenous to the Chaozhou region, formally known as the Shantou Metropolitan Region, located in eastern Guangdong province. It belongs to the category of Chinese folk ensemble music known as *sizhu* [silk and bamboo] which is typically performed indoors for the musicians' own private entertainment and makes use of a group of soft-sounding string and wind instruments and a few small percussion instruments. But unlike other Chinese regional sizhu ensembles, the *xianshi* ensemble almost always consists only of plucked and bowed string instruments. The characteristic string instruments are the *erxian* or *touxian, tihu,* big and small *yehu* [two-stringed bowed lutes], *pipa,* big and small *sanxian, qinqin, ruan, meihuaqin* (all plucked lutes), *zheng* [horizontal board zither with bridges] and *yangqin* [hammered dulcimer]. The percussion instruments consist of a hand-held wooden clapper [*muban*], a pair of hollow wooden blocks [*daban* and *fuban*], and a small drum [*zhegu*]. Aside from having its own distinctive instrumentation, system of notation, tuning, temperament, musical structure, and techniques of melodic development, *xianshi* music has a highly developed system of modes.[44]

2

From Pictures and Graphs to Words

Chinese is the only language with a graphic origin that is commonly used in the world today. During its early history, when its pictorial presentation was the dominant form and before it developed a phonetic system, Chinese shared many features with other graphic languages such as ancient Egyptian, ancient Semitics, and even Mayan script. This chapter explains how Chinese was born, grew and transformed from drawing to writing and from a system of pictures to that of characters and words made of graphic symbols.

For many decades historians have been debating about the origins and early times of Chinese writing. This debate most likely will continue as China unearths additional archaeological discoveries.[1] Although historians have different opinions about the exact date of the beginning of Chinese writing, they agree that archaeological examples of the earliest Chinese language so far discovered exhibit an established writing system that had possessed a long and complex pre-history.[2] This assumption is supported by the formal complexity and maturity that the earliest Chinese writing shared with those of similar pictorial scripts in Mesopotamia and ancient Egypt. All ancient graphic writing required several thousand years of evolution in visual presentation before systematic linguistic symbols were created. The sensibility of perception and subtlety of presentation were often carried into written forms.[3]

Chinese writing emerged from pictorial presentation that developed from its pre-history artifacts, as did the ancient Egyptian and Mesopotamian.[4] The increasing collections of Neolithic artifacts that have been unearthed throughout China during the past decades have provided illustrative clues as to how writing evolved from drawing and painting and how it abstracted from pictorial and geometrical images. Although historians have been debating about where drawing ended and writing began or when a pictorial representation could be called language, no one will deny the vital link between the symbols of drawing/painting and graphic writing.[5] Pre-history rudimentary markings carved into, painted or drawn on artifacts such as pottery, turtle shells, animal bones or other objects made of bone or jade are the most obvious footprints left by the long journey of Chinese writing.

Unlike the alphabetic language that was adopted to record the sound of an established spoken language, a graphic language began its development with long and slow accumulation of pictorial images. It created one sound and one word (character in case of Chinese) at a time. Initially, words simply occurred without any grammatical order, as seen in the pottery graphs of pre-history Chinese between the 6th millennium BC to the oracle bone inscription of Shang dynasty (14th to 11th century BC).

Until the end of the twentieth century, the earliest Neolithic signs found in China were at Dadiwan, a site (5800–5400 BC) discovered in the province of Gansu. The earliest phase of the research at the site yielded symbols painted on the inside surfaces of pottery basins.[6]

In 2003, tentative evidence of an early form of Chinese writing was found at Jiahu, an archaeological site (6600–6200 BC) in Henan province.[7] Some symbols that were found bore striking resemblance to certain modern characters, such as 目 [mù (eye)] and 日 [rì (the sun)]. The date of this site pushed the beginning of Chinese writing farther back to about five thousand years before the oracle bone inscriptions. Although it is difficult to establish direct connections between these inscriptions and a mature written Chinese language, it did provide evidence of the long-term evolution process of Chinese characters.[8]

In 2007, Chinese archaeologists found several thousand carvings in Damaidi, a site (6000–5000 BC) in Ningxia, Hui (ethnic minority) Autonomous Region. The pictographs seen in hundreds of these carvings shared the same size, shape, and meanings with the pictographs unearthed at later dates. They were also remarkably similar to the pictographs of ancient characters of later dynasties.[9] The relationship between these prehistory graphs and Chinese characters was further confirmed by the findings of Banpo and Jiangzhai of Sha'anxi province. Twenty-two Banpo pictographs were radiocarbon dated from 4770 to 4290 BC and the graphs of Jiangzhai were dated from 4020 to 3635 BC.[10]

The effect of three thousand years of linguistic evolution up to the oracle inscription appeared to be on the size of the vocabulary and the overall structure of the script. Just like the early Sumerian ideograms, the Banpo graphs were monophonic (character with single sound) and monosomatic (character with single meaning), each with only one component without any phonetic loan usage or semantic-phonetic compounding.[11] This demonstrated the primitive nature of this stage of linguistic accumulation. Verbal compounding only occurred during the next tens of centuries when language had exhausted the possible monophonic and monosomatic words. The Banpo graphs were also used individually on pottery and pottery fragments, unlike written language, which tended to occur in strings rather than isolated words (characters). Therefore, if or when these written words could be called language depends on the definition one uses.[12]

Like the ancient Mesopotamian and ancient Egyptian, Chinese writing emerged from a wealth of visual images manifested in painting and sculptured pottery. Along with the masterpieces of painted pottery in Majiayao culture, in Gansu and Qinghai provinces (3300–2000 BC), *machang* and *banshan* signs were discovered. The machang phase of the Majiayao culture (2300–2050 BC) produced many large and small two-handled jars, pitchers, bowls, and beakers. Decorative motifs on Machang-period wares were largely geometric and include curvilinear patterns and cross-hatching, lozenges, triangles, circles, and squares in an endless array of combinations.[13]

Many more complex signs were found on the east coast in Liangzhu pottery (3400–2250 BC). Some of these markings represented number, position, or ownership of the artifacts and they became more and more varied and precise. Many historians concluded that this was the proto Chinese writing before it became standardized, systematized, and stabilized, a process which took over ten more centuries to complete.[14] However, historians and archaeologists disagreed with each other on whether or not these symbols could be considered as a primitive type of writing. Many scholars thought that they could not be recognized as writing because they were found in isolation (as would be expected with ownership marks, clan symbols, number values or locations) rather than in sequences that were representative of the spoken language. As few of these artifacts exist, no evidence could be found concerning the processes fundamental to the beginnings of a true and functional writing system.[15]

The pottery inscription that showed steady consistency to the early development of Chinese writing was incised signs from the pottery of Dawenkou culture in Shandong, dating to c. 2800–2500 BC. This was the first time that the unearthed inscription could be directly linked to the Longshan culture, the recognized ancestral link to the Shang dynasty (1600–1046 BC), during which time the first undisputed Chinese writing appeared. At Dawenkou sites in Shandong, Lingyanghe and Dazhucun, nineteen pictorial symbols were found painted in sixteen pottery jars and shards.[16] Some of these symbols resembled axes similar to those at Banpo sites. Some symbols were variously described as resembling the sun above a cloud, fire, or the sun above a mountain-like mark. These symbols were very similar in style to Shang pictographs and early Zhou clan symbols.

The most important findings in the Dawenkou sites was that it was the first time that symbols came to have multiple components reminiscent of the compounding of elements in Chinese script.[17] For example, a graph depicting a circle-and-cloud resembled the Chinese character for 旦 [*dan* (dawn)] presented in a picture of a sun on the top of a cloud (a picture of sunrise). Another pictograph was the sun on top of a fire representing the later Chinese character 炅 [*jiong* (bright)].[18] These evidences proved that the evolution of Chinese pictographs shared the direction and the speed (about twenty centuries between the appearance of single to compound signs) of other pictographic systems in the ancient world.[19]

The findings of other Neolithic sites have also verified that the Dawenkou graphs were used as language rather than random and local marks. The motif of sun plus cloud and that of a bird perched on a mountain-like shape, for example, appeared at the sites of the Liangzhu culture (3400–2250 BC) in the Yangzi River Delta.[20] The Chengziyai site in Longshan township, Shandong province, has produced fragments of inscribed bones presumably used to divine the future, dating to 2500–1900 BC, and symbols on pottery vessels from Dinggong are thought by some scholars to be an early form of writing, although they did not look like the later Chinese characters.[21]

It appears obvious that Chinese script originated from pictorial symbols because even after several thousand years of evolution and transfiguration, there are still as many as six hundred Chinese characters that maintain their noticeable pictorial origins. Some of these are *ma* [horse], *ri* [the sun], *shan* [mountain], *shui* [water, (river)], *yu* [fish], *che* [wagon], *chen* [dust], and *jian* [to see]. The character ma had a horse head, four legs, a tail, and even hair behind its neck during the period of oracle bone inscription [*jiagu wen*] (1400–1200 BC). In the bronze script (1100–256 BC) ma had lost the depiction of its body yet still maintained its four legs and a tail. It took many more centuries for the pictorial graph horse to lose its legs, which were replaced by four dots. During the Han dynasty (207 BC–AD 220) the character horse came to have a horizontal stroke under its belly instead of four legs (abstracted four dots). By the same token, it took close to two thousand years of evolution and abstraction for the character yu [fish] to lose its pictorial tail while the depiction of a fish's scale became a linear line rather than a curved one.[22]

The earliest form of Chinese writing that the majority of scholars have agreed upon is the oracle bone inscription [*jiagu wen*].[23] The oracle bone inscription was primarily used in the royal house of the late Shang dynasty. The reason it was called oracle bone inscription was that these words were found in the front plates (plastrons) of turtle shells, or the shoulder bones (scapula) of oxen. The people of the Shang dynasty cut inscriptions in these bones with a sharp object and threw them into a fire. By interpreting the broken marks on the bone after it was burnt, they attempted to cast their fortune. This led to the English translation of Chinese *jiagu wen* (literally shell and bone inscription) into oracle bone inscription because its ritual function was perceived by Western scholars as similar to that of the oracles of the ancient Greeks.[24]

It was no surprise that the oracle bone inscriptions were pictographic when we consider that the prehistory pottery graphs had developed for thousands of years. Some important evolution had occurred during the gap between the pottery graphs and oracle bone inscription. First, the pictorial writing itself was conventionalized by simplification and linearization. This tendency continued during the next two hundred years after the earliest oracle bone inscription.[25] Second, sound (phonetic elements) began to play an increasingly important role in linguistic presentation, a development similar to the linguistic transition in other ancient graphic writing systems such as those of Mesopotamia and Egypt. By the time of the oracle bone inscriptions, phonetic loan graphs, semantic-phonetic compounds, and associative compounds became common in Chinese written language and represented almost forty percent of all words in the language, while pictographs had reduced to twenty-three percent.[26]

After many centuries, even thousands of years of accumulation of vocabulary and expansion of structural base, the oracle inscription represented a mature written language.[27] The number of different characters was estimated at approximately forty-five hundred (including about a thousand variant forms). As the inscription kept evolving and transforming, only about a thousand to fifteen hundred of these could be recognized by a Chinese writer of later dates. In the Zhou dynasty (1045–256 BC) bronze inscriptions, there are roughly four thousand different graphs, of which a little over twenty-four hundred are recognizable. The number of characters during the Warring States period (403–221 BC) was difficult to determine because of the variety of graphs scattered among silk, bamboo, bronze and stone inscriptions, but it was more than five thousand.[28]

Although it could function as a mature media, the oracle bone inscription was far from a standardized language. During the Yin and Shang periods, Chinese writing appeared to have a formal freedom that it lost and never regained during later times. As there were many different ways to envisage and depict the same objects, different words were invented to convey the same meaning. Writing followed the instinct of seeing and perceiving, and as the same subjects were seen from different angles and in different scope and depth, this naturally led to different pictorial graphs and therefore different characters that represented the writer's interpretation. Like the ancient Egyptian that had about seventy-five different pictorial signs for the word "man" (standing man, working man, sitting man, man with a tool, man with two hands up, man with a royal sign), Chinese scripts created dozens of different characters for the same man, each of which sounded and was written differently. Instead of adding a determinative (an additional sign) next to the pictograph of man, as in Egyptian, Chinese added simple strokes to the pictograph of man to create new words. Although strokes created more variations, they also created problems of visual distinction. For example, 刀 [a sword] and 匕 [small knife], 口 [a mouth] and 囗 [city wall], 内 [inside] and 丙 [the third] were often confused and mistaken for each other because visual distinction was too slight.[29]

As graphic words accumulated, their pictorial variations multiplied and the boundaries between words began to overlap. At this time, the distinctions were mainly pictorial: the same symbol indicated different meanings if it was presented in slightly different positions or in various proportions and sequences, single or double, up or down, upside down or inside out, leaning to the right or the left. With this purposeful alternation (to make new distinct meaning) or by accidental misuse (the writer meant one graph, yet used another by mistake), the shape of writing began to lose its precision and visual control. Thus, the form of characters was continuously in a state of flux because any alteration in the shape of the script would produce either confusion or repetition of the existing vocabulary. After centuries in which pictorial and ideographs continued to multiply and diversify, simplification became necessary. During this simplification, convention took over and graphs began to lose their visual edge.[30]

So, by the time of the oracle bone inscription, pictographic elements in writing contained only one-fourth of the total characters of Chinese. However, unlike the ancient Egyptian and Sumerian that transformed into phonetic languages, leaving their graphic features behind, Chinese remained graphic in its basic structure and component.[31] Through a long process of evolution, Chinese vocabulary gradually uprooted itself from pictorial imitation as semantic unity. At the beginning, words contained their graphical elements: the word mountain was an abstract image of three peaks, the sun, a circle with a dot, or the word vehicle, a man sitting on two wheels. Over time, the vast repertoire of pictorial characters became fragmented and abstracted into strokes and combinations of strokes while their meanings constantly redefined and transformed with every single visual alteration. This process of fragmentation and disfiguration was similar to the phonetic fragmentation that ancient

Semitic languages went through, from graphic words (often with one, two, or three syllables) to syllables, then eventually, to an alphabet. Think about tearing down an old building, salvaging the materials (beams, bricks) and then rebuilding, using a different floor plan. The difference was that Semitic languages had to work with phonetic elements while Chinese had vast stores of graphic components.

Despite its status as a fully functional and fairly established writing system, the oracle bone script was not completely mature. Some graphs changed meaning depending on context or occasion. This script gradually outgrew its inconsistency and became standardized by the early Western Zhou period. A graph when inverted horizontally generally referred to the same word, and additional components were sometimes present without changing the meaning. It was not until the more complete standardization during the Qin dynasty (when "seal script" established as the dominant script) that these irregularities ended.[32]

The Oracle bone script characters altered the shapes of their components in later writings. For instance, when an independent character came to be used as a component it changed its appearance. The character for a plant (of rice) 禾 [*he*] changed as it was used as a component of another character instead of as a character by itself. The character for autumn 秋 [*qiu*] now appears with 禾 as one component and 火 as another component. The transfiguration over thousands of years was the reason why the majority of characters found on the bone fragments were unrecognizable and many still remain undeciphered today.

Chinese historians have unearthed close to five thousand characters on oracle bones and only one third of them have been recognized as Chinese words found in later historic documents. Compared to the marks and graphs that appear on the Neolithic pottery, oracle inscription represented a language that had been used for a long time. One can also see that the transformation from pictographic to ideographic symbols has occurred. By the end of the period of the oracle inscription, although some visual elements of pictures from ancient texts remained — such as scales on the fish, the curved horn on the top of the sheep's head, and the big mouth of the tiger — the percentage of graphically derived characters had been reduced to about only thirty-seven percent. The number of phonetic characters had risen to about twenty percent.[33]

Unlike the Egyptian tomb hieroglyphs, whose meaning sometimes can be easily identified by a casual observer because of their pictorial quality, oracle inscriptions do not reveal their meanings to an untrained eye. This is an indication that the Chinese writing system had already become highly abstract.

Like the later cuneiform of ancient Mesopotamia, oracle bone inscription had begun to show the tendency to merge single characters into combined characters. These combined characters had grown to three hundred, one sixth of the total of the oracle inscription.

Inscriptions on Shang bronze were of a relatively uniform style compared to oracle inscription, although great inconsistency remained between typical characters and certain instances of clan names or emblems.[34] Like early oracle script, the structures and orientations of individual graphs still varied substantially in the Shang bronze, to the point where a particular character could be written differently each time rather than in a standardized way.[35] As in the oracle script, characters could be written facing left or right, turned 90 degrees, and sometimes even flipped vertically, generally with no change in meaning. However, Bronze inscription had an obvious tendency of standardization and formal control.[36]

The bronze inscriptions were almost all cast rather than engraved, and were relatively short and simple. Some expressed nothing but to identify the name of a clan or a family. Typical inscriptions include the maker's clan name and the posthumous title of the ancestor who was commemorated by the making and use of the bronze vessel. These inscriptions, especially those late period examples identifying a name, possessed a highly pictographic character and preserved the conservative and complex Shang form of writing as distinctive to the contemporary linear and simplified writing on other materials.[37]

The evolution and transfiguration of the word for tiger demonstrated the process from pictorial to abstract symbol. The word *hu* first appeared in Shang inscription as a picture of a tiger, complete with a head, a pair of eyes, a body, four legs, colorful fur, and a tail. It lost its head (which was replaced by a triangle) in the early oracle bone inscriptions. In later Shang, the body disappeared and was replaced by a vertical stroke. In middle Zhou inscriptions, especially those in bronze, the stripes and fur completely disappeared and were simplified into a stroke. The graph "to see" 見 [*jian*] is a more abstract character. In Shang it originally was written as a graph of a pair of eyes 目 [*mu*] on the top of a man. During the Zhou bronze inscription, the man was simplified into a pair of legs under the eyes. The word *to see* later became walking eyes (見) during the later Zhou and Han periods.

Shang bronze script was considered as a formal and official script. It was similar to, but sometimes even more complex than, the unattested daily (informal) script found on bamboo and wood books and other media. But they both were more complex than the Shang script on the oracle bones.[38]

The Chinese characters inscribed in Western Zhou dynasty (1045–770

BC) bronze basically continued from the Shang writing system without radical or sudden change. They were, like their Shang predecessors in all media, often irregular in shape and size, and the structures and details often varied from one piece of writing to the next, even within the same piece. Although most were not pictographs in function, the early Western Zhou bronze inscriptions have been described as more pictographic in appearance than those of subsequent periods. During the Western Zhou, many graphs began to show signs of simplification and linearization — the changing of rounded elements into squared ones, solid elements into short line segments, and thick, variable-width lines into thin ones of uniform width.

Some flexibility in orientation of graphs (rotation and reversibility) continued in the Western Zhou, but this became increasingly scarce. The graphs gradually became slightly more uniform in structure, size and arrangement by the time of the third Zhou sovereign, King Kang (1021–996 BC), and after the ninth, King Yì (885–878 BC), this trend appeared to be more obvious.[39] By the beginning of Eastern Zhou (770–221 BC), Chinese script became less pictorial as the strokes from which the characters were composed became fully linearized, the curved lines straightened, and disconnected lines were connected.

During the middle and late Warring States period (475–221 BC), the average length of inscriptions decreased greatly. Many, especially those on weapons, recorded only the date and maker. At this time inscriptions were typically engraved onto the already cast bronzes rather than being written into the wet clay of piece-molds, as had been the earlier practice. The engraving was often roughly and hastily executed. The bronze inscriptions continued trends from the earlier period such as the use of artistically embellished scripts (e.g., bird and insect scripts) on decorated bronze items. In daily writing, which was not embellished in this manner, the typical script evolved in different directions in various regions. The local styles of characters were cultivated independently of one another and crystallized into what are called the scripts of the Six States. There were also several variants for local scripts. For example, *niao chong wen* [birds and worms script], characterized by intricate decorations to the defining strokes, was used in the southern Kingdoms of Wu, Chu, and Yue.[40]

During the Qín dynasty (221–206 BC), Li Si (280–208 BC), with the support of the central government, promulgated the small seal script (commonly known as seal script) as the standard script throughout the newly unified Chinese empire.[41] The seal script was not invented during Qin, but by this time it had become more uniform and stylistically symmetrical than the vertically elongated script of the previous Warring States period while its structure remained unchanged. It was systematized by Li Si during the reign of Qin Shi Huang through elimination of most variant structures and it was imposed as the nationwide standard while other regional scripts were banned. Through Chinese commentaries it is known that Li Si compiled *Cangjiepian*, a non-extant work of character recognition listing some 3,300 Chinese characters in small seal script. Their form is characterized by being less rectangular and more squarish. The small cursive form clerical script came after the small script.[42]

After centuries of evolution and renovation of its written form, ancient Chinese maintained its graphic script. This is different from other ancient languages such as the Semitics that went through several linguistic re-orientations. As the languages of Mesopotamia changed from Sumerian, Akkadian, Babylonian, Assyrian, Canaanite, Phoenician, Aramaic, Hebrew, and Arabic, Chinese survived mainly because it abstracted its pictographs into ideograms and continuously simplified and standardized. To simplify writing, Chinese script was further reduced from graphic characters into strokes and combinations of strokes until they became a visual alphabet with its smallest components in image rather than in sound. Although concrete images had disappeared from the appearance of its script, Chinese maintained its visual structure and it remained organized by strokes and their combinations. These visual (as distinct from phonetic) distinctions still determine differences in meaning and connotation of the language.

These strokes had special order and were composed into graphic components. The majority of commonly used Chinese characters have 10 to 30 strokes. Certain stroke order was adopted to ensure speed, accuracy, and legibility in composition.[43]

The majority of Chinese characters have two parts: a graphic part to define meaning and a phonetic part to determine pronunciation. This combination order is the key to the understanding of the origins and development of meaning. This kind of graphic compound was called *xiangshengzi* [character imitating sound] by Chinese linguists and is a phono-semantic compound. Simple examples are: 河 [*hé*] (a river), 溏 [*tang*] (a pond) 流 [*liu*] (stream of flow), 浪 [*lang*] (*wave or to go with wave*), 活 [*huo*] (to move, to live or to be flexible) 源 [*yuan*] (fountain or river head) 湾 [*wan*] (a bay or grove) 湖 [*hú*] (lake), and 滑 [*huá*] (slippery). On the left side, each of these characters has a radical of three dots, a simplified pictograph for a water drop. This indicates that the character has a semantic connection with water. On the right-hand side of each character is a phonetic indicator. For example, in the case of 湖 [*hú*] (lake), the phonetic indicator is 胡 [*hu*], which by itself means the bottom of an animal's chin.

This seems logical and easy to understand; remember, however, Chinese characters are not always as they seem. For example, the last character 胡 [*hu*], without its three dots, is an ancient character first appearing in *Shijing*, an anthology of poetry collected by Confucius.

It refers to the above noted body part of an animal. However, it was already a compound character. It originally derived from two more components: 古 [gu] (old) and 月 [*yu*] (a radical), that had been simplified from a character 肉 [*rou*] (meat). In the latter case, there was no logical reason for 胡 to have the sound *hu* because neither of the components 古 [gu] or 月 [*yu*] had the *hu* sound.

From this deeper level of compounding, both the meaning and pronunciation of 湖 were not as transparent and arbitrary as they seemed. After many centuries of accumulation, the compounding and re-compounding of some of the internal components had become buried and forgotten. This disappearance of presentation also occurred to the sound of the compound characters. The relationship between 古 [*gu*], 月 [*yu*] and 胡 [*hu*] could well be in the vowel ending *u* which had obtained different tones that probably did not exist at the time of the compilation of *Shijing*.[44]

Compound characters are more complex and more difficult to pin down because not every component is clearly defined and straightforward. Their meanings and connotations often went through various detours and transfigurations (derivative cognates or reciprocal meaning) [*zhuǎnzhù*].[45] For example, 过 [*guo*] has multiple connotations: "to walk by," "to pass by (a place)," "to surpass," "to be better," and "to be mistaken." In *Zuo zhuan* (the earliest historical narrative compiled before 389 BC) and Lun yu (a collection of the words and acts of Confucius, compiled between 475 and 221 BC) alone, it was used for many different meanings, some close to its originals such as "to walk or to pass by"; others were used for extended meanings "to be over and better," and the most extended use was "to be wrong," implying that it had passed the limit to be correct.[46] 过 [*guo*] is being used today, but has confined its multi-dimensional connotations. It is often used as a component of a word rather than as a character. Some are 过 错 [*guo cuo*] (mistake), 过 矢 [*guo shi*] (accident), 改 过 [*gai guo*] (to correct a mistake) 过 期 [*guo qi*] (overdue) and 經 过 [*jing guo*] (to pass by). In each and every one of these occasions, the extra character functions as a determinative or definer of the connotation of *guo*, an overused and abused character after two thousand years of articulation and repeated writing.

The accumulation of Chinese characters was driven by two separate goals which were contrary and complementary at times: to create new characters by expanding the established boundaries of meanings and to distinguish the newly invented meanings from the existing ones. In other words, it alternately strengthened the boundaries of meanings by redefining graphic distinctions and relaxed them by adding increasingly refined distinctions. During this constant transfiguration, hardly any Chinese characters were (or are) the product of a single combination. Therefore it was impossible to simply specify the meaning of a character by merely identifying its graphic and phonetic parts. In Chinese language, one component plus another often did not become exactly two. The best example of this fluid relationship between graphic form and its meaning was the function of radicals, a highly abstract and simplified semantic determinative.

All Chinese characters are logograms of several derivative types depending on their origin and later transfiguration. They include a handful of pictographic [*xiàngxíng*] characters, a number of ideographic [*zhǐshì*] ones, and the vast majority that originated as phono-semantic compounds [*xiàngshēng*]. The traditional Chinese lexicography divided characters into six categories [*liùshū*, "Six Writings"]. As phono-semantic compounds continually increased, the boundary of categories overlapped. In the oracle bone inscriptions, roughly a quarter of the characters were pictograms while the rest were either phono-semantic compounds or compound ideograms. Only a few of these characters remain recognizable to modern readers, as their shape, usage and meaning have changed over time.

At present, more than 90 percent of Chinese characters are phono-semantic compounds constructed with elements that are intended to provide clues to both meaning and pronunciation. However, as both the meanings and pronunciations of the characters have changed over time, these components are no longer reliable guides. The failure to recognize the historical and etymological role of these components often leads to misclassification. Reconstructing Middle and Old Chinese phonology from the clues present in characters is a part of Chinese historical linguistics. In Chinese, it is called *Yinyunxue* [studies of sounds and rhymes]. In older literature, Chinese characters in general may be referred to as ideograms due to the misconception that characters represent ideas directly, whereas in fact they did so only through association or convention with the spoken word.[47]

The oldest type of Chinese character is *xiàng xíng zi* [character imitating physical form]. Examples are 木 [*mu* (a tree)] derived from a picture of a small tree with three branches and three roots spread out at the bottom. The combination of two 木 [*mu*] became 林 [*lin* (grove)], and three 木 [*mu*] became to 森 [*sen* (a forest)]. From characters that date back to the oracle bones inscription there is 鳥 [*niao* (a bird)] derived from the picture of a bird with a head, a crown of feathers, a pair of wings, a tail, and two feet. Over the centuries this character lost its distinction between the crown and head, its wings were reduced to two, then later, one horizontal stroke, and its feet and tail abstracted into a bottom stroke (in the modern simplified character).

As various pictorial characters were juxtaposed, they became ideographic compounds [*huìyì* (joined meaning)]. Two or more pictographic or ideographic characters were combined to suggest a third meaning. For example, the character 各 [*gè*] originally meant "to arrive" because it was a combination of the pictorial graphs 夂 [a foot (the inverted form of 止 *zhǐ*, originally a foot)] and of a 凵 or 口 (walled object), perhaps symbolizing a house. A foot in the door of a house became an abstract word meaning "arrive." The combination of two or more concrete characters to define an abstract word appeared to be an effective juxtaposition. For instance, to depict 人 [*ren* (a man)] leaning against a 木 [*mu* (a tree)] became 休 [*xi* (rest)]. From two 木 [*mu* (tree branches)] over 火 [*huo* (fire)] came 焚 [*fen* (burning)]; 爪 [*zhua* (a hand)] on a 木 [*mu* (bush) was 采 [*cai* (to harvest)]. The character 集 [*ji* (gather together)] showed three birds (隹) on a tree.

Jiǎjiè [Rebus (phonetic loan)] characters were formulated by borrowing or making use of the sound of another character.

Borrowed characters were used to write another homophonous or near-homophonous morpheme, comparable with using "4" as a rebus for English "for." The character 來 [*lai*] was originally a pictogram of a wheat plant and meant "wheat." As this was pronounced similarly to the Old Chinese word [*mlɔk* (to come)], 來 was also used to write the verb "to come." Eventually the more common usage, the verb "to come" became established as the default reading of the character 來 [*lai*], and a new character was devised for "wheat" [*mai*]. (The modern pronunciations are lái and mài.) When a character is used as a rebus this way, it is called a *jiajiezi* [loaned and borrowed character], translatable as "phonetic loan character" or "rebus character."

As in Egyptian hieroglyphs and Sumerian cuneiform, early Chinese characters were used as rebuses to express abstract meanings that were not easily depicted. Thus many characters stood for more than one word. In some cases the extended use would take over completely and a new character would be created for the original meaning, usually by modifying the original character with a radical (determinative). For instance, 右 [*yòu*] originally meant right hand or right side, but its sound was borrowed to write the abstract word 又 [*yòu* (again or moreover)]. In modern usage, the character 又 exclusively represents *yòu* [again] while 右, which adds the "mouth radical" 口 to 又, represents right. This process of graphic disambiguation was a common source of phono-semantic compound characters.

Most *Jiajie* [Rebus (phonetic loan)] characters were created during the

Han dynasty and the original (or loan) words and their new creations were well distinguished. Over ten centuries later during the Ming dynasty (1368–1644), these loan words and their creations became perceived as interchangeable borrowing [*tongjie*]. Therefore, the two terms, *jiajie* [phonetic loan] and *tongjie* [interchangeable or universal borrowing] became commonly used as synonyms.[48]

Phono-semantic compound characters [*xíng shēng zi*] sometimes were called radical-phonetic characters. Over ninety percent of Chinese characters were created by combining a phonetic (rebus) component with a semantic determinative component. This presents both an approximation of the correct pronunciation as well as an element of meaning. The semantic element, called a "radical," would be used centuries later to organize characters in a dictionary. Such compounds remedied the difficulty of using iconic forms to represent physically similar objects (such as dogs versus wolves), actions, and abstract notions, without creating undue homophony as simple rebuses would. Phono-semantic compounds appeared prior to the first attested Chinese writing on Shang Dynasty oracle bones.

As an example, the verb "to wash one's hair" was pronounced *mù*. Although difficult to draw a picture for the act, it happened to sound the same as the word 木 [*mù* (tree)]. So *mù* [to wash one's hair] could simply be written 沐, a pictorial of a tree, but disambiguated by adding a radical 氵 [*sandianshui*], which was an abstracted version of 水 [*shui* (water)], giving some idea of the meaning. Similarly, the water radical 氵 could also combine with 林 [*lín* (woods)] to produce the water-related homophone 淋 [*lín* (to pour)].

However, the phonetic component was not always as meaningless as this example would suggest. Rebuses were sometimes chosen to be compatible semantically as well as phonetically. It was often the case that the determinative merely constrained the meaning of a word which already had compounded. The character 菜 [*cai* (vegetable)] is a case in point. The determinative 艹 (an abstractive form of 草 [*cao* (plants)] was combined with 采 [*cai* (to harvest)]. However, 采 did not merely provide the pronunciation. In classical texts it was also used to mean "vegetable." That is, the character 采 extended semantically from "to harvest" to the things to be harvested, the vegetable. This semantic expansion was similar to that of the alphabetic language. The only difference was that alphabetic languages expanded semantically through phonetic inflection while Chinese expanded its meanings and connotations both graphically and phonetically.[49]

After several thousand years, Chinese characters often combined, compounded, and transfigured so many times that the origins of the word got lost. The distinction between roots and branches and between original and extended meanings began to overlap. To organize this increasingly swollen mass of characters, radicals were used as section headers for a Chinese dictionary [*bùshǒu*]. These radicals, also known as index keys or classifiers, classify characters in dictionaries from *Shuōwén Jiézì* (the first Chinese dictionary compiled during the late Han) down to modern times.

The term radical is not an adequate translation (for *bushou*) to depict the function of Chinese semantic determinatives. While radicals in the inflected words of European languages indicate the original meaning and prefixes and suffixes were added for case, time, and mood, the Chinese radical worked at lexicographic rather than grammatical levels, as seen in the European languages.[50] As the size of verbal repertoire grew, the relationship between the section headers and the characters under them became less exact. As semantic components became further abstracted, the semantic function of the *bushou* [section header] diminished. Some played a semantic role in the characters listed under them; others simply gave a hint of meaning or even were arbitrarily chosen as classifiers used to group characters for lexicographic convenience.[51]

Chinese possessed an open structure wherein new characters and words (combination of characters) could be continually created and added to the vocabulary. Unlike the glutting process of other languages, where words got longer and fatter, Chinese cultivated an elastic shape which expanded and retracted alternatively or simultaneously. In fact, at the earliest known stage of the Chinese script, it was not at all uncommon for two or even three syllables to be written together as a single graph, for example, *san wan* [thirty thousand] and *shiwu fa* [fifteen expeditions]. Bisyllabic graphs were also found in bronze inscriptions from the Zhou period. *Xiaozi* [little son], *xiao chen* [lesser vassal], *Wu Wang* [King Wu], and *Wen Wang* [King Wen] are examples. It is evident that at the earliest known stage of Chinese writing, there was still a clear understanding that graphs (and apparently lexical units as well) could have more than one syllable. However, by the Qin and Han periods the monosyllabicizing tendencies of the script had eliminated nearly all bisyllabic and trisyllabic graphs from the texts. This purification of written form did not diminish the intuitive sense that lexical items could be polysyllabic, and so graphs of more than one syllable continued to be created, such as *bu yung* [no need to], *er shi* [twenty], *san shi* [thirty], and *si shi* [forty]. Yet the pressure to conform to the monosyllabic constraints of the script was so compelling that character had to be compounded tightly into one space and one syllable. From this time on fusion of characters had to take different forms and combined components into a single character or characters into a single word rather than attempting to squeeze them into a single syllable.

During the early part of its verbal accumulation the majority of Chinese characters (85 to 90 percent) consisted of a component that conveyed sound (the phonophore) and a component that conveyed meaning (the radical or semantic classifier). Neither component, however, told the reader exactly what the character meant or precisely how it should sound, but only gave a more or less vague approximation of the meaning and pronunciation. For example, the reader might encounter a character whose semantic classifier consisted of three dots vertically stacked on the left side. This indicated that the graph in all likelihood (but not necessarily) had something to do with water or liquid substances, hence the reader might guess that the graph meant "wave," "splash," "shallow," and so forth. Judging from this "water" radical alone, he could not be sure exactly what the graph meant, only that it probably had something vaguely to do with water or liquidity. More than two thousand graphs share the 氵 [water] radical, with meanings running the gamut from "eternal" to "pure," "stream," "islet," "the Milky Way," "mercury," "float," "swim," "basket for catching fish," "bubbles," "varnish," "sap," "juice," "gravy," "oil," "wine," "briny," "drench," "drivel," "diarrhea," "spit," "damp," "stagnant," "mud," "licentious," "tears," and "Macao." Merely recognizing the semantic classifier of a character was not necessarily of much use in determining its meaning, reading and comprehension.[52]

Sometimes, a radical developed several different graphs, each of which served as a separate radical that branched out as separate wings of characters. For example, 口 [kou (mouth)] functioned as a variety of radicals and compounded different ways to form different characters. Most of these characters had something with do with the shape of a circle, to circle, or referred to an activity that was involved with some sort of confinement. They were as 囚 [qiu (to imprison)], 四 [si (four)], 囝 [zi (son or daughter)] 回 [hui (to return)], 因 [yin (reason)], 囡 [nan (child)], 困 [yuan (deep)], 囧 [jiong (bright)], 囫 [hu (complete)], 园 [yuan (circle)], 困 [qun (winding)], 固 [gu (solid)], 国 [guo (nation)], 图 [tu (a painting or a map)], 囿 [you (walled round piece of land)], 圁 [yin (the name of a river)], 图 [hun (stable of pigs)], 圃 [vegetable nursery)], 圄 [yu (jail)], 圈 [juan (pig house)], 圉 [yu (to raise a horse)], 圊 [qing (washroom)], 團 [tuan (circle)], 園 [yuan (to fence up)], 圜 [yuan (the universe)], and 𡇟 [luan (circle)]. As 口 [kou (mouth)], the graph of a mouth compounded with other graphs to form a variety of characters and it became 古 [gu (old or ancient)], 句 [ju (a sentence)], 另 [ling (to separate)], and 只 [zhi (only)]. When 口 was used as a radical on the left side of a character, the majority of newly compounded characters had a connotation of an activity involving the mouth: 叫 [jiao (to cry or shout)], 叮 [ding (to tell repeatedly)], 叱 [chi (yell at)], 叨 [tao (talk a lot)], 叽 [ji (to make fun of someone)], 吃

[chi (to eat)], 吐 [tu (to spit out)], 吓 [xia (to terrify)], 吟 [yin (to sigh)], 吠 [fei (to bark)], 吩 [fen (to advise)], 听 [ting (to listen)], 吮 [shun (to inhale)], 吰 [hong (sound of a bell)], 吵 [chao (to argue)], 吸 [xi (to breathe)], 鸣 [ming (to make sound)], 呪 [zhou (to pray)], 咕 [tie (to leak?)], 呬 [xi (to rest)], 咀 [ju (to taste)], 咍 [hai (to laugh at)], 咏 [yong (to sing)] and several hundred more. A doubled 口 could be put on the top or the bottom of a graph to create more characters such as 哭 [ku (to cry)], 嚴 [yan (urgent or rigid)], 嚣 [xiao (noise)], 嘽 [tan (at ease)], 器 [qi (tools or instruments)], and [jiao (in high voice)].[53]

Several thousand graphs share 氵, the "water" radical. Most, but not all, of the following characters have a connotation related to water: 汀 [ding (little piece of land in shallow water)], 汁 [zhi (juice)], 汃 [bin (the sound of waves)], 汊 [汊 [cha (tributary or small river)], 汋 [zhuo (sound of water)], 汍 [huan (a face with tears)], 汎 [fan (to flow)], 汏 [dai (to wash with running water)], 汗 [han (sweat)], 汝 [ru (you and the name of a river)], 江 [jiang, (river)], 池 [chi (a pound)], 汤 [tang (soup)], 汪 [wang (a water basin)], 汲 [ji (to get water)], 汸 [fang (a large flow of water)], 汹 [xung (fast flowing water)], 決 [jue (open a water channel)], 汽 [qi (steam)], 汾 [fen (the name of a river)], 沂 [yi (the name of a river)], 沅 [yuan (the name of a river)], 沌 [dun (unclear water)], 没 [mo (into water)], 沙 [sha (sand)], 沟 [gou (deep ditch], 治 [zhi (the name of an ancient river) and (to manage)], 河 [he (river)], 泄 [xie (letting out)], 沾 [zhan (to wet)], 法 [fa (law)], 泡 [Pao (bubbles)], 波 [bo (waves)], 泥 [ne (mud)], 注 [zhu (to pore into)], 泪 [lei (tears)], 泽 [ze (mash)], 洋 [yang (the ocean)], 潤 [ren (to wet)], 潦 [liao (潭 [tan (deep lake)], 涩 [se (not fluid)], 澎 [peng (big waves)], and 潜 [qian (to cross water)]. For such a large number of characters, it is not possible to determine the exact meaning by merely recognizing the semantic radical. The best example of how time had buried many original meanings of Chinese characters is the character of 法 [fa (law or punishment)]. The current character 法 has lost its original ancient graph, a complex pictorial compound of twenty-one strokes. It had three components, each of which referred to distinct meaning. The largest graph was *zhi*, the name (and graph) of a mythical animal (a deer with a single horn) that was believed to be able to differentiate between a righteous man and an evil one. Under this presiding animal was the character *qu* [out] symbolizing that the judge (*zhi*) would drive the evil (criminal) out of court. The last component was the familiar 氵 that emphasized that law (judgement) had to be as even as water.[54]

Another example of characters that had completely lost their original graph and associated connotations was 自 [zi (start from)]. 自, is an old graph that had been around at least as long as the Confucian classics. Unlike 法,

which was reduced from another graph, 自 co-existed and originally shared a part of the character of 鼻 [bi (nose)]. For centuries since the pre–Han period, the two characters developed a shared space of meanings. Although 自 had long departed from an associative meaning with the nose, it had been used as compounding component with other graphs to create characters that possessed connotations relative to nose or smell. 鼻 has always had a connotation of "beginning" until contemporary times.[55] Many characters, however, continued to be used in both abstract and concrete meanings. Chinese speakers and writers could effortlessly differentiate them according to the context. To mention a few: 足 [*zu*] means both the foot and sufficient; 云 [*yun*] both the cloud and to speak (say); 莫 [*mo*] both dusk and no one; 亦 [*yi*] both armpit and also; 又 [*you*] both hand and again; and 其 [*qi*] both basket and a possessive pronoun.[56]

Phonetic association alone did not clarify exact meaning. As in graphic features, the phonetic classifier of a character was not necessarily of much use in determining its meaning. For example, the reader might encounter a character whose phonophore might be fāng [a square], fáng [a house], fǎng [to visit] and fàng [to put down]. Each of these variations could further combine with another character to form a string of characters and words. Fáng [a house] could be extended to *fáng-jian* [a room], *fang-chan* [real-estate property], *fang-zu* [rent], *fang-zi* [a house], *zu-fang* [to rent out property], *mai-fang* [to buy property], and *kan-fang* [to view the property]. By replacing a consonant *f* with *a* or *t*, it became tāng [soup], táng [sugar], tǎng [to lay down] and tàng [to warm up]. With hundreds of characters that branched out by phonetic connection, clarifying semantic determinatives became useless or even redundant.

Even if one got the reading right, there were dozens of characters that had the same pronunciation. For example, scores of characters and words shared the same pronunciation, *shi*, that could mean a store of things, both concrete and abstract. The most commonly used are 式 [a form (or method)], 示 [to order], 士 [a civil servant, a commoner (as distinct from a noble man), the name of an official position in the government, a gentleman, a young man (as opposite to a young woman), a soldier, to take a government position, a surname, a student who participated in imperial examination], or 仕 (女) [a female model in a painting]. *Shi* could also refer to several nouns 試 [a test, the imperial examination], 世 [the world, the earthly (as opposed to religious) affairs], 事 [social status, personal or state affairs, a story, or a fact], 市 [the market, a city], or 是 [(it) is, (I) am, (we) are].

Only through the combination of its two components, the phonophore and the semantic classifier, could the practiced reader realize that this particular character stood for a morpheme pronounced *shì* (in one of the four tones) and the particular or intended meaning.

During the ancient times, a morpheme could occur as a word by itself and later occurred in combination with noun suffixes or near synonyms to form bisyllabic words. For example, *fang* [house] became *fang-zi* [a building], *fang-jian* [a room], and *lou-fang* [multistory building]. The above mentioned 事 [*shi*] could build an array of characters and words: *shi* (by itself) was a verb that meant to take care of business, to carry out a mission, to kill, to do a job, and as a noun, referred to an aspect or happening of life, a job, an affair. *Shi* (with combination) became more verbs: *shi-li* [to do manual work], *shi-huo* [to worship fire], *shi-zhu* [the planner (or plaintiff in court), *shi-gong* [achievement], *shi-you* [the origin of the affair], *shi-jian* [an event], *shi-dian* [maintaining regulation], *shi-wu* [material existence], *shi-gu* [accident], *shi-ji* [past experience], *shi-qing* [reality], *shi-li* [the reason of the affair], *shi-lui* [biography], and *shi-duan* [the origins of the affair].[57] This combination of a character and its semantic classifier can be seen in most world languages, but Chinese combination tended to be terse and brief; they commonly contained two characters instead of up to a dozen that one can observe in German or Sanskrit.

Although mindful of verbal efficiency, Chinese is a script of well over fifty thousand discrete units conveying both sound and meaning. It is a highly expressive media which demands long term education and high level of maintenance. Only those who devote great amounts of time to the language can achieve a reasonable degree of proficiency with it. Besides, the language has kept growing and the number of graphs rises constantly. At the end of the first century AD there were fewer than ten thousand characters. This number increased to about twelve thousand by the middle of the third century. More than ten thousand characters were added a century and a half later and another ten thousand from the fifth to the sixth century. By the beginning of the eleventh century, there were more than thirty thousand characters in written Chinese. It grew again to over 47,000 by 1716. As for modern dictionaries, *Zhonghua Da Zidian* (1916) contains 48,000 characters, the *Hanyu Da Zidian* (1989) has 54,678, *Zhonghua Zihai* (1994), 85,568 and *Yiti Zidian* (2004) has 106,230.[58]

Obviously, no one could possibly retain but a relatively small fraction of this large number of characters. The most rudimentary or basic literacy requires a thousand characters. Two to three thousand characters enables one to scrape by in most circumstances. A full literacy, which includes the ability to read a newspaper and exchange written communication on a variety of topics, would need more than four thousand characters. Six thousand characters is the standard for most computer word processing in Chinese and in typical desk dictionaries. It would be an extraordinary feat, and it is questionable whether anyone could actively command ten thousand or more characters. The customary restriction of most writing to a few thousand different characters is true not only today but even for Tang poetry, the narrative and descriptive zenith of Chinese literature. As for the other tens of thousands of sinographs, many of them have been used only a few times in history, and either their pronunciation or meaning (or both) is not definitively known. Nevertheless, font-makers must take them into account because they do occasionally appear in writing. Information processing specialists must be prepared to cope with at least twenty-five thousand separate sinographs on a fairly regular basis, even though most of them occur with a frequency of less than one one-thousandth of one percent in the majority of texts. They still show up from time to time in names, historical references, and lexicographical discussions.

Conclusions

As the only contemporary language that originated from pictorial origins, Chinese managed to maintain and expand its diverse repertoire of graphic characters. Compared to the alphabetic languages (Greek, Latin, Germanic, Romance, modern Semitics), literary Chinese developed and accumulated a language and vocabulary of high level graphical refinement. It achieved the balance between graphical refinement and phonetic sophistication through two opposite, alternating or simultaneous efforts that encouraged and increased variations and refinement while at the same time controlled its expansion by filtering its repertoire to increase efficiency.

3

The Music of Poetry

It took Chinese poets many centuries to establish a rhythm for their poetry that was suitable for Chinese language. During this process poetry was saturated with music at times and departed from it at others. The interaction and mutual influence between words and music drove poetic imagination as it redefined and clarified rhythm and tone.

There were three general stages of poetic evolution in terms of its relationship with music wherein poetry was inspired and relied on different kinds of rhythm. From the Shang and Zhou dynasties to the mid–Spring and Autumn period (770–476 BC), Chinese music and poetry shared a single form of expression: singing. Poetry was sung and danced and it was composed and recited according to musical scales (high/low) and duration (long/short).[1] At this stage, the sound of poetry took the form of primitive music and was similar to the recitative presentation of Greek (Homeric) epic that had a simple and repetitive beat. After Confucius' time, poetry evolved gradually into written form; it cultivated its own rhythm based on spoken language, a mixture of rhymes of alternate (long/short and high/low) sound that was inherited from singing and rhetorical stress derived from speaking. Now poetry sounded more like Latin poetry (such as Virgil's *Aeneid*). This new and non-musical rhyming scheme laid the foundation for spoken language as well as literary writing (both prose and poetry). It took several more centuries for poetry to develop its own music in regulated verse (three, four, five and seven characters per line) poetry that departed from spoken language and rhymed prose. Chinese classical poetry based on regulated length of lines, tonal pitch and stress matured during the Tang period (618–907). Song (960–1279) *ci* [poetry in uneven lines] marked another creative departure from the tonal and rhythmic unity that had been established by many generations of Tang poets. It represented a new attempt to enrich and extend the formal horizon of the regulated verse by assimilating music of songs accompanied by string instruments.

Formative Chinese poetry (as had the ancient Semitic, Greek and Latin) based its rhythm on an imitation of music that featured verbal repetition and duplication. *Shijing,* the first collection of Chinese poetry, reflected the characteristics of contemporary music that carried words. To create poetic flow, poets had to duplicate and repeat words and phrases to accommodate singing. In order to sing with a primitive and mainly percussion dominated music, the main form of shijing poetry was four characters per line and alliteration, as in the following:

Jūn	*zǐ*	*yú*	*yì*	
Bù	zhī	qí	qī	
Hé	zhì	zāi		
Jī	qī	yú	shí	
Rì	zhī	xī	yǐ	
Yáng	niú	xià	lái	
Jūn	*zǐ*	*yú*	*yì*	
Rú	zhī	hé	wù	sī
Jūn	*zǐ*	*yú*	*yì*	
Bù	rì	bù	yuè	
Hé	qí	yǒu	huó	
Jī	qī	yú	jié	
Rì	zhī	xī	yǐ	
Yáng	niú	xià	kuò	
Jūn	*zǐ*	*yú*	*yì*	
Gǒu	wú	jī	kě	

My man is away to serve the country;
I cannot know
How long there that he will stay,
Or when he'll be on homeward way.
The fowls are roosting in their nest,
The sun is setting in the west,
The sheep and cattle are getting rest.
To serve the country my man's away.
How can I not think of him night and day?
My man is away to serve the country,
I cannot know
When or if again we will meet.
The sun is already set,
The fowls have roosted in their nest,
The sheep and cattle have come to rest.
To serve the country my man is away,
Please keep him from hunger and thirst, I pray.

There were no more than four vowels (*a e u i*) each with four tones. With these simple words and simple diction, one almost could hear the musical beat of the drum. The alliteration here sounded much more primitive than that of *Beowulf.*

As pronunciation in the Chinese language grew longer and more complex, writers had to create increasingly varied beats to deliver poetry. They invented empty words (words void of meaning) to accommodate a more complex sound pattern and versatile rhythm. These empty words were utilized to carry a prolonged sound, weighty rhythm and more colorful narrative. Poets and critics called this primitive poetic delivery "yi chang san tian" [singing in one note or line and sighing in three]. For example the following poem "*Wang fong.Cai he*" had three lines. The first line was repeated twice with only one alternate word[2]:

> Bi cai ge   xi, yi ri bu jian, ru san yue xi.
> Bi cai xiao xi, yi ri bu jian, ru san qiu xi.
> Bi cai ai   xi, yi ri bu jian, ru san sui xi.

Repetition was typical of *shijing* style. Words and lines were repeated to lend a familiar and memorable tone to the poem.[3] The alliteration of "*Bi cai*" and "*yi ri bu jian*" at the beginning of all three lines was reinforced by six *xi*'s at the end of each half line. Although the degree of repetition varied in Shijing as it was compiled during more than five centuries, the function of exclamation words was common.

This complete unison of music and poetry did not last as long as the Latin tradition of the Middle Ages. Chinese poetry began to separate itself from singing and to search for a distinct rhythm of its own. As the compiler of *Shijing* pointed out in his preface: "When there are not enough words, it has to be sung; when there are not enough songs, it has to be gestured with hands, and danced with feet."[4] According to him, it was natural for poetry to graduate from song and dance as poetic language accumulated enough words and expression.

One of the best witnesses of this evolution was the changing function of empty words in poetry. Empty words were the most important instrument for poetic composition from *shijing* to *chuci*.[5] Chuci presented a new form of poetry that sprouted and blossomed in the area of Chu (present day Hunan and Hubei provinces) during the Warring States period (475–221 BC). As a new literary style, chuci abandoned shijing's four-character verses and adopted verses with varying lengths. Although composed in various line lengths, chuci continued to use empty words. Sometimes, the empty words, duplicated words, and exclamation words made up more than half of a poetic work. Like the poetry of ancient Greek and Latin that created its rhythm by alternating long and short vowels, Chinese poets used duplication and empty words (long vowels) to create musical beats by extending the sound of Chinese words, which were typically single-syllable.[6]

Gradually, the use of the word *xi* (originally derived from musical imitation) became an important part of poetic composition that emphasized its verbal rhythm. *Xi* in chuci established a stable position, often at the end of a half line and the end of the line. Its appearance in chuci did not only regulate the rhythm of the poetry but also created its verbal parallelism.[7]

Like the English poetry that evolved from alliteration (of phonetic repetition) to sonnet (of verbal regulation), Chinese poetry transformed its rhyme scheme from primitive shijing *and* chuci to regulated poem. The sound and structure of Chinese language at each developmental stage determined the difference in particular rhyme scheme. In theory, this was similar to the English poets who employed iambic pentameter when writing sonnets while their counterparts in the Romance languages more often adopted meters of hendecasyllable and Alexandrine. Unlike European poetry that was composed with multi-syllable words, most Chinese words up to the medieval times were single syllable. Therefore, in later chuci poetry, exclamation and empty words were used to create verbal balance as well as rhythm. Occasionally this rhetorical instrument was also used to form a rhythmic contrast in the same way that Germanic languages employ in modern poetry.[8]

Empty words gradually disappeared in composition after poets could find enough phonetic variations to create rhythm with new descriptive words and increase expressive efficiency. In the Han period poetic rhythm began to replace the end *xi*, which eventually made it possible to abandon the use of xi altogether. Liu Bang's (256–195 BC) "Da feng ge" and Xiang yu's (232–202 BC) "Gai xi ge" are illustrations:

> Da feng qi   **xi**   yun fei **yang**.
> Wei jia hai nei   **xi**   gui gu **xiang**.
> An de   meng shi **xi**   shou si **fang**!

Translation:

> Rise a great wind, oh! It drives the clouds away.
> Return to my birthplace, oh! The world is under my sway.
> Where can I find brave soldiers, oh! To defend the distant borders today!

> Li ba shan **xi** qi gai **shi**,
> Shi bu li   **xi** zhui bu **shi**.
> Zhui bu shi **xi** ke nai **he**,
> Yu   xi yu **xi** nai ruo **he**!

Translation:

> I pull mountains down, oh! my breath changes the world with might,
> But my good fortune wanes, oh! my steed refuses to fight.

Whether my steed will fight, oh! no longer I care.
What I am going to do with you, oh! my lady fair!

Here the end *xi* in both poems could be taken away without affecting
sound and rhythm. *Yang, xiang,* and *fang* in the first poem establish a tonal
rhyme as well as the *shi, shi, he,* and *he* of the second. *Xi* remained to separate
the half lines and continued to be employed well into Han.

These examples provide only a glimpse of the evolution of poetry from
the form of song to a distinct form of verbal composition. One can also observe
the same process in the *yuefu* poetry, which will be analyzed later in this chapter. Many yuefu were composed of lines of five or seven characters, a form
that was later adopted in classical regulated poetry. Regulated poetry had a
rhythm based on quantity, as did the poetry of ancient Greek and Latin.
However, Chinese poetry differed from these contemporaries with its tonal
parallelism which had emerged during its age-long saturation with music,
which formed a permanent influence upon the pronunciation and rhythm of
the spoken and written language.

During the post–Han period, court music went through an important
change from percussion based music to string and wind music. The dominance
of bells and chimes, the most important musical instruments for over two
thousand years, diminished. As a result, a new kind of music, centered on
strings, flutes, and vocals, became popular at both court and social functions.[9]

This marked the beginning of the new movement of poetry called yuefu.
The origin of the word *yuefu* came initially in the Qin Dynasty (221–206 BC)
and established in the Han Dynasty (206 BC–AD 220). *Yue* [music] fu [bureau]
meant music bureau and was the name of a court office that was responsible
for collecting, writing, and performing folk songs, ballads and music for ceremonial occasions at the imperial court. During and after Han, yuefu referred
to a kind of music that provided modal variety and quick setup in imperial
side-rooms and private homes other than temples and palace halls. In the
China of around 150–500, ensemble music blossomed in the private domestic
culture of the literati. After yuefu music became assimilated into court music,
it gradually lost its folk characteristics and became a kind of fine music. The
poems that were composed in these folk tunes later were called yuefu poetry;
however, at this time, it had already lost its original melody. As its original
words remained, it became a collection of Han folk poetry that served as the
basis of the yuefu, a form of literary poetry.[10]

These poems were significant in Chinese literary history because they
consisted of lines of varying lengths, some having a regular form of five syllables per line rather than the standard four-syllable line of traditional shijing
style. In this way, yuefu laid a foundation for the later classic *gushi* ["ancient-

style poetry"], with its broader use of rhyme and fewer metrical restrictions. Centuries later, many poets, including the great Li Bai (701–762) and Bai Juyi (772–846), continued to create poems in the yuefu tradition.

Shijing tradition was only one of the two pillars of poetry in ancient China. Chuci style lyrical poetry that evolved into *fu* [a rhyme-prose and descriptive poem] during the Han dynasty also made great contributions to the formation of Chinese poetry, especially the development of its imagery. Han fu was a mixed style of poetry and rhymed prose. It included introductory, concluding, or other interspersed passages that were composed in prose, especially as dialogue.[11]

A Han fu, typically very long, described a subject exhaustively from every possible angle, and was usually meant to display the poet's rhetorical and lexical skill rather than express personal feeling. Since it was meant to impress and display, the Han fu was termed the *epideictic fu*. One of the most well known Han fu was Sima Xiangru's (179–118 BC) "Tian zi you lie fu" [Rhapsody on the son of heaven on a leisurely hunt], which will be discussed in detail in the following chapters. Han fu was classified into *da fu* and *xiao fu*. Da Fu featured large volume, extensive structure, imposing manner and ornate vocabulary. Most of these were masterworks with tens of thousands of words. Representative writers of da fu included Jia Yi (210–169 BC), Sima Xiangru, Ban Gu (32–92 AD), and Zhang Heng (78–139). Most da fu was written to glamorize palaces and cities or to describe the king's hunting tours, or to narrate traveling experiences. Xiao fu, on the contrary, was short, lucid and graceful. They were written to satirize current affairs and to express emotions.[12]

During the Six Dynasties (220–589), fu remained a major poetic genre, and together with shi formed the twin generic pillars of Chinese poetry until shi began to dominate in the Tang dynasty. The typical Six Dynasties fu was very different from that of Han. They were much shorter, and often personal, expressive, and lyrical. Many contained no prose appendages, consisting entirely of rhymed verse in regular, usually hexametric, meter. Fu grew and included more and more poetic forms while shi assimilated fu imagery. A fine early example of this short lyrical fu [*shuqing xiao fu*] was Ji Kang's (223–262) "Qin Fu" ["Rhapsody on the Zither"]. Another representative work of this kind was Yu Xin's (513–581) "Ai Jiangnan Fu" ["Rhapsody in Lament of the South"].[13]

Equipped with the linguistic capacities that had been created by shijing, chuci, and fu tradition, the new yuefu poetry changed the ways in which poetry was composed. Instead of making speech rhyme and verse sing, poetry turned syllabic by filling words into popular tunes, called by some "scoring-prosody." Unlike Latin unity, where music was composed to convey the meaning of religious text, Chinese yuefu poets created lyrics fitting into established melodies. They made music and words into smooth euphony where instrumental timbers and strophic units of vocalized words merged seamlessly into a single flow of rhythm in real-time performance. The writing process of yuefu poetry was more similar to musical composition than literary writing.[14]

The purpose of poetic composition based on musical tune was to create a flow of sound that was pleasing to the ears. The challenge that Chinese yuefu poets encountered was to smooth out the prosodic disjointedness that occurred when the bell (and lithophone) sustaining tones hung in the air too long and drowned out various words. To solve this problem, two things happened. First, as the established melodies were repeatedly scored for new poetry, the extant lyrics for the new songs became streamlined into seven, four or five word lines. Second, as length of line of lyrics stabilized, poetry became capable of forming and transforming without melodic structure.

The latter transition from musical structure to literary structure in poetic composition would not have occurred without the constant compilation of a musical and poetic repertoire that regularized and tabulated poetic forms. This repertoire became a literary canon that inspired the composition of generations of poets.

The first poetic form that completely divorced from music in the Chinese literary tradition was *wu yan shi*, a regulated poem with five characters per line. Originating from shijing and chuci, five-character poetry evolved from the four-character poetry with the addition of a structural space, often with an exclamation word. This extra space changed the rhythm of the poetic flow. Chinese words during Han were monosyllabic (a syllable in each character); every line contained an even number of syllables. This created a simple and regular beat for chanting and recitation. However, the new regulated poetry was no longer a song, but rather a note beyond lines and a literary chanting without music.[15]

The exclamation word and other "empty" words — those that played a phonetic role yet had no or very little semantic function — became the tool to create rhythmic variations and raptures which made the poetic sequence of originally monotonic Chinese words sound more pleasing. In a longer historic sense, empty words were a temporary or transitional instrument that bridged musical rhythm to a more sophisticated tonal arrangement. Without this phonetic tool and later tonal variations upon which a brand new poetry was composed, Chinese would have sounded like medieval Latin or French. They were easy to set to music and yet difficult to function as a literary poetry because of a lack of rhythmic contrast, which was essential to build power of rhythm. The emergence of regulated poetry was the Chinese solution for the age-long struggle for unity between beat of stress and beat of duration, a process that drove centuries of poetic evolution of European languages.[16]

The transition from yuefu lyrics to regulated poems was made possible only by the creative labors of many generations of poets. The following poem, one of the early regulated ones, was a remnant of the customary repetition of shijing:

"Cháng Xíng Gē" ["A Slow Song"]

Qīng   qīng   yuán   zhōng   kuí,
Cháo   lǚ   dài   rì   xī.
Yáng   chūn   bǔ   dé   zé,
Wàn   wù   shēng   guáng   **huī.**
Cháng   kǒng   qīu   jié   zhì,
Kūn   huáng   huá   yè   **shuāi.**
Bǎi   chuān   dōng   dào   hǎi,
Hé   shí   fù   xī   **guī.**
Shào   zhuàng   bù   nǔ   lì,
Lǎo   dà   tú   shāng   **bēi.**

Sunflowers in the garden green,
Await the sun to dry the dew.
Spring spreads its nourishing light,
All living things become animated and bright.
I often fear the coming of the autumn drear,
When leaves turn yellow the red flowers sere.
A hundred streams flow eastward to the sea,
When they return west can they be free?
Those who do not make good use of their youth,
In vain will pass old age in sadness.

Even with a song-like title and some repetition, the piece was a poem rather than a song. Without the help of any exclamation words, it represented intense emotion with its calculated stops, parallelism, and varied tonal scale and rhythm.

This parallel yet varied rhythm was further cultivated into more structured poems like "Yong huai shi" ["Reflections"] by Ruan Ji (210–263).[17]

Yè   zhōng   bǔ   néng   **mèi**
Qǐ   zuò   tán   míng   **qín.**
Bó   wéi   jiàn   míng   **yuè,**
Qīng   fēng   chuī   wǒ   **jīn.**
Gū   hÓng   háo   wài   **yě,**
Xiáng   niǎo   míng   běi   **lín.**
Pái   hái   jiāng   hé   **jiàn,**
Yōu   sī   dú   shāng   **xīn.**

I can't sleep deep in the night;
Have to rise and play my lute.

> Sheer curtains reflect the moon bright;
> Cool breezes tug my lapels mute.
> A lonely swan shrieks over the plain,
> Hovering birds cry in north wood.
> What would I see, pacing in vain?
> My heart grieves in solitude.

Here, tonal parallelism begins to take shape. It had taken many centuries before a systematic tonal euphony and desirable sound effect in poetic composition could be established. This took place during the Qi dynasty (479–502).[18]

A century later, the five-character verse became more organized in both tonal and verbal senses as empty words almost completely disappeared in poetic composition. Wang Xizhi's (321–379) "Lan Ting Shi" ["In Orchid Pavilion"] reads:

> Sān chūn qǐ qǔn pǐn,
> Jì chàng zài suǒ yīn.
> *Yǎng* wàng bì tiān jì,
> *Fǔ* pán lù shuǐ bīn.
> Liào lǎng wǔ yá guān,
> Yù mù lǐ zì chén.
> Dà yǐ zǎo huà gōng,
> Wàn shū mò bù jūn.
> Qún lài suī cēn cī,
> Shì wǒ wú fēi xīn.

In this five-character verse, the tonal rhythm was not yet completely streamlined. There was hardly any verbal parallelism except for a few words here and there: *yang* [above] and *fu* [below].

> Spring came and all nature unfolded,
> We share our joy with the world.
> Above, we see a azure sky;
> Below, the stream's green waves flow by.
> The horizon is vast, endless and bright,
> Our eyes meet nothing but the light.
> All seems boundless, fair, and square;
> Things are different yet have equal share.
> In high and low they all are my view,
> But I see nothing but the new.

Chinese writers at this period shared the same concerns of the early medieval Latin writers who had adopted the Greek prosodic system which was alien to their native speech. But Chinese problems had more indigenous roots. The prosodic variations established by both shijing and chuci appeared to be inadequate for the rapidly evolving poetry. The alternation of long

(repetition and chanting in empty words) and short (consonantal and allit-
erative sequence), and the alternation of even [ping] and uneven [ze] tones
failed to specify the variety of tones and scales that new poetry needed and
demanded.

This disconnect between oral and literary language, although emerging
from different origins in Latin and Chinese, was the same engine that drove
prosodic transformation. While Latin turned to musical accompaniment to
provide variations that it needed, Chinese poetry went the opposite direction.
It created the music of its literary poetry by constructing an artificial tonal
arrangement.[19]

During later Han, Chinese language encountered the same threat that
Greek and Latin were facing. Chinese lost most of its consonantal distinctions
on both ends (initial and ending syllables) of its words, as singing and chanting
had eliminated many established consonantal distinctions. As rhyming emphasis shifted from initial consonants to vowel endings (as did English during
medieval and early modern times), the final consonants began to fall off of
the vowels. Once the consonants vanished, many vowels began to sound identical. (For example, if the English words bake, bait, bail and base dropped
their consonants, they would sound the same.) If Chinese had been an inflectional language like Latin and the Romance languages, it would be an easier
shift. It could simply change its prosodic emphasis from the initial to the final
syllables, as had been done in Italian and Spanish.

However, Han Chinese was already a mature language with an established grammatical structure. Without an inflectional structure which provided distinct and yet regulated endings, Chinese poetry was left with very
few sound options after it lost its ending variations provided by consonants.
In order to survive without losing its poetic inheritance, Chinese needed phonetic variations to sustain the rhythm of its speech as well as poetry.

Now, Chinese literary poetry needed a new system of rhythm that was
capable of maintaining its inherited form as well as keeping pace with linguistic
change. After centuries of experimenting with words and music, poets found
the solution in their large repertoire of vowel endings, which was divided into
two opposite tonal tendencies: *ping* [even] and *ze* [uneven] tone. They decided
to widen and reclassify the tonal distinctions that had already started to
develop after influence from foreign languages, such as those from southern
Asia. They began to formulate a tonal system by instigating and regulating
four tones of the language.[20]

This process, once known as musicalization of Chinese poetry, took many
centuries to complete and perfect, during which time a number of poetic
forms and hundreds of genres emerged. Since later Han, music was a prominent

element in poetic renovation. Instead of serving its text, as did ancient Chinese and medieval western music, Chinese poets attempted to fill words into musical notes *i-sheng tian-ci* [in accordance with musical notes or simply music first, then poetry].[21] This process presented a kind of music-word relationship that was different from that of Western languages until later Renaissance and that of earlier Chinese, as discussed in Chapter 2 (words were first, then music).

The musicalization of Chinese poetry began with an entirely different emphasis. In the fifth century, it was music first, then words, because Chinese poets realized that they could manipulate the tonal features of their language to enhance their expressive power. They classified these tonal features as level tone [*ping sheng*], rising tone [*shang sheng*], departing tone [*qù sheng*] and entering tone [*ru sheng*]. They subsequently began to employ these tones to establish desirable euphonic effects.[22]

Chinese poets inherited tonal features in the same way that ancient Greeks, Romans and Arabs had inherited their speaking rhythm. They chose to use them creatively in writing poetry in much the same way that Latin and English dramatists used speech on the stage. It took Chinese poets more than ten centuries to cultivate a prosodic system: the music of their poetry. Unlike the Greeks and pre–Islamic Arabs who had articulated poetry orally for centuries before they were recorded in writing, Chinese formative poetry left detailed written records about how it assimilated musical forms to create poetic diction. This formative history of poetry either was not recorded or has not yet been found in other ancient poetry.

The first Chinese poetic form without music was ancient *shi (gu shi)* and was written during the first century BC. They were transmitted orally without attribution to an author. It was not until the second century AD that gu shi became popular among literati, who were not songwriters. However, the first generation of poets composed their poetry using song as a model frame. The early shi poetry was constructed almost entirely of end-stopped lines of equal length (of either five or seven characters in each line), that were further organized into basic units of couplets with rhymes occurring at the end of each even-numbered line. This was the primitive form that fifth century poets started from as they began to experiment with the newly discovered tonal features of their spoken language.

In order to create an internal music of poetry, the poets attempted to infuse musical qualities into their writings by employing four tones to regulate resonance and create euphony. They believed that within every five-character line, all tones and final sounds should differ from each other, and that within every couplet, each word should differ in pitch. Shen Yüe (441–513), who has been credited with defining the rule of tonality, instructed poets to make these four notes alternate with the high and low sounds intermixed to form a rhythm. The poets were urged to balance the floating sound at the front and the intense sound at the rear and make the tones and final sounds of the words distinct in a single piece of writing. They were also encouraged to vary the light and heavy sounds within each couplet. Only when one understood this principle would he be allowed to discuss poetic writing.[23]

On this foundation of prosody, Shen Yue tried to use the four tones of Chinese parallel to the five notes on the pentatonic scale of ancient Chinese music, and in this way, create a sort of rhythm and melody similar to that of music. By drawing an analogy from music, Shen Yue emphasized variation and modulation. The following, a poem by Shen himself, illustrates this idea and his manipulation of the four tones:

"Lín gǎo tái" *["On the Height"]*

Gǎo tái bǔ   kě wàng,
Wàng yuǎn shǐ   rén chóu.
Lián shān wǔ   duàn jué,
Hé   shuǐ fǔ   yōu yōu.
Suǒ sī   jìng hé   zài?
Luò   yáng nán   mò tóu.
Kě   wàng bù   kě jiàn,
Hé   yòng jiě   rēn yōu.

Too close to mid day light,
You'll be terrified by the sight.
Hills stretch beyond the horizon,
While streams blend with heaven.
Where is the one that I miss?
South of Luoyang he is.
I can gaze but can't see,
The sorrow that will not leaven me.

If one looks carefully at the tonal marks on the original poetry, it is easy to see how rhythm was created with alternating tones. Shen Yue was practicing what he had preached and was creating a musical flow for the words by inventing and sequencing different tones rather than finding and lining up the similarities upon which natural rhymes were based. Four out of the eight lines of this poem consisted of four different tones and each of the two contained two to three tones. They also were alternated and yet echoed with regularity. According to these compositional principles, the regulated poetry of China established an artificial rhythm that manipulated and even streamlined speech.

The origins of the five-character verse [*wuyan shi*] have been the subject of a scholarly controversy. Although many yuefu were composed of five-character or seven-character [qiyan shi] lines, it took several linguistic changes to contribute to (if not determine) the increasing popularity of the regulated poems. The first of these changes was the emergence and widespread use of two character words, which gradually but fundamentally changed the rhythm of the language and its phrasing. The following poems exhibited the change of poetic rhythm by introducing two character words, the earlier version of which were of doubled single character.

Anonymous

Tiáo tiáo qiān niú xīng,
jiǎo jiǎo hé hàn nǔ.
Xiān xiān zhuó sù shǒu,
zhā zhā nòng jī zhù.
Zhōng rì bù chéng zhāng,
qī tì líng rǐ yǔ.
Hé hàn qīng yiě qiǎn,
xiāng qù fù jǐ xiǔ?
Yíng yíng yì shuǐ jiān,
Mò mò bù dé yǔ.

Translation:

Far, far away the Cowherd Star;
Glowing, glowing over the riverside Weaving Maid.
Slender, slender her fingers are,
Clack, clack her shuttle's tune is played.
She weaves all day, but none is done,
Like rain her tears drop one by one.
Heaven's River seems shallow and clear;
But how far are two stars, apart or near?
Where brimful waves separate two hearts,
They gaze, yet cannot speak their part.

The most primitive two character words that were used in early poetry were doubled single character, such as *Tiáo tiáo, jiǎo jiǎo, Xiān xiān, zhā zhā, Yíng yíng,* and *Mò mò* at the beginning of each line. Chinese double character words functioned more than merely as prolonged and emphasized sounds, like the double consonants in Arabic and Italian, but they also intensified the meaning of the single character word or clarified its imagery. For example, while *Tiáo* meant far away, Tiáo-tiáo meant very far away. In the case of this poem, the distance was from one star in the sky to another. Jiǎo signified brightness, but jiǎo-jiǎo conveyed not just brightness but a twinkling brightness (a specialized word to describe stars) or cold and remote brightness (to describe the moon). Mò normally referred to pulse and each beat of the heart, Mò-mò depicted the specific gaze between lovers that was full of emotion of longing and burning desire to speak to each other. In addition, these double character words slowed the rhythm of the four-character poetry that had been established in shijing style many centuries earlier. They also provided more and varied opportunities to alternate sound patterns, which later became the most utilized poetic model: five or seven character verse.

The three centuries of the Tang dynasty (618–907) were traditionally seen as the time of the fullest flowering and highest excellence of Chinese poetry. Regulated verse [*lü shi*] was the dominant form of poetic expression, just as fu was for the Han dynasty, ci for the Song (960–1279), and qu for the Yuan dynasty (1279–1368). However, during Tang, fu [rhapsody] remained an important genre of poetry and it declined only after Song ci inherited and assimilated its vivid and exquisite imagery into the new enhanced poetic writing.

The poetic evolution was an accumulation of various forms and styles wherein new and emerging forms were added onto the established repertoire of the older forms, which continued to be written, read, memorized, and recited. Therefore, Tang poetry had a wider spectrum of forms when compared to the old style verse.

By Tang, shi poetry had accumulated various forms. The most common of these was five characters per line verse. Since the second century AD, five character lines had been the most favored for shi poetry, and it remained so through the next dynasties, although verse in seven character lines became increasingly popular from the eighth century onward. In Tang the number of lines in a poem, or, more accurately, the number of couplets, was not prescribed. However, there was a pronounced preference for poems made up of multiples of four lines; the quatrain [*jüe jü*] was the lower (shortest) limit and two hundred lines (in one hundred rhymes) was the rarely achieved upper limit.[24]

The old style verse [gu shi] was the initial form from which regulated verse derived. The writer of gu shi was under no formal constraints other than line length and rhyme (in every second line). It had a much looser structure compared to the more recent style poetry. Thus, it was favored for narrative works and by writers seeking a relaxed or imaginative style. The best example of these are found in the works of Li Bai. His "Yue xia du zhuo" ["Drinking Alone with the Moon"] is one of his masterpieces.

> Huā jiān yì hú jiǒu,
> Dú zhuó wú xiāng **qīn**.
> Jǔ bēi yāo míng yué,
> Duì yǐng chéng **sān rén**.
> Yué jì bù juě yǐn,

Yǐng tú suí wó **shēn.**
Zhàn bàn yuè jiāng yǐng,
Xíng yué xū jí **chēn.**
Wó gē yué pái huí,
Wó wǔ yǐng líng **luàn.**
Xǐng shí tóng jiāo huān,
Zuì hòu gè fēn **sàn.**
Yǒng jié wú qíng yóu,
Xiāo qī miǎo yún **hàn.**

Amid the flowers, from a jar of wine
I drink alone with no friend,
Raised cup I invite the Moon,
she, my shadow, and I, three as companion.
The Moon does not know drinking,
my shadow follows me dancing.
For now I have them for friends,
to cheer me until the end of spring.
I sing and the Moon lingers to hear my song;
I dance and my shadow tumbles along.
Sober, we three remain cheerful and gay;
Drunken, we part and lose each in his way.
We are partners forever without earthly love.
We'll meet again beyond the stars above.

In exactly the same format, Du Fu depicted his dream about Li Bai in intimate tone, with free and moving imagery:

Clouds drift all day through the sky,
But you, like a wanderer, never stop by.
Three nights now I have dreamed of you,
Tender, intimate and real too.
And as you start to leave my bed,
You complain of your grueling trip ahead.
Of lakes and rivers with storms and wrecks,
You fear your small boat to be cracked.
On the way out, you rub your white head,
As if puzzled.
The capital city is crowded by rich officials,
But you are alone, poor, and helpless.
Who says the heaven is never unfair?
Though it brought you ill fortune as your end nears.
What use the fame of ten thousand years,
When you are gone, no longer here.

The "Recent-Style" or regulated verse [*jinti shi*] emerged during the 5th century. By the Tang period, it contained eight lines with required tone patterns and parallelism between the lines in the second and third couplets. This form was designed to ensure a balance between the four tones of Middle Chinese in each couplet. The four tones —*ping*, [level], *shang* [rising], *chü* [departing] and *ju* [entering]— were disposed in a binary opposition of "level" and "nonlevel or deflected," comprising the three nonlevel classes. In ideal form, the five character regulated poem demanded a mirror-image balancing of level and deflected tones in the words occupying the second and fourth position in the opposing lines of a couplet: xAxBx/xBxAx. For seven character lines the significant words were the second, fourth, and sixth: xAxBxAx/xBxAxBx.[25]

A non-native English speaker who is interested in English poetry can listen to English poetry being read or sung and can, without understanding the words or images, imagine mood, emotion and tone from the raw sounds of the words and their cadence. The best way for a non–Chinese speaking reader to understand regulated verse is to read in Chinese original according to its pinyin (romanized pronunciation) and to listen to its rhythm even without understanding its meaning.

The following is a small collection of Tang regulated verses in pinyin Chinese with the English translations. It is designed to let readers have a sense for the formal evolution of Tang poetry. Initially, reading pre–Tang poetry feels like reading Bob Dylan without his guitar and harmonica and Bruce Springsteen without his rock band. Sound imageries are scattered and thrown together disjointedly because they were not designed to be read but rather to be heard and carried by music. Reading Tang poetry, especially the regulated verse, sounds more like the poems of Leonard Cohen, which sound poetic and musical even without music. Chinese poetry since Tang has become silent; it is meant to be read and heard by the ears of the mind.

During the first decades of the eighth century the spread and establishment of regulated verse became the dominant form of poetic writing in China. The prosodic patterns of shi had been worked out previously in theory; many seventh century poets occasionally wrote poetry in a form close to the later regulated verse. It was only at this time that the tonal and verbal rules were employed with enough vigor to suggest the emergence and establishment of a new form.[26]

It took several centuries for poets to polish the parallelism of wording and bring them completely in line with the ideal regulation. The first generation of poets tended to take smaller formats in octave and quatrain, while describing limited imagery and momentary emotion. Wang Bo (650–676) was one of the Four Prominent Poets in Early Tang [*chu Tang si jie*] who promoted the new style of poetry. His "Song Du Shaofu Zhiren Shuzhou" ["Farewell to Vice-Prefect Du"] was composed in regulated verse, which reads:

Chéng què fǔ sān **qín,**
Fēng yān wàng wǔ jīn.
Yǔ jūn lí bié yì,
Tóng shì huàn yóu **rén.**
Hǎi něi zún ahī jǐ,
Tiān yá ruó bì lín.
Wú wéi zǎi qí lù,
Ér nǔ gòng zhān **jīn.**

You'll leave the town walled far and wide,
To a mist-veiled land by riverside.
Our parting feels sad and drear,
As both of us are strangers here.
A friend who is a world apart,
Can remain close to your heart.
Why would you linger at the fork of the road,
Wiping your eyes like a heart-broken child?

This poem described a sad moment of parting. Various images such as the "walled town" and "veiled land by riverside" portrayed the background and setting for the feelings of parting. The distance between this and the other side of the world [*tian ya*] was contrasted to the closeness [*bi lin*] of friendship that brought the parties together. They also came together during the lingering at the fork of the road and the ensuing tears of sadness. Parallelism was attempted and forcefully established, but was not as polished as in the later Tang poems, for example those of Li Bai, Du Fu, and Li Shangyin.

Luo Binwang's (?–684)'s "Zai Yu Yong Chan" ["The Cicada Heard in Prison"] was another poem of a moment and a single event. Luo's scope of imagery was very similar to Wang Bo's "Farewell to Vice-Prefect Du." Luo was Wang's contemporary and another of the four Poets, as was Wang. Luo's poem focused on the song of a cicada:

> At autumn the cicada sings,
> In prison I'm worn out with drear.
> How can I bear its blue-black wings
> That reminds me of my graying hair?
> Heavy with dew, it can't fly,
> Drowned in the wind, its song's not heard.
> Who would believe its spirit high?
> To whom I express my grief in word?

Wong Bo's "Teng Wang Ge" ["Prince Teng's Pavilion"], his most well-known poem, demonstrated more polished parallelism:

Téng **wáng** gāo gé lín jiāng **zhǔ,**
Pèi yù míng luán bà gē **wǔ**
Huà **dòng** chāo fēi nán pǔ yún,

Zhū lián mù juǎn xī shān **yǔ**.
Xián yún tán yǐng rì yōu **yōu**,
Wù huàn xīng yí jǐ dù jiū?
Gé zhōng dì zǐ jīn hé zài,
Jiàn wài chāng jāng kōng zì **liú**.
High Prince Teng's Pavilion stands by riverside,
No more ringing bells punctuate dancer's refrain.
At dawn its painted beams bar the south-flying cloud's ride
At dusk its open screens reveal the western hills' rain.
Day after day leisurely clouds over still waters hang,
Stars move from spring to autumn in the same sky.
Where is the prince who once enjoyed wine and song,
Beyond the rails the silent river still rolls by.

The memory and emotion concerning Prince Teng was completely activated by what the poet saw on the pavilion. Here we can see a series of images, sounds, and movements where past and present melded together through the use of tonal and verbal parallelism. *Jiāng zhǔ* [riverside] paralleled *gē wǔ* [sing and dance] by sound; *nán pǔ yún* [south flying cloud] paralleled *xī shān yǔ* [western hills' rain] by semantic construction. The third couplet highlighted was well woven together by sound, imagery, and meaning: *Xiàn yǔn tán yǐng* [leisurely cloud over still water]/ *wǔ huàn xīng yí* [stars move from spring to autumn] and *rì yōu yōu* [(rains) from day to day]/ *jǐ dǔ jiū?* [(from season to season) in a changeless sky].

The language of poetry during the middle and late Tang period became more terse and its imagery more distinct with the creative labors of the later generation of poets. Using a language equipped with increasing flexibility and agility, poets could change register quickly and portray a shifting mood by alternating not only a couplet but a line, or even one or two words.

Meng Haoran's (689–740) "Chun xiao" ["Daybreak in Spring"] was one of the best known of Tang poems.

Chūn mián bù zhī **xiǎo**,
Chù chù **wén tí niǎo**.
Yè lái fēng yǔ shēng,
Huā luò **zhī duō shiǎo**?

I'm lying in bed this spring morning,
Not to awake till birds are crying.
After one night of wind and showers,
How many are the fallen flowers?

Meng's friend Wang Wei (701–761) was a more accomplished poet of regulated verse. He earned his literary degree at the age of twenty, left more than four hundred poems, and became one of the five most famous of all Chinese poets. Wang depicted a much more grand imagery of nature that was filled with cosmic consonance. His seemingly simple style often masked perfection and complexities in tonal patterns. His "Han Jiang Lin Fan" ["A View of the Han River"] reads:

> Chǔ   sài   sān   xiāng   jié,
> Jīng   mén   jiǔ   pài   **tōng**.
> Jiāng   liú   tān   dì   wài,
> Shān   sè   yiǔ   wú   **zhōng**.
> Jùn   yí   fú   qián   pǔ,
> Bó   làng   dòng   yǎn   **kōng**.
> Xiāng   yāng   hǎo   fēng   rì,
> Liú   zuì   yǔ   shān   **wēng**.

> Three Southern rivers roll by,
> Nine tributaries are here gathered.
> Water flows beyond earth to the sky,
> Hills now appear, then disappear.
> Towns seem to float over rivershore,
> Waves make horizons rise and fall.
> Such amazing scenery as we adore,
> Made us drunken as did the world all.

The most musical and engaging Tang poet was Li Bai (701–762). He was in total command of the literary tradition before him, especially yuefu, which was the foundation for his unique and personal diction. His idiom played with his inherited language and poetic form in exuberant and even audacious ways. In his highly original diction, he exploited the untranslatable interplay between sense and sound.

Li Bai's fu were marvelous achievements, although neglected by critics in comparison with his shi. The rhapsodies "Ming-tang fu" ["The Hall of Light"] and "Da lie fu" ["The Great Hunt"] were composed in the grand manner of the Han epideictic *fu*. So was "Da Peng Niao Fu" ["The Great Peng Bird"] in which the gigantic bird of the Chuang Zi's opening passage was personalized into a symbol of the self-assured Li Bai himself. Li did not seem to always see generic distinction as important boundary; he moved easily among all types of poetry. While his other fu were shorter and more lyrical compositions, he also was expert in the briefest form of verse, the quatrain.[27]

Li Bai left over a thousand poems and eight fu that testified to his mastery and excellence in all poetic forms. His yuefu offered the most extensive canvas of topics and titles of any Tang poet. He sometimes treated a familiar theme with exceptional effectiveness utilizing variations of all previous poets, while other times, he surprised the reader with a fresh imagery that had never been envisioned by anyone else. His yuefu often exhibited a superabundance of rhyme and assonance.

One of the best-known of Li Bai's yuefu reads:

"Jiang jin jiou" ["Bring the Wine"]

Look!
The water of Yellow River is pouring out of heaven.
It races to the ocean, never to return.
Look!
In high chambers, one mourns white hair with mirror bright,
The black silk in the morning has turned to snow by night.
Be happy as one pleases, the man of good fortune,
Never tip his golden cup empty toward the moon!
Heavenly gifted talent has to be employed!
Spin a thousand pieces of silver, all of them returned!
Cook a sheep and kill a cow to satisfy my appetite,
Make three hundred cups of drink to quench my thirst.
To the old master, Cen,
And the young scholar, Danqiu,

Bring in the wine!
Don't stop drinking,
Let's begin singing!
Please pay attention and listen!
Bell, drum, delicate food, and jade no longer treasure,
I pray for constant slumber or to be drunk forever!
Old sages and sober men are forgotten,
Only the great drinkers leave their reputation.
In days past Prince Chen had banquets at the Palace,
And laughing, paid for a well of wine ten thousand coins.
Dear host, why worry about your money?
Go and buy more wine to treat your guests!
Take my flower-dappled horse,
My thousands worth of furs,
Give them to the boy to exchange for good wine,
We'll sweep away the woes of ten thousand years!

Li Bai was the most musical among the Tang poets because he had grasped the entire canon of pre–Tang poetry. He had the best ear for yuefu verse. Li Bai cannot be fully appreciated by an English reader unless he makes the effort to read and hear Li's poetry in original Chinese. Like the poetry of the Bible, Li Bai's power was in the sound, which had been lingering in the ears of Chinese, educated or otherwise, for thousands of years, as well as in his written form. Listen to this:

Rì zhào xiāng lú shēng zǐ **yān,**
Yáo kàn pú bù guà yán **chuān.**

Fēi liú zhí xià sān qiān chǐ,
Yí shì yín hé luò jiǔ **tiān.**

The censer under the sun exhales a wreath of purple cloud,
From far a cataract hangs from a high mountain.
Its torrent clashes and pours down long feet of three thousand,
Makes you wonder if the Milky Way has fallen from heaven.

Li Bai's "Guan shan yue" ["The Moon at the Fortified Pass"] reads:

Míng yuè chū tiān **shāng,**
Cāng máng yùn hǎi **jiān.**
Cháng fēng jǐ wàn lì,
Chuī dù yù mēn **guān.**
Hàn xià bái dēng **dào,**
Hú kuī qīng hǎi wān.
Yóu lái zhēng zhàn dì,
Bù jiàn yǔ rén **huán.**
Shù kè wàng páng sè,
Sī guī duō kǔ yán.
Gāo lóu dāng cǐ yé,
Tàn xī weì yīng **xián.**

Shining moon from the Mountain of Heaven
Seen through a sea of clouds so far away.
Coming from a distant place, the wind,
Breathes on and passes over the Jade Gate.
China marches its men down Baideng trail,
While Tartar troops peer across blue bay waters.
Battle field since the ancient times,
Has never seen soldiers once gone return,
Across the border, they turn around gazing,
Think of home, with tears running.
Those left behind in the upper chambers,
Toss and sigh worrying sleepless.

This poem became one of the most memorable poems of Chinese literature
due to its musicality and highly refined and varied diction.

In his famous "Shu tao nan" ["The Hard Way to Shu"], poetic imagery
and sound mingled into one easy flow:

Wéi hū gāo zāi
Shǔ dào zhī **nán**
nán yú shàng qīng **tiān**
Tiǎn cóng jí yú fú
Kāi guó hé máng **rán**
Ěr lái sì wàn bā qiān suì
Bù yǔ qín sāi tōng rén **yān**
Xī dāng tài bái yǒu niǎo dào

Kĕ yĭ héng jué é méi **diān**
Dì bēng shān cuī zhuàng shì sĭ
Rán hòu tiān tī shí zhàn fāng gōu **lián**
Shàng yŏu liù lóng huí rì zhī gāo biāo
Xià yŏu chōng bō nì zhé zhī huí **chuān**
Huáng hè zhī fēi shàng bù de guò
Yuán náo yù dù chóu pān **yuán**
Qīng ní hé pán pán
Băi bù jiŭ zhé yíng yán **luán**
Mén shēn lì jĭng yăng xié xí
Yĭ shŏu fŭ yīng zuò cháng tàn
Wèi tú chán yán bù kĕ **pān**
Dàn jiàn bēi niăo hào gŭ mù
Xióng fēi cóng cí rào lín **jiàn**
Yòu wén zĭ guī tí yè yuè
Chóu kōng **shān**

Shŭ dào zhī **nán**
Nán yú shàng qīng **tiān**
Shĭ rén tīng cĭ diāo zhū **yán**
Lián fēng qù tiān bù yíng chĭ
Kū sōng dào guà yĭ jué bì
Fēi tuān pù liú zhēng xuān huī
Pīng yá zhuăn shí wàn huò léi
Qí xiăn yĕ ruò cĭ
jiē ěr Yuăn dào zhī rén
hú wéi hū lái zāi
jiàn gé zhēng róng ér cuī wéi
yī fū dāng **guān**
wàn fū mò kāi
suŏ shŏu huò fĕi qīn
huà wéi láng yŭ chái
cháo bì mĕng hŭ
xì bì cháng shé
mó yá shŭn xuĕ
shā rén rú má
jĭn chéng suī yún lè
bù rú zăo huán jiā
shŭ dào zhī nán
nán yú shàng qīng tiān
cè shēn xī wàng cháng zī jiē

Oh, Shu Passway
Alas! how steep! Alas how high!
Climbing Shu Passway is harder than scaling the blue sky.
Since the times of Yu Fu and Can Cong,
As they established border, this land was found.
Forty-eight thousand years have passed,

Across the Qin line nobody has ever arrived.
From Middle Kingdom no road linking human dwellings,
Only a steep pathway, bird's path extending.
Leaving westward toward the evening stars,
Trailing across the forehead of the O-mei Mountain.
It crumbled in an earthquake and brave men were lost,
It's now a road of ladders and bridges rising toward heaven.

High, as on a tall flag, six dragons drive the sun,
While the river, far below, lashes its twisted course.
Even yellow cranes could not fly over the mountain,
Poor monkeys wail, unable to leap over the gorges.
Green Mud path turns round and round,
as many as nine curls in each hundred steps.
Climbing to the star, we gasp a breath in ground sinking,
And drew a long sigh, while we hold chests with both hands.
Oh, why we turned to the west, when will we be returning?
Afraid that we may not able to climb over these rocks protruding.
Hearing nothing but the voice of birds on old trees,
Male birds smoothly wheeling, following the females.
Melancholy songs of the cuckoos return,
under the lonely moon, on the empty mountain.
Climbing Shu Passway is harder than scaling the sky,
Even to hear of it turns the pink cheeks ghostly white.
The lofty peaks shoot up in rows, almost touching the stars,
Dry pines hang, head down, from the face of the cliffs.
Over one another, a thousand plunging cataracts roar,
Thunder of spinning stones tumbles ten thousand walls.

O traveler, why do you come hither on a road so dangerous,
In frightening height Sword Parapet Gate firm stands.
While one man guards it,
Ten thousand cannot force it.
What if the keepers are not your friends,
They may turn to wolves and leopards.
There are savage tigers to fear in the day,
and giant serpents in the night.
With their teeth and fangs ready
To cut people down like hemp, lick the blood with whet.
Many pleasures there may be in the Shu silk city,
You would be better to return to your home.
Climbing Shu Passway is harder than scaling the sky,
But I still face westward with a dreary sigh.

This example demonstrates the reason why yuefu as a poetic form continued to flourish and be written by many of the best Tang poets. Poetry was possible only when each word (character in the Chinese sense) in the language had been infused with clear meaning and vivid imagery. For several centuries yuefu provided a wide range of rhyme and assonance which had been excluded from the regulated poetry. By the Tang period it became the most flexible and diverse poetic form with its varying length and a wealth of rhythmic patterns that allowed Li Bai to craft his work.

Du Fu (712–770) was not as widely esteemed during his lifetime as Li Bai because his complex poetic form was ahead of his time. Poets and critics began to appreciate his work within two generations after his death and the popularity of his work crested in the eleventh century. It continued on unabated to the present day, and has made him into a cultural icon in the same way that Li Bai became a divine of Chinese poetry. Du Fu and his contemporaries (from the second half of the 8th century) pushed Chinese regulated poetry to new height and maximized its formal capacity.[28]

"Wang yue" ["Gazing at Mount Tai"], one of Du's early poems, reads:

> Dài **zōng** fú rú hé?
> Qí lù qīng wèi **hǎo**.
> Zào huà zhōng shén xiòu,
> Yīn yāng gē hūn **xiǎo**.
> Dàng **xiōng** shēng céng yūn,
> Jué zī rù guī **nǎo**.
> Huì dāng líng jué dǐng,
> Yī lǎn zhÒng shān **xiǎo**.

> A peak of peaks, so high it stands!
> A boundless green o'er spreads two states.
> A marvel made by Nature's hands,
> Divide light from darkness, nights from days.
> Cloud, layers and layers, rise from my breast,
> My eyes are strained to watch birds flee.
> I must ascend the mountain's crest,
> To see all peaks under my feet.

Du Fu's poetry, especially his regulated poems, had exceptionally wide ranges of style and penetrating imagery, and the tenor of his work changed registers rapidly from the direct and colloquial (the first line) to the allusive and self-consciously literary. Single character (gē in the fourth line, shēng in the fifth, and xiǎo of the last) often defined and activated the entire imagery.[29]

"Dēng Gāo" ["On the Height"]

> fēng jí tiān gāo **yuán** **xiào** **āi**
> zhǔ qīng shā bái **niǎ** **fēi** **huí**
> wú biān luò mù **xiāo** **xiāo** **xià**
> bú jìn cháng jiāng **gǔn** **gǔn** **lái**
> wàn lǐ bēi qiū **cháng** **zuò** **kè**
> bǎi nián duō bìng **dú** **dēng** **tái**

jiān   nán   kŭ   hèn   **fán   shuāng   bìn**
liáo   dăo   xīn   tíng   **zhuó   jiŭ   bēi**

Wind so swift, sky so wide, apes wail and cry,
Water so clear, beach so white, birds wheel and fly.
Boundless forest sheds its leaves in unending shower,
Timeless river rolls its waves with each passing hour.
I often grieve at autumn, a thousand miles, away from home,
Old and ill, now and forever, on this pick, alone.
Living in times so hard, it frosts my hair like pine,
Struck by poverty, I have to give up wine.

During the last years of his life, Du Fu concentrated on further exploring the formal intricacies of poetic form. During this period he wrote 400 poems in his powerful and densely juxtaposed style. He seemed to share John Keats' dictum that poetry had to surprise by excess. Du Fu believed that if his words could no longer surprise others, death would bring him no rest. Du's rich technical achievements during the last decade of his life were most often exhibited in old regulated poems, especially in lü shi of seven-character lines and jue ju. In these poems Du Fu presented a sometimes astounding, if not daunting, complexity of diction, symbol, consonance, and emotion, an involved inwardness that resembled the late sonnets of Gerard Manley Hopkins. The best example of his formal meditation and perfection was his eight-poem suite *Qiu Xing* [*Ode to Autumn*]. One of the Qiu Xing reads:

"Qiu Xing"

Yù   lù   diāo   shāng   **fēng   shù   lín,**
Wū   shān   wū   xiá   qì   xiāo   sēn.
Jiāng   jiān   bó   làng   jiān   tiān   yŏng,
Sài   shàng   fōng   yūn   jiē   dì   yīn.
Cóng   jú   liăng   kāi   tā   rī   lèi,
Gū   zhōu   yī   jì   gù   yuán   xīn.
Hán   yī   chù   chù   cuī   dāo   chŭ,
Bái   dì   chéng   gāo   **jí   mù   zhēn.**

"Ode to Autumn"

Jade dewdrops wither and wound maple trees,
Gorge and cliffs of Wu Mountain exhale fog heavy.
Waves of surging river storm to meet the sky,
Clouds over mountains draw shadows of darkness.
Chrysanthemum blooms twice, weeping for old days,
An only boat tugs at my homesick heart.
Hasty cutting and measuring to make winter robes,
Beating stones herald Baidi City at dusk.

The verbs that were previously used to activate imagery have disappeared and been replaced by several emotionally charged adjectives and adverbs (shang of line one, jiān of line three, jiē of line four, and jì of line five). In a complex construction of this series of imagery, the narrative retreated into the background and is assumed rather than stated. However, the poetic intent and its mood was portrayed by the way in which landscape was painted in front of the eyes of the readers' minds.

Li Shangyin (811?–859) made Du Fu's densely packed imagery more immediately felt with his diction that glittered with rich sensuality. Li Shangyin developed an original style to weave his imagery into his poem "wu ti" [an unnamed]. It gave a common theme of longing and sorrow a very moving and personal touch that was displayed in dizzying counterpoints of literary echoes[30]:

> 1
> You promised to come, but gone and left no trace,
> I wake to the moonlight bower the fifth watch bell.
> In dream my cry could not call you from distant place,
> Try to write you a quick note, the ink is too pale.
> The candlelight illumines half our broidered bed,
> The faint smell of musk sweetens lotus screen.
> Beyond my reach the far away fairy mountain spreads,
> But you're still farther off than the fairy mountain green.
>
> 2
> A misty rain comes blowing with a wind from the east,
> A thunder faintly rolling beyond the Lotus Pool.
> As doors locked and incense burned, I came at night,
> I went at dawn when windless pulled up water cool.
> You peeped at me first from behind a curtained bower,
> I'm left at last with but the cushion of a dame.
> Must human hearts bloom in spring, like all other flower?
> For inch by inch my heart is consumed by the flame.

Another poem of Li Shangyin titled "Jǐn Sè" ["The Sad Zither"] reads:

> Why should the zither sad have fifty strings?
> Each string, each bar chant distance springs.
> Morning dream bewitched be a butterfly,
> Longing heart sings with cuckoo's cry.
> The mermaid weeps pearly tears that drop in moonlit seas,
> Sun streams ocean of waves breathing and vaporizing!
> Will this feeling of the moment last forever?
> Before I know, it comes and begins away slipping.

Tang regulated verse became the zenith of Chinese poetry when it established its literary rhythm. As any literary form in history, regulated verse that had been an inspiration for hundreds of poets and millions of readers began to fossilize once used and reused by generations of poets. Its expression and allusion became worn out and emptied of meaning. Its imagery became increasingly polished, focused, and miniaturized after being seen, contemplated, and re-imagined from almost every point of view. The fresh, sparkling and vivid imagery that used to provoke feelings became pale, flat, meaningless, and eventually lifeless. The regulated form became highly rigid and superficial. This occurred especially when regulated verse became a subject of imperial examination and was attempted by many with or without heartfelt sentiment or emotional spark. It eventually hollowed and abstracted. This became a yoke on the shoulders of true poets, and poetry once again was looking for new and innovative form.[31]

Ci, the new form of poetry, derived from popular tunes. Ci originally meant lyrics of songs and was classified by the number of characters in each line. There were around 800 set patterns, each with a title, called *cípái* [name of lyrics] and set rhythm, rhyme, and tempo. Like classical music, where A major or C minor have nothing to do with the music itself, the title of a ci poem did not suggest anything about its content. Like the earlier yuefu, ci came from popular tunes that began to flourish during the sixth century. Ci was gradually cultivated and polished into a sophisticated literary form during the Tang dynasty and became widely popular during the Song (960–1279), when it appeared to provide a more diverse formal complexity that regulated poetry needed at the time.[32]

Song ci had two main categories: *xiǎolìng* [short tune] and *mànci* [slow tune], depending on the length and tempo of the poetry. After many poems had been written, the categories were reclassified later according to the number of characters. It was called xiǎolìng if it was under 58 characters, *zhōngdiào* [middle range tune] for 59 to 90, and *chángdiào* [long tune] for over 90. The single stanza ci was called *dāndiào* [single tune], mostly xiǎolìng written in pre–Song era. The majority was shuāngdiào [double tune] with two stanzas or *què* in identical or nearly identical patterns. In short, as poetic forms, ci regulated the length of line and the size of entire verse.

Compared to Tang regulated poems, ci maintained the stipulated number of characters but in uneven (long and short) lines. In place of the final rhymes of the even line, ci tightened its structure by regulating middle and final rhyming tones.[33] Moreover, ci redefined poetic forms according to a flow that paralleled that of music. *Xiaodiao* and *manci* corresponded to lyrics of short and fast tempo and those of long and slow tempo respectively. Poets began to observe not only level and oblique properties, but also the distinctions among the four tones as well as the timbre of the sounds of Chinese, such as initials, finals, and allotones.

The regulated poems of Tang brought various tunes of music into the sound of poetry. Song ci poetry further musicalized shi, the poetic language that established in Tang. It turned grammatical and even prosodic rules that used to govern verbal composition into a musical syntax. This more refined and flexible syntax could move and turn words much more quickly and facilitate the evolution of a complex and intricate writing form (an entire orchestra of words) that was not possible in rigidly constructed Tang poetry. Ci could isolate a phrase or add a single long line as if an after-thought. It could formally enact a sudden shift, an odd association, a flashback, an image left hanging. Shi tended to balance and complete utterances.[34] Ci, on the contrary, deliberately left things seemingly out of order, incomplete, and isolated. It would be impossible in shi to put together the same sequence of imageries and passage in the same straightforward and economic manner as did Li Qingzhao in her "Spring End" in the turn of "A Dream Song":

> Last night there were gusty winds and sparse rain.
> Deep sleep did not release me of the effects of wine.
> I asked the maid who rolled up the blind,
> "Don't you know the red should be lean and green plump?"
> "Don't you know that the crabapple still the same."
> She replies.

The poem made readers realize that there was a relationship between the state of the mind of the wine affected lady and her confusing conversation with her maid, but ci allows the components simply to be thrown together in ways that were impossible in shi. Only ci could make such swift turns of thought expressed with the utmost economy of words. Although some Tang poets attempted to mix elements in such an indeterminate fashion, they had to counterbalance the indeterminacy by the second, often parallel, line. Ci made it possible to cut the parallel line off and directly and rapidly juxtapose alternatives. Ci poets could imply rather than state their connotations. This made expression terse, direct, and efficient.

This ability to abruptly shift and juxtapose distilled an ordinary shi line, "The sorrow of being apart can be cut but not severed," into the following three character lines:

> Jian bu duan
> Li huan luan
> Shi li chou
> Bie shi yi ban zi wei zai xin tou.
>
> Cut, but not off,
> Organized, but tangled again.
> This is the anguish of being apart.
> a special flavor of the heart.

In the first two lines, the topic, the "sorrow of being apart," the two predicates referring to a topic in the speaker's mind, was stated in clarity in the third line. If this topic was presented in a conventional shi form, it would be rendered in a straight-forward descriptive manner: The sorrow of separation was portrayed as bleak landscape, an endless river rolling away, a cloud floating off the horizon or a lonely sail disappearing in blue sky. This ci version offered a more gestural and dramatic claim: the sorrow of being apart felt like being cut, a messy heart, and a lingering bad taste that refuses to go away. Compared to the calm shi's narrative, ci presented a dramatic voice crying out that was filled with the emotions of irritation, impatience, sadness and bitterness.

The final line adds another qualification in which the experience of this emotion was objectified as a flavor that was lingering in the mouth. As the feeling could now be tasted, it became an agony that could be savored and judged; both immediately as a taste in the mouth or reflective, as an aftertaste. Here, ci poetry renovated the worn out emotion of parting into something new and refreshing. Parting was no longer an act (as physical separation) and a scene (miserable weather and tears) but a deep and long felt tormenting emotion that was cut but not severed (still pulling), organized but still messy, and gone, yet leaving something behind.[35]

The following poem by Su Shi (1037–1101) illustrates how imageries could be intuitively combined to achieve a strong emotional effect:

"Dreaming of My Deceased Wife on the Night of the 20th Day of the First Month"

Shí náin shēng sǐ **liǎng máng máng!**
Bù sī liàng,
zì nán **wàng.**
Qīan lǐ gū fén,
wú chù huà qī **liáng.**
Zòng shǐ xīang féng yīng bù shí,
Chēn mǎn mìan,
bīn rú **shuāng.**
Yè laí yōu mèng hū huán **xiāng.**
Xiǎo hān **chuāng,**
zhèng shū **zhuāng.**
Xiāng gù wú yían,
Wéi yǒu lèi qīan **háng.**
Liào dè niàn niàn cháng duàn chù,
Mīng yè yué,
duǎn sōng **gāng.**

For ten long years here I wander and there you lie.
I don't often think about you, yet how can I forget!
You are in a lonely grave a thousand miles away,

How can I tell you my chilling sorrow?
You wouldn't recognize me even if we met now,
My face is covered with dust, my temples glazed with frost.
Last night, suddenly a dream brought me home.
I saw you by a window, doing your hair and makeup.
We looked at each other, could not say a word,
With thousand tears streaming down.
Every year, I think of you in that heart-breaking place,
Where moon shines bright on your tomb guarded by bare pine.

Readers can easily realize that ci had a much looser rhyming scheme. The uneven length of line gave the poets ample opportunity to change register and alter rhyming tones whenever they saw fit. (Remember, there were more than eight hundred set tune patterns to chose from.) The changing rhyme that set apart the brilliant poets of the Tang dynasty had now become an established rule of Song ci. Short, terse lines and more changeable rhyming patterns also condensed the poetic delivery and forced imagery to become sharper and more focused.

The following ci poem, also by Su Shi, painted a more focused and more vivid imagery of the poet himself:

"To the tune of 'Lin Jiang Xian'"

Yé yǐn dōng Pō xǐng yòu zuì,
Guī lái fǎng fú **sān gēng,**
Jiā **tóng** bí xī yǐ léi míng.
Qiāo mén dū bù yīng,
Yī zhàng tīng jiāng **shēng.**

Cháng hèn cǐ shēn fēi wó yǒu,
Hé shí wàng yù **yíng yíng,**
Yé **lái** fēng jìng gǔ wēn **píng.**
Xiǎo zhōu cóng cǐ shì
Jiāng hǎi jì yú **shēng.**

I drink all night at East Slope, awaking drunk once again
Then return home at maybe midnight.
The servant-boy snores like thunder,
Nobody answers to my knock.

Leaning on my stick, I listen to the river,
Hating the body that I can't move,
Wondering when I can escape this misery.

The night now deep, the wind quiet, the waves smooth;
I drift away on a boat,
and let the river and sea take care of the rest of my life.

Here the story line is sketchy and vague. The reader does not know for sure if the poet was awake, still drunk, somewhere in between, or if he plans to or already has disappeared in the sea as he wished. However, all of these are irrelevant to the emotion that the poem portrays. The imagery of helplessness is vivid and the subject's intent is clear: he has decided to give up.

The scope of Su's imagery sometimes reminds one of that of "Because I Could Not Stop for Death" by Emily Dickinson (1830–1886). However, in Chinese ci, imagery has a fluidity that does not exist in nineteenth century English. This poetic subtlety was also not available to the Tang poets in China. When one compares Su's imagery to those of "A View of the Han River" (Wang Wei) and "Yue Xia Du Zhuo" (Li Bai), readers can easily recognize that the Tang natural imagery, although vivid, powerful, and provocative, was perceived by the poets. Poets could coexist, talk to, dance, or drink with nature but never disappear into it. In Chinese poetry, the clear boundary between life and death (Dickinson's carriage, Li Bai's wine), consciousness and unconsciousness, and between reality and imagination became penetrable only in Song ci. Ci was the language that fragmented, highlighted, and punctuated the natural world and made it possible for the mind to inhale it or melt into it.

The following poem illustrates this poetic world where time, space, emotion and ideas freely flow into one another. "Shui Long Yin" by Su Shi reads:

> Looks like a flower, but not a flower,
> no one cares when it falls.
> Discarded and scattered at the roadside.
> Not moved,
> But I imagine
> wounded tendrils tangle
> Lovely eyes full of sleep
> About to open, yet still in dreams.
> Taken by the wind ten thousand miles,
> dreaming of lost love,
> but startled, again, by the oriole's cry.
>
> Don't pity the flower that flies away,
> For the sorry western garden, messy with fallen red, hard to lean
> After morning rain
> What's left?
> A pond full of broken weed.
> The fragile three parts of spring,
> Two turn to dust,
> One to flowing water.
> Look carefully:
> These are not catkins
> But drops and drops of tears
> from parting lovers.

The surprising ending that referred back to the beginning hinted at the real subject matter of this poem: the broken heart of the parted lovers. The wounded and bleeding heart was portrayed as a completely destroyed garden after the rain. Don't worry about the tears (flowers), look at the heart (garden): it is in complete ruin and beyond repair.

Li Qingzhao's (1084–1151) "Chong Jiu" in the tune of "Zui Hua Yin" also painted an imagery of sorrow with sound and smell:

> Bó   wù   nóng yún   chóu yǒng **dàn**
> Reì   nǎo xuāo jīn   **shòu**
> Jiā   jié yòu   chóng yáng
> Yù   zhēn shā   chóu
> Biàn yé   liáng chū   **tòu**
>
> Zhōng lí   bǎ   jiǒu huāng hūn   **hòu**
> Yǒu   àn   xiàng yīn   **xiòu**
> Mò   dào bù   xiāo hún
> Liàn juǎn xī   fēng
> Rēn   bì   huáng huá   **shòu**

"The Double Ninth Festival"

Light mists and heavy clouds made day unbearably long,
Burning incense is dying away in a golden censer.
Again, comes the lovely Double Ninth festival;
Midnight cold penetrates my screen of shear silk
and chills through my jade pillow.

By the grass edge, drinking wine after twilight,
My sleeves smell the fragrance of the plants.
Oh, I cannot say it is not enchanting,
Only, when the west wind stirs the curtain,
I realized that I am thinner than the yellow flowers.

Ci gave Chinese poetry a new life by equipping it with a new repertoire of details to express overly repeated and worn out motifs such as love, sorrow, and longing.

The best example of the new emotional details is found in Li Qingzhao's "Untitled" set to the tune of "Sheng-sheng Man" [slow song]. To give readers a sense of the compact composition of the imagery in the original and to illustrate how the Chinese words (imagery) are juxtaposed, the example is presented in three different ways. The first and second parts illustrate the pinyin versions of the original and the direct character-by-character translation from Chinese script into English, then a finished translation of the poem is given.

> (version 1)
> **Xún   xún   jiàn jiàn**
> **Lěng   lěng qīng qīng**

Qī qī căn căn qī qī
Zhà nuăn huán hán shí hòu
Zuì nán **jiāng xī**
Sān beī liăng zhăn diàn jiŭ
Zĕn dí tā wăn lái fēng **jí**
Yàn guò yĕ
Zhèng shāng xīn
Què shì jiù shí xiāng **shí**
Măn dì huáng huā duī **jī**
Qiáo cuì suĕn
Rú jīn yŏu shuí **kān zhāi**
Shŏu zhuò chuāng ré
Dú zì zĕn shēng dé **heī**
Wú tóng gèng jiān xì yŭ
Dào huáng huēn **diĕn diĕn** dī dī
Zhè cì dì
Zĕn yī **gè** chóu zì liăo **dé**

(version 2)
Search search seek seek
cold cold empty empty
chill chill bleak bleak sad sad
just warm return cold time
most hard to relax
three glass two cup weak wine
how resist next night coming wind strong
goose pass have
It broke heart
but are old time mutual recognize
entire ground yellow flower pile up
haggered damaged
and now (where) any who able (to) pick
watching window
alone self how can endure darkness
firmiana again comes with misty rain

(version 3)
Searching and searching, seeking and seeking,
so chilly, so empty,
dreary, miserable and lonely.
The season just began to warm up, cold again
It is most difficult to rest.
Two or three glasses of weak wine —
how can they resist the sharp wind of night?
The wild geese flying away —
that's what hurts most —
and yet they're old friends.

Chrysanthemum covers the ground in piles,

Haggard and damaged —
Who can pick them now?
Watching out the window,
All alone, how can I survive till darkness?
Misty rain falls on firminana's leaves,
Drop by drop, drop by drop, as twilight approaches.
How can one sad word sum all this up?

This ninety-seven character ci is about a single word, "sorrow," which had been envisaged, meditated, and composed upon by Chinese poets for centuries. The tone of Li's poem was slow, sad, and punctuated by seven reduplicated pairs of fourteen words. Li's imagery of sorrow included visions (deserted garden, weak wine, approaching twilight, lonely gaze from a window...), sounds (rainfall, flying geese, honking with their wings beating the air), and discomfort (cold, bleak weather, chilly wind, insomnia, loneliness...). A reader could imagine Li seeking and searching in despair for that which she had lost in the war: her husband, her home, and her happy life. This is exactly what ci contributed to the Chinese language of fine poetry.[36] When shi became replaced by ci as the dominant poetic form, it did not only change its word account (from regulated to unregulated poetry) as did yuefu centuries earlier, but it provided two services to the evolution of Chinese poetic accumulation. First, it liberated poetry from fixed rhythmic and verbal sequence to a more diversified framework. Second, it oriented the function of musical influence away from strictly phonetic to that of literary structure. While the regulated verse focused on the sound of the poetry, ci expanded this focus to imagery. Ci intensified the cultivation of more vivid and more provocative images in the Chinese literary mind. As these images were reread and rewritten, the sounds, pictures, movements and textures were experienced in the imagination of readers and the poetic nature of Chinese language refined further.

Conclusions

The capacity to envisage and to depict is shaped by the degree of maturity of literary language that is inherited by any given writer. The texture of literary vision becomes richer, more complex, and more refined as the language evolves. Formal evolution of language drives the creation and transformation of literary vision and the scope of its ideological choices. It determines how a writer sees, envisages, and describes the world around him, and how he relates to the horizon, depth, and details in his vision. Every time this vision is re-imagined by his reader and rewritten by another writer, it becomes more varied and is enriched.

PART II

PAINTING, THEATRE AND THE IMAGERY OF POETRY

Part Two is a history of the accumulation and refinement of Chinese imagery within its multimedia environment. It demonstrates how literary Chinese adopted and assimilated various images that were presented in visual and performing arts to enrich its visual repertoire and enhance its expressive capacity. It challenges the established assumption that the origin of imagination lies within the universal facility of the mind. It demonstrates that the mind's visual ability (specifically, the ability of the Chinese mind) to imagine with minimal or no physical reference was cultivated by centuries of reading, writing, and performance. It was a consequence of a long process in which literary language absorbed visual and dramatic images wherein words were not only read but also seen in colors and shades, heard and gestured on stage. As these images were repeatedly envisaged and recreated by writers, painters, performers, readers, and their audience, literary language gradually acquired more vivid and yet distilled imagery that in turn, constantly activated the minds of its speakers and readers. Compared to other languages, literary Chinese sharpened one's ability to depict and distinguish various sensual experiences that allowed one to see, hear, smell, touch, and feel as poetic imagery became varied and refined with subtle nuances.

Theatre and performing art played an important role in the development of literary Chinese. However, unlike distinguished world dramatic traditions such as those of Greek, Latin, Renaissance English and French, Chinese theatre was not a theatre of formative language. Instead, like the Italian, Spanish, Russian and Arabic theatres, Chinese musical theatre flourished after it had become a mature literary language whose poetic had been polished without theatrical display. Similar to the English stage of the twentieth century, Chinese theatre was driven by playwrights who focused on characterization rather than plot, and performance rather narrative structure. As visual images became verbalized, they tended to become clarified and focused. Words often created more distilled and condensed imagery as they carried these vivid images. Words spoken on stage became dramatic and included many levels of meanings. Literary Chinese became richer, more mature and refined as it was constantly recycled and reprocessed by its various art forms. As a result, words began to sing and paint while song and painting began to speak. This is a phenomenon that we can now see in the contemporary cultural scene of the west; a phenomenon that has appeared in Chinese culture for many centuries.

4

History of Painting

Like its language, Chinese painting is one of the oldest artistic traditions in the world. The earliest painting elements have been found in prehistoric pottery pieces unearthed in the Yellow River valley and are dated from 5000 to 3000 BC. By the time of the Neolithic cultures (3000–2000 BC), pottery painting became more complex and refined. The ancient villages of the lower Yellow River region (2300–500 BC) produced distinct colorful pottery painting of human figures, animals, birds, fish, trees, insects, and abstract patterns. This level of presentation laid the foundation for the forthcoming bronze art.[1]

Painting (drawing) and writing in pre-history China are believed to share a common origin. In ancient Chinese literature both writing and painting were referred to as *xie* (literally "to write") because they used the same writing implements: brush and ink.[2] It is believed that formalized painting and writing began during the time of Huang Di [Yellow Emperor] (2479–2379 BC?). Cang Jie, the legendary inventor of the Chinese character, was the court historian for this emperor, while Shi Huang, another minister of the imperial court, drew and painted for the royal residence. Although Cang Jie, Shi Huang, and their emperor are fictional rather than historical figures, the association between writing and painting (as visual presentations) is evident and has been repeatedly verified by historical records and archeological findings. While historians still continue the debate about the exact date that drawing evolved into writing, no one can deny the close relationship of these two types of expression.

Natural objects inspired both writing and painting. Legend said that Cang Jie created the primal characters of Chinese language from the shapes (captured in drawing) of the sun, moon, stars, clouds, lakes, oceans, birds and animals. Shi Huang excelled in painting because of his ability to capture images of natural objects in the sky and on the earth.[3]

From Zhou Dynasty on, the imperial court always employed painters who were responsible for producing portraits and decorating the palaces and temples with murals. Jing Jun was a skillful painter for Qi (a state), and his king ordered him to decorate the newly built nine-story royal terrace, a lengthy assignment. Jing Jun was not allowed to go home and he missed his wife. He painted a portrait of her and took the portrait to work so he could see her every day. The king saw the portrait, and taken by her beauty, offered perpetual wealth to Jing in return for his wife.

The court painter of Qin dynasty (255–206 BC) was the legendary Lie Yi. As the story goes, Lie could take ink in his mouth, spurt it on the wall and make pictures of dragons and beasts. His paintings of phoenixes were so real that people would tiptoe around them because they were afraid that the sound of footsteps would startle the beautiful birds and they would fly away. His carved animals looked as if they could move. In order to keep the painted birds and animals on walls and in the palace (without them becoming alive and running away), the artist often painted and carved their eyes without pupils. But Emperor Qin Shihuang did not believe that painted or carved beasts could run away. He ordered someone to paint pupils into one eye of each of a pair of jade (carved) tigers. Days later, the tigers disappeared. In the meantime, the people in the nearby mountains began to report seeing a pair of one-eyed white tigers that appeared to be very different from any local tigers that they had ever seen. The emperor sent hunters to capture the tigers and discovered that they were actually the carved tigers from the palace.[4] These stories sound purely fictional, but they indicate that during ancient times, good painting was measured by how realistic the images were. Chinese tradition of visual art began with natural imitation, as did Egyptian, Mesopotamian, Greek and Roman.

This critical tendency for realistic painting continued in the Han dynasty (206 BC–AD 220). The painting of Liu Bao, a court painter, could make people feel as if they were standing in front of a real object. Liu's painting of the Milky Way made viewers feel warm, while his painting of north wind made them shiver with cold. Another painter, Xu Mo, is mentioned in literary records. The story went like this: the Emperor Mi of Wei was traveling along Luo River and saw a beautiful white otter. He took great fancy for it but failed to catch it. Xu Mo had a suggestion. He told the emperor that otter liked perch and that they would risk their lives to get them. Xu Mo painted a picture of perch and set it upon the riverbank. A crowd of otters raced to the spot and they were finally captured by the emperor.[5] Unfortunately none of the works of these great painters has survived or has yet been found.

Like ancient Greek and Roman civilization, Chinese visual presentation began with three-dimensional forms because without an adequate language to describe an object, before a sufficient verbal media was invented, the only way to reproduce a natural image was to make a touchable copy. The wealth of pre-history visual arts in China was unknown in the West until recently. It took Chinese artists many centuries to be able to reduce three-dimensional images into realistic images in drawing, relief, and eventually painting (a two dimensional picture with a convincing three-dimensional image). But when they did, Chinese paintings of the human figure were much more realistic than were those of ancient Egypt.[6] The most illustrative way to observe this evolution is to compare the Han Flying Horse (sculpture) with Han Kan's (Tang) famous painting of white horse. Although Han Kan followed basically the same linear conventions in depicting his horse, his image completely out-grew the archaic flat representation and created a superbly articulated, per-sonality-charged animal. It was a realism that Chinese artists had been struggling to achieve for many centuries.

The earliest surviving material evidence of the Chinese representation of nature was found in cast metal dated to the Late Zhou period. There were often stylized trees, animals, birds, or mountains on bronze mirrors and inlaid bronze vessels, and rare findings in carved jade. Mountains and rivers also appeared in stone relief and stamped pottery tomb tiles. Mountain patterns were used as a baseline for paintings of magical birdmen, the symbol of the spirits of mountains and untamed nature. A tile presented the two mountain styles together on three friezes, one above the other. The uppermost, with the birdman, used the continuous wave mountain range. It consisted of linear and rhythmically undulating mountain symbols of a cloud-like nature. Inher-ited from later Zhou, this shape was used for clouds, mountains, or even as a linear decoration out of which landscape elements could sprout. Other stamped tiles from West China showed a surprisingly real and spacious setting for a hunting scene.

The Chinese linear landscape setting further developed in the later Han Dynasty and was found on much stamped and glazed pottery. By this time, cliffs, mountains, rocks, and trees were clearly differentiated but lacked a sense of relative scale. These, too, served as settings for animals and mythical figures.[7]

Like the medieval books in English, the earliest Chinese books consisted of words and illustrations. They were painted not as book page but rather as a diagram of cosmic order wherein everything, both words and pictures, had to be properly arranged as a picture or a diagram. The writer-painter was afraid that if the text or picture was out of place, it would threaten the natural order, and cosmic collapse and evil catastrophic events would occur. The best example of this diagram was the Chu Silk Manuscript (475–221 BC), the oldest existing written work found to date.[8]

This silk manuscript has 926 characters of ancient Chu script concerning the astrological almanac. The text, although written in words, is painted as a picture. It contains three parts: the first segment was written right side up, the next is inverted, and the third portion runs along the four outer edges. In the margin of four sides, twelve mythical figures (deities of zodiac signs) are organized in groups of three with short descriptions. There are stylish pictures of trees in each corner, rendered in green, red, white, and black, probably symbolizing the four seasons or four pillars holding up heaven. The silk textile varies in tone from dark to light brown, with red pigmentation in some areas.

Among the earliest surviving examples of Chinese visual artwork (dated to the Warring States Period, 481–221 BC) are paintings on silk or tomb murals on rock, brick, or stone. The earliest painted landscapes in the modern sense are found in the Han Literary accounts that depict magnificent wall murals in palaces, temples and gardens of the Han emperors. Since these structures were all built of wood, none of them have survived. Another technical reason for the non-survival of the pre–Han arts is the poor quality of Han blue and Han purple, the mineral paint that was used from Zhou to the end of the Han dynasty. They tended to fade away with sunlight and weather change and were not as resistant as the more modern paints, such as Maya blue.[9] To verify the literary record of painting, art historians turned to Han tombs to get some idea of the artistic production of this epoch.

Painted mountains, clouds, trees, and buildings appeared in Han relief carvings, textile designs, mirror backs, and inlaid metal objects. However, the natural objects were rendered in a highly symbolic and abstract manner. Trees and mountains were painted in geometrical shapes and the imagery was overly simplified and sometimes hardly recognizable. This derived less from the limited skills of the Chinese painters than in the predominantly literary culture. Chinese painters were in many ways highly competent, even sophisticated. However, like the works of medieval European artists and illustrators whose work was monopolized by religious doctrine, Chinese visual images were designed to serve literature. Paintings concentrated on the human figure, and painters devoted their major effort and time to depicting scenes from literary and religious texts, myths, legends, history, and filial piety, and they showed little interest in landscape as an independent subject.

The best example of illustrated arts in Han is burial pictorial art, especially Daoist art. The art of drawing emerged well before the formation of religious doctrine. However, arts became very important to illustrate the attainment of postmortem immortality. One of the earliest human figures depicted was a Daoist priest who appeared in a Leshan tomb (*Mahaomi*). He was standing, wearing a long robe and a tall hat. He held a ceremonial staff (*jie zhang*) in his left hand and a medicine bag in his right hand. About one hundred similar figures were found in stone sarcophagi with carvings. They often stood in front of a half-open gate representing the Heavenly Gate [*tian men*] or Gate of Soul [*hun men*]. Inside of the gate was a deity on a throne adorned with dragon and tiger.[10]

The Daoist symbols of dragon and tiger appeared on many different occasions in carvings during the same period. Daoist deities were often portrayed as riding a dragon and tiger or accompanied by them, a motif derived from Daoist literature. For example, Daoist script described how dragons and tigers appeared on the road of the (Dao) Master Zhang Ling as he was making his Divine Elixir to the Nine Heavens [*jiutian shendan*]. Although it is difficult to determine which of the words that depict mountains and the story of dragons and tigers or their images were created first, the close association between recorded story line and visual images is apparent.

A money tree was another popular motif during the Han period. One of these artworks was a bronze sculpture in glazed earthenware. This tree had an abundance of round coins with square holes hanging from the branches. When it appeared at a burial site, it was meant to provide guiding light for the deceased, who would ride on a winged ram up the ceramic mountain to the bronze tree of paradise. This image of the money tree was a later distortion of the tree that symbolized heaven (paradise) where gods lived. Like the trees and rivers that are described and illustrated in heaven of the west, Chinese heaven was originally a tree. It was envisaged as the shelter for gods who rested and slept throughout its multi-leveled branches. There were also heavenly horses, giant hares, musicians and dancers. A later version of the tree kept the original image of the Queen Mother (Goddess) of the West [*Xiwangmu*]. She remained on the top of the tree sitting on her tiger of the west and dragon of the east throne, representing yin [darkness] and yang [brightness]. The tree was decorated with scenes of paradise containing magical creatures and immortals including the sunbird, the moon toad, the deer who found the main ingredient for the elixir of immortality and the clever monkey who stole the elixir.[11]

In addition to stone and bronze carvings and murals, the most significant art works were paintings on silk that were buried with emperors and wealthy individuals. One of the earliest known paintings of this kind was unearthed in 1949 from a grave in Chenjia Mountain in Hunan province. It was called *Dragon, Phoenix and Beauties* and is dated to the period of 475 BC to 221 BC. During this period many kingdoms fought for dominance in the land of China. The Chenjia Mountain was in the middle of the kingdom Chu, where Qu Yuan lived and composed his legendary poetry, *chu ci*. There was an image of a woman in the middle of *Dragon, Phoenix and Beauties*. Above her, images of fictional figures of dragon and phoenix (auspicious signs, like angels in Christian literature) were painted to guide her to heaven.

Another important silk painting was unearthed from the Mawangdui tomb near Changsha, Hunan province, dated roughly to 165 BC. Among the eleven silk paintings from this site, the two T shaped banners that were used in the funeral were most beautiful and sophisticated. They were called *fei yi* [flying garment] in the tomb record. This name derived from the traditional belief that the deceased would go to heaven and become a celestial being in another world. This garment was designed to fly with her after death.

The painting depicted the journey of a soul going to heaven as the fabric was extended. The top section of the T clearly represented heaven, where the sun's crow, moon's toad, a jade rabbit, Zhu Long (a mythical god in heaven), and heavenly guardians were illustrated. There was also a large mulberry tree shining in moonlight and a young woman was flying with a dragon. She looked as if she had escaped the chores of earthly life, and totally rejuvenated, was dancing with the divine dragon in a celestial world. In the middle section, the deceased (who was the wife of the Marquis of Dai) was dressed in colorful lavish cloth, and was attended by three maids. She was walking through a large hall and the servants were kneeling in front of her. As she was ascending slowly to heaven, her family was offering sacrifices to assist her journey. They had set up banquet tables with plates of food and glasses full of wine. As there was no master present (she was busy ascending to heaven); the assembled people were not eating and drinking but were bowing forward as if they were seeing the master off. On the bottom section of the banner, the underground, a giant was holding up the earth.

It appeared that Han painting continued the tradition seen from the *Dragon, Phoenix and Beauties* of the Warring State period. But the Han painting was more sophisticated compared to those of early periods, which contained only simple lines that conveyed symbolic meanings. The Han painting was drawn with more elegant and fluid lines achieved by sophisticated technique. Black ink was used to draw an outline and colors were filled in afterwards. The mineral pigments of cinnabar red, malachite green, azurite blue and chalk white still have remarkable original color after more than two thousand years.[12]

Literary dominance continued and it was not until the Six Dynasties period (265–589) that landscape painting as a distinct genre of visual art began to emerge. The first verifiable and celebrated Chinese artist and the father of Chinese classical painting, Gu Kaizhi (344–406), was a great painter, calligrapher, and poet. The major subject of his painting was the human figure. None of Gu's original works, which are recorded in literature, have survived except copies of three silk hand scroll paintings. The "Admonitions of the Instructress to the Palace Ladies" (in a Tang dynasty copy) portrayed nine stories from a political satire about Empress Jia. The theme of the "*Luoshen* [Goddess of the Luo River] Appraisal" was drawn from the article of the same title, written by Cao Zhi (192–232), son of the Wei Emperor Cao Cao. It depicted the meeting of Cao Zhi and Goddess Luoshen at the Luo River. The painting vividly illustrates their emotions when they first met and when they were finally forced to separate. Gu emphasized the expressions of the figures — the stones, mountains and trees in the picture; however, they were only ornamental. "Wise and Benevolent Women" (a Song copy) portrayed a subset of the women described in the Han dynasty work *Biographies of Exemplary Women*. This 5 meter long scroll was divided into 10 sections, each of which contained a group of women with a short description in texts.[13]

In contrast to the medieval Christian painting that had lost its Hellenistic naturalism, Chinese figure painting placed a great emphasis on depicting the inner spirit of its characters. Gu Kaizhi's painting demonstrated lifelike charm, as he paid particular attention to the eyes of his portrait subjects, whether human, gods or Buddha. He emphasized that one's spirit and lively personality all showed in the eyes. He shared the naturalist tendency of the ancient Greeks and believed that a well-painted figure with lively eyes should provide an invitation for the viewers to talk with it.

In a well-documented story about Gu's skills, he promised that he would donate a large amount of cash to a Buddhist fundraising event. Everyone was laughing in disbelief because even the wealthy people in attendance could afford to give only a small fraction of his pledge. Gu Kaizhi began to draw a portrait of Weimo (a Buddha at the time of Sakyamuni) but refused to draw the eyes until the next day when the spectators would be required to make a substantial donation for the privilege of observing his technique. As the news spread, large crowds of people rushed to the temple. Gu Kaizhi cleansed himself, lit some incense, and prayed silently. Then, he made two strokes in the position of the eyes. Suddenly the Weimo had become alive; his eyes shone with a kindness that spread to light up the temple. The audience was highly impressed and generously donated their money; before long, several times Gu's original pledge was collected. This traditional ceremony of painting the eyes has passed down from Gu's time and is continued even today in modern Japan.

In contrast to live human figures that were painted with highly polished skill, the landscape of the Han continuous scrolls, in which figures dominated the scene, was quite primitive. For example, the landscape was too small in proportion to human figures in the same fashion as the Italian Primitives of Giotto. Natural setting was little more than a decorative framework for human activity. The mountains in the foreground were so stylized that at first glance one could hardly recognize them, and the trees, climbing up the slopes and standing in front, had no consistent relationship in size, either among themselves or to the mountains. A tree could soar high above the tallest peak; a willow could be the same size as the mountains. Each part of the work, the mountains, the figures, the trees, the pathways and buildings — were painted almost as a unit in themselves. Neither in space nor in perspective did the painter succeed in fusing the parts into a whole.

Although none of Gu's landscapes have survived, a detailed description of how he portrayed a real or imaginary landscape has been preserved in his essay "Hua Yun-tai-Shan Chi" ["How to Paint the Cloud-Terrace Mountain"].[14]

"I would make purple rocks stand erect at the top of the next peak, and thereby form the buttressing element of a left hand watchtower. The steep cliff, lofty and dark, is linked on the west with the Cloud Terrace so as to indicate a road. The left-hand watchtower peak has a precipice for its base, and below this is a void. I will combine several boulders in a layered effect to support the precipice so that together with it they face the eastern gorge. To the west, a rocky torrent appears. However, as it adapts to its steep confines, I will make it to flow down through the ridge as an underground stream that emerges after awhile to the east. It pours down the gorge as a stony brook that sinks into a deep pool. The reason for its falling now to the west and now to the east is that I wish to make the painting seem natural."[15]

If Gu's writing stated the intention of the painter, the words of the critic provided the perception that the actual painting gave to its viewers. The discrepancy between the two illustrates a perspective of the limitation of Gu's effort and skill. Zhang Yenyuan, a Tang critic who lived five hundred years later, had seen famous paintings of Wei and Jin dynasties, including those of Gu, and testified that those landscapes were filled with crowded peaks. Their effect was like that of filigree ornaments or horn combs. Sometimes the water did not seem to flow, while other times the figures were larger than the mountains. The views were generally enclosed by trees and stones which stood in a circle on the ground. They looked like rows of lifted arms with outspread fingers. The relation between the figures and the mountain in the painting appeared to the eyes of the audience as absolutely not naturalistic, although the mountain itself, with its rising peaks, deep valleys, and dropping cliffs, was rendered very convincingly.[16]

It was clear that Gu did his best to make his painting look natural and real, but he was apparently struggling with his ability to portray the depth and texture of the space. Another of Gu's paintings (a Song copy) in which figures are seen in a landscape presented the tale of the nymph of the Lo River in a continuous scroll, and illustrates the primitive kind of landscape typical of the period.

During the sixth century landscape depiction developed further, although its function remained decorative. The finest and most famous works are the stone sarcophagus that represented stories of filial piety. For the first time, the figures were rendered in proper proportion to the setting, and they moved among the trees and rocks in a natural and convincing way. There was also a real feeling of space, with the eye of the observer being led into the distance. The free-flowing line, employed with both skill and elegance, highlighted the picturesque shapes of the trees and rock formations. However, even here the artist's main emphasis was upon a story of literary text, and the landscape was merely a setting for the main figures.

During the Tang dynasty, landscape finally became a separate genre of painting. As Tang predominantly was a literary culture, where visual imagination was shaped by texts, this dynasty did not produce many brilliant painters, especially landscape artists. Tang painting, like the later medieval church painting in Europe, remained the servant of literary narrative. Like its poetry that set up the tonal regulation for classical poetry, Tang's gallery of painting was an arena to sharpen basic skills of presentation such as the clarity of line, refinement of composition, the utilization of more brilliant color and meticulous detail. This technical evolution left prominent footprints in the paintings of the human figure. For example, Han Gan's (706–783) painting was characterized by controlled line and clear composition. History has recorded his wall paintings on Buddhist and Daoist themes, but he is best remembered for his paintings of horses. Han emphasized the strength and nobility of the animal. Zhang Xuan (713–755) was best known for the painting *Court Ladies Preparing Newly-Woven Silk* (survived in a copy painted by Emperor Huizong of Song [1100–1125]) and *Spring Outing of the Court Ladies*. Zhou Fang (730–800) was an influential painter of the mid–Tang Dynasty who was inspired by the pure and detailed style of Gu Kaizhi. His works included *Court Ladies Adorning Their Hair with Flowers*.[17]

The best example of this technical advance was *gong bi* [fine brush] style. Gong bi strove for extremely meticulous realism in depiction that was achieved by painstakingly slow work of fine brush strokes and shading in ink and color. This style tended to be visually complex and descriptive rather than interpretive of the subject matter. Gong bi paintings were often highly ornamental and refined, and had an aristocratic and haughty aura. Gong bi paintings became particularly popular in the flower-and-bird genre but were also seen in figure painting and less frequently in landscape.[18]

The Tang painter who had the most enduring influence on later landscape painting was Li Sixun (651–716). Also called General Li, he and his son Li Zhaodao (General Li junior, 675–730) were the founders of what historians refer to as the Northern school of landscape painting. Their early style was mainly characterized by prominently pushing the use of blue and green color. To create space and texture in landscape painting, both used strong brushes and bright paint to illustrate high mountains and cliffs, with rivers, rocks, and trees. They paid much more attention to realistic detail than the later Song painters, especially those of the Southern school, who sought to create an atmospheric impression. The landscapes of the two generals were heavily colored with mineral pigments, especially blue azurite and green malachite. The most well known Tang blue and green landscapes are *The Emperor Ming-huang's Journey to Shu*, a copy of a composition sometimes attributed to Li Zhaodao, and *Ocean of Mountains in Sea of Cloud* and *Visiting Friend in Spring Mountain* by Li Sixun.[19]

Li Sixun's landscapes have an elevated mood and a very unique style. He beautifully captured the real space and texture of the mountains and rivers with the strokes of his brush. Li Zhaodao put more emphasis on technique in his portrayal of mountains, rivers and wild animals. Emperor Xuan Zong (685–762) once summoned Li Sixun to the royal court and commissioned him to paint a mural at the Da Tong Palace. When Li Sixun completed the mural, the emperor told him that he could hear the sound of a river when he gazed at the work. Li was considered the master of landscape by his contemporaries. According to their accounts, Li Sixun painted elaborate landscapes with palaces, pavilions, bridges, and terraces all brightly colored in blues, greens, reds and whites composed with a wealth of detail in a meticulous and refined manner.

Many painters and critics disagreed with the emperor and Tang critics. They considered Li's landscape as dry and lifeless. This partially was due to the fact that they disliked gong bi style and preferred much freer, more expressive and dynamic styles. The latter has emerged as the main tendency of landscape painting since Tang. The first painter who was said to have dynamic brush stroke was Wu Daozi (710–760), who became the major artistic personality of the late Tang period. According to records, Wu painted over 300 murals and more than 100 scrolls, only one of which (*The Portrait of 87 Immortals*) has survived. In addition to human figures, Wu drew mountains, rivers, flowers and birds. Unlike his predecessor, Gu Kaizhi, whose line strokes were slender and forceful but lacked variety, Wu's strokes were full of vigor, expressing the internal world of his subjects. Wu's works exhibited an expressionist style.

According to tradition, his contribution to the development of landscape painting was considerable. Zhang Yanyuan, a famous Tang painter-calligrapher and critic, wrote only a century after the death of the artist that Wu was one of the pioneers in the evolution of Tang landscape painting. He pointed out that although the old technique of painting gradually changed, Wu's contemporaries still shaped stones like dripping ice crystals and drew every fiber and carved every leaf of the trees. Among these conventional and technical painters, Wu Daozi's brushwork was outstanding and full of energy. Zhang noticed that Wu Daozi painted strange rocks and broken river banks on temple walls. He was obviously working in a new and more expressive style. Zhang also added that Wu's landscape transformed the art of landscape painting.

Many Chinese critics stressed the boldness and power of Wu's brush stroke. For example, legend says that Wu once completed a panorama painting of over three hundred li (over a hundred kilometers long) in a single day and it was a much looser, freer type of painting, a style very different from that of Li Sixun. In another story, when the emperor asked to see his sketches, Wu replied that he had none, for he had set them down in his heart. It is also said that the Emperor Ming Huang commissioned General Li to do a painting for the same building and that it took him several months to complete the project. The emperor commented that what Li Sixun achieved in several months, Wu Daozi could get done in a single day. Both of these artists were excellent in their own way.

Although this story must be legendary, since Li was no longer alive at the time of Wu Daozi, it nevertheless illustrates the style of painting associated with these two artists during the Tang period when their works were no doubt readily available for scholars and connoisseurs. Of course wall paintings such as these would deteriorate rapidly, and today we have no idea of what they looked like.

The most influential instrument for more expressive painting was the ink and wash [*shui mo hua*] technique, which was invented during the Tang dynasty. Like gong bi it was another important contribution to the development of landscape painting. The application of color on existing ink and then wash painting enriched the language of painting and revolutionized the way in which natural scenery and objects were portrayed. By replacing simple, thin lines with strokes in black or color, landscape painting moved further away from natural imitation and linear narrative (story telling with line). Strokes could not only reproduce the appearance of the subjects, but also capture and illustrate soul. For example, to paint a flower, the painter was not limited to perfectly matching its petals and colors, but rather he could convey its liveliness and fragrance. Ink and wash technique also made visual language (line, color, and texture) much more efficient, as the painter had to put upon the paper the fewest possible lines and tones — just enough to convey form, texture and effect.[20]

Ink and wash painting was a radical departure from Tang's gong bi painting of meticulous blue and green landscape. It was a formal revolution of painting similar to the impressionist and abstractionist movement in the modern West. This revolution took place in China during the late Tang and early Song dynasties when the interest of painting shifted from the subject matter to its presentational and expressive forms. Unlike the west, where classical realism and modern expressionism coexisted and competed with each other for decades, Chinese realistic was retained only in narrowly defined genres, such as figure painting and painting of birds and flowers in landscapes. Landscape painting as a whole outgrew visual imitation, and came to focus on impression and expression. New generic distinctions emerged not in basic impressive assumptions but rather in specific technique and different focuses in subject matter.

The northern school frequently used a technique known as *fu bi cun* [ax chopped strokes]. This technique was aggressive and forceful, leaving the surface of the paper or silk with grotesque marks that adequately reflected the powerful and vigorous geography of north China. The southern school preferred *bi ma cun* [hemp fiber strokes], which was more suitable in depicting the luxuriant vegetation and the moist and gentle texture of the southern landscape. Another essential difference between north and south schools was that the monumental northern landscapes gave the viewer a grand perspective that could be captured at once, sometimes referred to as "full-view" landscape. The northern tendency to glorify the power and vastness of nature was opposite to the more lyrical southern landscapes, which usually brought the view closer to the audience to create a more intimate feeling.

The tenth century has been regarded as the best of Chinese landscape painting. The first surviving masterpiece of this time was the *View of the Mountain Lu* by Jing Hao (855–915). Jing was one of the earliest Chinese artists who employed ink washes [*shui mo*] to simulate depth and atmospheric perspective. While inheriting the Tang approach, Jing re-clarified and redefined the ink wash technique to distinguish higher and lower (parts of objects), and to present shallowness and depth with a gradation in ink tones and texture. He added his bold brush strokes to define ink wash (providing structure for his brushwork) in order to accurately transcribe the landscapes of Shanxi province, where he spent his entire life.

Jing described his brush stroke [*cun fa*] as a way of allowing the heart to follow after the brush. He insisted that the image had to be seized without hesitation so that the representation did not suffer. If the ink was too rich, it lost its expressive quality; if too weak in tone, it failed to achieve a proper vigor. In other words, he sought to allow denser forms to take shape spontaneously out of ink wash, like rocky crags jutting forth from misty basins. He insisted that the type of brushstroke used in a painting must correspond to the inner nature of the object being depicted. Rocks needed to be painted with broad, hard brush strokes, flowers with delicate, thin brush strokes, etc. In *Bifa Ji*, Jing argues that an artist must strive to find a delicate balance between communicating the physical resemblance of an object and conveying the emotional character it possesses, or, in the words of historian Michael Sullivan, an artist must strive for harmony between form and spirit. The search for such a balance between the real and the abstract would form the basis of Chinese art criticism for centuries to come.[21]

This embrace of spontaneity was readily apparent in his surviving works, such as *Mount Lu*. The work is a tight, vertical composition, employing Jing's newly developed *cun fa* technique to compress the landscape into layers of jutting rock-pillars between chasms of mist. The enclosed space of the composition enhances the monumental characteristics of the mountain, which fills some 90 percent of the scroll. Humans and buildings, though drawn with remarkable realism in a manner that contrasts sharply against the atmospheric landscape surrounding, were reduced to an almost unnoticeable scale, clustered at the foot of the mountain at the very bottom of the scroll, further conveying the intimidating grandeur of the natural world over the transient activities of man.[22]

Jing Hao's pupil, Guan Tong (906–960), favored the use of "ax chopped brush strokes" [fu bi cun] in depicting the angularity of the northern mountains, and focused on the cyclical seasons of nature in his painting. The best example of this technique was his *Drinking and Singing at the Foot of a Precipitous Mountain*. Although Guan Tong had no less than ninety-four landscapes listed in the catalogue of the imperial collection, few of his works survive today. The most convincing of these is the *Ford of the Mountain Stream*. The art of landscape painting had evolved considerably during the several decades that separated the paintings of Jing Hao and Guan Tong. In contrast to the Jing painting in the same collection, Guan Tong's brushwork was far more spontaneous and does not appear either dry or mechanical. The subject was again the familiar one of lofty mountains, trees, shrubs, houses, rocks, water, and tiny figures. However, the treatment of space and atmosphere shows a marked advance when compared to the Jing Hao scroll. The rocks and mountains give a far greater sense of both mass and depth, and by using mist and aerial perspective the artist has succeeded in conveying a true feeling of space.

The leading artist of the middle of the tenth century was Li Cheng (919–967), who was particularly well-known for his winter landscapes and picturesque trees. In an essay by the artist entitled "The Secrets of Landscape Painting," Li Cheng describes the proper methods of painting landscapes during different seasons: "The atmosphere of the mountain in spring is clear and charming; the trees in summer are thick and luxuriant; the autumnal forest is forlorn and solemn; and the winter trees are resigned and death-like. The roots of the trees should penetrate the soil like a dragon's claws gripping its prey. The stony ground is full of sharp edges, but its base is covered with soil."[23]

Apparently even by the eleventh century, the genuine works of Li Cheng had already become rare. Mi Fu (1052–1107), a painter and critic, lamented the fact that he had only seen two authentic scrolls among more than three hundred imitations. Of those preserved today the most convincing was *Travellers Among the Snowy Hills*. The subject, which is very similar to that painted by Jing Hao and Guan Tong, represented mountains, water, trees, buildings, and in the midst of the wild setting, a few miniature figures climbing up a mountain road. In contrast to the earlier paintings, however, Li used a somewhat different treatment of the background. Here the sky soars over the mountains, and to the right of the rocky mass there is a series of smaller ranges. The rendition of the trees, with their writhing branches, was typical of Li Cheng's manner of painting, as was the great economy of his brush stroke.

Mi Fu elaborates on Li Cheng's work titled *Pine and Rocks*:

> Trunk thrusts upward in a majestic curve, and the branches cast shadows with their luxuriant growth. Where the knotholes are indicated, he did not use circles of ink but put down one big dab to run throughout the trunk, going over it lightly with a palely inked brush. Thus it is like the work of nature. On the opposite side, a textured boulder juts up, rounded and glistening; at the crest of a bank the brushwork ends. The foot of the rock is on a level with a rock in the water, and below that he used light ink to indicate an appropriate amount of water. Hence this is a ledge that goes straight down into the water. It is not like those of common imitators that are done in vertical or slanting strokes and, even worse, lack ground and water effects beneath, seeming to float in midair.[24]

It is this inspired quality of Li Cheng's brushwork which is praised again and again by later critics and which made him, especially in the eyes of the Yüan dynasty artists, one of the most renowned painters in the history of Chinese art.

Another painter who was noted for his treatment of atmosphere and space was Dong Yuan (934–962). *The Xiao and Xiang Rivers*, one of his best-known paintings, demonstrated his unique techniques and his sense of composition. The clouds broke the background mountains into a central pyramid composition and a secondary pyramid. By softening the mountain line he made the immobile effect more pronounced. The inlet broke the landscape into groups and made the serenity of the foreground more pronounced. Instead of simply being a border to the composition, it was a space of its own into which the boat on the far right intruded, even though the boat was tiny compared to the mountains. Left of center, he used his unusual brush stroke techniques to give a strong sense of foliage to the trees which contrasted with the rounded waves of stone that made up the mountains. This gave the painting a more distinct middle ground, and the mountains an aura and depth which made them appear grand. Everything that the earlier tenth-century artists had been striving for was here perfectly expressed, and the result was a painting of almost magical power.

Dong Yuan used color to paint *Cave of the Immortals*. The theme was once again the familiar mountain landscape with a body of water, trees, buildings, and tiny figures. The view was somewhat different, as the landscape was seen from a high point in the foreground rather than from a level position or looking up from below. This was designed to show receding groups of mountains and thus increase the illusion of space and distance.

Dong Yuan was a master of the southern hemp fiber technique. He combined it with another technique that he was famous for called *dian zi cun* [dot technique]. The dot technique came to represent vegetation and helped to merge separate parts of the landscape into a whole. The southern school carried a more lyrical mood and was to some extent more subtle and intimate than the monumental northern landscapes. Dong Yuan's painting often instantly evoked a tranquil and laid-back mood of a warm, hazy and calm afternoon, glittering water, peaceful fisherman, and smooth lush hills all coming together in a captivating image of an enjoyable afternoon in nature.

Ju Ran, who helped to introduce and develop different versions of the southern hemp fiber technique, was also active at the end of the tenth century. Ju Ran excelled in creating misty atmospheric effects and high spacious views of mountains and rivers. He pushed the moisture, softness, and subtlety of southern brush to a new height. Although Ju had at least one hundred and thirty landscape paintings listed in the Imperial catalogue, the surviving paintings attributed to him are hardly distinguishable from his Yuan imitators. To get a sense of how Ju Ran paintings appeared in the eyes of his admirers, one had to be satisfied with the words of his contemporary connoisseurs:

> Whenever he set down his brush, it was like some author or man of arts at the moment of composing in poetical form; a veritable spring would gush forth in

abundance from the tip of his brush ... the great riches within his breast gave an inexhaustible fertility to his brush. Ju Ran's landscapes beyond their peaks and ranges and gorges, will descend by way of wooded foothills; there he will set such things as big boulders, pine and cypress, scattered bamboo, vines and grasses, all helping to bring each other out. His somber ravines with their tiny trails dipping and turning, winding and enclosing; his bamboo fences and thatched huts, his high-hung bridges and perilous cause-ways, are as real as actual mountain scenery.[25]

Northern Song landscapes contained the principle elements of mountains and trees, which are portrayed by an extensive repertoire of well-developed form types. For example, there were clearly defined systems of texture strokes or dots to depict different kinds of rock surfaces. Trees were painted as a mixture of deciduous hardwoods and coniferous evergreens, and leaves were represented by a variety of dotted or needle patterns.

Landscape in the style of Fan Kuan (960–1030) was neither a realistic portrayal nor a romantic personal vision. It emphasized the vastness and complexity of nature. His composition had a strict order of three levels. The foreground was executed in crisp and well-defined brush works: a boat was landing at the foot of a tree-covered bluff. At the middle distance, travelers headed toward a temple retreat. Rising mountain peaks suspended and fitted into the background. There was a suitable break between the foreground and the towering central peak. Human figures in this scene appeared to be overpowered by the magnitude and mystery of their surroundings.[26] Fan Kuan was considered a painter of the northern school who surpassed all of his contemporaries.

Contrasting Fan Kuan's dramatic scope of the land was the tranquil and private world of a pair of birds painted by Emperor Hui Zong (1082–1135) entitled *Finches and Bamboo*. It was a painting derived from meticulous observation and portrayal of the natural world. The bamboo leaves, whose tips were browned by a harsh winter, had regained a lush jade-green hue and pink tendrils sprouted from each branch. The spring stalks provided secure perches for the birds. The sleek male on the lower stalk, tail and wing tips pulled back, was attentive to the female, who was rather aloof but enjoying his attention. However, by this time, bird depiction had highly stereotyped into conventional form and brush patterns. Hui Zong's painting remained a frozen image; even the dots of lacquer in the birds' eyes failed to add life.

Guo Xi (1020–1090) was the most accomplished academic painter of his time. He developed an incredibly detailed system of idiomatic brush strokes which became influential for later painters. His most famous work, *Early Spring* was and still is considered as one of the most important landscape paintings. It vividly captured the movement and subtle dynamism that took place with spring's arrival. The entire surface of the painting looked as if it was breathing and alive, reflecting the changes and awakening that spring evoked on earth. Some of the more well-known aspects of *Early Spring* are its twisted trees, an element that employed a variety of techniques in order to reach a three-dimensional effect and the wide range of ink tone that showcased his innovative techniques for producing multiple perspectives, which he called "the angle of totality."

The following excerpt from Guo's treatise "Mountains and Waters" illustrates the thinking behind his three dimensional techniques:

> Clouds and the vapors in a real landscape differ through the four seasons. They are genial in spring, profuse in summer, sparse in autumn, and somber in winter. If a painting shows the major aspect and does not create overly detailed forms, then the prevailing attitude of clouds and vapors will appear alive. Mists and haze (on mountains) in a real landscape differ through the seasons. Spring mountains are gently seductive and seem to smile. Summer mountains seem moist in their verdant hues. Autumn mountains are bright and clear, arrayed in colorful garments. Winter mountains are withdrawn in melancholy, apparently asleep.[27]

Contrary to traditional methods that provided a window where one could see nature from a fixed viewpoint, Guo Xi developed a strategy to depict multiple perspectives, more like moving a camera around the subject and yet putting all of the images together into a single frame. Like most Song landscapists, Guo Xi used textured strokes to build up credible, three-dimensional forms. Strokes particular to his style include those on "cloud-resembling" rocks, and the "devil's face texture stroke," seen on the surface of larger rock forms. Guo Xi's reputation was based upon his landscapes and pictures of dried trees which were recognizable for their "crab-claw" branches. He painted tall pines, lofty trees, winding streams, craggy cliffs, deep gorges, high peaks, and mountain ranges cut off by clouds and mist or hidden in haze, representing them with countless variations and forms.[28]

Chinese artistic vision turned inward at least eight or nine centuries earlier than did the Western arts. During the eleventh century the subject of painting began to subordinate to the personal expression of the artists. Thus for the painter, visual phenomena served only as "raw material" to be transformed and charged with individual feeling through the means of style and brush technique. The mind of the artist himself was now the real subject of his painting.[29]

But Chinese painting had not yet completely uprooted itself from physical representation, as did the abstract art of modern West. The tradition of painting had been an accumulation of forms to deal with issues of representation that included shapes of height, distance, mass, space and atmosphere in landscapes, movement and texture in birds and animals, color and spatial ordering in flowers, posture, foreshortening, and individual characterization in figures. The major achievements of the Tang and early Song dynasties derived from the context of these basic issues. As a result, since painting substitutes, in a sense, for the thing depicted, it had to have a reasonably convincing likeness of that thing.[30]

During the Southern Song period (1127–1279), court painters such as Ma Yuan (1190–1225) and Xia Gui (1195–1224) used strong black brushstrokes to sketch trees and rocks and pale washes to suggest misty space. Contrary to the monumental and total vision of the northern school, Ma Yuan put great focus on the bottom corner of the painting, creating a closer, warmer, and more intimate atmosphere. This intimate but boldly defined corner foreground gradually evaporated into the background in lighter tones of ink, driving the viewers' eyes into a great mysterious and remote void.

Ma Yuan's painting, much like ci poetry, had a simple and poetic aura that eliminated all but the most essential and unavoidable details of the landscape through the use of forceful and dramatic brushstrokes. His landscapes were so simple that they could be captured with one glance and represented a departure from the more intricate works of the northern landscapists. This highly idealized abstraction gradually became popular among the Yuan, Ming and Qing painters who explored alternative channels in order to take this tradition to new places.

Xia Gui used more extreme abstraction and economy of stroke, a technique which only slightly suggested what might have been hidden behind heavy mists and boundless distance. Xia deliberately left the upper half of his landscapes empty. The viewer was invited to freely wander with his imagination to remote places where only little tones of ink wash suggested life. The stark contrast between the two halves of the painting suggested the boundless distances that the mind could travel as it departed from the concrete safety of the mountains in the foreground. Another important characteristic of the Ma/Xia school was the reconciliation of techniques of both southern and northern schools. In addition to southern lyrical approach and hemp fiber technique, they were also skilled in presenting variations by applying the more bold northern techniques.

Xia's *Mountain and Lake Landscape* also showed the subtlety of the tonal effects and the firmness and quality of Xia's brush strokes. Various scenes were shown, but all of them conveyed the same mood of profound peace. A lake portrayed with the line of the shore barely visible in the mist was the most revealing of the economy and beauty of his work. There were three tiny, face-less figures in a long narrow boat and to the right, some rushes extended into the water. Most of the surface of the silk was empty, suggesting the loneliness and mystery of the ultimate Daoist idea better than any detail or color could achieve.

Another Xia Gui paintings, *Sailboat in the Rain*, showed the same subtle beauty of tone and brush, but portrayed a more dramatic scene of trees in a rainstorm with branches and leaves blowing in the wind. On the water was a boat in full sail, and in the distance, the edge of the mountain peaks were barely discernible in the heavy air. Xia had compressed the essence of the majesty of nature and man's place in the universe with a little boat.

The Yuan dynasty witnessed a revolution in Chinese landscape painting as it departed from the works of Song masters, especially their various degrees of visual realism. Yuan painters, who were more often leading scholars rather than professional artists patronized by the imperial court, emphasized the expressive qualities inherent in brush and ink as a means of portraying personality, thought, and emotion. Simplicity, transcendence, and elegance were the main characteristics of their work, which was usually composed in ink monochrome or with washes of light color. They were often unconvincing as images of a possible outer reality; the world they depicted was essentially an interior one.[31]

Huang Gongwang (1269–1354) was the eldest and the most prominent of the four great landscapists of the Yuan Dynasty and his work exercised more influence than any other on the development of the "School of Chinese Literati Painting" during the Ming and Qing dynasties.

The works of Huang Gongwang could be divided into two general stylistic types. In one type of painting he used light purple color, whereas the other type was executed in black ink only with the portrayal of the surfaces of rocks and trees being much more simple in structure and technique. In both types, Huang created contrast of shape and visual rhythm by interweaving thick and dry brushstrokes. He painted darker brushstrokes over lighter ones and drier brushstrokes over wetter ones to create rich textures and a strong sense of tactile surface.

The best illustration of this method was *Dwelling in the Fuchun Mountains*. Beginning with a vast expanse of river scenery at the right, viewers were driven to move on to the mountains and hills, then back to areas of river and marsh that end at a conical peak. They finally came to the end of their wandering through the landscape as it ebbed out in the distant ink-wash hills over the water. The composition was first laid out in light ink and then finished with successive applications of darker and drier brushwork. Sometimes shapes were slightly altered, contours strengthened, and texture strokes or tree groups added here and there. Finally, brush dots were distributed across the work as abstracted accents. Buildings, tree limbs, and foliage were reduced to the simplest of forms as if nature had been translated into the artist's terms of brush and ink. Huang once confessed that he created this design in a single outburst of energy during one sitting. He worked on the painting on and off whenever the mood struck him over the next three years.[32]

One of Huang's best-known compositions was *The Stone Cliff at the Pond of Heaven*. It represented a real place, located on Mount Hua near Suzhou (Jiangsu province). As an intricate construction of simple forms within its frame, it was the most abstract painting since the beginning of Chinese landscape. A precisely arranged foreground, made up of trees on a rocky bank, occupied a triangular space in the lower left. A valley opened in the right corner and proceeded upward, dividing into two valleys that extended diagonally toward the upper corners. The left-hand gorge hung with mists and moved back along a relatively flat course, widening finally until its sides were lost in fog. The right, by contrast, climbed steeply to a high pass and was tightly set with trees, boulders, buildings, and waterfalls which provided a formally episodic exercise for the ascending eye.

Embraced by these diverging valleys is a mountain ridge which occupied the central and dominating position that in older landscapes of this type was given to the "host mountain." Huang's mountain ridge was not (as in Northern Song landscapes) a single coherent mass but a composite of dynamically interacting parts. Its unity, and the unity of the painting as a whole, was thus one of development rather than stasis. Some early painters had attempted to break the total pictorial structure but they failed to keep the consistency of the framework that held fragments together. It was only here in Huang's painting that clusters of smaller forms rose to the status of a new, modular principle of composition based on the clear organization of units consisting of simple, repeated shapes merging into a complex whole. Huang's orderly construction can be analyzed to reveal the rules that it follows. Rounded, swelling forms alternate with dark bands of trees as one ascends; squared outcroppings break the progression at carefully spaced intervals, and at several points, flat-topped ledges extend sideward. As one nears the top the momentum subsides, the staccato interruptions become fewer and the enclosing upper contours longer and more gently curved, until the peak ends the whole movement in a quiet silhouette that makes a final leftward thrust and drops off into the mist.

Also entirely new was the way in which all elements of the picture were made to serve clear compositional functions. Trees were depicted with trunks and branches bared so that their direction of leaning could be incorporated into larger movements; plateaus slanted and boulders were regimented into rows with the same purposefulness. By means of this relentless subordination of variety, detail, and individual characterization in the parts of his picture, Huang Gongwang was able to achieve, within an essential simplicity and clarity of design, a formal complexity that had been unknown in Chinese painting since the Northern Song period. As is the case with the cubists centuries later in the West, his was a solution more intellectual rather than pictorial or emotional. Like them, he seemed to have disassembled the visible world and rebuilt it on new, more dynamic, more intelligible patterns. However, Huang's picture, as Chinese brand of abstract painting, could still (in contrast to most cubist works) be read easily as a landscape.[33]

Wu Zhen (1280–1354) was known as a painter of landscapes, especially scenes with fishermen. In some of his landscapes the lines were smooth, curved and flowing, which was an abstract reinterpretation of traditional landscape paintings through brushwork focusing on balance. His *Fisherman* was a night scene. The surface of the water reflecting the moonlight was painted more pale than the sky, to which a thin gray wash had been applied. Despite the title and inscription of "in a fisherman spirit," Wu did not paint any fishing gear. Instead, a scholar appeared sitting at ease in the boat gazing at the scenery while the boy in the stern sculled placidly along the marshy shore. The mood was calm and relaxing. He explained that only the rustle of a light wind in the reeds and the occasional splash of the scull reached the ears of the musing scholar. The boat and figures were small and did not invite any emotional reaction. The vertical trees and horizontal shorelines served to stabilize the tension-free scene. Wu's personal touches could be found in his mode of drawing, in the blunt, vertical dots, and in the repetition of certain favored shapes, particularly the conical hills in the distance. The inscribed poem on the painting revealed and clarified this abstract imagery[34]:

> West wind blows tree leaves, with sighing sounds,
> Blue hills press on the river shore in ten thousand folds.
> With the sorrow of old age, one enjoys rod and line.
> How often, with coat and hat, has he fished in wind and rain!
> He claps his oar west and east on silent waterweeds,
> His song ripples waves, and wind blows tassels of the reeds.
> With deep night behind, fish break the surface, splash at dawn.
> Clouds disperse, the sky is clear, the misty water stretches on.

Wu's renowned painting *Eight Views of Jia He* was an illustration of a guided tour of Wu's hometown, Jia He (now, Jia Xing, Zhejiang province). As the scroll rolls out, Wu showcased local landmarks and monuments, such as a pond that had once harbored a dragon, and a hall visited long ago by the great Song poet Su Shi. There was added written commentary above the scenes, poems, and identifying notes. Viewing this scroll involved reading as well as seeing. In the last passage of the scroll, Wu depicted a temple among the trees, *Jing de Jiao* temple, and next to it a well, the *Yu lan* spring. The viewer was told that the water of this well was ideal for brewing tea. Next to the well was a small pavilion. Further on was another temple, *Ji xiang da sheng*, whose pagoda was seen above the treetops. Still further on, as the scroll ended, Wu wrote the name "Wei tang," without any specific image.

The abstract tendency can be detected in Wu's *Central Mountain*. Here most of what we have been led to expect of Chinese landscape painting was missing. The picture seemed only a matter-of-fact presentation of the most ordinary scenery. Arranged in a roughly symmetrical plan, seven peaks surround an eighth, the tallest, the central mountain of the title. The larger peaks all had a distinctive truncated conical shape with slightly convex sides that belonged to Wu's limited repertory of favorite forms. Smaller mountains and hills, rising and falling like ocean waves, were seen between and beyond these. They repeat, larger or smaller, darker or lighter, in a few simple shapes. There was no real distance, only peaks beyond peaks. Groves of trees, drawn large so as to reduce the mountains to a modest scale, were in the valleys, and bushes on the summits.

Ni Zan's (1301–1374) landscapes push the abstract tendency of Yuan painting further. Initially he was determined to paint a plain scene: no vegetation other than trees, and no attempt at variety in the hills and rocks. He portrayed the sense of loneliness and seclusion by placing the figure in the middle, dwarfing him against the scale of the trees and turning him away from the viewer who was forced to move past rocks and trees and under the roof to reach the human figure. By 1363, when Ni Zan painted his *Mountains Seen from a River Bank*, he had left behind his early landscape plan and arrived at his ultimate formula. It was a foreground bank with a few trees and a four-posted shelter, a broad expanse of water separating the two landmasses and hills marking a high horizon. Although extremely simple, the composition was stabilized by strong vertical and horizontal emphases, and in particular, the flat bases on which all the earth forms rest. However, the transition from land to water to land appeared to be awkward and lacking of a smooth passage across onto the farther shore.

In order to overcome this weakness, Ni Zan developed a new technique wherein he created an extreme sparseness and thinness and a greatly stretched interval between foreground and distance. "Six gentlemen," a picture of six trees that looked undernourished in the foreground and a horizon with low hills placed high above, was an early example of his attempt. A similar but much finer painting, *Autumn Clearing Over a Fishing Lodge*, greatly improved the compositional balance. It included a poem to clarify what the viewer was seeing in a scene of an autumn evening. The painting itself was extremely plain and the composition was extremely simple, lacking even a rest shelter or imposing hills. The trees were more spindly, the shorelines less adorned than is usual even in Ni Zan's works. Its widely separated upper and lower limits, the base of the foreground bank and the horizon were strictly horizontal. The knoll on which the trees grow slants upward to the left in a diagonal and is paralleled by the graded heights of the trees and echoed less distinctly in the distant shore, setting up an easily perceptible relationship that helped the eye bridge the gap between them. The effect was of having one's consciousness somehow absorbed in scenery which held little that was compelling, as may happen when one is in an abstracted mood. That was exactly the experience that Ni Zan intended to convey. The artist and viewer regard the minimal landscape in a detached, contemplative frame of mind. A poem written by a contemporary on another of Ni's paintings caught this mood perfectly[35]:

> Autumn trees make no sound, clouds cast no shadows,
> On the long deep river mirror flat.
> Distant hills sink in mist as bright moon rises,
> Sitting in a shelter on the bank watching the tide.

This soundless and soulless landscape became a completely private vision shared only by someone who was looking seriously and sympathetically for solitude.

A typical appreciation of one of his landscapes by a later connoisseur, Juan Yüan (1764–1849), is this: "In landscapes painted by other men, which make use of real, existing scenery, one can roam over their terrain and enjoy it. With Ni Zan, one is given a withered tree or two, a squat building, 'remnants of mountains and residual waters,' drawn onto a sheet of paper — decidedly the ultimate in loneliness and remoteness, the most dilute and withdrawn. If one were to enter bodily into this world, he would find it without flavor and would be emptied of all thought."[36]

This characterization could be applied to all of Ni Zan's paintings. He depicted essentially the same scene, over and over, throughout his life. The essence of Ni Zan's paintings, as the Chinese critics recognized, was their "plainness and blandness" [*ping-dan*], which is what Juan Yüan means by "without flavor." Contrary to the busy realist landscape, they deliberately appear pure or chaste in that they have been purified of all the objects and elements that seemingly stimulate and invite sensory participation.

The Jungxi Studio was the supreme exemplification of this aspect of Ni's style. The drawing, done with a slanting brush lightly loaded with dilute ink, carried no sense of nervous energy or impulsion. The strokes, soft and sensitive, were not by any means individually distinct but merge into the forms. The tonal range was kept narrow, generally pale, with only the sparsely placed, sidewise dots, the mosslike foliage of the trees, and a few of the shoal lines serving as darker accents. The forms were self-contained, placid. Nothing intruded forcibly on the consciousness of the viewer. The painting, an expression of a state of consciousness, visualized the same fastidiousness, the same attitude of withdrawal from human involvement, the same longing for peace that we know were the motivating forces in Ni Zan's character and lifelong activities. It was a moving statement of alienation from a corrupt and contaminated world.[37]

The youngest of the Four Great Masters was Wang Meng (1308–1385). While Ni Zan pushed landscape painting toward the abstract, Wang Meng preferred to allow the components of his composition to run together by packing them densely and blurring their junctures with vegetation.[38] The "fisherman-recluse" depicted a man sitting in the bow of his boat, at the bottom of the painting, who presided over the opening of the composition without dominating it. His villa was seen above at the head of an inlet, behind a row of willows; his wife stood in the doorway. Thus far all of these were stable, with parts closely interlocked. To the right of the buildings, a ridge began to rise, taking up the diagonal direction of the foreground trees, and curved upward, humping and dipping, shifting from side to side along the way. It culminated in a slanting-topped mass, a variant of the familiar Tong zhü mountain-peak shape, which was a favorite motif in Wang's formal repertory. From this point the rising line of force was divided; one could follow up the steep slope at the left of the summit or continue smoothly across the valley to the right, where another curving hill caught the movement and turned it leftward and up to the same summit. Between these two lines of ascent was a village; at the right was a man on a path, and above, in still another bay, was another fisherman who provided a distant echo of the foreground and a quiet close.

The texture strokes were no longer the straight, stringy "hemp-fiber" stroke of the earlier and more traditional style, but curled and interwove restlessly. The dotting was heavier and in places turned into a kind of stippling. These systems of repeated strokes gave Wang's earth surfaces their distinctively furry appearance and produced, along with the diversified and tight-packed foliage patterns, an overall denseness that contrasted with the extreme thinness of fabric that Ni Zan utilized. From this denseness the blank areas of water in his painting served as relief.

Derived from Hung Gongwang's method, Wang Meng developed a different composition (from Ni Zan's simplification and abstraction) that set separate, activated, richly textured forms against water areas of distinct shape. Like Huang, he worked to reconcile strength and clarity of structure with textural variety and profusion of detail. He was organizing a wealth of sensory and emotional experience for orderly, intelligible presentation. But as his material became more profuse, more diverse, his problem was compounded. Here the reconciliation was effected with a success that amounts to tour de force; in other presumably later works, the balance was broken and Wang gave up the insistence on orderly structure, employed a virtue of unclarity, and eventually, allowed no relief at all.

Wang Meng's *Dwelling in the Qing Bian Mountains* is one of the most astonishing, overwhelmingly original works in Chinese painting. It is also an isolated achievement. There is no evidence in his other works nor elsewhere of any painting that quite follows up the new ideas it presents. It stands as the product of some extraordinary burst of creative genius that evidently proved unrepeatable, even for the artist himself.[39]

Although the combination of painting and poetry initiated from the Song dynasty, it was during Yuan and Ming that the adoption of written inscription (calligraphy) in painting became general practice of the majority of artists.[40] It became common, especially since later Yuan works, to affix an explanatory preface to the painting. The poem, like the image, was a lyrical expression of what the artist saw and felt, concentrating more on the essence of the experience while leaving the visual imagery to provide the details of the scene. These verbal images provide clues to the true meaning of the artist's "mind landscape." It also evoked a long chain of imageries by building references to the repertoire of imagery and allusions accumulated during the historical progression of literature and painting. It did not only connect imagery of painting with literary images inscribed in writing, but also reinforced this imagery in the memories of its viewers and readers who were educated in the tradition. By bringing painting and writing (image and text) together in the same composition, the personal expression of the artist became more precise and efficient. Besides being an entertaining footnote to the painting, the inscription gave some insight into the painter's attitude toward artistic creation as well as the symbolism behind imagery.

Qian Xuan (1235–1305) inscribed a poem, "Pear Blossoms," to the left of his image to indicate that the real subject was not pear blossoms but his profound sorrow at the destruction of Song civilization[41]:

> Alone by the veranda railing, teardrops drench the branches,
> With face unadorned, she retains old charms.
> Behind the locked gate, she is filled with sadness on a rainy night.
> And looks different, as bathed in golden waves of moonlight.

Unlike Hui Zong's *Finches and Bamboo,* which demonstrated a commitment to an accurate rendering of nature, *Pear Blossoms* and the faded beauty that it represented were expressions of the artist's personal feelings. To create a mood of cool detachment reflecting his state of mind, Qian drew in a fine calligraphic line and used flat, schematic patterns in elegant pale colors. The tender lyricism of the poem was echoed in his calligraphy, and its brush strokes repeat the languid, twisting movement of the pear-branch leaves. Here painting, poetry, and calligraphy were completely integrated into a single work that moved away from objective representation and traditional symbolic and allegorical conventions. The subtly interwoven literary and pictorial images, purposely vague but evocative, defy simple interpretation. Literary readers supply their own imagery while reading a poem. A rendition of a flower beside the poem would substantially focus the motivation, feelings, and intentions of the author, thus engaging the viewer-reader with the artist's creative consciousness. This compels the viewer-reader to explore within himself and relate to his own personal experiences.[42]

Lu Guang's (1271–1368) *Spring Dawn After Returning to the Lake Tai Area* was painted to celebrate his reunion with his friend after many years of war and separation. It depicted a Taoist temple at daybreak, nestled in a mountain ravine. Lu accompanied the painting with a poem that expressed his feelings of joy and contentment at the reunion with his old friend:

> For ten years I wandered,
> homeless and detached from worldly entanglements.
> Now, returning home by the river,
> I see things differently from most others.
> Jade like vapor floats in the sky,
> it is spring but no rain,
> Elixir rays emitted from a well turn into clouds at dawn.
> Standing in the wind I lean on my dragon staff,
> I have long missed hearing your mouth-organ music by moonlight.
> I am happy to be with the venerable immortal,
> And away from the military strategists;
> We sit looking at paintings and talk about literature.

Lu Guang treated his painting as the writing of ideas using calligraphic brushstrokes to "write out" his feelings. Comparing Lu's work to the twelfth-century landscape in the style of Fan Kuan (990–1020), it can be seen that the visual structure of landscape painting had changed by late Yuan times. Lu Guang's calligraphic brushwork was very different from the descriptive style of Northern Song. The loosely directed kinesthetic strokes build, layer upon layer, until the landscape forms emerge. Yet they were not just energized, abstract brush patterns; they represented an illusionistic technique of fused brush line and ink wash that suggested blurred forms in atmospheric space. Lu Kuang's landscape forms were physically connected organic masses. All the elements of near, middle, and far distance were fused as parts of an integrated vision that extended along a continuous, receding ground plane. Late Yuan landscape painting shows a fully realized, realistic spatial structure.

Lu Zhi (1496–1576), a Ming painter of Wu school, specialized in landscape and bird and flower painting. His *Planting Chrysanthemums* was presented to his friend, Tao, in exchange for some rare chrysanthemum cuttings. Lu cultivated flowers at his retirement home below Zhi Xian Mountain on the shore of Lake Tai. He evoked the beauty of autumn in his poem inscribed on the painting:

> I hear you have opened up a Tao path near the ocean,
> Where clouds of leaves and frost-covered blossoms
> Vie in wondrous splendor.
> I too have built a new residence at Zhi Xing Mountain;
> May I share some of your autumn colors along my eastern hedge?

The first two lines allude to the well-known story "Peach Blossom Spring" by Tao's illustrious namesake Tao Qian, a famous poet of the fifth century who told a story of a hidden utopia resplendent with blossoming peach trees. In the last two lines, the painter suggests that he had planned his own utopian retreat and refers to the growing of chrysanthemums, a passion that he shared with Tao Qian. Awash in soft colors, the crystalline mountains rising from mist in Lu's painting evoke perfectly the dreamlike Peach Blossom Spring, a hermit's paradise. Structurally, although the Yuan painters were concerned with the problems of creating depth and recession and the treatment of forms in space, the Ming painters increasingly turned to issues of surface abstraction through surface pattern and stylization. Compared to Lu Guang's solidly built mountain forms which move magisterially in space, both Lu Zhi's mountains looked paper-thin and they were consciously cut and framed by the picture borders in an increasingly attenuated format. Lu Zhi's ethereal mountainscape with peaks superimposed along its narrow, vertical picture plane seemed to exist in its own time and space. Like fissures in a moonscape or crackles in glass, the abstract brushstrokes are beautifully held together by their own tension and apparently seamless internal structure.

Chen Shun (1483–1544), another Ming painter, depicted superb still-lifes executed in bold calligraphic brushwork. He painted flowers brilliant with color and full of life. On one of these he wrote a poem:

> In steamy summer the days are unbearably long,
> With a linen kerchief and a palm-leaf fan, I mount my rattan couch;

When the flowers' shadows meet with a cool breeze from the water,
Where else would you find such a heavenly White Jade Hall?

By the end of the sixteenth century, Wu school paintings began to show signs of fatigue. Scattered bursts of new creative energy appeared in late Ming works that experimented in new forms, often glorying in eccentricity.

Conclusions

A unique characteristic of Chinese painting is its close relationship to writing. Brushwork was not the only common instrument for painting and calligraphy. Pictorial and verbal modes of expression also accumulated simultaneously in the course of history. They became integral to and inseparable from each other at various times and in individual works of art. However, it took several thousand years for writing to return to the same page with painting. During the interval, writing and painting cultivated separate repertoires of idioms.

The richness and complexity of Chinese painting and calligraphy derived from its thousand-year-long history of accumulation and innovation. After establishing basic visual descriptive language (up to the Tang period), landscape that emerged initially as a background for figures became an independent subject in the late ninth and early tenth centuries. It developed a unified compositional structure, culminating in the successful creation of illusionist depth by the end of the thirteenth century. As painters began to explore meaning and beauty beyond nature's physical phenomena, they turned away from formal representation to self-expression, as did the poets. Artists increasingly integrated calligraphic technique into their paintings (Song, Yuan to Ming). By the seventeenth century, landscape painting adopted calligraphic vocabulary for visual depiction.

During over ten centuries of brush strokes, painting elevated Chinese expression (including writing) into a language of visions and expanded the horizon for the eyes of the Chinese mind. The next two chapters illustrate how Chinese literary language, especially poetry, absorbed and adopted visual imagery and eventually became able to project images into the imagination of the reader. This repertoire of imagery enhanced the descriptive and expressive capacity of literary Chinese.

5

Imagery and Narrative of Nature

This chapter is a brief history of the formation of the language of nature in Chinese literature up to the end of the Han dynasty. Like language of painting, it took literary language at least a thousand years to accumulate the vocabulary, imagery and composition scheme to describe a natural world distinct from that of man. During this process words needed to be created (by capturing physical images) defined and classified as they accumulated. They also had to develop narrative forms that were fluid and engaging. Eventually, literary language developed an ability to evoke pictures in its reader's mind with words alone. Literature re-trained the mind of the reader to be able to imagine the connection between what was visible and what was beyond vision. This process is presented here as a snapshot of the transformation of literary imagery from oral and written poetry to prose writing, from myth to history, and from ritual to science.

Like the pre–Tang painting, natural images in Chinese literature initially developed within the description of human activities without forming a separate world. As in the background images of figure painting, nature was a rhetorical method to decorate the human-centered story. For example, the following poem from Shijing reads:

> The genial wind from the south
> Blows the heart of the jujube tree,
> Mother's heart was as tender.
> What toil and pain did she endure!
>
> The genial wind from the south
> Blows the branches of the jujube tree,
> Our mother is wise and good;
> But among us no one is as good.

There is a cool spring
Below (the city) of Jun.
We are seven sons,
And our mother is full of pain.

The beautiful yellow birds
Sing their pleasant song.
Seven of us,
Cannot please mother's heart.[1]

In this poem the described nature (as in specific objects) served as nothing but a frame for the poetic delivery. Another poem reads:

O Sun, O Moon,
illuminate the earth!
Here is the man,
Who does not treat me well by ancient custom.
How could he be like that?
Would he then not regard me?

O Sun, O Moon,
overshadow the earth!
Here is the man,
Who is not friendly to me.
How could he be like that?
Would he then not respond to me?[2]

Here, "sun" and "moon" referred to a more general nature before the more abstract words like God or cosmic universe were coined. Shijing was compiled during the period when words such as "sun" and "moon" began to refer to nature in a more general term in addition to specific objects. The word "Heaven" [*tian*] eventually replaced this context of sun and moon. The original meaning of "heaven" was the sky (the sun, the moon, and stars) and referred to a single natural thing. It gradually expanded to include a connotation of an overlord residing over both natural and human worlds. The context of this poem seems to fall during the transitional period when the sun and the moon carried the additional and more abstract meaning that would soon be replaced by the word "heaven." They were used here more like God (the Father in Heaven) as commonly phrased at the beginning of a prayer.

This vague connection between the sun, the moon and the universal overlord began to be clarified when the word heaven was used in a situation involving human affairs.

Xuan Niao ["Black Bird"]

Heaven commissioned the raven,
To descend and give birth to (the father of) Shang.
His sons dwelt in the land of Yin, and flourished.

Ancestral king in heaven appointed the warrior Tang,
To regulate the boundaries throughout land.
In four quarters he appointed the princes,
And successfully possessed the nine regions.
The first King of Shang,
Received and completed the mission.
It is [now] held by the descendant of Wu Ding.
The descendant of Wu Ding,
Capable of dealing with emergency, a warrior king.
Ten princes, with their dragon-emblazoned banners,
Bear millet in large dishes.
The royal domain reached a thousand li.
where the people reside,
Their trade reached beyond border to four seas.
From the four seas they came (to our sacrifices);
Many of them came
King pushed his frontier to Weihe River.
(The King of) Yin should have the right to be commissioned.
He should have the right to be commissioned.
(Its king) sustains and should be dignified.[3]

In Chinese, the word heaven carried a much wider range of connotation than its English counterpart. In addition to the religious and metaphysical meanings of English, heaven could also refer to the visible sky or a general (non-religious) realm beyond human vision (Heaven in English). The word heaven as used during Shang and early Zhou periods had yet to evolve into a notion of universal head equivalent to the European concept of God. Even after heaven established itself as a notion of a universal overlord it remained grounded in the realm of concrete meaning (heaven or simply sky). As Chinese language does not have case distinction (Heaven and heaven), the precise meaning of the word (concrete, general, or abstract) must be determined by context.[4]

For over a century, prominent sinologists have translated the "Ancestral king in heaven" (line four) into "god" due to a lack of historical sense for the evolution of the word *di*. The Chinese word *di* has two meanings. First, it is a general name for a sovereign (king) and refers to any king. The Old Testament monarchs King David and King Solomon are examples. However, *di* could refer to both a monarch on earth and a sovereign in heaven (which later evolved into a concept close to the concept of God in the West) interchangeably due to lack of complete abstraction. This is similar to the biblical word king, which sometimes referred to the king (of Heaven) or lord to describe God. In Western tradition, which had been built on translation (from Hebrew to Greek, Latin, and European languages), human king and God-like man grew farther apart and not interchangeable with God. In Chinese context, *di*, the living sovereign of a state, became sovereign in heaven (beyond the earth) after death. Therefore, the dead ancestral king was referred to as the ancestral king in heaven [*gu di*] by his surviving family. Before *di* in heaven elevated into a notion of universal godhead, the communication between the heavenly and earthly kings of this time was concrete and void of religious (in Christian sense) and metaphysical meanings (in sense of philosophy). These non-concrete notions did not begin to formulate until the time of Confucius. The dialogue (including that of sacrificial ceremonies) was a personal one between the *di* in heaven and the king of the earthy realm. Secondly, it was only after the third century BC (Zhan Guo Ce), that *di* obtained a more restricted meaning. *Di* of the ancient times was replaced by *wang*, a sovereign of the earthly kingdom. As a concept, *di* in heaven was now a step closer to an idea of God; however, it would take many more centuries for this high god in heaven to oversee a separate kingdom in the imagination of Chinese literary minds.[5]

Regardless of their titles, Chinese monarchs, like the kings and emperors of any other cultures, did attempt to claim divine origin. However, as there was no concept of a universal god in China between the fifteenth and the second century BC, Chinese monarchs had to elevate themselves above ordinary man and assume a divine quality by creating stories of miraculous acts in the same way that many of the world's religions initially created their gods. The divine quality of Shang kings was depicted as a physical relationship with elements of the natural world and actions of superhuman abilities.

There was a wealth of divinely inspired stories of miracles in Chinese antiquity similar to those in ancient Egyptian, Semitic and Biblical Hebrew. One went like this: The ancestral king sent a black bird to drop an egg in the pond in which his wife was taking a bath. She became pregnant with ten sons who came to be mighty stars: ten suns. According to specific order of their queen mother they were supposed to ascend to the sky by turn. These suns bathed everyday in a pool of water and dwelt on the branches of a mythical tree (the Mulberry Tree) after their daily journey through the sky. They were portrayed as partially sun and partially bird.

The idea of putting sun and bird together was customary for the ancient Chinese, who often created a new character (word) by putting two characters (pictorial graph) together. But sometimes the exact way to combine the two could differ. A passage from the Shanhaijing, a classical collection of mountains and seas, (14/65a–b) described that the suns were carried by birds from and to the sky, but the Huainanzi [a book of Huai Nan philosophers], (7/2a) told us that the birds were inside the suns. The latter image appeared to be more popular because it was also mentioned in Chuci and illustrated in tomb paintings of the Han Dynasty.[6]

Here, the nine off-duty suns were portrayed as living on the branches of the Mulberry Tree when they were not crossing the sky. They took the shape of orange discs. The disc at the top of the tree in the left-hand corner of the pendant contained a black bird, possibly a raven, that stood on two legs. The sun-bird boys were all very young and loved to play. One day they tired of their mother's routine and decided to all go out to the sky and play together. This foolish act created a disaster on the earth. With all of these suns in the sky at the same time, the world was set afire. Metal was melting and stone was cracking. All of the vegetation died. A hero archer named Houyi (or Yi) shot down nine of the ten suns and saved the world and all that was on it.[7]

There is a popular assumption that this story had originated from Shang, but there is no record of it in the Shang oracle bone inscription, the earliest known written record (according to commonly accepted assumption). The reason might be that the oracle bone inscription was written in a pre-narrative language. Although much information about the natural religion of Shang could be garnered from the inscriptions on the bones and later bronze, the Shang written language was a simple dialogue used in ritual ceremonies. Patterns of Shang divine worship could be observed; many names were mentioned, but there was no explicit narration. There was a gap of many centuries between Shang, when the story was said to take place, and the writing of the earliest texts which record this event. During this gap, the Zhou dynasty defeated Shang in the central plains of China and replaced the stories of Shang divine origin with its own. Before a mature narrative scheme evolved there was no record of mythical narratives included in any expository writing and there is no direct evidence supporting the myth and the logic underlying the ceremonial rites. Nevertheless, the pattern of names and ritual suggested an earlier myth from which the Mulberry Tree and Shang original traditions derived, and these traditions provide a key to interpretation.[8] Most historians believed that the myth of ten suns rising from the Mulberry Tree and the story of the archer Yi shooting them down first appeared in Zhou and then was re-imagined later in Han writing. The assumption has been that the Shang had a myth of ten suns and that the Shang ruling group was organized in a totemic relationship to these suns. This myth was specific to Shang dynasty, endorsed, and rectified by the royal family. When the tribe of Zhou, who believed in one sun, conquered the Shang, the ten-sun myth lost its earlier meaning and integrity. However, both Shang and Zhou were local kingdoms whose oral and written language had not yet reached the prominence that took place several centuries later. The stories and their multifold motifs continued to be re-imagined, rewritten, and transformed in other literature and cultural contexts.

According to the commonly accepted chronology, prose writing in China began during the second half of Eastern Zhou (770–221 BC) when memoir and instruction rather than clan insignia appeared on bronze vessels. *The Book of History* [*Shu*] was one of the earliest written narratives at the beginning of record keeping (or retrieving). It consisted of 58 chapters, 33 of which are generally considered by historians as authentic works of the 6th century BC. The first five chapters of the book intended to preserve the sayings and recall the deeds of emperors Yao and Shun, legendary rulers between 2358 and 2195 BC. The next four chapters were about the Xia Dynasty (2100–1600 BC); the following 17 chapters were devoted to the Shang Dynasty and its collapse. The responsibility for this decline was placed on the last Shang ruler, Di Xin, who was described as oppressive, murderous, extravagant, and lustful. The final 32 chapters covered the Zhou Dynasty until the reign of Duke Mu of Qin. *The Book of History* predates the *Historiai* of Herodotus as a historic narrative by a century. Many sections have been confirmed in the bamboo slips texts from the tombs of Guodian, in Hubei, dated to 300 BC.[9]

Writing initiated Chinese transformation from the recording of myth to the recording of history. The first mission of Zhou historic narration was to streamline the story of royal origin. Zhou tradition held that there was only one sun in the universe and the king was the son of Heaven. This idea quickly became the official version of recorded history. For example, Confucius once confirmed it by saying, "Heaven does not have two suns; the people do not have two kings."[10] However, Zhou tradition did not write the story of Shang divine progeny completely out of existence. The divine king who was called *xuan wang* [the Black King] in the Shijing, was now renamed in prose as *Xie*. Zhou texts reclassified royal linkage, and consistently defined *Xie* as the initial ancestor of the Shang dynasty in contrast to *Qi*, the ancestor of the *Xia* dynasty, and *Houji*, the ancestor of the Zhou dynasty. Houji established his divine inheritance by a similar progeny. It was said that Houji's mother was impregnated by stepping on an ancestor's (the same black bird who was said to have impregnated the ancestors of the Shang dynasty) footprint.[11]

Another motif that had survived rewriting was the tradition of the Mulberry Tree [*fu sang*] because it appeared much less threatening to the literary establishment of Zhou. (Extra suns had the potential to suggest the legitimacy of more than one king/state.) The mythical Mulberry Tree has been well preserved by repeated painting and writing. However, without the excitement of the sun association, it became nothing more significant than a decoration of the moon and endless moon associated stories. Until early modern times, mythical images of the moon always contained a mulberry tree.

During ancient times, the Mulberry Tree was a heavenly tree to which the sun(s) went as they set. The original pictorial graph of mulberry in the oracle bone inscription was a tree with many mouths (open pockets) among its branches which indicated the places where the suns perched. The first written narrative associated with the tree was in Shanhaijing (300 to 200 BC), "Above the Tang Valley is the *Fu Sang*" [Mulberry Tree]. The valley was where the ten suns used to bathe. It was north of the Black Tooth Tribe. In the swirling water was a great tree. The suns dwell on its lower branches. On the top of a mountain named Nieyaojundi is the Fu Tree. Although its trunk was three hundred li in size (about a hundred and fifty kilometers), its leaves were tiny, like those of mustard.[12]

The mulberry tree was revived in Han Dynasty tomb paintings. The imagination of the last several centuries had added many interesting details. The region beneath the earth (the underworld in Greek mythological sense) was a yellow spring that was depicted with turtles, dragons, and large fish-like creatures. The earliest literary reference to the yellow springs was in a passage from the *Zuo Zhuan* (compiled in the fourth century BC) in which a yellow spring was noted as the underworld or world of death.[13]

Thus the universe in the minds of ancient Chinese had a unity that, rather than being portrayed in empty and abstract (philosophical) words, was animated and manifested in concrete images. Water ran beneath the earth [*huang quan*] as the sky surmounted it. If one dug a hole in the ground in one place, he could find the same water (yellow spring) that another person found from a different hole in another place. The world could be safe and in peace if the sky stayed where it was, the sun went up and down as scheduled, and underground water maintained in its realm. If water was out of control, as in a great flood, it threatened to rise up and mix with the sky, and the world would be in great danger. This concern was reflected in the language of ritual ceremony which was recorded on the oracle bone inscriptions. The entire business of ceremonial ritual was to keep the world in order by pleasing (or even bribing) heaven with sacrifice.[14]

The first natural image that inspired the Chinese notion of heavenly god was the sun, as in many ancient civilizations. How could the sun fly up to the sky every day without wings, and where did it go after dark? A bird or a chariot driven by horses must have helped the sun and took it up every morning and returned it to its resting place. Now the sun-bird went to work across the sky from Sun Valley and was bathed by its mother Xi He in a pool of water to cool it down. Xi He was the wife of Di Jun (the ancestral king), mother of the ten suns. Initially Chinese graphic characters did not have consistent degree of precision and phonetic distinction. Many names had the same or similar sound. Many mythical characters played similar roles in the story. For example, the Shanhaijing (16/76a) named two other women beside Xi He as wives of Di Jun. One was Chang Xi, the western counterpart of Xi He. Chang Xi was said to have given birth to the twelve moons that she bathed in a pool of water in the West, just as Xi He bathed her sun-children in the East. Because of the similarity of the sound of her name, Chang Xi sometimes was associated or even identified with Chang E, the goddess who fled to the moon after stealing the elixir of immortality from Archer Yi and Chang Yi, the second wife of the ancestral king. These confusions all derived from the same vowel endings of Xi (*xia* in ancient Chinese), E [ngâ] and Yi [ngia], which were within the same word family and closely related phonetically. In other words, every single variant sound of a word could spawn a new mythical character and a new repertoire of stories.

The name of the ancestral king itself could hardly escape the confusion. Yi Jun might be related to Shang Jun the son but not the successor of Shun. Di Jun has been identified with both Di Ku and Shun whose wives, Chang Yi (Di Ku) and E Huang (Shun), he shared. Jun was the personal name of Di Ku, the progenitor of the Shang. Shun, the second emperor of ancient kingdoms and the Emperor of Xia (2200–1700), and Jun sometimes also were identified because of the phonetic similarity of jun and shun and on an overlap of roles and relationships including their common wife, E Huang. Jun might be a phonetic borrowing for Shun in *Shanhaijing* (16/73b). This suggested that the names were variants. The roles of Shun and Di Ku (Jun) were also occasionally perceived as interchangeable.[15]

Rewriting mythological tales did not only clarify the inherited textual confusion and streamline diverse story lines; it also created a history out of mythical tales which carried increasingly defined moral tones. In the new writing, the origins of Shang were said to take place in the historical rather than mythical time of Yao Di (King Yao, 2358–2258 BC). The history of Shang began with a description of a time of perfect peace. People could entrust their infants to the safety of nests and place their excess grain at the head of the fields. Tigers and leopards could be pulled by the tail; vipers and snakes could be trod upon. But the peace was broken when the world was overly heated by the ten suns. As the heat withered the crops, killed the grasses, and burned animals, famine began to spread. Various monsters also appeared, until Yao (the ancestral king) ordered Yi to punish the rebellious and chaotic ten suns by shooting them down. Because of Yao's success, he became the first ruler.[16]

In Huainanzi (8/5a–b), which was compiled in 139 BC by Liu An (179–122 BC), the king of Huai-nan, the Shang myth was placed in the context of a larger cosmogony myth which has certain structural parallels to the "Yao dian" [chronology of Yao dynasty] (in Shang Shu). The time of Yao which was overly heated by ten suns was followed by the time of Shun (2255–2205 BC), the second king. During Shun's reign, a great flood occurred because Water God, Gong Gong, out of rage, smashed his head against Buzhou Mountain, one of the several pillars holding up the sky. The pillar suffered great damage and caused the sky to tilt towards the northwest and the earth to shift to the southeast. This also created the tilt of the earth. This caused great floods and water reached the Hollow Mulberry where the sun used to set. If water and sky became mixed, it would mean the end of the world. King Shun appointed Yu to dig the river channels and open up passages so that the water could run into the ocean.

In historical writing, natural force carried increasing moral and judicial messages. Like the biblical story of the flood during Noah's time, the following Chinese flood story was closely mingled with the virtue and wisdom of rulers.

Lords of Shang had long been the favorites of Heaven.
When water overflowed, Yu divided the regions of land,
Arranged boundaries of states all over [the kingdom].
Then the State of Song began to flourish,
Heaven raised up and founded [the Family of] Shang.

The black king exercised an effective sway,
He commanded small and large states with success.
He followed his rules of conduct without error,
People responded to his instructions.
[Then came] Xiang-tu, all-ardent,
And all [within] the seas, beyond [the middle region], acknowledged his restraints.

The favor of God did not leave [Shang],
And in Tang was found the subject for its display.
Tang was not born too late,
And his wisdom and virtue daily advanced.
Brilliant was the influence of his character [on Heaven] for long,
And God appointed him to be model to the nine regions.

He received the rank-tokens [of the States], small and large,
Which depended on him, like the pendants of a banner;
So did he receive the blessing of Heaven.
He was neither violent nor remiss,
Never too hard nor too soft.
Gently he spread his instructions abroad,
He was blessed with all wealth and dignities.

He received the tribute from all the states.
As he supported them as a strong steed [does its burden]
So did he receive the favor of Heaven.
He displayed everywhere his valor,
Unshaken, unmoved,
Unterrified, unscared:
He collected all the dignities.

The warrior king raised his banner,
And with reverence grasped his axe.
It was like a blazing fire,
Which no one could put it down.
The root, with its three shoots,
Could not advance,
He secured all nine regions,
After smitten [the princes of] Wei and Gu,
He dealt with [the prince of] Kun-wu, and Jie of Xia.

Formerly in the middle of the period [before Tang],
There was a time of shaking and peril,
But truly did Heaven [then] deal with him as its son,
And sent him down a minister, named A-heng,
To assist the king of Shang.[17]

There were many tales of the heroic deeds of Yu the Great. For example, he left home and his new bride four days after their wedding and spent the next thirteen years fighting against the flood. Although he passed by his home three times, he did not return until the raging water was finally under control. Because of his good service for the people, Yu was elected as the new ruler instead of the less worthy son of the King Yao. Yu's rule initiated a new dynasty called *Xia* (2100 to 1600 BC). Before his death, instead of passing power to the person deemed most capable to rule in the same manner as Yu himself, he passed power to his son, Qi, setting the precedent for dynastic hereditary system of rule. Yu was the only Chinese ruler posthumously honored with the appellation "the Great." The Xia dynasty included a succession of sixteen kings during its five hundred year reign, but none of Yu's offspring accomplished a body of achievement that was comparable to the founder.[18]

In the pre–Han historic writings, nature as a subject matter had three roles. First, it was often perceived as altered by the decisions and actions of an ancestral king. Second, nature was the supreme judge of the behavior of a ruler, and reacted to either his virtue or vice. Third, the naturally derived notion of divine gradually transformed from physical inheritance to moral superiority. With an increasing moral tone, which kept being written into myth/history, the virtue of the ruler, rather than his divine origin, played an increasingly important role in maintaining the universal order and political stability of the realm. Personal virtue of the ruler, such as that of Tang, the founding king of the Shang dynasty, and the selfless dedication to people's welfare promoted by Yu, the founding king of Xia, were modeled as the sacred template for a sovereign, whose good deeds were rewarded in Heaven. A failure to please Heaven also began to be perceived as the primary cause of the decline of previous dynasties. In short, nature and humanity were seen as living in a common world and sharing a mutual fate.

Nature began to separate from the world of man as language accumulated enough words, phrases, and narrative forms to create a world that was detached from physical imagery. One can detect the footprints of this process in many writings about the origin of the natural world. In the beginning, the universe was nothing but a lightless and shapeless chaotic mass. All was a dark swirling confusion. The first shape that occurred was a cosmic egg that slept for 18,000 years and the emerged (or woke up) as Pan Gu. Pan Gu was usually depicted as a primitive, hairy, horned giant clad in furs. Pan Gu set about the task of creating the world. He separated the earth and the sky with a swing of his giant axe. To keep them separated, Pan Gu, with enormous strength, stood between them and pushed the sky up over his head. This task took another 18,000 years, during which the sky grew a little higher and the earth grew a little wider each day as Pan Gu continued to grow. In some versions of the story, Pan Gu was aided in this task by the four most prominent beasts: the turtle, the *qilin* (a mystic animal, whose sculptures are still standing in the Imperial Palace in Beijing), the phoenix, and the dragon.

Pan Gu's breath became the wind; his voice, the thunder; his left eye, the sun and his right eye, the moon. He turned his body into mountains and streams. His blood formed rivers; his muscles, the fertile lands; his facial hair, the stars and Milky Way; his fur, the bushes and forests; his bones, the valuable minerals; his bone marrow, sacred diamonds. His sweat fell as rain and the fleas on his fur were carried by the wind and became the fish and animals throughout the world. However, after this long and stressful work of creation, Pan Gu was exhausted and laid down to rest. He never got up and he died giving his life to the earth and its people.[19]

Now the world was a beautiful place with its landscape, wild animals running in its forests and fishes playing in its water, but it remained empty and dull for the gods when they came from heaven to roam around. Nüwa, a goddess with a dragon's body and a human-like head, became weary of this empty world. After long thought, she picked up a lump of clay from the ground, mixed it with water and fashioned the shape of a new creature. It had the same head as hers but instead of a dragon's body it had two arms and two legs. She gave it life and placed it back upon the earth, and this new creature, human, started to dance and sing. This pleased the goddess. Excited by the result of her labor, Nüwa made many more humans and they all danced around her. As they (her sons and daughters) left her and disappeared into the vast land, a new thought came to Nüwa. What if they died? She had to find a way for them to produce their own children. She gave the gift of marriage and procreation. The next blessing for the humans came from another god, Fu Xi. Fu Xi taught them to hunt, fish and make fire and even provided the signs for writing.[20]

Initially in a language without any abstract concept, both continuity and change in the world has to be described in terms of natural phenomena. The most immediate natural continuity that man could immediately see and think of was human regeneration and family linkage. Thus Chinese writers created the story of the emergence of the royal family of Shang that interacted with the birth of the natural world. Its jumbled universe of gods and goddesses became streamlined into a family as in Greek mythology, where a large-scale group of various gods and goddesses were organized into a dysfunctional divine clan.[21]

Greek literature eventually elevated myth into philosophy. Chinese writing also reorganized the animated world into an interactive system that alternated between chaos and order, unity and separation, harmony and rapture. Excess was believed to lead to disaster. Too many suns would overheat the earth while too much water would flood it. As in ancient Semitic and Biblical Hebrew narration, Chinese mythology used nature (raging water) as the means to reorient the earthly realm and bring change in human history. It recounted that the ancient Chinese knew the wrath of Heaven, as did the Israelites during Noah's time, who also became victims of a terrible and all consuming flood. Unlike the Greek myth that used violence to force separation and regeneration, Chinese tales made every possible effort to maintain harmony and balance.[22]

This rudimentary dual logic was initially cultivated in written dialogue (collection of sayings). For example, Confucius' (550–479 BC) teachings were written by his disciples in Lun-yü [Analects], a set of sayings. According to the Analects, Confucius viewed the early Western Zhou as a fully moral culture, guided by kings and ministers who correctly followed the ethical dictates of righteousness and benevolence. However, he argued, the morals and ritual traditions of the Zhou had slowly decayed, resulting ultimately in a loss of sovereign authority for the Zhou kings and a full breakdown in morality throughout society at large. Confucius saw his own world of the Eastern Chou as in a state of decline, and he called upon his contemporaries to put in place once again the moral and ritual traditions of the Zhou. This would involve everything from, at the highest level, a recognition of the Zhou king as the one proper ruler for all of China to, at a lower level, an attempt by the elite of society to cultivate themselves through practicing the rituals of the Zhou. In short, the ideal society for Confucius was not located in an afterlife or in a distant mythical past. He believed that an ideal moral society had been realized by mankind only a few generations earlier and that it could be realized once again simply through acts of proper moral cultivation.[23]

Confucius died disappointed and frustrated because his contemporaries ignored his teachings. His recorded sayings reflected a stage of Chinese literary writing when nature was not yet written as a realm independent from that of man. The only way that literature could relate to nature was through a single word and idea: Heaven. Heaven at the time of Confucius had already departed from its meaning of concrete natural phenomenon (sky) and came to represent all of the things beyond man's world. What did the Heaven contain besides a collection of dead people? How was Heaven related to man's world other than as an aloof receiver of human sacrifice and praying? What Heaven wanted (from man) had never been expressed or heard because of the non-specific concept of Chinese Heaven. It had neither face nor mouth, as did God in the Bible.

Post-Confucius writers invented the language to describe a grander nature within and beyond Heaven. The first attempt to define that which was before the existence of Heaven was *dao*, as defined in the following:

It is from the unnamed *dao* [way]
That Heaven and Earth sprang;
The named is but
The Mother of the ten thousand creatures.
If a *dao* can be defined, it is not the enduring *dao*.
If a name can be named, it is not the enduring name.
Nameless is the beginning of heaven and earth,
Named is the mother of the ten thousand things.
Thus, without desire [*wu yu*], we can sense the world;
with desire [*you yu*], we have to participate in it.
These two are the same experience but are defined differently.
Together, we call them mystery.
Beyond the mystery flows the *dao*, which was the gate to a world of wonders.[24]

The text indicates that dao, unlike Heaven, did more than create a realm beyond the world of man [*ren*]. It also opened a horizon that perceived thousands of natural wonders that could be specified (invented) because it pinned down naming as the very origin of the human perception and reconstruction of nature. Nature was a world that was beyond man's initial capacity to comprehend, so he started to gather knowledge by naming (classifying) the things that surrounded him in his habitat. This yet to be named and spontaneous nature was larger and more boundless than that of any religious concept of the natural world because it did not include an outer boundary, such as that defined by god, spirits, or science.

Dao proposed a completely different notion of nature compared to early Confucius *tian*. Tian was an anthropomorphic moral agency with the ability to sanction administration and government through its mandate. For Lao Zi, the assumed author of Dao De Jing, nature was an impersonal and immoral realm that treated humans like straw dogs, or scraps of waste paper left over from a celebration. Lao Zi saw nature as a universe operated through a constant process of generation and decay; things were naturally born, and then they naturally died. Everything emerged from oneness and, ultimately, returned to it. The act of differentiation, although perfectly natural, was thus a movement away from oneness, from stillness, from emptiness. The goal of the true sage, therefore, was to become still and empty and thus achieve a state of returning to this oneness. Such a state was referred to as attaining the *dao*. Insofar as the text places a higher value on the undifferentiated than on the differentiated world, it is not surprising that the additional creation of anything artificial by humans was strongly opposed.

More newly discovered ancient manuscripts illustrate that this notion of nature in antiquity had evolved during a long period of time. It began with the nature named *tian*, employing a host of expressions built around that root concept: *tian dao* [the natural way], *tian zhi dao* [the way of nature], *tian di zhi dao* [the way of heaven and earth], and *tian di zhi heng dao* [the constant way of heaven and earth]. It was often difficult to state definitively the precise meaning of *tian* in a particular classical text. In part, this was due to the ambiguity mentioned previously: *tian* could refer to the natural order as a whole, to nonhuman nature, or to the sky/heavens. But it was also due perhaps in even greater measure to the wide range of meaning of *tian* in the classical corpus. For Mo Zi (470–391 BC), tian was a fully personified, religious force like God, that when displeased would bring ruin on the world. For Xun Zi (312–230 BC), tian was once again an impersonal nature operating impervious to the machinations of humans. As he pointed out, the sun, moon, stars, planets, and auspicious periods of the calendar remained the same during the time of a sage king or that of a wicked king.[25]

In Lao Zi's writing, tian (dao) was an impersonal and detached nature void of morals. Heaven and earth were impartial with unceasing flow of four seasons. Heaven with all its light was not concerned with the darkness in which the people lived. People opened their doors and windows and each took light from it, while heaven was simply there, not taking any active part. With its endless bounty, the earth did not burden itself with the poverty of the people. As people cut trees and gathered firewood and each took his riches from the mother earth, the earth did not participate in giving. These words in fact took soul and moral conscience out of nature.[26]

Nature was depicted as spontaneously self-generated and it all began as the following:

> The Great One gave birth to water,
> Water in turn assisted "Taiyi,"
> in this way heaven is created.
> Heaven in turn and assisted "Taiyi,"
> in this way the earth is formed.
>
> Heaven and earth separated and collaborated with each other,
> in this way they breed below and above.
> above and below repeatedly interacted with one another,
> in this way Yin and Yang are evolved.
>
> Yin and Yang repeatedly reinforced each other,
> in this way four seasons were developed.
> Seasons repeatedly circulated from one to the other,
> in this way hot and cold were produced.
>
> Cold and hot repeatedly collaborated each other,
> in this way which led to moist and dry.
> Moist and dry constantly facilitated one another,
> Circle of the year came to an end of process.
> Thus, the year was formed by dryness and moisture,
> Dryness and moisture came from cold and hot.
> Cold and hot, and the four seasons
> were evolved from Yin and Yang.
>
> Yin and Yang were formed by above and below.
> Above and below came by heaven and earth.
>
> Great One produced heaven and earth.
> The Great One is concealed in water
> and moves with four seasons.
>
> It completes a cycle, but is ready to be
> the source of ten thousand things.
> It is depleted at first, then it is full,
> This beginning serves as the principle of ten thousand things.
>
> This is the One that heaven can't destroy,
> One that the earth can't conceal,
> and the One that Yin and Yang can't bring to closure.
> It should be known as (the dao?).[27]

In this description, essence and its form became one and the same:

> In ancient times, these attained oneness:
> heaven became clear as it attained oneness,

earth became peaceful as it attained oneness,
spirits became mighty as it attained oneness.
valleys became full as it attained oneness,
myriad creatures became alive as they attained oneness,
princes and kings acted as the world's example, as they attained oneness,
All this was created by oneness!

A Heaven without its according clearness will fear to tear. Earth without according peace will fear to tumble. Spirituality without according efficacy will fear to vanish. Valleys without according abundance will fear to dry up. Countless creatures without adequate fertility will fear to die out. Rulers without according role models will fear to fall.

In other words, *dao* was nameless, formless, empty and unfathomable. With harmony as its function, it operated in a *wu wei* [nonimpositional] fashion. It was the undifferentiated ground from which the phenomenal world of the myriad things arose:

At the outset of constant undifferentiatedness,
there was a far-reaching indeterminacy, a great emptiness.
In its emptiness and indeterminacy, it constituted the oneness.
Perpetually one, it abided...
Obtaining it, birds fly.
Obtaining it, fish swim.
Obtaining it, animals run.
Obtaining it, the myriad things are engendered.
Obtaining it, all undertakings are completed...
Heaven and earth, yin and yang,
the four seasons, sun and moon,
the stars, constellations, clouds and qi,
things that crawl, those that move like worms
and those that have roots —
all take life from it
yet the Way does not become diminished;
all return to it
yet the Way does not become augmented.

This passage, both in style and content, echoed Lao Zi's assumption that all things arose from and returned to dao. Each was what it was because of the dao. Myriad things were able to coexist and flourish to realize their inherent potential as fish, birds, and humans, because of dao, the natural order which was an all-pervading, universal harmony. As the underlying unity of the cosmic natural order, dao was called *yi* [one, oneness]. All creatures which were crawling, breathing with beaks, flying with fanlike wings, or wriggling like worms did not lose their constancy because of the natural order called "one."[28]

The wealth of literary creation from the end of Zhou and the Spring and

Autumn period made it possible for the Warring States period to witness the emergence of the most diverse ideas of nature. On the one hand a steadily declining belief in supernatural spirits and deities occurred. On the other, there was a dramatic increase in the understanding of the universe in naturalist terms, stimulated by the Yin-Yang and Five Elements thinking of Zou Yan and his fellow Jixia Academy philosophers.[29]

The concept of Yin-Yang was probably the single most important and distinctive theory of Chinese philosophy from which science and medicine emerged. The principle of Yin-Yang was extremely simple, yet very inclusive and profound. One could seemingly understand it on a rational level, and yet, continually find new expressions of it in literature. Since the early modern period, Yin-Yang has been interpreted as the same or similar to Western dualism based upon the opposition of contraries (which was the fundamental premise of Western philosophy that began with Aristotelian logic). According to this logic, contraries (such as "The table is square" and "The table is not square") could not both be true. This has dominated Western thought for over 2,000 years. The Chinese concept of Yin-Yang was radically different. Yin and Yang did not only represent opposites but also complementary qualities. The boundary between the two was fluid rather than solid and exclusive like that in German philosophy. In Chinese thinking, each thing or phenomenon could simultaneously be itself and its contrary at the same time. *Yin* contained the seed of *Yang* and vice versa; thus, contrary to Aristotelian logic, A can also be non–A. A and non–A were not a choice by coexistence; logic that sprang from this dual concept could be two dimensional rather than linear.

The earliest reference to Yin and Yang was found in Yi Jing [*The Book of Change*] dated to the sixth century BC. In this book Yin and Yang were represented by hexagram (symbols of broken and unbroken lines). The combination of broken and unbroken lines in pairs forms four pairs of diagrams representing utmost Yin, utmost Yang and two intermediate stages. The addition of another line to these four diagrams forms, with varying combinations, the eight trigrams. Finally, the various combinations of the trigrams gave rise to the 64 hexagrams. These were the first rudimentary symbols that were intended to depict all possible phenomena of the universe, and it therefore illustrates that all phenomena ultimately derived from the two poles of Yin and Yang.[30]

The philosophical school that developed the theory of Yin-Yang to its highest degree was called the Yin-Yang school, one of many institutions of thought that arose during the Warring States period (476–221 BC). The Yin-Yang school, as in the pre-classical philosophy of ancient Greece, drew its basic concepts from a formative language that had accumulated simple words depicting natural phenomena. These words were arranged in pairs such as day and night, water and earth, light and darkness. One of each pair corresponded to Yang, the opposite one corresponded to Yin. This marked the first observation of the continuous alternation of every natural phenomenon between two cyclical poles, one corresponding to Light, Sun, Brightness and Activity (Yang), the other corresponding to Darkness, Moon, Shade and Rest (Yin). As the sun rose in the east and set in the west, the former was Yang and the latter, Yin. If one faced south, east would be on the left and west on the right. In Chinese cosmology, the compass directions were established assuming that one faced south. This was also reflected in imperial ceremonials when the emperor faced south towards his subjects, who faced north. The emperor thus opened himself to receive the influence of Heaven and Yang (south). In ancient Chinese maps, south, therefore like Heaven, was at the top; north, like Earth, was at the bottom.

These were the basic pairs of concepts:

Yang	Yin
Light	Darkness
Sun	Moon
Brightness	Shade
Activity	Rest
Heaven	Earth
Round	Flat
Time	Space
East	West
South	North
Left	Right

From this point of view, Yin and Yang were represented in a duality, an alternation of two opposite stages in time. Every phenomenon alternated through a cyclical movement of peaks and bases and the alternation of Yin and Yang was perceived as the motive force of change and development. Day changed into night, summer into winter, growth into decay and vice versa. The development of all phenomena was the result of the interplay of two opposite stages, symbolized by Yin and Yang and every phenomenon contained within itself both aspects in different degrees of manifestation. The day belonged to Yang but after reaching its peak at midday, the Yin within it gradually began to unfold. Thus each phenomenon might be classified as either Yang or Yin but always contained the seed of the opposite stage within itself.

To represent the yearly cycle one only needed to substitute "Spring" for "dawn," "Summer" for "noon," Autumn" for "dusk" and "Winter" for "midnight." From a different viewpoint, Yin and Yang stood for two stages in the process of change and transformation of all things in the universe. Everything went through phases of a cycle, and in so doing, its form also changed. For example, the water in lakes and seas became heated during the day and was transformed into vapor. As the air cooled down in the evening, vapor condensed into rain, returning to the surface.

The density of any form could vary. Yang symbolized the more immaterial, rarefied states of matter, whereas Yin symbolized the more material, dense states. Using water as an example, its liquid state pertained to Yin, and the vapor resulting from heat pertained to Yang. This duality in the states of condensation was often symbolized by the duality of "Heaven" and "Earth." Heaven symbolized all rarefied, immaterial, pure and gas-like states of things, while "Earth" symbolized all dense, material, coarse and solid states of things. In short, Heaven was an accumulation of Yang, Earth was an accumulation of Yin.[31]

Unlike the early European duality wherein two opposites were exclusive of each other, the Chinese contrary states of condensation or aggregation were not independent of each other, but rather they evolved into and substituted for each other. Yin and Yang could also symbolize two distinct states of aggregation. Lie Zi, a Daoist philosopher (300 BC), said: "The purer and lighter [elements] tending upwards made the Heaven; the grosser and heavier, tending downwards, made the Earth."[32]

However, the opposition of Yin and Yang was relative because nothing was totally Yin or completely Yang under all circumstances. Everything contained the seed of its opposite. Everything only pertained to Yin or Yang in relation to something else. For example, as hot pertained to Yang and cold pertained to Yin, the climate in Rome was Yang in relation to that in Stockholm, but it was Yin in relation to that in Cairo.

Although everything contained Yin and Yang, the combination was never presented in a static proportion in any given time. The components of Yin and Yang existed in a constant, fluid and dynamic balance. Yin and Yang, although opposites, were also interdependent: one could not exist without the other. Everything contained opposite forces which were mutually exclusive, but, at the same time, they depended on each other. Yin and Yang were in an enduring yet fluid balance, which was maintained by a continuous adjustment of their relative levels. When either Yin or Yang was out of balance, they necessarily affected each other and changed their proportion, and in this way found a new balance.

To substantiate the unity and fluidity between the opposites (Yin-Yang and resulting other pairs), nature was also defined as *qi* [air, breath, energy].

Qi, like tian and dao, had multiple meanings. However, unlike tian, which represented one of the two opposite states, qi could be represented as either or both under certain circumstances. Unlike dao that had dropped off its concrete connotation completely when used as the natural way (form), qi maintained its concrete and sometimes contrary connotations. Qi was the primordial substance in which both spirit and matter originated. Qi was also the general term which represented the material element in all the myriad transformations of the cosmos. In short, qi simultaneously had three distinct meanings: primordial substance, or as spirit, or as matter. These three aspects of the same word actually were characteristics of qi as it operated through all stages in the evolution of the cosmos.[33]

Qi was believed to be able to exist in two different states. It could either be at rest or in motion, and it could contract or expand, giving rise to the two states, yin and yang. It could also flow (transform) from one state to the other, as there were two components of qi operating in nature, one yin and one yang, each of which overwhelmed the other successively in a wave-like motion. This could be best illustrated by the *Taiji* diagram: half of the diagram was yin and the other half was yang. In this diagram of the Taiji, yin and yang rotated around the center, illustrating how yin and yang took over from each other successively in a wave-like action. Thus yin and yang were both opposite and complementary to each other.[34]

The Five Elements [*wu xing*] — water, fire, wood, metal and earth — were coined during the Warring States period and added new vocabularies and categories to the depiction of nature in Chinese literature. The word "elements" [*xing*] was invented to convey a qualification that was more general than single and concrete natural phenomena such as water, fire, wood, metal and earth. Initially, the qualification of nature was called *fu* [a seat of government], a commonly used word to classify governmental position (function), or *cai* [ability, talent, or material], a more ambiguous concept. The word "abilities" was not impersonal and abstract enough to describe natural states. *Xing* [element] was not only a more precise and concise way to refer to abstract types of constituent qualities of nature, but also carried the connotation of movement and processes, phases of a cycle. It was the first Chinese word that combined inherent qualities and existing capabilities of change.[35]

First of all, the Five Elements symbolized five different inherent qualities and states of natural phenomena. All of water, fire, wood, metal, and earth had distinct features that could be seen, heard, tasted and even manipulated. Water moistened downwards, fire flared upwards, wood could be bent and straightened, metal could be molded and hardened, earth permitted sowing, growing and reaping. That which soaked and descended [water] was salty;

that which blazed upward [fire] was bitter; that which could be bent and straightened [wood] was sour; that which could be molded and become hard [metal] was pungent; that which permitted sowing and reaping [earth] was sweet. In the latter case, the Five Elements indicated not only the actual flavor of things but also their inherent qualities (like their chemical composition, in modern terms).

The penetrating and inclusive meanings of the Five Elements also caught the invisible movements of nature. Accordingly, the structure of the living cosmos manifested in five phases. Each phase had a complex series of associations with different aspects of nature. There were mainly two types of natural processes: generating and restraining. For example, natural generating [sheng] processes included: wood fed fire; fire created earth (ash); earth bore metal; metal carried water (in a container, or water condensed on metal); and water nourished wood. Wood in turn, absorbed water; water rusted metal; metal broke up earth; earth smothered fire; and fire burned wood.

The second process was a natural restraining (overcoming) process: wood parted earth (such as roots or trees preventing soil erosion); earth absorbed (or muddied) water (or earth dam controlled the water); water quenched fire; fire melted metal; and metal chopped wood.[36]

Chinese were not the only ancients who abstracted nature into chemical elements. During the sixth century BC, Greek philosophers developed the concept of four elements. Thales (624–565 BC), the founder of the philosophical school of Miletus, regarded water or moisture as the essence of all things. Anaximenes (570–526 BC), another member of the same school, chose air as the ultimate principle, and he even accidentally called it breath [*pneuma*], as did the Chinese. He also did not see them only as static elements of nature, but also as changing movements. He noticed that air became fire when rarefied; but when air condensed it became water; when water condensed it became earth. Anaximenes' concept of air was extended by Diogenes of Apollonia (400 BC), who pointed out that every substance in the world was formed out of air through a process of condensation. Life itself, according to him, consisted of warm air moving like currents through the veins, thus preserving the strength in the body. The language of nature in ancient Greek was further abstracted by the Pythagorean school in the Greek colony in south Italy during the fifth century BC. The Pythagoreans used the four regular solids in geometry that they then knew to represent the Four Elements: the four-sided pyramid (tetrahedron) to represent Earth; the six-sided cube to represent Air; the eight-sided octahedron to represent Fire; and the twenty-sided icosahedron to represent Water. Later on they discovered the twelve-sided regular solid, the dodecahedron, and they took this to represent the universe. These five solids were made famous by Plato (427–347 BC) and became known as the "Platonic Bodies."

Empedocles of Acragas (490–435 BC), a Pythagorean and the creator of the Four Elements theory, made an observation similar to that of Chinese about the interaction of the four elements. He pointed out that water was opposed to fire but shows affinity to earth and air. Earth is opposed to air but shows affinity to fire and water. Each of the elements is formed by a pair of Four Primary Qualities — heat and cold, and moisture and dryness. These Primary Qualities also show affinity and opposition among themselves. Empedocles thought that the alternately predominating forces of affinity and opposition caused the Four Elements to be in constant change.

There was a parallel development of language of nature in ancient Greek and China until the emergence of Greek classical philosophy. In Chinese and Greek, nature has been described both as concrete phenomena and as principle elements. These basic elements represented the diverse qualities in natural phenomena and their inherited capacities of change. So far the mode of natural change was depicted in semi-abstract words such as water, fire, earth, metal, and air. These words are used here as principle elements of nature rather than the concrete things in nature such as river, sun, dirt, bronze, or mist. However, there was no case distinction in both ancient Chinese and Greek. (Ancient Greek was written in capital letters throughout its text while Chinese was not a Romanized language which had an option of two distinct cases.) Here Chinese and Greek had different solutions when literary language diversified into that of philosophy and science.

In ancient Greece, the description of nature had a long and yet linear evolution from concrete to abstract language. The earliest (materialistic) philosophers, like the earliest Chinese philosophers at the age of Confucius, initially wrote in poetic (rhyming) form. Then, they wrote prose in concrete language depicting visible and tangible nature beings, as did the writers of pre–Han and Han periods. While Chinese writers attempted to elevate their concrete words such as water, fire, and earth into abstract words such as *Yin-Yang* and *Five Elements*, they created a complete verbal context where each of the concrete words in the language could be obviously (visually) connected to these abstract words. Thus the connection between abstract words such as *water* was not limited to water but rather an array of words that had verbal and logical connections with the phenomenon of water. This connection was also reinforced by the visual components of writing. (For example, there were more than several hundred words that had a water radical and indicated meanings concerning water, including teas, sweat, river, ocean, string, and wetness.) Each of the concepts of Yin and Yang would have half of the verbal universe under their wings.

In short, when Chinese needed abstract words to depict something beyond vision, they could easily create those by extending their graphical writing without completely uprooting from the inherited repertoire of vocabulary. This was not possible in any alphabetic language, including ancient Greek. The concrete words that were used by early Greek philosophers, as well as their poetic delivery of nature, had mostly disappeared from the writings of post–Socratic philosophers. The language of nature in ancient Greek sharply diversified into pure Pythagorean mathematical and the abstract language of philosophers such as Plato and Aristotle.

Pythagoras (582–507 BC) saw numbers as the fundamental unchanging entity underlying all structure of the universe. For Pythagoras and his followers, matter was made up of ordered points that were arranged according to geometrical principles into triangles, squares, rectangles, and the like. On a larger scale, the parts of the universe were arranged on the principles of a musical scale and a number. For example, the Pythagoreans held that there were ten heavenly bodies because ten was a perfect number, the sum of 1 + 2 + 3 + 4. The Pythagoreans held that mathematical language (number) was the most precise and concise language to describe the natural order of the universe.[37]

Like the Pythagoreans, Plato (427–347 BC) found the ordering principle of the universe in mathematics, specifically in geometry. It was said Plato had inscribed at the entrance to his school, the Academy, "Let no man ignorant of geometry enter."[38] The story, like Chinese myth, might contain a grain of truth because in his writing, Plato repeatedly emphasized the importance of geometry. Plato was known more for his contributions to the philosophical basis of the scientific approach to nature rather than particular and specific concepts and descriptions. He maintained that all things in the material world were imperfect reflections of eternal unchanging ideas. In a general sense, Plato, like Confucius and Lao Zi, was pursuing an ultimate truth, although these truths were defined in different languages. Chinese philosophers called their versions of truth *tian* or *dao* depending on various schools of thought. The Platonic concept of idea was also repeatedly and variously redefined by his Greek and Latin disciples. As Greek idea was translated into Germanic and Romance languages, the conceptual link between concrete and abstract words, which was originally weak in Platonic Greek, became an unbridgeable gap. While Platonic truth should be found through rational demonstrations, analogous to the demonstrations of geometry, Chinese philosophers believed that it could never be found within the describable world, including that of God, literature, or science, in an English sense.[39]

This conclusion was found both before and after the Chinese had developed its various branches of ancient science: mathematics and astronomy.[40] What made Chinese different was that they spent many centuries building a literary language capable of filling the gap between nature as phenomena and their underlying logic, and between nature's constantly changing appearances [*xing*] and its enduring underlying logic. This historical attempt has been recorded every step of the way throughout its literary history.

Like their Greek counterparts, the Chinese depicted nature in the two distinct approaches of concrete and abstract. The former further developed into various disciplines and branches of sciences such as mathematics, astronomy, and medicine. The latter elevated narrative into highly general and sometimes abstract argumentation of the major issues of cosmology. What made Chinese experience different from that of other parts of the world was that both science and philosophy shared the same vocabulary and narrative language, rooted in common and concrete words and grounded even after they were used in abstract speculation.

The overlapping of speculative and practical pursuit of nature in China derived from the literary language that both branches (philosophical and scientific narratives) shared. The best illustration of this characteristic was the evolution of the concept of *qi*. The term *qi* sometimes was the reminder of the concept of the psyche, or "spirit" that was introduced by the Greek philosopher and naturalist Aristotle to distinguish between living and non-living things. According to Aristotle, plants had vegetative spirits, animals had vegetative spirits and sensitive spirits, and man had a vegetative spirit, a sensitive spirit and a rational spirit. The Chinese philosopher Xunzi had gone a step further by saying: "Water and fire possess subtle spirits [*qi*], but no life [*sheng*]. Plants and trees possess (also) life, but no perception [*zhi*]. Birds and animals possess perception, but no sense of justice [*yi*]. Man possesses spirit, life, perception, and in addition, the sense of justice. Hence he is the noblest of earthly beings."[41]

At this stage, the word *qi* had both concrete and abstract connotations. The following earlier texts illustrate the case:

> There was a Man from the state of Qi, who thought that the heavens might collapse, fall into pieces, and leave him no place to live. He was so worried that could not sleep or eat. Another man took pity on him and tried to enlighten him, saying, "The heavens are nothing but an accumulation of air [*qi*], and there is no place where air [*qi*] does not exist.... Why then should you worry about a collapse of the heavens?" The man said, "If it is true that the heaven is only an accumulation of air, why do the sun, the moon and the stars not fall down upon us?" His informant replied, "Those bright lights are only shining mass of condensed air themselves. Even if they did fall they would not hurt anybody."[42]

This story was referred to by later philosophers in a continuing debate. Lie Zi (4th century BC) said: "Those who believe that heaven and earth will pass away, and those who believe the contrary, are both wrong. We can never know what will happen to the heaven and earth. If they go, we shall go with them; if they stay, we shall stay (without knowing the end). The living and the dead, the going and coming, knows nothing of each other's state. Why then should we worry whether the world will be destroyed or not?"[43]

The continued debate about the origins and presumed end of the universe demonstrated the fluidity of word *qi* between original argument and its repeated rewriting and reinterpretations. By the time of Zhu Xi (1130–1200), qi had become a cosmic principle and a vital form (matter-energy) driving the entire circulation of the universe.[44]

The closest European example of overlapping of natural philosophy and science was the work of Aristotle (382–344 BC), who was actually making philosophy rather than just contemplating it. Unlike the Chinese, who had developed their dialectical reasoning by reductional argumentation [*Reductio ad absurdum*] for many centuries before they gravitated into natural philosophy and science, Aristotle was part of merely the second generation of post–Socratic philosophers who were never considered to be writers in a modern sense. His recorded dialogue was far from polished and refined.[45] However, Aristotle was the final philosopher who spoke a non- or semi-philosophical language. By the time of Euclid in Alexandria (300 BC), Greek mathematicians had developed a language of their own that was unintelligible to that of the philosophers. His *Elements* [*Stoicheia*], which consisted of thirteen books, was a collection of mathematical and geometric treatise, definitions, postulates (axioms), propositions (theorems and constructions), and mathematical proofs of the propositions. Euclid's presentation was limited by the mathematical ideas and notations in common currency for his era, and this made his treatment seem awkward to nonprofessional mathematicians.[46]

During the period between Han and Song dynasties, the literary Chinese that was being promoted and refined in the writings of mathematics, astronomy, medicine, physics (metallurgy), and mechanical and hydraulic engineering was shared by philosophers. They elevated it into a more abstract realm to carry out their speculative reasoning. The best example of this conceptual expression and juxtaposition (between concrete and abstract words and between the language of science and that of philosophy) was the way in which Zhu Xi (1130–1200) identified the words *qi* and *li*.

Zhu Xi the most prominent philosopher of the Song dynasty, juxtaposed *qi*, a major concept of daoism with *li*, a Confucian concept. He said: "Throughout the universe there is no *qi* without *li*, nor *li* without *qi*."[47] He maintained that all things were brought into being by the union of two universal aspects of reality: *qi*, and *li*. In order to seal this union, Zhu reinterpreted an old philosophical concept, *taiji*, [Supreme Ultimate] as the ultimate origin of the universe.[48] By replacing qi and dao with taiji Zhu Xi completely uprooted the concept of universal unity from the last remnant of the physical world and opened the door for its li. As he put it, li was one, but its functions were many. Consider heaven and earth and the myriad things, they have one unitary li. Each man possesses in himself one unitary li. Throughout heaven and earth, there is li and there is qi. Li is the dao that organizes all forms from above, and the roots from which all things are produced. Qi is the instrument to composing all forms from below, and the tools and raw material with which all things are made. Thus men and all other things must receive this li in the moment of their coming into existence, and obtain their specific nature [*xìng*]. They must also receive this qi in order to get their form [*xíng*].[49]

If this sounds like neo–Platonism, Chinese philosophy did not depart from natural science by creating its own vocabulary and abstract reasoning as the West did. If philosophers attempted to elevate scientific reasoning into speculative logic, science provided the detailed description of natural phenomena with which philosophers applied their theories into the most minute forms of nature. The best example is the following story of snowflakes.

The first literary record of hexagonal snowflake crystals was in 135 BC's edition of *Hanshi waizhuan* [*The Outer Commentary to the Book of Songs by Master Han*]. It pointed out that all flowers of plants and trees were generally five-pointed. However, flowers of snow [*ying*] were always six-pointed. Zhu Xi was the first person in China who had an explanation for why snowflake crystals were always six-pointed. He said: "The reason why snowflakes are six-pointed is because they are only half-frozen-rain [*xian*] split open by violent winds, and so they must be six-pointed. If one throws a lump of mud on the ground it will splash into a radiating, angular petal-like form. Now 6 is a yin number; and gypsum also is six-pointed with sharp prismatic angular edges. Everything is due to the number inherent in nature."[50]

The explanation of Zhu Xi might not be scientifically sound by modern physics, but European scientists did not recognize the symmetrical hexagonal form of snow crystals until the time of Johann Kepler, in 1611. In the thirteenth century Albertus Magnus mentioned that the crystals were star-shaped and in 1555 Olaus Magnus illustrated twenty-three different forms of snowflake crystals in many kinds of curious shapes, such as crescents, arrows, bells, and the like.[51]

Another similar example can be found in Huainanzi (139 BC). It was believed that *chemica* and other substances in the earth were produced in a certain definite order:

When the *qi* of the central regions [*zhengtu*] ascends to the dusty heavens [*aitian*], the latter produce *jue* [realgar] after five hundred years. *Jue* after five hundred years produces yellow dust, which after five hundred years produces yellow mercury. Yellow mercury after five hundred years produces the yellow metal (i.e. gold). The yellow metal after another five hundred years gives birth to a yellow dragon. The yellow dragon, entering into hiding, produces the yellow springs. The dust of the yellow springs ascends and turns into yellow clouds. Yin and yang beat upon one another to produce peals of thunder and flash out as lightning. Thereupon (rain) descends and the running streams flow to unite in the yellow sea.

When the *qi* of the eastern regions [*piantu*] ascends to the caerulean heavens [*qingtian*], the latter produce azurite [*qingzeng*] after eight hundred years. Azurite after eight hundred years produces green mercury, which after eight hundred years produces the green metal (i.e. lead). The green metal after eight hundred years gives birth to a green dragon. The green dragon, hiding in a place, produces the green springs. The dust of the green springs ascends and turns into green clouds. Yin and yang beat upon one another to produce peals of thunder and flash out as lightning. Thereupon (rain) descends and the running streams flow to unite in the green sea.

When the *qi* of the southern regions [*mutu*] ascends to the red heavens [*chitian*], the latter produce red cinnabar [*chidan*] after seven hundred years. Red cinnabar after seven hundred years produces red mercury, which after seven hundred years produces the red metal (i.e. copper). The red metal after seven hundred years gives birth to a red dragon. The red dragon, entering into hiding, produces the red springs. The dust of the red springs ascends and turns into red clouds. Yin and yang beat upon one another to produce peals of thunder and flash out as lightning. Thereupon (rain) descends and the running streams flow to unite in the red sea.

When the *qi* of the western regions [*ruotu*] ascends to the white heavens [*baitian*], the latter produce white arsenolite [*baiyu*] after nine hundred years. The white arsenolite after nine hundred years produces white mercury, which after nine hundred years produces the white metal (i.e. silver). The white metal after nine hundred years gives birth to a white dragon. The white dragon, entering into hiding, produces the white springs. The dust of the white springs ascends and turns into white clouds. Yin and yang beat upon one another to produce peals of thunder and flash out as lightning. Thereupon (rain) descends and the running streams flow to unite in the white sea.

When the *qi* of the northern regions [*pintu*] ascends to the black heavens [*heitian*], the latter produce dark grindstone [*xuanzhi*] after six hundred years. Dark grindstone after six hundred years produces black mercury, which after six hundred years produces the black metal (i.e. iron). The black metal after six hundred years gives birth to a black dragon. The black dragon, entering into hiding, produces the black springs. The dust of the black springs ascends and turns into black clouds. Yin and yang beat upon one another to produce peals of thunder and flash out as lightning. Thereupon (rain) descends and the running streams flow to unite in the black sea.[52]

This description was also illustrated by the *Hetu* diagram [river map] where everything fell into place and was precisely numbered. Right in the center are the numbers 5 and 10, and Earth — the color of which is yellow, and in the passage from Huainanzi are the numbers 5 and 10 for 500 years and 1000 years, and the yellow color; on the left are the numbers 3 and 8, the cardinal point East, and Wood — the color of which is green, and in Huainanzi there is the number 8 for 800 years, the eastern regions, and the green color; at the top are the numbers 2 and 7, the cardinal point South, and fire — the color of which is red, and in Huainanzi there is the number 7 for 700 years, the southern regions, and the red color; on the right are the numbers 4 and 9, the cardinal point West, and metal — the color of which is white, and in Huainanzi there is the number 9 for 900 years, the western regions, and the white color; and finally at the bottom are the numbers 1 and 6, the cardinal point north, and water — the color of which is black, and in Huainanzi there is the number 6 for 600 years, the northern regions, and the black color.[53]

Conclusions

The description of nature in formative Chinese drove the evolution of literary language from myth to history and then to philosophy. It gradually widened the horizon and depth of literary vision of nature from a part of the human world to an independent universe, and from diverse and fluid phenomena to the essence of its spontaneous movement and transformation.

The ten centuries between the end of Han (206 BC–AD 220 and Song dynasty, 960–1279) witnessed the widest separation of language of nature as concrete and abstract notions. Similar to the period of later Renaissance and the pre-modern period of Western Europe, this conceptual gap nurtured the most creative energy in China where science and philosophy flourished.

Like in the history of Chinese painting, the naturalistic description in Chinese literature was but a passing fashion. Literary language became internalized and descriptive precision channeled into structured worldview. However, equipped with refined natural imagery, the literary mind expanded into a natural world instead of retreating into a mystic world, as did the later Latin literature. The next chapter illustrates how natural imagery created a highly vivid and yet private world of poets.

6

Rhythm and Imagery of Feeling

This chapter is a history of natural imagery in Chinese poetry. Unlike the prose that gradually created a natural world distinct in vocabulary and composition from the human world, poetry took natural phenomena as stimulus, raw material, and metaphor to create an increasingly personal worldview. From pre-history to the Song period, although the concept and boundary of nature had been repeatedly redefined, poets continued to explore natural imagery as they searched for a distinctive vision. As ink and brush had for mature painting and calligraphy, poetic expression of nature became an alternative way to project creative ideas, vision, feeling, attitude, and personality.

During the pre–Han period, poetry was a vehicle to pursue and communicate with the god(s) in Heaven. At this time the clear division between man and god, nature and the supernatural had yet to formulate in literary language, and a poet could put his ideas into the gods' minds and his words into the gods' mouths while imagining a divine journey as if he was a god himself. This intimacy between man and his god(s), shaped by formative literary language, was common in many languages of the world. The most representative of this stage of literary development in China was Qu Yuan's (340 BCE–278 BC) *Nine Songs* [*jiu ge*].[1] In his hymns Qu Yuan addressed his deities by human names such as *jun* [Mr. (Sir)], *dong jun* [lord of the East], *yun zhong jun* [master in (of) cloud], *Xiang jun* [Mr. Xiang], *Xiang furen* [Mrs. Xiang] (commonly translated to River Goddess), *shan gui* [mountain spirit], or *ji gui* [spirit of rite]. The only title among these that he gave to his nine gods and goddesses that could be correctly translated to god was *dong huang tai yi* [supreme king of the east]. This supreme king, adjectivally juxtaposed with *tai yi* [The One] and *dong* indicated that there was still a local king because the idea of an overlord would suggest a hierarchy of gods, a connotation that was not yet established.

Qu Yuan depicted the journey of the Sun God:

Coming from the east land I am glowing,
On my porch by the Fu-sang tree I am shining.
To a steady gallop, I slap my steeds,
night lights up as the day breaks.
In my dragon chariot I ride on thunder,
Like a waving cloud, I carry a stream of banner.
Beginning to take off, I heave a heavy sigh,
As my heart falters, I look back with care.
Sound of music and beautiful women are so attractive,
The audience is frozen and forgets to move.
Harps played with drumming,
Bells are rung with chimes shaking,
Fifes sing and pipes are blown;
Music like the player is wholesome and comely,
Fairies fly with wings and suddenly gather,
To join the dance poetry is recited.
Music with matching rhythms and pitch harmonized,
The fairies come until the sun is covered.
In gown of green cloud and white rainbow mantle,
I raise the long arrow and shoot Heaven's Wolf,
Sinking back with yew-bow in hand,
I seize the North Dipper to pour out cinnamon wine,
Clutching my reins, I am soaring high in haste,
off through darkness voyaging east.

The life story of the Sun God was well known in Qu Yuan's time. It was said that there were ten suns in the universe; they resided in the branches of the *fu-sang* [mulberry] tree at the Sun Valley. As a duty, every morning one of them would make the journey across the sky to light up the world. The first four lines described how Sun God woke up in the morning and was getting ready for his daily trip across the sky. Then, the next section portrayed what he saw through his journey, the spectacle on the earth that his presence had activated.

There were nine hymns for various gods, goddesses, and spirits. As more detailed imagery emerged, gods seemed to become closer to men in behavior and character. The first three gods, the Great God, the Sun God, and the God of the Clouds, rule over the world from afar. The Greater and Lesser Masters of Fate [*da si-ming, xiao si-ming*], while still celestial deities, were more intimately connected with specific human existence, controlling the length of men's lives and the birth of their children.

Even closer to humanity were the gods who actually inhabited the earthly domain, such as the *Xiang* River deities [*Xiang Jun, Xiang Furen*], the Yellow River god, and the mountain spirit [*Shan-gui*]. Like the Greek gods and goddesses, they had real human-like personalities. They were calm at times, moody and stormy at others. These active and capricious features of gods were demonstrated in their direct encounters with mankind. Gods and goddesses had human lovers whom they loved, desired, and longed for when they were separated from them. As gods and goddesses embraced their human traits, their thoughts became more human and their speech became more intensely emotional.

The lyrical culmination of the song cycle was the hymn of the "Mountain Spirits." Unlike most of the hymns, this poem was sung entirely in a three-beat, pause and three-beat again rhythm, like the final section of the "Master of the East." While it contained formulaic lines describing the symbolic gathering of certain flowers as seen in other poems, it seemed to present a more unified scene and mood than did the poems before it.

The dense, forested hills with their howling apes, the divinely induced clouds and rain, and the eroticism coupled with intense loneliness were strikingly similar imagery:

> Someone at top of the mountain,
> Wearing fig leaf cloth and dodder vine ribbon.
> With bright eyes and smile she says:
> I am elegant and ready to amuse.
> She drives a red leopard and followed by a wildcat,
> With a flower flag she rides on a magnolia cart.
> Coat of orchids and belt of asarum she wears,
> She blows sweet fragrance to whoever she loves.
> "I live in bamboo grove and never see the sunlight,
> the roads are hard and I came late."
> Upon the mountain's summit alone she stands,
> Surrounded by an ocean of flowing clouds.
> The sky darkens and light disappears,
> East wind blows, god sends down showers.
> "Waiting for my lord, I am sad and forget to return.
> What flowers can I deck myself with, so late in season?"
> She picked flowers from the mountains,
> From piled rocks and spread vines.
> "It is your fault Sir, I am confused and have lost my way.
> Perhaps, you are thinking of me but can't stay."
> The lady of the mountain is fragrant with pollia,
> She drinks from springs and finds the shade of trees.
> Thinks of me, but she holds back, uncertain.
> The thunder rumbles, rain darkens,
> Apes scream and monkeys chatter,
> Trees rustle and wind sighs,
> I think of you, Sir, but can't escape the sorrow.

This hymn movingly conveyed the underlying theme of all the foregoing poems, the desire for union with god. Through divine sexual encounter, the physical and spiritual regeneration of the human community can be ensured, and man could feel more at one with the divine natural forces.

The poet who spoke for both man and god could bridge the two worlds by conjuring up the divine through a structured succession of images. Changing voices and speech patterns became a vehicle that could drive communication between them whether they were apart or reunited. The prescribed incarnation of the gods, the intervention of the supernatural, allowed the poet to carry out his quest and the narrative to progress to a rapid modification, producing another equilibrium where a harmony, albeit fragile, was restored.

But the poet did not always reach the god(s). Of the seven pieces that mention love trysts, consummation was achieved in only three or four. These early gods have imperfect personalities much like their counterparts in Greek and early Hebrew literature. They could be moody and biased, granting or withholding favors, and act generously or selfishly, just like the men who created them. Perhaps because of their fickle natures, which were known by the poet, worshippers often attempted to manipulate or even take advantage of their gods by employing ambiguous language of ritual ceremony.

But on a deeper level, these attempts of uncertain courtship with the gods revealed a fundamental attitude held by the poet. At best, the union he was seeking would be a brief one. While there was a desire to contact the god, there also must have been a fear of being obliged to become his pliant instrument.

Qu Yuan's "Encountering Sorrow" ["*Li Sao*"] was the most famous poem in his *Chu Ci* [Songs of the South]. In this poem, the ambiguity of the identity of the speaker was clearly defined. It became the single voice of the poet who had transformed from an anonymous worshipper representing humanized divine into an individual who declared his identity from the first lines. He began with a genealogy and a description of himself, confirming a consciousness of his place in a historical continuity and an existence extending through time. He also became, instead of an ordinary worshipper, a magician who could summon gods and immortal spirits to do his bidding, and could roam at will to the utmost ends of the universe.[2]

The remaining element of belief in myth is what gives power to the poem's poetic vision. The "magical" effects are produced in much the same ways that they were in the *Nine Songs*, that was, through ingenious structuring as narrative and through the use of special effects of language.

The ritualistic presentation of objects, particularly flowers, in the first stanzas of the poem led readers to sense the sacred dimensions of the poet's actions. As in his *Nine Songs*, the flowers accrue meaning through repetition in the narrative until they come collectively to embody abstract qualities. The plants were never presented as if observed in their natural state. Always, the poet was manipulating them within his intentional framework:

> I inherited brilliant innate beauty,
> I added to it skill and talents as adornment.
> In selinea and shady angelica I dress,
> And I wear a belt of autumn orchids.
> Swiftly I am on my way to pursue
> Afraid time would race on and leave me behind.

> I grew fine fields of orchids,
> Planted hundreds of rods of melilotus.
> I have raised sweet lichens and cart-halt flowers,
> And asarum mingled with fragrant angelica.
> I longed to see them yielding blossoms rare,
> In season to harvest such a fine share.

Many commentators, attempting to pinpoint political allegory in the poem, have tried to match historical figures to the various flowers and herbs. But for the most part, the flowers seem to be invoked for their ritual appropriateness to the poet's character and actions rather than for their correspondence on a one-to-one basis with abstract behavioral qualities or specific people. Taken as a totality, they seem to indicate instances where sacredness and purity are either present or absent.

As in "The Great God, Lord of the Eastern World," where the human celebrants made the divine manifest by creating a sacred atmosphere, in this poem we have a similar transformation from the mundane to the extraordinary through ritual actions. In the first eight lines, Qu Yuan identifies himself and proclaims the human purity of his character. This opening is followed by a long section (lines 9–120) declaring his inability to lead the ruler of his kingdom along the correct path, and describes the many ritual actions he has performed in vain. Finally, a quarter of the way through the poem, he decides on his course of action:

> Suddenly I turned back gazing at the distance,
> I longed to visit the world of four quarters.
> Splendid my ornaments together surround,
> The fragrance all wafts far and wide.
> All men have pleasures in many ways,
> From a beautiful mind I take mine.
> I would not change, even my body dismembered,
> How could dismemberment hurt my mind?

The narrative is interrupted here while his handmaidens try to dissuade him, but his resolve is firm, and he travels to the site of Emperor Shun's grave to make his plaint. Having done this, he is infused with the power to make his journey:

I heaved despair in many sighs,
Regretting my birth in unfortunate times.
I plucked lotus petals to give my tears a wipe.
I stumbled on the riverbank and fell, my coat got wet.
Then knelt on spread skirt to pure my plaint,
It clarified my truth, my feelings manifested.
I yoked jade dragons to a phoenix chariot,
On a dusty wind I suddenly soared.

It is only at this point that the poem carried the reader to the supernatural realm where man and deities interacted and spoke to and for each other. It continued:

At daybreak from the land of trees gray,
I came to paradise by the end of the day.
Hoping to stay in sacred grove to rest,
But the sun was sinking into the west.
I begged the father of the sun to stay,
Towards the setting rays we sped away.
The road was long and filled with gloom,
I was up, then down chasing disappearing dreams.
In the Pool of Heaven dragons quenched their thirst,
On Fusang Tree I tired their reins.
I broke a sprig of Ruo tree to strike the sun,
First I wanted a roaming ride for fun.
Ordering the driver of moon's chariot to lead,
following me the Wind God swiftly succeeded.
The Bird of Heaven cleared my way,
The lord of thunder urged me to delay.
I bade phoenix to search the heaven wide,

And fly onward by day and by night.
Whirlwinds appeared to gather in my sight,
Clouds and rainbows accompany my flight.
Merging and departing in chaotic train,
Above, below, rushed into a glittering rain.
I asked the Heaven's porter to open his palace,
But he leaned on his door to inspect my face.

The day grew darker and close to spent,
Idly my orchids into wreaths I bent.
Muddy and impure world undiscriminating,
It tends to veil beauty out of jealous feeling.
In the morning I crossed white waters,
On Langfeng Mountain I tied up steeds.
Looking around, I burst out weeping,
From this lofty hill there was no fair lady dwelling.

I wandered eastward to the House of Spring,
I broke a jasper branch on my girdle adding.

I vowed that before jasper flower fade,
I should give them to the loveliest maid.
I order Fong Long ride the clouds
To search for the home where nymph lay.
As a pledge I offered my girdle,
I appointed Lame Beauty to negotiate.
Many meetings and fleeing like clouds,
All wills and caprices she hard pursued.
At dusk she retired to the mountain withdrawn,
And washed hair in the stream at dawn.
She guarded her beauty with proud disdain,
She worshipped there, no whim could reign.
Fair she might be, but she lacked all grace,
Forget her and search for another place.

Four quarters of earth I sought my bride,
Pushing my journey through heaven wide.
I gazed jade tower's glittering splendor,
Found Lord Song's beautiful daughter.
I sent off magpie to entreat the maid,
But magpie replied that my suit was denied.
The magpie flew, I heard its chatter,
A fellow of dishonest and annoying barter.
My mind was irresolute and still,
I wished to go, but could not find the will.
The phoenix had accepted wedding gifts,
As I feared that they had arrived from the prince.
I wished to travel far, a place my mind could bear,
Aimless and wandered, not knowing where.
Before the young Prince was marriage bound,
The two royal sisters might still be found.
My matchmaker was weak and dumb,
I knew I had little hope to succeed with him.
The world is dark and envious of the able,
Eager to hide man's virtue and praises evil.
Wise kings were unapproachable in Palace deep,
They could slumber not waking from their sleep.
The thoughts in my heart will never be said,
How can I bear this silence until life's end?

With mistletoe and herbs of magic,
I urged Ling Fen to tell my future.
She said "Beauty always finds its mate,
But who would your virtue long to greet?
Think of nine continents in a wider world,
Why waste time here to look for your maid?
"Go farther" she cried, "set fainted heart aside."
If you seek beauty, no one here could vie.

> All the world has flower fair,
> Why is the native land your only care?
> The world is blinded by folly of the vain,
> When people cannot see the virtue within.
>
> ....
>
> Gather the flower of youth before it fades,
> While the good season still remains.
> Beware the shriek before the equinox,
> When all the flowers lose their fine fragrance.
>
> ...
>
> The age is in chaos, in constant change,
> Among them how much longer can I remain?
> Orchid and iris have lost all of their scent,
>
> Having changed to straw Flag and melilotus.
> Flowers change as each day passes,
> All transformed into mugwort useless.

During the poet's celestial journey the narrative covers great distances at high speed. Qu Yuan seems to be traveling ever westward, as if trying to catch the sun before it sets. It was the imaginative power that the poet was able to generate in these lines which made the ending so abrupt and poignant:

> Ascending to Heaven's splendid vastness,
> Suddenly I catch a glimpse of my old home.
> My groom is grieved and my horses are yearning,
> Arching their backs they refuse go on.

The emotional attachment of the poet to earthly realm was expressed by the reaction of the horses when they saw the glimpse of the poet's old home on earth. They, which were highly humanized by being sensitive to the poet's feelings, began to arch their backs and demand a stop.[3]

Chu Ci [*The Songs of the South*], of which "Encountering Sorrow" and "Nine Songs" were a part, was composed at a time when nature had not yet been depicted in literature as a world distinct from that of man. Qu Yuan, as lyric protagonist, could only refashion the world through his own perceptions and render it in a highly symbolic and distinctive imaginary form. Nature was seen and therefore portrayed as scattered and isolated phenomena only loosely connected. The poet took and envisioned it for symbolic meaning. He described his entourage at some length, with dragons pulling jade-hubbed chariots and phoenixes bearing pendants, but these picturesque images also were devices for expressing his newly assumed divine power and ability to animate the universe. When the reader tried to visualize the lands he passed over or the route that he followed, the scenes evaporated. Although the places had evocative names such as Flowing Sands and Red Waters, they had neither physical detail nor geographical framework to tie them together.

In the "Nine Songs," the height of the poet's power and lyricism was elicited by his passion. In the beautiful songs to the Xiang River goddesses and the mountain spirit, the entire world of nature seemed to exist only in order to evoke the longings and promise of union with the divine. Qu Yuan was seeking gods, but his quests were immersed in a framework which was, from beginning to end, a process of personal exploration through history, and through his life over time. His personal alienation from the world precluded his finding solace in an intermediary. He confronted the totality of the world directly. The metaphor for his attempt to conquer it was the journey. The height of his lyricism was reached in those passages where his soul soared above the world. For a short time he could control the elements; marshal the gods to do his bidding. And as he rushed through space, keeping pace with the sun, he was metaphorically conquering time.

In "Encountering Sorrow," the reader had heard only one voice. The protagonist was not only a worshipper of God but also a painfully self-aware individual. He expropriated the imagery, the grandeur, and the power of the gods, but the main concern was the human affair. Natural imagery was but ink and color that he utilized to portray his sorrow for the injustice and disgrace of his time. This sorrow, with vivid imagery and passionate emotion, has been revisited by billions of Chinese during the ensuing two thousand years.[4]

Chu ci imitation became a completely exhausted genre well before the end of Han. The new innovations in poetry during the period were largely inspired by forms of song called yuefu, initially collected from the common people and later composed by literati. However, chu ci's lyrical tradition, which put the poet himself as the true subject, continued in yuefu poetry. In Han and post–Han poetry, natural imagery continued to evolve but gradually completely lost its mythical theme and political overtone, as had chu ci, leaving behind isolated and micronatural phenomena to describe specific feelings that poets intended to illustrate or project in the minds of readers. Imagery further clarified and specified, since natural objects were taken as the theme of poetry. For example:

"A Rare Tree"

by an anonymous writer

A rare tree stands in courtyard quiet;
Among green leaves where flowers run riot.
I bend a branch and pluck its bloom
To send to my far off dear groom.

Its fragrance fills my breast and sleeves,
The journey, so far away, I grieve.
I don't mind this light gift bloom sweet-hearted,
But I am sad, too long since we've been parted.

"To an Autumn Fan"

by Lady Ban

Fresh from the weaver's loom, silk so white,
You are as clear as frost and snow is bright.
Fashioned into a fan, a love taken,
You are as round as a brilliant moon.
In my lord's sleeve as in or out he goes,
You wave and shake, and a gentle breeze blows.
I am afraid of the coming autumn day,
As chilling wind drives summer away,
Abandoned in a lonely place,
You take leave of my lord and fall into disgrace.

Like the early poetry, natural imagery was well selected to suit a specific descriptive environment. However, the trees, the moon, breeze, and fragrance had lost their grand cosmic scope and moral connotations. Sometimes, even the poet painted a larger picture of nature with various details centered in a single or single-minded feeling. An example of this was the poem of Cao Cao (155–220), a highly complex personality in Chinese history[5]:

"The Sea"

I came to see the ocean boundless
from the Stony Hill on the shore.
In rhythm its water rolls,
Islands stand amid the roar.
From peak to peak, tree upon tree grows,
Grass on grass is lush far and thick.
Surge up high the monstrous billows,
Autumn wind blows drear and bleak.
The sun by day, the moon by night
appear to rise from the ocean deep.
The Milky Way with stars so bright
sinks down into the sea to sleep.
How happy I feel at this sight,
I hum this song in my delight.

While this grand vision of seascape was designed to express delight and celebration, a different sight of a similar scale was adopted to portray a completely different mood:

"Though the Tortoise Lives Long"

by Cao Cao

Tortoise is blessed with long life, yet at the end he has to die.
Winged serpents ride high on the mist, they turn to dust at last.
Old war-horse may be stabled, yet it longs to run a thousand miles.
A noble man in advanced years never abandons his proud spirit.
It's not only up to heaven, man lives long or short.
To enjoy living to the fullest, we can live a great old age,
if we keep fit, cheerful and gay.
Here, with joy in my heart, I hum this song.

Even when Cao Cao utilized the mythical themes and characters, they had lost their context in ritualistic narrative and didactical tone. Although an important political feature (Cao was the Emperor of Wei), Cao's poetry no longer functioned as a moral and political medium.

"Mulberry on the Fields"

by Cao Cao

Driving rainbows,
Riding crimson clouds,
I ascend the Nine Peaks to the Gates of Jade.

I crossing Heaven's River, Milky Way,
To Mount Kunlun, gate to world of immortals,
I pay respect to the Sun and Western Goddess.

Chisong is my companion,
With Xianmen I am friend
I learn to nurture my spirit with the Dao that transcends.

I eat lingzhi for the immorals,
I drink from fragrant waters,
I wear an orchid crown and hold a staff of flowers.

No mortal affairs or troubles,
No limits to where I travel,
As swift as the wind in the universe go.

Though the shadow has moved not,
A thousand miles I've passed,
Ageless as the mountains but forgetting not the past.[6]

Compared to Qu Yuan's *Li Sao*, Cao's mythical ride was filled with his contentment of life and peace with the world.

Poets of Cao Cao's time (commonly referred to as Jian An poets) established subgenres and themes that were to endure throughout much of subsequent literary history. Like the later landscape painters who gradually focused on specific objects, such as mountains, trees, boats, and mist, Jian An poets wrote about history, feast [*yen-hui*], and sightseeing [*yu-lan*]. They invented poems of presentation and response [*zeng-da shi*], poems on roaming into the world of immortals [*yu-shien shi*], and poems on lonely or abandoned women [*yüan-nü shi* or *qi-fu shi*]. In all of these, natural imagery became the ink that the poet utilized to paint various imagery of emotions: separation, political turmoil, personal aspirations and frustrations, praise for superiors, longing for the parted, and sorrow for hardships and the plight of dispossessed women. Xu Gan's (171–218) "A Wife's Thoughts" was one of these:

> The floating cloud flows like an ocean,
> Will it deliver my heart's passion?
> On rolling cloud I can't ride,
> I pace up and down with a sigh.
> Others part but return and meet again,
> Why are you alone and still far away remain?
> Since you left me and went away,
> My mirror gets dustier with each day.
> My thoughts of you like a river flow,
> O when can they stop to grow?

Parting was one of the most common themes of poetry during this and subsequent times. However, its imagery became more and more detailed and specific to the various feelings. If Xu Gan's poem painted a vivid image of longing, the following poem by Zhang Hua (232–300) provided more detailed impressions of the same emotion:

> **"Love Poem"**
> Soft breeze ripples curtains drawn,
> Alonely in a moonlit room at dawn.
> My love remains in a far off place,
> My orchid room sees not a guest.
> In vain I embrace moonlight,
> over empty bed on my thin quilt.
> I used to regret happy days in flight,
> But now complain of long, sad night.
> Tapping my pillow, deep I sigh,
> With broken heart I cannot cry.

Here the reader can see the beginning of a tighter correspondence between the imagery and emotion: soft breeze, lonely moonlight, empty bedroom, thin quilt, and the long, long sad night. These familiar imageries were further refined and polished during the Tang period.

Li Bai's "Seeing Meng Haoran off at Yellow Crane Tower" illustrated a refinement of imagery which painted a vivid vision of parting of a friend as the sail was gradually swallowed by the rolling water at the edge of blue sky:

My friend has left at the Yellow Crane Towers.
To visit Yangzhou in misty month of flowers.
His sail, a single shadow lost in the blue sky,
Till now I see only the river rolling by.

In the following poem, Li Bai's natural imagery carried a spiritual journey.

"A Song of Lu Mountain to Censor Lu Xuzhou"

I am a madman from Chu country
Who sang a mad song laughing at Confucius.
Holding a staff of green jade,
I have crossed, since morning at the Yellow Crane Terrace,
All five Holy Mountains, regardless of distance,
Spending my entire life travelling holy mountains,
Lu Mountain stands beside the Southern Dipper.

In silky clouds of nine layers extended its screen,
its shadows in a crystal lake with brightening water green.
The Golden Gate opens into two mountain-ranges,
A silver stream hangs down to three stone bridges.
Mighty Tripod Falls are seen from afar.
Ledges of cliff and winding trails lead to blue azure.
In blue shadow a flush of cloud reflects the morning sun,
no flight of birds could be blown into Wu.

Climb to the top to survey the entire world,
I see a long river that runs without looking back.
Wind drives Yellow clouds to fly miles of hundred,
While waves in nine streams glide down the snow peak.

I am singing a song of Lu Mountain,
A song born of the breath of the Mountain,
Where the Stone Mirror has again purified my heart.
And green moss has buried the footsteps of Xie (sage),
Taken the immortal pellet and rid of the world's troubles,
Before the lute's third play, I have achieved my element.
Far away I watch the angels riding colored clouds
Toward heaven's Jade City, with hibiscus in their hands.
I have traversed the nine sections of the world,
I will follow Saint Luao and fly up to the Great Purity.

Here nature was not only displayed but also animated as it responded to the journey of the poet: wind drives cloud, waves glide through snowing mountains, gate opens to mountain ranges, red cloud reflects morning sun, and silver stream hangs down. These naturally spontaneous movements are punctuated by the poet's mountain travels as he sees, investigates and is purified by nature.

In other poems, Li Bai illustrated single characteristic imagery with various emotional images. For example, the following poem was about a single imagery — a temple high in the mountain and close to heaven:

"Sleeping at the Mountain"

I could pluck stars with my hands,
in a temple on the top of the mountain.
When speak, I lower my voice,
afraid to disturb the residents of Heaven.

"The Love for Peony Flower" by Bai Juyi (772–846) was also a poem about a single feeling:

I am worried about the red peonies at my steps,
they have only two surviving blooms.
If a wind starts to blow in the morning,
it might wipe all of them away.
At night with candles burning,
I have one last look at my blooms remaining.

Another poem of peonies in bloom by Liu Yuxi (772–842) illustrated a completely different kind of feeling:

"Drinking Before Peonies in Bloom"

Today I drink with blooms.
Don't care if I drink too many cups!
But I am afraid to be told,
"Our bloom is not for you, you are too Old!"

Wang Wei (699–761), a poet and painter, often created poetic imageries as vivid as those in his painting:

"The Dale of Singing Birds"

Osmanthus blooms fall, I'm absent minded,
When night comes, green hills dissolve into void.
The rising moon startled birds to singing,
Their fitful twitters fill the dale with spring.

"Villa on Zhong-nan Mountain" went as:

In my middle years I came to much love the Way
and late made my home by South Mountain's edge.
When the mood comes upon me, I go off alone,
and have glorious moments all to myself.
I walk to the point where a stream ends,
and sitting, watch when the clouds rise.
By chance I meet old men in the woods;
we laugh and chat, no fixed time to turn home.

Meng Jiao's (751–814) "Sadness of the Gorges" (third of a set of ten) was translated as follows:

> A thread of sky above the gorges,
> Cascades twine a thousand cords.
> High up, slants splintered sunlight,
> And below, curbs the wild heave of waves.
> Moving and then another gleams,
> In depths of shadow frozen for centuries.
> Sun rays do not stop at noon between gorges,
> More hungry spittle, the straits are perilous.
> Trees lock their roots in rotted coffins,
> Hang tilted upright, twisted skeletons.
> Branches right as the frost perches,
> Remote and clear in mournful cadences.
> A spurned exile's shriveled entrails,
> Scald and seethe in fire water as he wails.
> A life is like a fine-spun thread,
> The road ascends with rope at the edge.
> His tears pour to ghosts in the stream,
> Where on the waves they gather and gleam.

Later Tang natural imagery and human imagery became completely woven into a single vision. The best illustration of this new development was the later works of Du Fu (712–770). In this refined type of verbal tapestry, imagery of nature and fabric of feelings and characters became one and inseparable:

"The Harvest Moon"

Moon, the flying mirror dazzles in mine eyes.
I, like a broken sword, have no hope to go home.
Wandering o'er the earth like creeping weeds!
Seeking elixir of life, but Heaven is too high to climb.

Imagine the Moonlit waters made of snow and frost.
Moonbeams shine on feathered birds in the woods.
I fixed my gaze upon the Rabbit in the Moon,
as if I hope to count the hairs upon his snowy coat.

Within each gaze of a poet was an entire galaxy of imagery that had accumulated during thousands of years of writing and reading. That which he looked upon (the object) became increasingly insignificant compared to what he could see and feel there (his imagination). This was the reason why in both painting and poetry the repertoire of subject matter shrunk as a more refined and inspired imagery flourished and multiplied. Mountain Tai was one of the favorite inspirational places for poets to express themselves throughout the ages. Here is what Du Fu could see in it:

"Gazing at Mount Tai"

What shall I say of the Great Peak high stands!
Boundless green covered two ancient states.
Inspired and stirred by nature's hands,
Day and night rotates by Yin/Yang forces.
Open my chest to layers of clouds,
My sight is restrained to see bird fleet.
To view all mountains in a single glance,
I must reach the top and hold peaks under my feet.

This combination of natural and human imagery created a tradition of allusions where animated natural imagery and types of feelings juxtaposed and compounded. From a repertoire of highly stylized allusions, poets had to imagine (invent) new imagery and new associations to make their voice unique. The following poem by Hao Jing (1223–1275) demonstrates how and what a post–Tang poet had to do to reinvent the old, sometimes even rustic, allusions to express something new and original:

"Fallen Flowers"

As rainbow clouds over darkened door, red petals shower,
On jadeite branch leave the trace of fallen flower.
Of peach and plum in eastern breeze dream butterflies,
Over moonlit hills and northern walls cuckoo cries.
Jade railings stand in chilly mist amid bare trees,
The beauty gone in Golden Val, wine cups displease.
Don't sweep the blooms in the yard away,

Like the shrinking subjects of landscape painting, there were fewer numbers of poetic themes and the scope of nature became smaller, yet more focused. A single category of nature such as flowers, insects, pine trees, or even fish or horses became the subject for the entire work of a painter's career. Form rather than natural object presented the essence of an artists' contemplation. The same process occurred in the evolution of Chinese poetry. The following poem by Du Fu illustrates this microscopic imagery of nature:

"Ballad of the Old Cypress"

An ancient cypress in front of Confucius' shrine,
with a trunk of green bronze and a root of stone.
The girth of its white bark needs arms of forty men
its dark blue tip reaches a thousand feet toward heaven.
Great kings and their statesman have come and gone,
Their tree is still admired by many as residuum.

Clouds come to it from far away Wu cliffs,
And the cold moon glistens on its peak of snow.
East of Silk Pavilion yesterday I found kings and statesmen

I worshipped in the same temple,
whose tree with curious branches, ages the entire landscape
although with fresh colors on the windows and the doors.

So wide is the deep root maintained underground,
That its solitary lofty boughs can dare the weight of winds,
Its only protection the Heavenly Power,
Its only endurance the art of its Creator.
Though oxen pull, ten thousand heads cannot move a mountain.

Yet if beams are needed to restore a great house,
Though a tree writes no memorial, people understand
that not unless they fell it can use be made of it....
Its bitter heart may be tenanted now by black and white ants,
But its odorous leaves were once the nest of phoenixes and pheasants.

Oh, wise and ambitious men, sigh no more:
Using timber this big was tough!

A similar example was Li Bai's "A Dream of Tian Mu Mountain," where a single mountain scene activated a mystic journey:

Seafaring visitor tell of the Eastern Isle of Bliss,
which was lost in wild and mystic sea waves.
But Yue people talk about Tian Mu Mountain in the south,
which still is seen through glimmering clouds.
Like a road to the sky stretching across the leagues of heaven;
it rises above all the peaks, and shadows the entire land.
The Tien-tai Peak a thousand miles tall,
Staggering and tilting toward the southeast.

As I dream of the south lands of Wu and Yue,
I fly across the Mirror Lake all night.
The moon's reflection companies my flight,
and carries me to the town of Yen Xi.
Here still stands the mansion of Prince Xie,
Where green waters swirl and monkeys shriek.
Wearing Prince's pegged boots,
I climb a ladder of blue clouds.
Half-way up the sky-wall I see the morning sun,
and hear the heaven's cock crowing in space.
Later among a thousand peaks and valleys I lose my way,
Flowers lure me, rocks ease me. Day suddenly ends.

Roaring bears and howling dragons tremble cliffs and forest and shudder overhanging peaks.
Clouds on clouds gather above, threatening to rain;
Waters gush below, breaking into mist.
A peal of blasting thunder
It shatters an entire range of mountains.
The stone gate of the heaven opens wide,

Revealing in its pit a grand lake of blue deep water.
Sun and moon shine together on gold and silver palace.

In rainbow garments and riding on the wind,
Cloud Goddesses descend like showering flowers
where tigers play lute and mythical birds dance,
row upon row on fields of hemp, a parade of fairy figures.
My soul flies and is terrified,
I lift myself in amazement, but alas!
I wake up and find my bed and pillow —
gone was the radiant world of gossamer.

As with all pleasures of life
Ten thousand things run forever like water flowing east.
So I leave you now not knowing for how long.
But let me, on my green slope, raise a white deer,
to ride to visit your lovely mountains when I need you!
Why does the pursuit of wealth service the powerful,
always stifling my soul?

It appeared that self-animation into a natural (mythical) environment in which he was completely emerged set a stage for the poet to express his feelings, attitude and philosophy of life. In this highly personalized vision, nature had lost its physical consistency and became selected and reconstructed according to the rhythm and pace of the flow of narrative. The following two poems by Li Bai are the most representative of "unnatural" nature:

"Long Yearning" I

I am yearning forever
to be in Changan.
Autumn insects hum by the gold brim of the well;
A thin frost glistens like little mirrors on my cold mat;
as high lantern flickers; my longing grows deeper.
I lift the shade and gaze upon the moon,
and see beautiful Chang E at the end of a cloud.
Above, I see the sky, blue and deep,
below, I see the water green and restless.
Heaven is too high, earth too wide for my sorrow to fly,
Even in dream my soul can't pass the mountain gateway.
Long yearning
Makes my heart break.

"Long Yearning" II

The sun has set, and mist lingers on flowers;
the moon grows pale and I am sad and sleepless.
A Zhao harp has just stopped on its phoenix holder,
a Shu lute begins to sing with its mandarin-duck strings.
As nobody could deliver the words of my song,

Hopefully spring wind would carry them to Mount Yanran.
I think of you far away, beyond the blue sky,
And my eyes that once sparkled are now a well of tears.
Oh, if you don't believe my broken heart,
Come back and look at me in my mirror bright!

After repeated juxtaposition by generations of poets, nature with each of the specific rivers, mountains, towers, and flowers became stereotyped and designated to specific types of feelings or human characteristics. For example, flowers were often used as symbols of female beauty; fallen flowers became the metaphor of the short life of this beauty or the swiftness of its impact on the feeling of male admirers.

"Plum Blossoms"

by Chu Shu chen (early 12th century)

The snow dances and frost flies,
We see vaguely through the bamboo blinds.
Sparse shadows of plum branches,
Unexpectedly a cold perfume
came with the sound of a Tatar flute
blown to our bed curtains.
Surrounded by puzzling scented wind,
Who can appreciate such a subtle joy?
I quickly get up
with uncombed cloud of dark hair.
We taste the stamens and
adorn ourselves with the blossoms,
Frowning and smiling,
Still drowsy with wine.

Song Qi's (998–1062) "To the Fallen Flower" was a second person depiction of flowers in their decay:

Your red blossoms and white petals fall with regret,
Parting from mist-veiled green mansion you can't forget.
Before reaching the ground, you dance in wind with grace,
Fallen, still revealing the hidden fairness of your face.
Sea sheds pearly tears when sailors go ashore,
Beauty leaves behind sweet scent though she is no more.
You can't leave your honey to the butterflies.
Confide your sweet heart to beehives before it dies!

Wang Qinghui's "Men jiang hong" projected the life of a flower from a woman's perspective[7]:

The lotus of Taiyi Pond is pale
and has lost its color of the past.

I remember imperial favor
Like rain and dew shower last.
In the Emperor's golden bed of the jade palace,
my fame spread like orchid incense
amongst the queens and concubines.
I blushed like a lotus blossom
As to my Lord's side I was summoned.
Suddenly one day, war drums beating,
came like thunder off the sky tearing.
It came to an end all my glorious splendor.
Generals scattered like dragons and tigers.
Courtiers fled like wind blown clouds.
To whom can I express
my everlasting sorrow?
Facing the vast land of the mountains and rivers,
Tears mingle with blood on my sleeves.
I startled and woke up from dreams of dust and dirt.
Fleeing in the dawn, our palace cart
Through the mountain pass rolling,
under the moon setting.
I pray to Chang E,
The girl who took refuge on the moon,
and ask her to allow me
to follow her to rise and wane.

A different kind of flower might be adopted to describe a gender neutral noble character. For example, the following poem "To the Mume Blossom" by Lin Bu (967–1028) expressed different ideas about flowers. Instead of being fragile, short-lived, and weak, they were strong, resilient and seeking a different kind of company:

Alone you bloom as all flowers fade,
You own the entire garden night and day.
Across clear shallow water sparse shadows lay,
Gloomy fragrance floats at dusk in dim moonlight.
Seeing your purity, white birds appear and alight,
Knowing your sweetness, butterflies would lose their heart.
Is your friend only a lucky poet,
Who can tell sandal clappers and golden goblets apart!

Another imagery of the same flower was written by Wang Anshi (1021–1086):

"Mume Blossoms"

At the wall corner mume trees grow;
Against the cold they bloom apart.
How could we know they are not snow?
Only with unseen fragrance they impart.

Various kinds of trees, without exception, were also taken for their symbolic meanings and connotations. Willow was often present in parting scenes and it inspired the following two poems:

"The Willows"

by Liu Yuxi (772–842)

Thousands of willows stand by winding stream clear
Under an old wooden bridge of twenty years
Here, my lady left and went away.
Sadly, I've not heard from her to this day!

A similar imagery of the willow was found in "Gazing Afar in the Evening from the West Tower of Xianyang" by Xu Hun:

On city wall I see grief spread for miles and miles,
Over reeds and willow as entrenched on banks and isles.
The sun behind cloud sinks into waterside bower,
The wind, before mountain storm fills the tower.
In abandoned Qin garden only birds fly still,
Amid yellow leaves in Han palace cicadas shrill.
O wayfarer, don't ask about things of past days,
I come from east, only hearing what the river says.

Willow became the main subject of the following poem by Yong Yuzhi (785):

"To the Riverside Willow"

Your long, long branches are waving by riverside,
Your green green leaves like rings of smoke afloat.
"Make them into unbreakable ropes," she sighed.
"To tie up my beloved one's parting boat!"

The utility of willow could be given to its more symbolic connotation in "The Bridge of Love's End" by Yong Tao (805–?)

Why should this bridge be called "Love's End,"
As love is always hard to end?
Plant willow trees for parting friend,
Your longing for him will never end.

By the later Tang and Song period, natural imagery and emotional imagery (presented as natural forms) had become one and the same throughout poetic description. Nature had feelings corresponding to that of the poet, as men and women had become a part of landscape as in painting.

The following two poems illustrate how the willow imagery shrunk and lost its physical shape entirely in Song poetry. It was no longer about the willow but rather about its impact on artificially constructed and meditated scenery:

"To One Unnamed"

by Yan Shu (991–1055)

Your fragrant cab, never again come in sight,
It disappears as clouds in dreams without a trace.
Country yard pear blossoms steeped in moonlight,
The pond is rippled by willow down in the breeze.
So many lonely hours can't be washed away in wine,
I feel even more desolate on Cold Food Day.
How can I send you letters or even a line?
Everywhere mountains and rivers block the way.

"The Willow Branch Song"

by Zheng Wenbao (952–1012)

The painted boat on vernal lake has tarried long
Until half-drunk no one will sing a farewell song.
Despite mist and rain the boat goes on,
Carrying sorrow and wave unto the southern shore.

Instead of focusing a single object that conveyed a single idea or event, poetry created a more grand imagery to convey a more specific mood. Su Shi (1037–1101) was one of the best to express such highly elevated moods:

"On My Way to New Town"

The eastern wind knows that I will go to the wood,
It blows off endless songs by rain on the eaves.
The mountain crowned with rainbow cloud's silken hood,
Rising sun, a brass gong that hangs over leaves.
Peach blossoms smile over the bamboo fence not tall,
By clear sandy paved brook sway and swing.
Folks in the Western Hills should be happiest of all,
They send food to those working in fields of spring.

"Impromptu Verse Written in Exile"

I

My unkempt white hair flows as the wind frost spreads,
In my small study I lie ill in wicker bed.
Knowing that I am having a sweet sleep in spring,
Daoist priest strikes the morning bells, they softly ring.

II

Alonely I, Master of Eastern Slope, lie a sick man,
My straggling white beard flows as the frost spreads.
See my crimson face, my son is happy that I am fine,
I laugh, for he does not know I had some wine.

"The Fairy Hills Viewed in Rain from Yueyang Tower"

I

Living through many dangers made my hair grey,

Now I've survived in Three Gorges in deadly hour.
Before reaching southern shore, I laugh so gay,
To face the twelve Fairy Hills from the Yueyang Tower.
II
Leaning alone on rails, I see the tempest break,
The twelve peaks stand like tresses of the Fairy Queen.
I wish I could view them from the floating lake,
Amid silver waving mountain to see twelve hills green.

After centuries of poets meditating upon these images and utilizing them in similar scenes, natural images had acquired specific symbolic meanings and served certain themes. For example, moonlight often came with the feeling of loneliness and emotional distance. It was the most commonly used imagery in the poems of parting. Parting and longing were also a common theme in poetry, each time uniquely described in different natural images of different combinations. The moon was the most prominent imagery for longing because it was assumed to be seen by people far away from each other who were sharing the same vision. Zhang Jiuling's (673–740) "Gazing at the Moon and Longing for One Far Away" rendered:

Over the sea the moon rises bright;
We both gaze at it far, a world apart.
You might complain too long is the night,
And you would rise, lovesick at heart.
I blow out candle, but there's still light,
I don my coat soon moist with dew.
I can't hand you these moonbeams white,
But go to bed and to dream of you.

The most well-know verse of this theme was Li Bai's "A Tranquil Night":

Before my bed a pool of light
Can it be frost on the ground?
Glance up, I find the moon bright,
Glance down, homesick I am drowned.

Du Fu's "A Moonlight Night" depicted a longing of a different kind:

She must now gaze at the moon, far off Fuzhou,
Watching it alone from the window of her chamber.
We were poor children, boys and girls,
Early life in Chang An, we were too young to remember.
In fragrant mist her flowing hair is damp,
Her jade-white shoulder is chilled by moonlight.
When again on our screen shall we lie together,
While the moonlight dries our shining tears?

Yet the moon inspired entirely different feelings in Wen Tong (1018–1079):

"The Moon Viewed After Rain in the Mountain"

The sparse pines filter moonbeams
Falling shadows paint a land of dreams.
Pacing up and down,
I can't sleep for long.
Afraid Lotus leaves roll in the breeze;
Rain spoils fruits falling from the trees.

Who would sing with me or ponder?
While crickets' songs fill the forest.

Sometimes the moon was one of an array of imageries of longing filled with vision, sound and sense of touch. Li Shangyin's (813–858) "To an Unnamed Lover" was one of these:

It's difficult for us to meet and harder to part,
The east wind is too weak to revive flowers dead.
Spring silkworm spins till the death of heart,
Candles burned to ashes no tears to shed.
At dawn I grieve as your hair turns gray,
At night you chill while I croon by moonlight.
To the three mountains it's not a long way.
For the blue bird to fly to see you on the height!

And another of his "To an Unnamed Lover":

She promised to come, but gone without a trace,
I hear watch bell when on the tower the moon slanting.
My dreaming cries can not find her anyplace.
Ink is too thin to flow when in haste I attempted writing.
Flickering candle illumines half our emerald bed,
Sweet musk still faintly clings to lotus screen.
Beyond my reach the far-off mountains spread,
You are farther than ten thousand hills green.

Ci, a poetic form of the Song dynasty (960–1279), represented a compositional revolution in the history of Chinese poetry. Ci provided an innovative means to reframe fresh meanings and particular connotations in a repertoire of worn out imagery and allusions, and overly abstracted and generalized words. After centuries of rewriting, the poetic imagery could not be saved and kept alive through the accumulation of innovative connotations alone. Poetry needed a fresh formal framework to juxtapose phrases, lines, and stanzas that could make its expression more economical, precise, and emotional. The internally complete couplet and linear and highly regulated forms of the century old poetry *shi* restrained poetic imagination. The formal asymmetries of ci made possible certain moves and flexible compositions that were impossible in shi. Ci could isolate a phrase (without its parallel phrase) and add a single long (or short) line as if an after-thought. It also could formally enact a sudden shift, an odd association, a flashback, or an image left hanging. While shi tended to balance and complete utterances, ci could leave things incomplete, asymmetrical, and standing alone.

Song lyric worked with and reconstructed clichés, normative responses, and commonplace categories of feeling, such as sorrow and longing. However, the real interest of the genre lay in representing particular and original experience, often involving a reflective relation to the normative category of feeling. Precise objectification of one's own state of mind made a changing relation possible. For example, rather than simply "being in love," one might express exasperation at finding oneself helplessly in love. The song lyric's continual reflection on the categories of feeling was not a dispassionate distance but the means by which the real emotional up and downs, and the real shifts of mood, could be represented. The sorrow of presently being apart was no longer a commonly read universal experience but rather a flavor of its own kind in the heart. Sorrow of parting as a subject was uninteresting in its own right; what animated it was the tone in which we imagine the statement was made and, inferred from that, the way that the speaker felt individually and experienced personally.

In the new ci poetry, each time when a passage from early poetry was recited, it had to be reframed into a new, often more vernacular form. For instance, *"i-jiang chun-shui xiang tong liu* [a riverful of spring water flowing to the east]" was a very conventional "poetic" line of seven-character regulated verse for centuries. If this line was set in its originally correct context, an early Tang poet could have made it a convincing closing for a poem, a universal truth of nature that would in some way serve as the displaced embodiment of the poet's response. By the ninth and especially by the tenth century, such a closing line would have become painfully banal, a device that had become all too familiar and even boring. But when this same line was reframed in a markedly different diction: *Jiasi ijiang chunshui xiangdong liu* [it's just like a riverful of spring water flowing to the east], the conventionally poetic image loses its autonomy in the longer line and its status as simple natural fact. Thus, a natural imagery that originated from a physical observation became uprooted from reality and reduced into an image (expression) that had occurred in the poet's mind. This internalized and framed image turned a cold and static worn out image into an immediate poetic image.[8]

Compared with natural imagery that was based on observation of the eyes, poetic images could travel much longer distances in shorter lines of composition. For example, a common poetic image, a parallel pair of compounds such as spring flowers or autumn moonlight, could not possibly appear before a person's eyes simply because they occurred in different seasons. They could only be seen together by a mind that was not restrained by natural time. In other words, if the poet replaced natural imagery with mental imagery (image in the mind), he would enjoy much more freedom to juxtapose his ideas. His imagination literally grew wings and he could take the reader anywhere.

Ci, originally composed for singing, adopted a musical rather than visual or verbal (parallelism) organization and gave poets the potential for a new kind of emotional complexity. One stanza might tell of the past, another of the present, or one might relate an event and the other, focus on simple imagery. When a poet (Wei Cheng is one example) typically wrote "across" the gap (between stanzas) with no disjunction in time frame or in style of language, the musical component would break the depicted event into two parts. (Refrain lines typical of stanzaic poetry in the West were avoided in the lyrics, though the music probably involved repeated phrases.) The result was the creation of an underlying relationship between the stanza, which fostered the sense that emotion was flowing through and infusing the whole.

This reconstruction of compositional scheme is best illustrated by the introduction of *manci* (a popular form of song) in ci composition. *Manci* changed the rhythm of Chinese poetry during the eleventh century. In traditional seven-syllable lines of Tang poetry, there were eight beats. The seventh syllable was either followed by a pause, or, if it was a rhyming syllable, prolonged to two beats to fill the eighth unit. Notes of only two durations, either one beat or two beats, were needed in composition. The *xiaoling* stanza (averaging only two more syllables than a quatrain) required little or no adjustment to match this eight-beat measure. Where there were eight or more syllables in an eight-unit measure, notes of half-beat duration would be used.

In *manci*, however, the poet encountered large numbers of lines of three, four, five, and six syllables, some ending in rhyme, some not. Analysis has shown that these lines were probably squeezed into four-beat measures with more half-beat syllables being used. When one of these short lines seemed to correspond to a line of eight beats in another stanza, as long as it contained at least five or six syllables it could be slowed down to make an eight-beat measure without having to exceed the two-beat maximum for any syllable. Once a singer noticed whether a line ended in rhyme (a two-beat syllable) or did not end in rhyme (which meant it would be a single-beat syllable or, if there were only three syllables in the line, a pause on the fourth beat), he had a limited number of patterns of single- and half-beat syllables from which to choose.

In the longer *manci* form, the poet did not only have more room to tell a story, but he also could fill that space with extended reminiscences of love images and descriptive details. He had flexibility within stanzas to create a variety of units bound by rhyme and comprising one, two, three, or four lines, most of which were shorter than seven syllables. This variation of stanzaic form shifted the rhythm between and within these substanza units and the tensions between the regular and irregular beats. The enriched rhythmic scheme made it possible for poetry to engage and express more sophisticated emotional experience. Ci became capable of isolating a phrase or adding a long line as if an afterthought. It could also enact a sudden shift, an odd association, a flashback, or even leave an image hanging. The resultant tendency of the lyric to present itself as an exploration of feeling reached its full potential as a result of the innovations of Liu Yung (987–1053).[9]

An example of this freedom of composition is illustrated by the following ci by Lu You (1125–1210):

In the tune of "Chai Tou Feng" ["Phoenix Hairpin"]:

> Red soft hands, yellow rippling wine,
> Willows by palace wall, spring fill the town.
> East wind is biting, happiness is thin,
> heart full of sorrow, many years apart.
>
> Wrong, Wrong, Wrong!
>
> Spring turns old; people are empty and thin.
> Red sheer silk spoiled by tearstain.
> Peach blossoms falling, glimmering pond freezing,
> Oath remains paramount, Brocade book fails to hold.
>
> Can't, can't, can't![10]

This poem is about lost true love. In it, a biting east wind was metaphoric of the traditional male view about women. This view contributed to the demise of his first marriage. "Brocade book" was another metaphor for his ambition of unifying China. But he did not seem to be successful in either of marriage or career. He also used antithesis, which was very popular in Chinese poetry. It matched both sound and sense in two poetic lines, like "heart full of sorrow" pairing with "years apart" and "paramount oath" pairing "brocade book." The sounds match perfectly in Chinese.

Li Yu (937–978) was the first poet of ci; his "Yü Meiren" ["The Mermaid"] was another example of the terse and precise imagery of ci that could transcend supernatural time and space:

> Spring flowers and autumn moons,
> when did they end?
> I can't remember,
> how many things had happened and gone.
> East wind buffeted my tiny chamber,

again last night.
My hometown in moonlight,
is too much a sight for me to bear.

The marble steps and carved balustrades are still there,
Only ladies' rosy cheeks are not as fair.
How much sorrow can a man bear?
As much as a river of spring endlessly flowing east.[11]

A more scattered spring imagery was put together to describe a different mood:

The wind again stirs my little courtyard,
Overgrown with weeds of green,
The willow appears to sprout
spring after spring.

Leaning against railings for half a day,
All alone, with nothing to say.
The sound of flute and crescent moon
seem to be the same.

Pipes and songs are still heard,
and wine cups remain.
The ice in the pond begins to melt,
The candles do not wane,
Faint fragrance lingers in my painted room.
But it's hard to believe I allowed my temples to all turn white.

Another spring imagery of his brought not a new life but deadly sorrow and self-pity:

East wind blows over water,
the hill embraced by sun.
My day still filled with idleness, although the Spring has come.
Fallen blossoms scatter amid wine and tinkling pendants by the rail.
I hear music and song beyond my drunken daze,
With pendants still and evening dress undone.
To whom should I make my hair?
Oh, my rosy face will fade as time slips on,
On friendly rail I lean once more alone.

Following Li Yu, Liu Yung's (980–1053) poems firmly established ci as a new form of poetic composition. The most critical formal innovation was Liu Yung's production of a significant number of lyrics in the manci form, which had previously been confined to popular lyrics. A century early, isolated manci by poets like Tu Mu (803–852) had failed to have any impact on the elite practice of poetry writing, but most (more than 90 percent) of the 204 lyrics in Liu's collection were in this longer format. Liu used this additional length to dramatize genuine feelings and to bind various imageries into a moment in time; it contributed to the formation of a character, real or legendary.[12]

Liu Yung's "To the Tune of 'Rain-Soaked Bell'"

A cold cicada, sad and desolate
faces the long pavilion at twilight,
The showers have just stopped.
Of the city gate, I take a long drink in the tent.
I want to linger more times,
but the magnolia boat can't wait to start the journey.
Holding hands, we look into each other's tearful eyes,
Without words, throats choked,
I think of my voyage through a thousand miles of mists and waves,
Where the evening clouds are somber and the distant skies vast.

Lovers have suffered the sorrows of parting since ancient times,
The clear autumn season makes my solitude more unbearable.
Where am I going to wake up from my drink tonight?
Willow banks, the breeze at dawn, and the waning moon.
During the next long year of separation,
all fine moments and lovely scenes will appear to me in vain.
Even if I have a thousand kinds of tender emotion,
To whom could I impart them now?

Up to the Song dynasty, Chinese poetic expression had become highly terse and compacted. Every word (character) was pregnant with a wealth of imagery. For example, the first six lines of the following poem in English translation were expressed in the Chinese original with only two lines of nine characters each. The slow song form created more space for additional narrative details and vivid imagery of feelings.[13]

"To the Tune of 'Young Gentleman'"

On the long river the waves are shimmering,
At Huai, my hometown in Chu, I am landing.
Over the misty islet the rain has just passed,
The fragrant grass is as green as just dyed.
I press on, packing books and my sword.
Here, on this fine day and fine vista I am facing,
I feel my sorrows are many, my ailments increasing
Heartsick of traveling.

There, I see boundless wilderness,
Dark and gloomy evening clouds.
My trip intrudes into the hues of night,
At a village inn in the bends I rest.
The destination is near appearing,
To another the boatmen are calling,
To a distant spot where their lantern light is falling.

Here, Liu's personal voice disappeared as he narrated his sorrowful experiences as a sojourner distressed by life's hardship and his unsuccessful official career, mostly expressed through scenic description containing repeated and varied imagery: for example, "press on" [*qu qu*] (packing books and sword) in line 5, "boundless" [*chen chen*] (wilderness) in line 9 and "dark and gloomy" [*an an*] clouds in line 10. The four characters "fine day and fine vista" [*hao tian hao jing*] in line 6 depicted a nice day in contrast with the ill feelings described by another four characters, *duo chou duo bing* ["many" "sorrows" and "endless ailments"] in the following line.

This poem illustrates the characteristic of imagery in Song ci, its terseness, precision and flexible framework of composition. Only a word (character) or two were sufficient to create an image and a chain of imagery in the mind of readers rather than an entire scene or complete sentence.

Ouyang Xiu's (1007–1072) "To the Tune of 'Picking Mulberries'":

> I always love the darling West Lake.
> A crowd came around the red wheels,
> Riches and honors are floating clouds,
> Look up and down, the years flow on, twenty springs have passed.
>
> Now returned, I look like a crane from the distant east.
> The people are around the city walls,
> Everything I can see is new.
> Who could recognize their old masters?

Another poem by Ouyang to the same tune:

> After blossoms are gone, the West Lake is charming.
> Tattered scraps of remnant red,
> Mist of cotton catkins flying,
> Weeping willow by the railing follow sun and wind.
>
> Pipes and song scatter and cease, visitors depart.
> Spring starts to feel empty,
> Curtain falls back down,
> Swallows turn home through the drizzly rain.

These two poems, set at West Lake and sung in the same tune, express entirely different landscapes that provoke different sentiments. The first poem focuses on change of time (old v. new). This change is depicted in the imagery of people (crowds) who flow and change like the seasons and years. The second is a quiet scene of late spring that focuses on the word *empty*: flowers are gone, music is stopped, curtains are down, and even the birds are going home.

During the time of Li Qingzhao (1084–1151), ci as a poetic form had attained the apex of its perfection. Li became one of the most accomplished ci poets, especially for those who preferred an elegant, restrained style. Li employed a limited repertoire of natural images: flowers and plants, such as plum, cassia, crabapple, chrysanthemum, grass, willows, wild geese, egrets, gulls, and other birds. She also used the familiar motifs of the sun, moon, stars, wind, clouds, snow, frost, dew, and mist. Li seldom relied on classical illusions to connect nature and man and to achieve emotional effect. Instead, she preferred to use fresh metaphors and similes to juxtapose inanimate objects, animals, or birds with mankind, as in the following example:

> Sunny breezes, warm drizzles,
> Take the chill from the air.
> As the world sets to warming,
> Like a girl's eyes, the willow is sprouting.
> With rosy cheek the plum is blooming,
> The heart of spring now starts its stirring.

In "Late Spring" to the tune of "Wu ling Chun," she ingeniously used spoken language to create the metaphor of "grasshopper of a boat" to bring smallness of the boat into charming relief (line 13):

> The wind has subsided,
> The flowers have faded.
> In the muddy earth hangs a lingering fragrance of petals,
> I'm in no mood to comb my hair as dusk falls.
> Things remain. But all has been lost.
> Now he's no longer here.
> My words are choked with tears.
>
> I hear sweet gurgling of Twin Brooks
> With the breath of spring.
> How I'd too love to go rowing
> On a tiny skiff.
> But at Twin Brooks I fear
> My grasshopper of a boat,
> Wouldn't be able to bear
> The grief of such a heavy load.

Another example of her animated imagery of nature is illustrated in the following poem titled "To the Late Peony" (to the tune of "Celebrating the Clear Serene Dawn"):

> To seize the last days of spring,
> Palace curtains are suspending,
> Protected by exquisite crimson railing.
> Delicate, unadorned,
> Nature's very image untrampled!
> Let all other flowers hide away!
> To you alone the dewy breeze of morn bring
> A hundred charms after your early toilet

Envied by the wind and at the moon laughing.
In love with you God of Spring falling,
He has no wish to be departing.

Perfumed carriages jostle one and others,
Through the southern streets,
To Brook Side Hall where sun bathes
East of city hall.
Who can replace you after you become fragrant dust,
And when the banquet ends?
Let all the golden cups be drained,
And all the candles gutter and melt,
As the yellow twilight fall quietly disappears!
But miss not your branches,
That nestle beside the Palace of Brilliance!
In the sun's first soft embrace.

As Li Qingzhao created more vivid and animated imagery, her poetic expression became extremely suggestive and moving. Her "Sorrow of Separation" in the tune of "Yi jian mei" made a highly conventional theme sound refreshing:

The lotus has wilted, only a faint perfume remains,
On the bamboo mat a touch of autumn chill stays.
Softly I take off my silk dress,
Alone I step on board my skiff of orchid.
Who sent me the letter of Brocade
from beyond the clouds?
When the wild geese returns
The chamber will be filled with moonlight flooding.
Flowers drift away and falling,
On water flowing,
after their destiny.
This is our yearning
Both sides far apart enduring
A never-ending melancholy feeling.
Began from the eyebrow lifting,
In the heart continues surging.

"In Memoriam" (to the tune of "A Southern Song" [*"Nan ge zi"*] reads:

In heaven the Milky Way turns,
On earth hang low all curtains.
A chill creeps on to my pillow-mat
Damp with tears.
I sit up to unloosen my robe silk,
To myself idly ask:
"What is the hour of night?"

The kingfisher-embroidered lotus-pods are smaller,
The gold-stitched lotus leaves more sparse.
The same weather, the same clothes
As of old.
But quite another are my feelings
Than those of past years.

"Loneliness" (to the tune of "To Rouged the Lips") ["Dian jiang chun"]

Alone in my secluded chamber,
Sad thoughts made my heart ache.
Regret, soon spring will be fleeing.
Fine rain hastens petals falling.

Impossible to get out of this mood of sorrow,
Moving from one end of the balustrade to the other.
Where is he, my beloved?
I can't glimpse the road by which he might return,
Just withered grass touching where the farthest skies appear.

As emotional expression in poetry became increasingly refined, natural imagery fragmented further. It was no longer about a certain flower or its blooms; it had refocused upon a single element of that flower such as appearance (in parts, in whole, during different seasons or different time of the day), its fragrance, or its inner characteristics. As imagery became fragmented, it could project and juxtapose into an entirely different landscape. Li's "To the Cassia Flower" [to the tune of "Partridge Sky"] reads:

Fair flower!
Dark, pale, light and yellow,
Soft and gentle by nature.
Aloof and remote,
A subtle fragrance trails behind you.
What need for light green or deep crimson,
You have the best color of them all!

Let plum blossom be ashamed,
Chrysanthemums envious!
You are the queen of mid–Autumn crowned
at the grand exhibition of flowers.
How wrong Qu Yuan, the poet
To be toward you so cold,
As to deny you a post
In his masterpiece poem!

The secret of Li Qingzhao's success as a poet lies in her ability to enchant her readers with vivid imagery and rhythmic charm produced by original arrangement of words, mainly nouns and verbs. Many of her lines and phrases became engraved in the minds of millions because of their extreme emotional effect and their economy of words. For example, the half line of seven characters in the poem titled "Sorrow of Separation," "*hong ou xiang can yu tan qiu*" [The lotus has wilted, only a faint perfume remains; on the bamboo mat there is a touch of autumn chill], painted a lucid picture of four highly selective images. They depicted scenes both within and outside of the room: bamboo mat, autumn chill, wilted lotus and its faint perfume. This compact imagery portrayed her feelings of loneliness after her husband departed. This remarkable verbal succinctness reminded one of the poetics of Du Fu.

After three centuries of distillation and abstraction of poetic expression, the natural imagery during the Yuan dynasty became more vivid and provocative. In a way, if the Song era perfected poetry into vivid painting in verbal form, Yuan poetry began to give this painting movement. The following by Ming poet Yuan Zhongdao (1570–1623) projected a highly animated moonlight, an image which had stopped being static and became an activating natural force to create a chain of other images:

"Fountain in Moonlight"

> On lightened hills the birds begin their cries,
> Frozen with cold, frost on rock now lies.
> Steeped in moonlight, the fountain flows,
> They turn into a stream of snow.

As imagery began to move, it created a different kind of rhythm, the rhythm of feelings that played musical notes according to the flow of emotion. Poetry began again to imitate music, but this time, not as songs but a symphony which was played by many different instruments. The following poem, "Fallen Flowers" ["Luo Hua"], by Hao Jing (1223–1275), juxtaposed a variety of seemingly isolated imageries, which included movement, sound, and touch. These imageries, colored cloud, rainbow, petals of flowers, jade green, red rain, butterflies, breeze, (fragrances of) peach and plum, soul (of bird), moonlit hills, jade railing, chilly mist and bare trees, like instruments, played a music of sadness.

> Rainbow clouds darken door, red petals shower,
> On jadeite branch is the trace of fallen flower.
> Wind blows peach and plum to butterflies' dreams,
> On moonlit hills and northern walls a cuckoo cries.
> Jade railings stand in chilly mist among bare trees,
> Beauty is gone in Golden Val, wine can no longer please.
> Don't sweep the blooms in the yard away,
> Let vernal beauty stay until the end of the day!

The following poem by Liu Yi (1240–1293) added a voice into the symphony:

Full of the gloomy thoughts, I'm depressed and drear,
At dead of night I face the empty mountain high.
Cliffs are whitened by frost of autumn clear,
The moon appears o'er the clouds flooding the sky.
The rocky valley echoes with my stirring strain,
On wine flooded river of stars my shadow appears.
Drunken, I hear the ape whisper to the crane:
The world hasn't been so fair for o'er a hundred years!

Conclusions

Accumulated poetic expression was the key element that integrated Chinese literary language during and after the highly technical description of nature that occurred after Han. In poetry, like in painting, nature description had never been an end itself, but rather a means to illustrate the intention of the writer-poet. However, as the natural imagery became more refined and polished over time, the ability of poetic language to specify and elaborate emotional states increased. As language became more terse, efficient, and provocative, it could project more complex and distinct imagery of feelings.

7

Poetry on Stage

This chapter illustrates how literary poetry in China was refined on stage as it was reinterpreted and performed in musical theatre. From the Yuan dynasty, literary poetry that had been meditated and polished by intellectuals over the centuries became spoken (oral) poetry once again and its sound became engraved in the memories of millions through the media of theatrical performance. It became a language of presence (rather than only in the mind) through its song, dance, masks, costumes, body movements, and hand gestures. It was heard not only in literary and standard language but also in local vernaculars and regional dialects. This animation of poetry substantially increased the expressive power of Chinese language. On stage, poetry could be recited, sung, danced, and gestured in many different ways simultaneously or alternately, sometimes even by the same actor. As language was resurrected through speakers and singers, poetry returned to its origin, a form that was heard and seen, a form that had been lost in the writing process of previous years. Spoken words could provoke a more immediate reaction from an audience who became immersed in the personal expression of the performers.

Theatre also made it possible for the literary language to create more focused and dramatic plot, more intricate narrative, striking characterization, and more compound imagery. Unlike European theatre of the early modern period that relied on visual effect and lavish staging, Chinese theatre, a theatre of a mature literary tradition, employed only modest stage scenery and props. With highly polished performance, theatre provoked and captivated the imagination of the audience suggesting (rather than displaying) the connection between story line, acts, and interpersonal relations. The lack of visual cue provided ample opportunity for poetry to activate the emotion and intellect of spectators.

Initially poetry of the Yuan dynasty (1279–1368) took an innovative form: *sanqu* [separate songs]. Like ci of the Song dynasty, Yuan *sanqu* was sung. However, unlike the later Song poetry that had lost its music and had become formalized in structure (number of characters per line and rhyming schemes, for example), Yuan *sanqu* were sung individually or in groups in live theatre. Since music portrayed specific mood, Yuan tunes used a specific key or mode that dictated the content of the verse to some extent. Yuan music consisted of various kinds of inherited musical traditions, including the Tang dance music [*daqu*] and Song *ci* music. The former, a simple repetitive music with variations, had diminishing influence (under 10 percent of the Yuan musical repertoire) because it could not keep up with the increasing complexity and demand of poetry. Song *ci* music had more refined and specific tunes for various shades of emotion.

Yuan music further developed and refined these traditions and chained them together into *zhu gong diao* [set songs]. Dramatic narrative and theatrical performance became tools that linked separate songs to set songs. These sets had distinctive features and functions in storytelling, rather than a momentary mood as in Song *ci*. Sporadic dialogue on the stage also provided necessary linkages between songs and sets of songs and between lyrical and narrative expression. *Sanqu* lyrics were written to fixed musical modes and could contain several arias or lyrical song segments in one suite (similar to the instrumental piece in classical music). It could also be composed in single discreet sections.

Sanqu flourished in Yuan *zaju* [variety theatre or opera] that was popular at the time. The basic structural unit of musical drama, *qu* (song or aria), that gave momentum to the spread of *sanqu* could be separate or woven into a play. Many of the tunes were the same and could be used both in arias of drama and as stand-alone songs. Unlike Song *ci* poets, *sanqu* writers often wrote long song sets [*diao shu*] (a separate group of songs) as the basic form of a scene in drama. Sets were not unique to the Yuan. However, they had never before been so well organized in a musical format or so intrinsic a part of composing verse. Single songs [*xiao ling*] (a single tune standing by itself, as opposed to sets of songs) comprise the majority of *sanqu* that have survived. It was a lyrical form that could be relatively easily executed even for the casual writer. Songs in sets had to be in the same mode and have the same rhyme throughout, which required considerable skill in versification though set phrases and clichés. Conventional subject matter made composition less arduous.[1]

There were perhaps a dozen or so major writers of *sanqu*. The most outstanding among them are Ma Zhiyüan (1250–1321), Guan Hanqing (1225–1302?), Bai Renfu (1226–1306), Qiao Ji (d. 1345) and Zhang Kejiu (1317?). Zhang Kejiu left behind songs that demonstrated his exceptionally polished style and mastery of allusion, greatly admired in later times. Li Kaixian (1502–

1568), the leading critic of the Ming dynasty, referred to him as the Du Fu of *sanqu*. The strongest characteristics of his verse were the descriptive power of his lines and his ability to evoke a subtle mood. His use of classical phraseology and allusion was more like that of earlier poets who employed the *shi* or *ci* forms. It was his refined style that made his poems very popular among Ming and Qing writers.[2]

If Ming critics considered that Zhang Kejiu as the Du Fu of *sanqu*, then Qiao Ji was their Li Bai. He was in the entertainment world for forty years, "a scholar of the mists and clouds, the drunken sage of the lakes and streams."[3] A long-standing friendship with a lady inspired many poems and his relationship with her invested these works with special significance. In his poem "Song of Hands" ["*Yung shou*"], slightly conflicting imagery becomes beautifully evocative in her hands "secretly give rise to spring [i.e., feelings of love]" in an otherwise innocent and casual scene, as they reach up to adjust her hair, are "painfully lovely."[4] In a comparison of his verse to the work of Zhang Kejiu, it is often easier to discover a voice behind his lines and to envision the individual in them.

Guan Hanqing, one of the four great Yuan dramatists, was best known for his plays; however, his stylistic excellence carries over to fifty-seven separate songs and thirteen song sets. In these he wrote mainly about the sadness of parting or the longing of love. He was capable of evoking vivid emotions, as in the last three lines of "*Bie qing*" ("Parting"): "The stream winds away, / The hill screens the view, / And you are gone." In a set of nine songs he recounted a clandestine tryst of two young lovers.[5] The first four songs describe a young man who waited outside the window as agreed, saw no sign of the one he desired, and was afraid someone would discover him standing under the shadows of the flowers. Just as he was about to give up she appeared, looking as beautiful as he had dreamed. As their passions rose, the earth became their couch, the moon their lamp: "A pleasant breeze opens the peony ... a moment, shuddering, they lie languid." In the last song, the young lady straightens her hair and, as she is about to return to her boudoir, she suggested, "Maybe you could come a bit earlier tomorrow." One of his best-known song sets was "*Bu fu lao*" ["Refusal to Get Old"].[6] He portrayed himself as someone who was still able to do all that the young could do, and even better. He vowed never to stop his drinking, singing, and loving of women until the god of hell, Yama, ordered his soul to be drawn out of him and consigned to oblivion.[7]

Ma Zhiyuan wrote fifteen plays of which seven survive, but he also left 115 songs and 16 song sets. In these there are two exceptional poems, both called "*Qiu Si*" ["Autumn Thoughts"]. One was a short descriptive poem composed as a tour de force almost entirely in noun phrases expressing a sentiment of perennial interest to the Chinese: a traveler looking at a pleasant and tranquil evening scene and thinking of home. Many poems can be compared to this, the best-known *sanqu*, but few surpass it:

> Over old trees wreathed with rotten vines fly evening crows,
> Under a small bridge near a cottage a stream flows,
> On ancient road a lean horse goes walking into the wind that blows.
> On the west is the sinking sun,
> Far, far from home is the heartbroken one.

In Ma's other "Autumn Thoughts" song set, the world-weary poet set forth questions about life and fame. His conclusion was that seclusion was the best. He began by describing how life passed as if in a dream: spring was here today and flowers withered tomorrow, so one should drink quickly: "It is getting late and the lamp is dying." What becomes of the great, he asked, and their palaces? What good was wealth if one must be a slave to it? Now he too had reached the end of life, his hair was white, and his days were few; if others laughed, then he had played the fool well in his time. But now there was no time for fame and "the world no longer vexed me here"; his life was simple, nature was his domain, and his days were filled by it. If anyone asked, he was drunk beneath the east hedge.[8]

Some of his best descriptive songs painted scenes in his readers' minds. For example, *"Yuan pu fan gui"* ["Returning Sails"] included the usual static tableau: an evening scene, the sun setting, the flag drooping outside a wine shop, boats slowly coming to shore, and evening settling over the rooftops. The last line surprised the reader, "At the old bridge, fishmongers leave for home." One almost hears, as if in the distance, the quiet gathering up of things and a few words of farewell. As he describes the warm weather which brings with it spring fever, even the butterflies are too lazy to play and the birds are too tired to sing. "No wonder the fallen petals hardly stir, the evening breezes lack the strength."[9]

Another important writer of the period is Bai Renfu (1226–1306). Fifteen plays have been attributed to him, of which three have corresponding extant editions: *The Tale of East Wall* [*Dong-qiang ji*], *Over the Wall and on Horseback* [*Qiangtou mashang*], and "Paulownia Rain" [*Wutong Yu*]. The last was based on Bai Juyi's long poem "A Song of Unending Sorrow." It further enriched the love story between Emperor Xuanzong of Tang and his consort Yang Guifei by adding social and moral content. Enchanted by Lady Yang, Emperor Xuanzong indulged himself in seeking pleasure all day long. He appointed Lady Yang's elder brother, Yang Guozhong, as the first prime minister and bestowed the title of ladyship upon her three sisters. Then Yang Guifei and Xuanzong took a vow to the stars of Vega and Altair in the Palace of Longevity that they would never betray each other.

In order to please his lady, Emperor Xuanzong once spent a large amount of money and manpower to transport fresh lychees from Hainan Province to the capital city, Chang'an. The horses kept running for thousands of miles, destroying plants along the roads and kicking innocent people to death. Attracted by Lady Yang alone, Emperor Xuanzong paid less and less attention to the running of the empire. Instead, Yang Guozhong (the brother of Lady Yang) and An Lushan were given more and more power. Eventually, An Lushan launched a rebellion, and Emperor Xuanzong, along with his trusted ministers, was forced to flee Chang'an. On the way, his escort troops launched a mutiny and demanded that the chief criminals, Yang Guozong and Lady Yang, be put to death. The emperor had no choice but to have Lady Yang strangled with a bridle rein. Before her death, Lady Yang confessed her deep regrets to god and was forgiven.

Emperor Xuanzong then went back to Chang'an and suppressed An Lushan's rebellion. Although he had recovered his throne, Xuanzong could not help missing the late Lady Yang and cried with great sorrow day and night. When the bells rang or the moon rose he would only sink deeper in his despair. He was often seen crying before the statue of Lady Yang. Finally, the goddess Vega, granddaughter of the Emperor of Heaven, was moved and arranged their reunion in the Moon Palace. This became one of the most celebrated Yuan *zaju* and also a rare example among traditional dramas of a predominantly tragic motif. During the next centuries this story has been rewritten and repeatedly adapted in a variety of Chinese theatres, including the Peking opera.

Guan Yunshi (1286–1324) was one of the best *sanqu* poets. His themes tended toward romantic love and parting; some verses expound on the carefree life. His strongest quality was his mastery of language. Although he had much of the smoothness of Zhang Kejiu, his phrasing was sometimes more colorful and imaginative. The best illustration of this was the nine terse verb phrases in three lines of a song describing two blissful lovers who forgot time and were surprised by the sounding of the dawn watch.[10] Guan's "A Quilt of Reed Catkins" ["*Lu hua bei*"] demonstrates his imagery:

> The reed catkins you gathered are now clean,
> They used to fill my quilt straw cloak green.
> Western wind blows my dreams to autumn boundless,
> I am covered with fragrant snow by light moon shade.
> My hair and bones grow old with the earth and sky,
> My fame won't fade in time or modern sages high.

Don't envy silk quilt on which the love birds sing!
For in a fisherman's song emerges another spring.

Zhang Yanghao (1270–1329) was one of the *sanqu* writers whose 161 songs and 2 song sets were preserved in a separate anthology. The poems and songs from his later life were deeply moving. He witnessed the helplessness of mankind at the hands of fate and bad government[11]:

"Thought on the Past at Tong Pass"

As if gathered together, the peaks of the ranges.
As if raging, the waves on these banks.

Winding along these mountains and rivers,
the road to Tong Pass.
I look west and lament hesitant,
Where opposing armies passed.
Palaces of countless rulers, now but dust.
Empires rise, people suffer.
Empires fall, people suffer.

Like the Italian opera, Yuan opera emerged from ritual and street performance. At the turn of the Song (960–1279) and Yuan (1279–1368) dynasties, regional theatre became the main vehicle for artistic creation. *Zaju* [variety theatre] was developed from *yuanben* [drama in written form] and *zhugongdiao* [all modes of tunes] in North China, while *nanxi* [southern opera] prevailed in the south. During the period between the 14th and 17th centuries, Chinese theatre evolved into two major types: *chuanqi* [romance play] and *zaju* [variety drama], each of which had distinct artistic features. The average chuanqi was characterized by 30 to 50 changes of scene and the frequent and free change of end rhymes in arias. Singing parts were probably more languorous than those of zaju and were distributed among many actors, not just the hero and heroine. Plots were often taken from popular accounts of historical figures or from contemporary life. In the Ming Dynasty (1368–1644), the term *chuanqi* was used to denote romance plays, like *The Moonlight Pavilion* and *Tale of the Lute*. Ming critics noted the differences between *zaju* and *chuanqi*.

Zaju had a northern accent, while *chuanqi* carried a southern tone. There were only four acts and a single singer in each *zaju*, while in *chuanqi*, there were more acts and more actors for different singing roles. *Zaju* focused on one event and was usually short and concise. In contrast, *chuanqi* described the entire life of the character and often left a lingering aftertaste. As time passed, *chuanqi* grew in popularity while *zaju* declined. The orchestral instruments for *zaju* were not loud enough to spread far and wide, whereas the *chuanqi* music was accompanied by resounding and lively drumbeats, attracting a wider audience.

Over time, the term *chuanqi* underwent several changes in its connotations. For instance, the classical Chinese short stories of the Tang Dynasty were also called *chuanqi*. But in drama, this term was specified to mean a long play with standardized literary patterns and regular musical schemes. The scripts of *chuanqi* were often stories with intricate and fantastic plots and detailed descriptions of emotions and romances designed to achieve thrilling and dramatic effects.

The scripts of *chuanqi* could be sung in diverse local tunes of different regions. Four major tunes prevailed in the South (the areas south of the Yangtze River) by the end of the Yuan Dynasty and the beginning of the Ming Dynasty (1368–1644). These tunes were the "Yuyao," "Haiyan," "Yiyang," and "Kunshan," whose names derived from the names of the four regions from which they initially emerged. The *Kunshan* tune was applied to singing *chuanqi* scripts and the singers simply sang the arias without wearing stage make-up. Singing as a part of the dramatic performance came later. *Kunqu* opera (opera sung in "Kunshan" tune) developed into a mature opera genre only after the reform of the Kunshan tune. The local tunes of Yuyao, Haiyan, and Yiyang areas used to be more popular than the Kunshan tune. The Haiyan tune used the official language and its elegance catered well to the scholar-officials and the literati. The Yiyang tune was welcomed by the common people for its sonorous liveliness accompanied by gongs and drums. The style of the Kunshan tune was similar to that of the Haiyan tune, though not as exquisite.

The first Yuan theatres were constructed as round stages surrounded by tiered seats, like a circus. The show began with the sound of loud gongs and drums to attract the audience. Before the main drama started, a clown performed. He wore a colorful cloth robe, a black kerchief around his head, and a long pin through his hair. His face was made up in black and white. He sang, danced and performed various conjuring tricks. The opera then began, to the accompaniment of music played on traditional stringed and woodwind instruments.

Although Yuan opera had no unified form or structure, the performances were strictly ordered. Performances proceeded continuously, with no curtain rise or fall between acts. Dramas were in four acts — a beginning, a small climax, a big climax, and the finale. Sometimes the show went on for days.

Zaju performances comprised both singing and talking. Only the leading actor or actress sang while the minor characters either spoke or just appeared and acted in mime. At present about 160 Yuan *zaju* manuscripts have been discovered, a small portion of the estimated 450 to 700 recorded or noted dramatic *zaju* titles attributed to writers of this period.

Nanxi [theatre of the south] evolved from ancient traditions of mime, singing, and dancing during the Song Dynasty of the 12th century. It began as a combination of Song plays and local folk songs and ballads, and used colloquial language and a large number of scene changes. As with Western operetta, spoken passages alternated with verses [*qu*] set to popular music. Professional companies of actors performed nanxi in theatres that could hold thousands of spectators.

Nanxi had seven role types, many of which were inherited by later Chinese opera forms. *Sheng* was the heroic male character and *dan*, the heroine. *Mo, jing, chou, wai,* and *hou* (also called *tie*) were less defined roles, and actors in these role types could portray a variety of characters in the same play. Later forms of Chinese opera, tracing their nanxi roots, further clarified these roles and gave them strict definition.[14] Unlike the later and more polished operas, *nanxi* used coarse language, rough prosody, and unsophisticated literary style. Its theatrical form disappeared and was replaced by more modern theatres during the mid–16th century. *Nanxi* developed into a more complex dramatic form known as *chuanju* [Sichuan opera] during the end of the Ming dynasty (1368–1644) and the beginning of Qing (1644–1911).

Compared to other forms of regional theatre, *chuanju* was more dramatic than operatic. Its performance was highly polished. Face (mask) changing and gesture highlighted the action. An actor could change more than 10 masks in less than 20 seconds. By raising the hand, swinging a sleeve or tossing the head, he used different masks to show different emotions, expressing invisible and intangible feelings through visible and tangible masks. From green to blue, red, yellow, brown, black, and gold, these masks portrayed fear, tension, relaxation, slyness, desperation, outrage, and so on.

Kunqu (*Kunju*) was another of the oldest and yet most refined styles of traditional Chinese theatre. It was a synthesis of drama, opera, dance, poetry choral, and musical recital, which drew from earlier forms of Chinese theatrical performances such as mime, farce, acrobatics, ballad recital, and medley, some of which went back to the third century BC. In a *kunqu* performance, recitative is interspersed with arias sung to traditional melodies, called *qupai* [song tune], which were the same as the tune titles of the ci poetry. Each word or phrase is also accompanied by a stylized movement or gesture that is essentially part of a dance, with strict rules of style and execution, much like classical ballet. Even casual gestures must be precisely executed and timed to coordinate with the music and percussion. The refinement of the movement is further enhanced with stylized costumes that also serve as simple props.

The basic rules of the musical form of *kunqu* were established by Master Wei Liangfu around 1530 in his *Qu lü* [*Principles of Kunqu Singing*]. Originally, Wei was a student of the Northern singing style and turned to refine nanxi.

He completely reinvented nanqu [song of the south] and turned it from a plain and straightforward song tradition into a sophisticated and subtle singing. He could sing smoothly through various vocal ranges and intervals like "waves of silk." Wei's book summarized his technique of singing and became an important theoretical guide for the vocal training of Chinese opera. His advice inspired generations of kunqu singers and actors.

The Wei reform of the "Kunshan" tune covered three aspects. The first aspect was the improvement of its singing techniques. It was required that the modulation should abide by the rules of the level, rising, falling and entering tones, the four tones of classical Chinese pronunciation and intonation. As Wei Liangfu put it in his book, the five notes of music were based on the four tones of the classical Chinese language. If an actor could not articulate the four tones correctly, he would not be able to sing the five music notes successfully. An actor should study the level, rising, falling and entering tones one by one to make sure that he could pronounce them precisely and properly. If he was not careful enough and made mistakes, his singing would not be pleasant to the ear. He also demanded that an actor be precise in articulating the consonant, the vowel and the last syllabic sound (designated respectively as the head, the end, and the tail by kunqu specialists) in each Chinese character in the three stages of producing, dragging out and ending the sound. Only by so doing could the actor reach the standard of "being suave and mellow when starting to sing and being melodious and smooth when drawing it to an end."[12]

The second aspect of the reform lay in the innovation of the original tune, processing the chanting with more elaboration to make it sound softer and finer. This is the reason that the refined tune was referred to as the milling tune (as if being polished finely with a water mill) by critics. The third aspect was to incorporate more vigorous elements into the "Kunshan" tune. A southern tune in origin, the "Kunshan" tune used to be more gentle than strong. As a result, it could not fully express ardent emotions. In the course of the reform, using his training in Northern singing, Wei compensated this weakness by drawing on many elements from northern dramas to make the "Kunshan" tune more forceful and expressive.

From the perspective of musical accompaniment, Wei Liangfu and other artists enlarged and modified the traditional orchestra by picking the essence out of the various zithers, wood and bamboo pipes, drums and clappers from both the northern and southern dramas. A new form of the accompanying band was introduced, with string, wind, and percussion instruments.

The reformed "Kunshan" tune captured people's attention with its clear, soft, pleasant and harmonious effect and soon became very popular. Before long, Liang Chenyu (1521–1594) tried the new tune on the stage in his play *Wansha ji* [*The Tale of Silk Washing*], which became the first chuanju play sung in the reformed "Kunshan" tune. It was an instant success and spread all over the country. Thereafter, the "Kunshan" tune became all the rage and soon developed from a single tune into a nation-wide major operatic form. People then began to call the tune kunqu opera.

Following the success of *Washing Silk*, many famous *chuanju* playwrights started to write scripts for kunqu opera, which in turn improved both stage acting and aria-singing without stage makeup. The fifty years (1570–1620) under the reign of the Ming Emperor Wanli witnessed the expansion of *kunqu* opera during which a large number of writers and excellent works came to the fore. Great dramatists like Tang Xianzu (1550–1616) and Xu Fuzuo (1560–1629) emerged in this period. They produced many famous works that have survived for centuries: *The Peony Pavilion* [*Mu Dan Ting*], *The Nanke Dream* [*Nanke meng*] and *The Handan Dream* [*Handan meng*], *The Tale of the Gallant Hero* [*Yi xia ji*], *The Tale of Red Pear Blossoms* [*Hong li ji*], *The Tale of the Jade Hairpin* [*Yu zhan ji*], and *The Tale of Red Plums* [*Hong mei ji*]. Records verify that more than two hundred dramatic scripts were written. [13]

Composition and performance were complex matters. First of all, the script had to be read and reread thoroughly, and the tones and rhymes were analyzed systematically. The oblique tones had to be clearly distinguished into the rising, the falling and the entering, and the two level tones into yin and yang. Efforts had to be made to ensure a good understanding of the settings, arias, recitations, emotions and plots. All the tunes and words had to be studied in accordance with the context. Actors had to submerge themselves into the roles so as to perform naturally. Actors' facial expressions, such as smiles and frowns, ought to follow precisely with the plots. Successful performances had to be true to life, bringing forth emotional reaction from the audience.

Mirror of the Heart, a guild book for acting, advised that an actor should take his own heart as a mirror and examine his performance in the "mirror" to ascertain ways that his portrayal could improve. The chapter "Ten Defects of Acting" was of key importance. In addition, there were also chapters on the "Six Musts of Recitation" and "Eight Musts of Postures." *The Treasure Mountain*, with six guiding principles, was a supplement. This thorough exposition gave a theoretical summary of the kunqu opera performance from various aspects covering singing, reciting, acting, dancing, hand gestures, eye movements, body postures, techniques of maneuvering the body and gait.

During the Qianlong Period of the Qing Dynasty (1736–1795), the costumes and stage props of kunqu opera were finally standardized. They were designed and formed into suites for the convenience of stage performance, and were symbolic rather than copies of contemporary or historical style. In this way, the same costumes and stage props could be used at any time, regardless of the historical period of the staged story. In addition, the makeup of kunqu opera also became strictly standardized into *junban* [light makeup], *lianpu* [face painting], *bianlian* [rapid change of masks], and *rankou* [whiskers]. As for the stage itself, it was usually shaped with three facets exposed to the audience. The backstage was separated from the exposed parts by a bulkhead. On the back wall of the stage hung a heavy decorative curtain called a *taiman*. On each side of the stage there was a door used for entrances and exits. Horizontal inscription boards and vertical boards of couplets hung not only on the upper part and both sides of the stage, but also on each pillar. A desk and two chairs might be the only stage props when the play was intended to show an indoor setting. If the plot took place in an outdoor setting, there could be either nothing at all on the stage, or a feint bridge, pavilion, tower or city entrance signified by a few desks and chairs. Such a stage format was shaped out of the Chinese tradition of placing actors in the central position, highlighting an important feature of Chinese drama performance. This system was standardized in kunqu opera.

Strictly speaking, the name *kunqu* refers to the musical element of this theatrical performance. *Kun* refers to Kunshan and *qu* means music. The name derived from the fact that one of the principal types of regional music that went into the making of kunqu came from the district of Kunshan near Suzhou, in Jiangsu Province. This type of regional music dates back to the 14th century. It was expanded in the 16th century by Wei Liangfu and others who combined it with three other forms of southern music and with northern tunes from the drama of the Yuan dynasty. Wei Liangfu and his collaborators standardized the rules of rhyme, tone, pronunciation, and notation, making it possible for this regional form of music to become a national standard. By the end of the 16th century, kunqu spread from the Suzhou region to the rest of China, and for the next 200 years was the most prestigious form of Chinese drama.

Kunqu was first and foremost a performing art. Performances were valued not only for their riveting synthesis of drama, singing and dancing, but also for the literary refinement of their poetic libretto. The plot was usually familiar to the audience, or else made available through a prose summary. In fact, most *kunqu* plays would take several days to perform in their entirety. So any given performance generally consisted of a few selected scenes from one or more well-known plays. In a *kunqu* performance, three media worked simultaneously and in harmony to convey the meaning and desired esthetic effect:

music, words, and dance. An accomplished *kunqu* performer had to master the special styles of singing and dance movement to convey the meaning of its poetry.

There were two easily distinguished styles of text and music. Arias, sung and accompanied by the orchestra, were elaborate poems of high literary quality. Prose passages (monologues and dialogues) were neither sung nor spoken but chanted in a stylized fashion comparable to the recitative of Western opera. Sometimes there was a combination of the two styles wherein one of the characters sang while another one chanted in response or in unison.

The language of *kunqu* was not the dialect of Kunshan or Suzhou as people might assume, nor was it standard Mandarin. It was an artificial stage language, a modified Mandarin with some features of the local dialect. Since the language in which *kunju* plays were written had eight tones (rather than four tones of the regulated poetry), the composition of the libretto was a complex undertaking. Typically, the author had to continuously refine the libretto and musical notes until the word melody of libretto and the melody of the set song fell into harmony. In fact, an ideal harmony was seldom fully realized. Since the creation of a new *kunqu* play presented such a great challenge to the author, almost all kunqu playwrights were poets themselves. The libretto typically had significant esthetic value in its own right, and many *kunqu* libretti were highly regarded as examples of refined Chinese literature.

In addition to music and words, dance movements and highly stylized gestures formed an integral part of the performance. As in classical ballet, the whole body of the actor was engaged, but the movement was much more grounded. The movements conveyed an intricate language of gestures and body movements that was similar but much more complex and extensive than the mime of classical ballet. Although the meaning of some movements was immediately understood even by the uninitiated, other movements were stylized and conventional, involving not only the body but also the costume (especially the sleeves) and props held in the hand, such as a fan.

As in all traditional Chinese theatre, and modern and contemporary Western theatre as well, *kunqu* used a minimum of props and scenery. This permitted the performers to more easily express their stage movements in the form of dance. The performers appealed to the audience's imagination and conjured up a scene or a setting (such as a door, a horse, a river, a boot) with words, gestures, and music. The costumes were elaborate exaggerated versions of the style of dress during the Ming Dynasty and made no attempt to fit the period or place of the action. For instance, in many roles, the performers wore robes with extremely long white sleeves called "water sleeves," which essentially served as props to accent their dance movements. One of the signs of accomplished *kunqu* performance is the skill with which the players manipulate their water sleeves and fans to enhance movement.

The costumes and simple props often conveyed additional information about character. Peonies on a young man's robe might indicate a playboy, or the carrying of a magnifying glass might indicate social blindness. A Buddhist nun always carried a duster to ward off evil spirits.

The meaning and comprehension of *kunqu* performances was further enhanced by well-defined role types. These roles differ not only in the type of character (young man, young woman, clown, etc.) but also in the vocal requirements and the form in which the body is presented. In fact, the stylized movement associated with each role type constitutes an art form in itself. The three most popular types of roles in *kunqu* are young women [*dan*], young men (scholar or civil officer) [*sheng*], and the clowns [*qao*]. Other important role types include the old man role [*lao sheng*], old woman role [*lao dan*], and the painted face [*jing*].

A small instrumental ensemble, generally consisting of 6 to 10 musicians, accompanied the *kunqu* performance. This ensemble was divided into two sections: *wen-chang*, the section composed of wind and string instruments, and *wu-chang*, the percussion section. The primary function of *wen-chang* was to accompany singing, led by the *dizi* (a horizontal bamboo flute). Depending on the play, it might also include a *san xian* [a three-stringed lute], an *erhu* [a two-stringed fiddle], a *sheng* [a bamboo wind organ or pan pipe], and a *zither*. The *wu-chang* section consisted of a Chinese *xiqu* drum, *ban* [wooden clappers], *xiao luo* [small gong], *da luo* [big gong], and *nao bo* (cymbals). It was led by a drummer who performed with a small drum and a pair of wooden clappers to set the pace of the play, while the gongs and cymbals were used to punctuate the action and emotion. The drummer was also the conductor of the orchestra.

Kunqu was and remains the most refined and literary of all forms of Chinese theatre, and reached its peak during the periods under the reigns of Emperor Kangxi (r. 1661–1722) and Emperor Qianlong (r. 1736–1795). However, it started to wane in the periods of Emperor Daoguang (r. 1820–1850) and Emperor Guangxu (r. 1875–1908). Toward the middle of the 18th century, Peking opera emerged. With the support of the Emperor Qianlong, it quickly began to supersede *kunqu*.

Peking opera retains many of the features of *kunqu*, but uses fewer and less sophisticated sets of melodies. It also uses different lead instruments in the accompanying orchestra. For example, while the bamboo flute was the main accompaniment to *kunqu* singing, it was generally the *jin-hu* (a string instrument with a louder sound) that provided the principal accompaniment of singing in Peking opera. To broaden its public appeal, Peking opera also added acrobatic elements. There were no acrobatic movements in a traditional *kunqu* play, and instead, all of the martial art (fighting) movements were expressed in dance form.[14]

A more subtle difference between *kunqu* theatre and Peking opera was the type of stories and the way that they were presented. In all Chinese theatre, the basic plot was generally based on some historical event or well known story that had been told and retold repeatedly for many centuries. However, the plots of *kunqu* tended to focus more on human relationships and the inner life of an individual, while Peking opera focused more on public moral conduct. Peking opera also reduced the vocal requirements for some of the role types. For example, in Peking opera, the clown role rarely sang, relying almost exclusively on spoken dialogue. In *kunqu* theatre, vocal quality was an essential requirement of each of the major roles, with subtle difference in the vocal technique required for the clown, young man, and young woman roles.

Contrary to what its name might suggest, Peking opera did not originate in Beijing. Like the majority of Chinese theatrical forms (there were more than three hundred of them), Peking opera evolved from the amalgamation of Anhui opera (*huiju*) and the Han opera of the south. In the process, it absorbed facets of other theatrical arts (such as the popular local drama genres, *bangzi*, Beijing tune, *kunqu* opera and native dialects) to develop into an entirely new type of opera. The forerunner of this amalgamation was the Anhui theatre troupes who went to Beijing in 1790 to perform at an imperial party in honor of Emperor Qianlong's birthday and continued to perform afterwards in Beijing. When Han opera (Han tune) from Hubei province arrived in Beijing in 1828, it combined with Anhui opera and Peking opera was born. Han opera was a local opera popular around the Hanshui River in Hubei Province which began to circulate into Beijing at the end of Emperor Qianlong's reign. There had already been frequent mutual exchanges between Anhui opera and Han opera. So when the Han opera actors went to Beijing, they joined the Anhui troupes there rather than set up their own troupes for performances. This merger made it possible for the performers to combine elements of two forms of theatre.[15]

The major tunes of Han opera were *xipi* and *erhuang*. *Xipi* was derived from *bangzi* opera in Northwest China. *Erhuang* originated from Jiangxi Province, spread into Anhui, and extended further into the provinces of Hunan, Hubei and Guangxi. This explained why the two tunes were also jointly called the *hu-guang* tune. *Xipi* was a northern melody, whereas *erhuang* was from the south. Having been polished by actors from Hanshui and Anhui, the two were merged into *pi-huang* tune (sometimes referred to as Han tune or Chu tune). The following statement reflected how delighted the contemporary artists and critics were about the new operatic creation[16]:

> With instruments of *yueqin, xianzi* and *huqin,*
> What a perfect harmony they are reaching!
> The tune shifts so well with the plots,
> With joy it smiles, when sad, it deplores.
> For singing, fandiao's sad tune sounds weeping,
> *erhuang* chants slowly, and *xipi* goes sweeping;
> *Daoban* pitches high, and *pingban* falls down,
> Each sound is round, clear and dragged far and long.

Popular around Hankou (presently Wuhan in Hubei province), the Han tune began to circulate throughout China. Although the *pi-huang* tune did exist in Anhui opera, it was not fully developed. The merger of the Hanshui and Anhui troupes enriched and reformed the Anhui opera tunes. As a result, the performance given by the Anhui troupes gradually changed from a jumble of different tunes into a new musical form with *pi-huang* as the main melodic form. As for the techniques of singing and reciting, the rules in the book *Pronunciation in Central China* became the standard. The local pronunciation in Hubei was maintained for the four tones, and some Beijing accents were assimilated to promote communication between the actors and the audience. Thus the criterion for performances by the Anhui troupes was established.

It took between fifty and sixty years for Peking opera to establish its own characteristics in theatrical programs, tunes, articulation and performing arts. In terms of music, an integrated system had been worked out by the Anhui opera troupes. In this system, the *pi-huang* tune played a major role, and the auxiliary tunes were the "Kunshan" tune. At that time, the tunes and beats of both *xipi* and *erhuang* had become quite sophisticated. As for the pronunciation on stage, the acquisition and assimilation of the Beijing accent became a new feature. During the reigns of Emperor Daoguang and Emperor Xianfeng (r. 1850–1861), the Beijing dialect was gradually absorbed into Anhui and Han operas in the capital and finally became an integral part of the performances.

At that time, some regular patterns of pronunciation had been fixed, for example, "*shisan zhe,*" "*yunbai,*" "*shangkou zi*" and "*jiantuan zi.*" Shisan zhe was a set of thirteen rhyming categories for singing and reciting verses in dramas. They were based on the characteristics of the Anhui dialect, the Hankou dialect and some Beijing pronunciation. *Yunbai* was a unique way to articulate dialogues on the stage in the four tones of classical Chinese. It drew on the opera tunes of Anhui, Hankou and Kunshan, with the Hubei dialect as the strongest element. It also employed the characteristics of the Beijing dialect to sound more melodious and understandable to the Beijing audience. The term *shangkou zi* referred to a special way to articulate *yunbai* in Beijing opera. Actually, it retained traces of certain local pronunciation from *kunqu* opera and Hankou opera during the development of Peking opera, and incorporated a blend of the three source dialects. In short, *shangkou zi* was a unique phonetic standard for stage. *Jiantuan zi* referred to another standard to pronounce the initial consonants of some Chinese characters. The correct way to pronounce *jiantuan zi* was mandated in *Pronunciation in Central China* that outlined the correct singing and reciting of northern dramas. This combination of the Beijing accent and the hu-guang dialects (the dialects of Hunan, Hubei, Guangdong and Guangxi provinces) finally brought about the standardization of singing and speaking in Peking opera.

Scripts that were specifically written for Peking opera mushroomed. In fact about 3,800 titles were specifically written, although only a small number were actually staged. The themes of these operas were broad, with politics and history as the favorite topics. Most of the classical pieces of Peking opera, such as *The Injustice Done to Dou E, Zhao Family Orphan, The West Chamber, River-Watching Pavilion, Zhaojun Goes Out of the Pass,* and *Attending a Meeting Single-Handed,* were adapted from Yuan zaju and its recent regional theatres. However, Peking opera had some distinctive features as compared with the pi-huang scripts. For example, the language of Peking opera was clear and standardized, with fewer dialects. Peking opera used formalized stage settings and props, costumes, and make-up, which made it stand out from regional productions.[17]

Peking opera followed the traditions of classical Chinese operas. Initially, there were five major characters: *sheng, dan, jing, mo,* and *chou.* Later, *sheng* and *mo* merged into one (*sheng*). The characters of opera were and still are divided into four major role types according to their sexes, personalities, ages, occupations and social status. Different role types employed specific features in their singing, reciting, dancing and body gesture routines.[18]

Sheng was a general type of male role that was subdivided into *lao sheng* [middle-aged man], *xiao sheng* [young man], *wu sheng* [martial man], *hong sheng* [man with red face], and *wawa sheng* [little boys]. Different types of *sheng* were identified by different types of makeup or painted masks. Except for *hong sheng* and *wu sheng,* the other *sheng* types had *jun ban* [handsome make-up]. Their facial paint was very light to make the figures look good. *Lao sheng* wore a beard representing a middle aged or old male's performance that specialized in singing, acting or acrobatic fighting. *Xiao sheng* did not wear whiskers and their stage appearance was usually delicate and handsome, even feminine in a Western sense. In stage singing, they applied both true voice and falsetto, a specially trained voice which sounded shrill and high-pitched like the tenor in Italian opera. *Xiao sheng* could also be subdivided into *wen xiao sheng* [civilian role] and *wu xiao sheng* [martial role]. The civil type could be further classified into *xiao sheng* wearing gauze hats, usually young scholarly officials. *Xiao sheng* holding a fan was usually a figure in a love story, who impressed the audience with his easy and elegant bearing. *Xiao sheng* with two long feathers on his head as decoration was usually handsome and had a martial bearing. *Wu xiao sheng* could be further divided into those in long garments, wielding a long weapon, and those in short costumes, fighting at close range with short weapons.

Dan actors played different types of female roles with different social statuses, ages and personalities. The roles of *dan* were divided into *qingyi*, *huadan*, *wudan* and *laodan*. Their different costumes in various colors signified moral and social status. *Qingyi* [literally black garment] played the role of young or middle-aged female characters who were usually morally righteous, demure, and dignified, such as understanding wives, loving mothers, and chaste widows. *Huadan*'s role was lively and cheerful young girls with witty minds and quick motions. Most *huadan* actors wore short costumes like short gowns, short trousers, short coats and short skirts, always in bright colors. They also often lived in the bottom of society and had loose moral consciences. *Laodan* referred to the matriarch, and *wudan* was a female who excelled in the martial arts.[19]

Most Peking opera scripts were written anonymously and devised by actors who treated them as vehicles to display their own performance skills. Many of them have never been published and existed as private possessions of the performers. As they were performance (rather than script) driven, even published plays contained no directional instruction or description of action. The only things recorded were the words that were spoken and sung in performance, the plot and descriptions of the characters.

Most of the plot was not original, but was inherited from the *chuanqi* plays of *kunqu* and other familiar stories that had been played by older theatres before *kunqu*, such as *nanxi* and Yuan *zaju*. In other words, Chinese theatre kept reviving and reactivating the traditional themes, plots, and characters. The difference that each theatrical form as well as each new production presented was rooted in the original ways in which the plot was delivered and characters were portrayed through acting. As for each performance, it was not about the words and their meanings but rather about how the words were spoken, sung, and gestured (delivered).

On stage, a character could give the spoken language colorful and multiple meanings by the skillful use of gesture, mask, body movement, and tone change. There was a lot of repetition in Peking opera. However, unlike the primitive poetic repetition that simply made up the rhythm (a chant), repetition in opera served by adding more shades, color, and imagery to the emotions of the characters.

Drunken Imperial Concubine is one of the most frequently performed Peking operas. It portrays the emotional ups and downs of Lady Yang (Yuhuan), the most favored concubine in Chinese history. Yang's singing carries the entire scene, often performed entirely without or with only minimal staging. As her words describe what she sees (such as the moon, the Moon Goddess, the moon-light world, the birds and geese) and how she feels (happy, beautiful, depressed, drunkenly confused and lonely), the audience can see and feel through the gestures of her eyes, hands, arms, feet, and dance movements with white sleeves and a peony fan.[20] This was one of the masterpieces by Mei Lan-Fang, the best known performer of Peking opera. Mei had made this play famous with his vivid portrayal of Yang's disappointment, her drunken charm, and her shameless display of her beauty.[21] The following script illustrates how this performance works with speaking and singing. The translation is mine.

Yang (Yuhuan) sings:

> The icy wheel starts to rise over the island in the sea,
> Look, the Jade Hare again leaps up from the east!
> As the icy wheel departs from the island,
> It brightens heaven and earth.
> The moon shines in the sky,
> Like Chang E I'm leaving the moon palace.
> Like Chang E I'm leaving the moon palace.

As she was singing the last line, Yang made the pose *"Bao yue shi"* (a gesture to imitate Change E leaving the moon). At this moment she reveals her emotional climax, feeling beautiful and happy like the rising moon and the Moon Goddess, Chang E.

Introducing herself to the audience:

> True beauty is heaven grant, not one's own,
> So bestowed grateful, I served the throne.
> Among all of three thousand concubines,
> he adored me alone.
>
> ...
>
> I am Yang Yuhuan, my lord's favorite.
> Last night he ordered me to arrange a feast at Fragrance Hall today,
> Mr. Gao and Pei, is the feast well prepared?
> Now lead on to Fragrance Hall.

...
A jade bridge over a stream, I take the rail and lean.
Now two ducks come to play.
Golden carp swim in the stream and watch me.
Ah, swim and watch me.
Boundless space, geese in flight.
Hi, wild geese, fly, I rejoice to see you!
Wild geese in pairs ascend,
Hearing my singing settle in the shade of flowers.
This landscape intoxicated me,
Without notice, I have arrived at the Fragrance Hall.

A few minutes later, after a few cups of wine, she lost control of her singing and repeated exactly the words of her eunuchs (eunuch Pei and eunuch Gao):

> YANG: (sings)]
>> Leaning over the balustrade of the jade stone bridge,
> PEI: (speaks)
>> The mandarin ducks playing on the water
> YANG: (sings)
>> The mandarin ducks playing on the water
> GAO: (speaks)
>> Golden carp play on the surface of the water
> YANG: (continues singing)
>> Golden carp play on the surface of the water
>> ....
> PEI: (speaks)
>> Mistress, life on earth...
> YANG: (singing)
>> Life on earth is like a short spring dream
> GAO: (speaks)
>> To drink with abandon...
> YANG: (continues singing)
>> To drink with abandon, several cups,

Listening and watching her singing, the audience could imagine as Yang described through gestures of her eyes, arms, legs, feet and movements of her silk fan and sleeves that she was impersonating the movement the duck, the fish, and flying geese.

In the second drunken scene, Yang was drunk out of her mind and her speech was slurred. She presents her drunkenness by singing to her lost sober self:

> YANG: (sings)
>> Yang Yuhuan is in a dream night,
>> Remember the time you first entered the palace
>> How kindly the emperor treated you

How much he loved you,
But today suddenly is forsaking,
Can it be from today the two shall forever part!

These examples are only three of her many singing and speaking voices that reveal different sides of her role and personality, a concubine, geese, birds, fish, and Moon Goddess. These voices also present her changing emotions: happiness, loneliness, and despair.[22]

During the Qing dynasty (1644–1911), as seen in the theatres of the modern West (rather than those of the developing theatres of the Renaissance and Baroque), the emphasis of Chinese music drama shifted from narrative (plot) and presentation to the refinement of performance and characterization. The best example of this historic change was in the development of Peking opera.[23] Derived and refined from regional musical dramas, Peking opera developed a highly refined vocal and stage presence. Peking opera produced four levels of singing: singing with music, verse recitation, prose dialogue, and non-verbal vocalizations. The conception of a sliding scale of vocalization created a sense of smooth continuity between songs and speech. The three basic categories of vocal production technique are the use of breath (*yongqi*), pronunciation (*fayin*), and special Peking opera pronunciation (*shangkouzi*).[24]

Like classical opera, Peking opera consisted of artificially trained singing. Well controlled breath moved and delivered the melodic passages [*zhong qi xing xiang*]. Breath was visualized as being drawn up through a central breathing cavity extending from the pubic region to the top of the head. This cavity should be under the performer's control at all times, and he (or she) developed special techniques to control the air as it moved in and out. Breath should not be expended all at once at the beginning of a spoken or sung passage, but rather expelled slowly and evenly over its length. Most songs and some prose contain precise written intervals to indicate when breath should be exchanged or stolen. These intervals are often marked by carats.[25]

Pronunciation is conceptualized as forming the throat and mouth into the shape necessary to produce the desired vowel sound, and clearly articulating the initial consonant. There are four basic shapes for the throat and mouth, corresponding to four vowel types, and five methods of articulating consonants, one for each type of consonant. The four throat and mouth shapes are "opened-mouth" (*kaikou*), "level-teeth" (*qichi*), "closed-mouth" (*hekou* or *huokou*), and "scooped-lips" (*cuochun*). The five consonant types are denoted by the portion of the mouth most critical to each type's production: throat, or larynx (*hou*); tongue (*she*); molars, the jaws, and palate; front teeth; and lips. Chinese opera even invented a special operatic way to pronounce certain Chinese syllables to ease vocal performance.[26]

These complex techniques and conventions of vocal production were used to create the two main categories of vocalizations in Peking opera: stage speech and singing. There were three major types of stage recitation [*nianbai*]. Monologues and dialogue, which made up the majority of plays, consisted of prose recitation. The purpose of prose speech was to advance the plot of the play or inject humor into a scene. They were usually short and were performed mostly using vernacular language. However, they also had rhythmic and musical elements achieved through the stylized articulation of monosyllabic sound units and the stylized pronunciation of speech-tones. The second main type of stage speech consisted of quotations drawn from classical Chinese poetry. This type was rarely used in Peking opera; when it was, the poetry recitation was intended to heighten the impact of a scene. However, *chou* and *huadan* characters might deliberately misquote or misinterpret the classical lines to create a comic effect. The final category was conventionalized stage recitation [*chengshi nianbai*]. They were composed in rigid formulations which were inherited from earlier Yuan plays. For example, the entrance speech [*shangchang*] or self-introduction passage [*zi bao jiamen*] included a prelude poem, a scene setting poem, and a prose scene setting speech, delivered in that order. Another conventionalized stage speech was the exit speech, which might take the form of a poem followed by a single spoken line. This speech was usually delivered by a supporting character to describe his or her present situation and state of mind.[27]

Chinese theatre that developed from the thirteenth to seventeenth centuries was a post-literary theatre. It was more similar to Italian opera and modern Western theatre of the twentieth century rather than to Greek, Roman and English theatre of the Renaissance, which were written in formative languages. Like the West, Chinese theatre took its initial form from dramatic performance of religious ritual. However, in China there was a gap of three thousand years between pre-literary public performance (from the middle of the second millennium BC) and the emergence of dramatic writing for musical theatre in the thirteenth century.[28] Due to this long delay a higher degree of refinement was cultivated and manifested in literary expression when compared to that of surviving Western languages at the beginning of their musical theatre. The following poem by Zhang Zhongsu (769–819), a song of grief, sadness and longing of a person with dead emotions, illustrates the capacity of Chinese poetry to describe these feelings in vivid yet subtle imageries. It was a sadness which was strong yet more subtlely presented compared to the ancient Chinese poetry (in *Shijing* for example) and early Italian poetry accompanied by music. Chinese theatre emerged from a literary heritage that was no longer a naked poetry describing physical scenery, simple emotion, and linear ideas.

"The Pavilion of Swallows"

Upstairs dying lamp flickers with morning frost,
The lonely widow rises from her wedding bed.
Sleepless all night long, lost in mournful thoughts,
The night seems endless as the boundless cosmos.

The pines before his grave filter sad smoke,
In Swallows' Pavilion she suffers in silence.
Her songs are hushed by dust on his sword,
Her scented dancing dress had ten years for perfume to fade.

Wild geese from her lord's grave have gone way,
Now the swallows come with spring again.
Flute and zither she has no zest to play,
Lie buried in spider's web, dusty they remain.

With a literary language that could produce dramatic narrative and project emotional images without stage and music, Chinese dramatic writing redirected its focus from plot to its presentational form, as did the modern theatre of the twentieth century. In other words, Chinese drama of the thirteenth century did not begin with a plot described by writing; it had never needed a story line, as did Wagner's opera. The early formal core of the Yuan zaju, its *qu* [song], began to emerge during the Jin dynasty (1115–1234) before the golden age of drama of the Yuan. These songs, or more precisely these chains of songs, often drove the development of plot and wove acting scenes together. Usually they made no excursions into lengthy poetic elaboration at key points in the action except for good theatrical reasons, such as to intensify atmosphere or to heighten dramatic tension. The very manner in which these songs were arranged, both musically and prosodically, tended to contribute to the tightly constructed movement of the narrative and to the precise emotional moment of the main character. The thoughts and feelings of the protagonist were confided to the audience or to other characters on stage, as well as his provision of scenic, historic, or other background, or his moral or philosophical interpretation of the action.[29]

The dramatic effect of Yuan *zaju* derives not only from literary content but also from the types of sounds heard from the stage. Yuan theatre was carried by characters, the portrayal of their development, and the emotional journey that they took. A prose section of the performance could be one character's extended monologue or a dialogue; humor played a significant part and puns or vulgar language were commonly used to reveal the inner world of stage personae. The lyric sections were sung rather than spoken by one main character per act. In Yuan dramatic lyrics, Chinese poetry delivered the strongest emotions, distinct from the polished and subtle emotion that was projected by classical literary poetry:

"Injustice of Dou E"

by Guan Hanqing

Sun and moon hang high night or day;
Gods and ghosts over life and death hold sway.
Alas, Heaven and Earth!
You should know how to distinguish fair from foul.
How could you confuse vice with wise!
Let those who have done good deeds poor and early die,
While those who have done wrong enjoy luxury and long life.
Alas, Heaven and Earth!
How could you fear the strong and be cruel to the weak,
An opportunist, how could you support only the winner?
O, Earth, shame on your mighty name,
If you can't separate right from wrong!
O, Heaven, how could you be a paradise
If you can't tell wise from vice?
Alas! Now all I have is but two streams of tears.

Yuan drama had a unified rhyming system. Not only was poetry prefer-ably used as lyrics (as in Italian opera), but Yuan zaju allowed only one poetic rhyme throughout a complete act. There could be over a hundred words in the same act all rhyming with one another. The great majority fell at the end of the line, but internal rhymes were also allowed. This was only possible for a language that had cultivated its poetry for centuries and had accumulated a huge repertoire of resources for dramatic writing. However, unlike French, whose verses were always rhymed according to the complex and inflexible rules of Racine and others, the lyrics of *qu* followed a varied and relaxed for-mula. This was because Chinese poetry arrived at its most formal rigidity during the late Tang dynasty (618–907), three hundred years earlier, and Chi-nese poetic form had since gone through several transformations to relax its prosodic rules. During the Yuan dynasty poetry did not have to mirror gram-matical structure. Sentences could spill across line-boundaries, as seen in later works of Milton and Shakespeare. The language of *qu* had already broken free from a small stock of learned poetic words and assimilated the vast reper-toires of spoken language and regional dialects.

The language of Yuan *zaju*, as an established literary theatre, also pro-vided additional formal freedom in literary and tonal rhyme. Whereas earlier poetry had rules laid down in a most detailed manner as to which groupings of tones actually constituted rhyme, the Yuan system allowed greater flexibility within the same rhyme group as to which tones were acceptable.[30] As a result, any risk of monotony due to the single rhyme throughout the act was reduced. This flexible tonal arrangement, which was possible only in a poetry consisting of various prosodic forms, also avoided the problems of many operas of the early Western languages in which mediocre, even bad, poetry had to be included in the libretto because it made beautiful music.

A further device that promoted variety was that the meter of the lyrics was comparatively free. It is true that there were prescribed syllables, but it was possible to add nonmetric words. Sometimes the nonmetric outnumbered the prescribed syllables. The addition of nonmetric words may not have affected the basic rhythm, but it did suspend it, making the poetic lines and songs much more fluid and brisk. It has been argued that the irregularity of line length and rhythm by the use of non-metric words enhanced the natural flow of poetry. This was considered as the hallmark of *qu* as a poetic genre. Since *qu* was sung to the accompaniment of musical instruments, if and how the nonmetric words were used depended on the types of instruments used in the play. In the plays of Southern China, the musical beat was clear and definite as produced by many percussion instruments. This discouraged the use of nonmetric words. In the North where singing was accompanied by strings, *zaju* lyrics included more nonmetric words.[31]

Like European opera, music enjoyed different degrees of dominance over words of different national or regional styles and modes of theatre during various periods of their development. At the early stage of musical drama, as in the early Italian and French operas, word sense was dominant in China and music ideally served as a willing vassal and helper. However, like the more mature European opera, later forms of Chinese drama gave sound and forms of singing greater emphasis over the delivery of lyrics.[32] The Chinese composers, like their contemporaries of nineteenth century Italian opera, exhibited this expertise as they created dramatic sound imageries.

Unlike the European opera where distinct, sometimes, contrary styles (Latin/German music, singer/orchestra, melody/polyphony, and simplicity/complexity) took several centuries to resolve in the works of Verdi and Wagner, Chinese music drama constantly combined regional and stylistic variations into new dramatic forms because they shared the same literary language and classical poetic tradition.[33] During five hundred years of theatrical development, dramatic writing absorbed both Northern and Southern forms of music, prosody, rhythmic schemes, and tonal composition in a number of national forms of music drama. For example, *kunqu* opera, which emerged during the Ming dynasty (1368–1644), was a combination of *chuanqi*, an established literary form and *kunqu* ("Kunshan" tune), a musical form.[34] The process of combining distinct forms of poetry and music formed the creative labor of generations of playwrights. Some of them paid close attention to the intonation of their lyrics in order to set to melody; others focused on music, solos, duets, chorus, or a combination of them.

While modern Western theatre generally attempted to refine every scene of a play, Chinese theatre had outgrown the episodic approach and turned instead to perfecting every single hand movement, glance of the eye, gesture of a finger, and configuration of steps.[35]

In Peking opera, traditional Chinese string and percussion instruments provide a strong rhythmic accompaniment to the acting. The acting is based on bodily gestures: hands position, arm and footwork, and dance movement to express actions such as riding a horse, rowing a boat, or opening a door. Spoken dialogue is divided into recitative and Beijing colloquial speech, the former employed by serious characters and the latter by young females and clowns. Character roles are strictly defined. Elaborate make-up designs portray the identity (role) of each character. The traditional repertoire of Peking opera includes more than 1,000 works, mostly taken from historical novels about political and military struggles.

Musical theatre had made substantial contributions to the refinement of literary Chinese. As songs were compounded into dramatic narratives on stage, literary imagery through musical accompaniment juxtaposed into more complex representations. The following poems in opera demonstrate how natural images became completely internalized and humanized[36]:

"A Waterfall Revisited" [*Chong kan pubu*] to the tune of "*Shuang Dao. Sui Xian Zi*"

by Jia Mi

After the loom of the sky stops, the moon shuttle rests.
The stone cliff hovers, the silk like snow is cold.
Threads of ice carrying rain hang from the sky;
It will never dry up in a thousand years.
Cold dew chills and startles man in thin cloth.
Like a white rainbow drinking at the stream,
and a jade dragon descending the mountain,
snow under a clear sky is flying on the riverbank.

Another waterfall poem that seemingly depicted a similar cold and snowing natural scene was meant to describe the cold, dark inhumanity of man's world.

"The Waterfall Tian Tai" [*Tian Tai pubu Zi*] to the tune of "*Zhong lu.Hong xiu xie*"

by Zhang Kejiu

At top, the peaks gather like swords of snow,
On sheer cliff, the stream hangs like a curtain of ice.
In trees, monkeys play with high clouds;
Among the blood flowers, the cuckoo calls.

From the dark caves the Wind-God howls...
Compared to men's hearts, mountains hold no peril.

Legend has it that the red color of the azalea comes from the cuckoo who sings until it spits blood.[37]

The juxtaposition of human heart and mountain had a long history in literary language. The metaphor was based on the imagery of the darkness, danger and harm that they presented.

Poetry became further classified and refined as it was sung and acted by a variety of characters who expressed different shades of emotion. In Peking opera, lyrics were subdivided into six modes: narrative [*xushu*] lyrics, emotional [*shuqing*] lyrics, condemning [*chize*] lyrics, descriptive [*xingrong*] lyrics, argumentative [*zhengbian*] lyrics, and lyrics of separate minds in shared space [*tongchuang yimeng*].

Peking opera further distilled lyrical expression into various shades of descriptive emotion and tones of descriptive mode. Spoken and sung in a theatrical context, poetic language projected a much wider variety of meanings by utilizing the six types of song lyrics according to dramatic role. Each employed the same basic lyrical structure, differing only in kind and degree of emotions portrayed. Lyrics were written in couplets (*lian*) consisting of two lines (*ju*). Couplets could consist of two ten-character lines or two seven-character lines. The lines are further subdivided into three *dou* (literally means "pause"), typically in a 3-3-4 or 2-2-3 pattern. Lines may be augmented with extra characters for the purpose of clarity. The lyrical meaning was substantially stretched by the distinctive singing styles of opera performers who made extensive use of vocal vibrato during songs in a way that was "slower" and "wider" than the vibrato used in Western operas. The Peking opera aesthetic for songs is summed up by the expression *zi zheng qiang yuan* [accurately and precisely delivered words and weaving and rounded singing sound].[38]

Emotional [*shuqing*] lyrics expressed an introspective direct statement of a character's feelings. In many cases it occurred when the character was alone on the stage speaking, as in Shakespearean monologues. But instead of speaking to the audience, the Chinese actor sang his lyrics. The following song of Silang in his first scene in *Silang Visits his Mother* illustrates:

> Yang Yanhui in the palace
> Sighs reflecting events of years past,
> How sad and depressed!
> I am like a bird in a cage,
> I have wings, but can't stretch.
> I am like a tiger forgotten in the mountain,
> alone and suffering.

> I am like a wild goose from the south,
> lost from the flight.
> I am like a dragon out of water,
> besieged on a sandbank.

Condemning [*zhezi*] lyrics were sharp and direct statements of a character's feelings while confronting and criticizing another character. The wife of Silang sang the following words after she had learned that her husband had taken another wife while she was faithfully awaiting his return:

> I am unhappy with your words.
> You married the Iron Mirror Princess!
> Because of you I did not wear flowers on my hair,
> Because of you I did not wear embroidered shoes,
> I did not eat and I could not drink tea.
> For fifteen years I have not sat down at my dressing table
> to do my coiffure....
> (How could you take another wife when I was waiting for you!)

The subtlety of this indirect expression is also revealed in the lyrics of different minds in shared space [*tong chuang yi meng*] (literally means sleeping together having different dreams). This type of lyric was presented as two songs sung by two different characters who were on the stage at the same time yet unaware of each another. This left the audience in the middle hearing both sides. Many plays that involved love affairs used this type of lyric. Each lover sang about his or her feelings and thoughts alternately. The cross passages would become progressively shorter until they finally met. In the play *Black Dragon Residence* [*Wu long yuan*], two lovers who had bitterly quarreled were locked into a single bedroom by the girl's mother who hoped that this arrangement would encourage a reconciliation. On the stage the two lovers, Song Jiang and Yan Xijiao, awoke alternately and sang about their feelings and intentions towards one another, then resumed sleeping:

> SONG: The watchtower has announced the first part of the
>   night.
>   In silent melancholy I retreat to serious thought.
>   Suddenly I have a desire to make peace with her...
>   But she treats me like a stranger,
>   a real stranger.
> YAN: The watchtower slowly drumming
>   recalls to me his kindness.
>   I want to embrace him....
>   But I have sworn to break up,
>   to cut him away.
> SONG: The watchtower has sounded the third time.
>   My anger shoots up high from my heart.

I will go ahead to settle my score with her...
But a man should think twice before he acts, yes, think
twice.

YAN: The watchtower strikes the fourth part of the night.
A murder instinct comes over me;
With these scissors I could stab his heart...
But I'm afraid it'll ruin my plan, my long held
plan.

Sanqu (separate song) was not the only genre through which Yuan poetry had excelled.[39] The dramatic imagery that cultivated in drama was also reflected in poetic creations of more traditional forms which portrayed a picture of the world wherein the boundaries between nature and man became a seamless one:

"Bamboo Branch Song" [*Zhu Zhi Ci*]

by Ni Zan (1301–1374)

The old men talk about the kingdom's fall and rise,
For captive king and general slain they give deep sighs.
evening wind breaks willow branch with might and main,
The brimming lake is veiled in green mist and rain.

"The Lady of Stone" [*Shi fu ren*]

by Sa Dula (1300–1355)

Alone by riverside proudly she stands,
No one accompanies her but songs' waters.
Her hair hasn't be combed for a thousand years,
Yet her beauty remains for as many springs.
Gentle wind blows snowflakes to powder her face,
Dewdrops color her cheeks under sun bright.
Don't say there is no mirror to reflect her grace,
The moon will shine on the Lady of Stone all night.

Conclusions

Chinese theatre came later in its literary history compared to those of western European languages. Hardly any pre-literary theatre existed in China. With a long-standing rather than a formative literary tradition and indigenous music, Chinese theatre cultivated a stable relationship with its literary establishment. Stage presentation was never out of step with the literature from which it drew plot, narration, vocabulary, as well as expressive forms. Chinese theatre, with its multiple artistic and regional forms, constantly enriched and reinforced its literary canon.

There was a different kind of interaction between literature and music/ dance that encouraged different evolutions of theatre. This contribution to literature can be observed in the various ways that British and American theatre evolved during the late nineteenth and the first half of the twentieth century. While the English playwright maintained his literary control of the theatre, American theatre became completely swept and carried by music and dance numbers for several decades before American English cultivated its own dramatic tradition. As American dramatic writing swiftly matured during the middle of the twentieth century, it transformed theatre as well as its language. American English became able to penetrate the inner world of its characters and activate deep emotions of its audience and readers.

Dramatic writing and performance played a prominent role in the development of literary language only during the transitional periods of a given literature. In the post-literary period, theatrical performance provided a space wherein literature was further refined and objectified on a stage that could present various options. Modern British and early modern Chinese theatres are the best examples of this enrichment.

8

A Few Final Words

This work is an outline of the history of Chinese language that focuses on how Chinese accumulated an exceptionally diverse repertoire of expression and how it obtained a high degree of descriptive refinement. After five thousand years, almost every sound and vision created by Chinese can be heard and seen in other languages, but none of these languages has the same capacity to portray a minute and animated vision that is as immense and fluid as that of Chinese.

In this Chinese world, god (in the widest sense of the word, including the god that is renamed as nature or science in the West) has been buried in countless words and mosaic images that describe his concrete and immediate presence. God is not dead or forgotten, but he has lost his universal name, his visible boundary, and his referential authority as he is manifested in distinctive humanity that is constantly redefined and meticulously depicted by individual poets and writers. In a world without rigid division of god/man and object/subject, creative energy obtains a high degree of freedom. Imagination can fly beyond the visible and imaginable world without losing its footing on the physical ground. Images from various worlds can be presented in a single piece of literature.

This poetic, rather than religious or scientific, universe is a world without a god (an absolute center) and his gravity. Everything is in constant flux in this universe, which can be seen from various angles, and its images move in various directions and can be organized in different sequences. If metaphysical vision is represented by paintings which imitate the visible world as expressed by different hands of various degrees of skills and faith, poetic vision is motion pictures made by individual artists. Every frame in the movie is shot and edited by a single mind and portrayed by a distinctive worldview. It announces that this is the way in which the world is seen through one pair of eyes. In this sense, the Chinese literary world is a film festival without a judging panel, where millions of rival visions have been showing and competing for many centuries. The intention of creation is not to win the highest prize (because the best creation always defies the judgment of its own time), but to present and be seen and remembered by viewers for generations to come.

With this highly poetic vision, Chinese intellect preferred artistic rather than economic pursuits until the mid twentieth century. Several economic and social reforms that occurred in the rest of the world did not occur in China. The industrial and scientific revolution in the West escaped China during the early modern period, although China accumulated advanced scientific knowledge and made important discoveries during ancient and medieval times. Technical and commercial development did not trigger social change in China as it did in the West. Instead, Chinese society evolved during periodical alternations of dictatorship and war or social anarchy because language alone, without state politics, failed to establish an authority similar to that of Western laws.[1] Without the authority of words (as inherited in Christian traditions), Chinese minds did not recognize that words of law had absolute binding power overriding ordinary words. Politicians often pursued their own words (wishes) beyond the boundaries of law. Words of Chinese constitution often needed the support of an army and its weapons; law could not function without political rhetoric that overwhelmed legislated principles. In a highly poetic language, law and politics are often indistinguishable and this allowed authoritarianism as well as social anarchy to entrench as acceptable conditions in society.

This study of Chinese language also aims at providing an alternative approach to the study of language. As time is an important factor for the development of language, the Chinese experience can illustrate what might happen to other languages as they age. During the past decades, the study of Chinese language has been eliminated by established linguistic and sociological theories which are constructed in much younger languages. These theories reduced the linguistic and literary experience of the Chinese people during the past five thousand years to fit within rigid scientific typologies and disciplinary frameworks such as linguistic forms (grammar and phonology), conceptual and generic evolution of literature, tonality and harmony of musical systems, and visual and performing presentations. This book demonstrates that the real dynamic of linguistic evolution in China is the historic accumulation of expressive variations and multitudes. It has provided ample examples of the interaction of written language with various forms of non-literary expression (dance, music, poetry recitation, theatre, visual images, and performing gestures) and illustrates how these forms collided with, altered, and eventually enriched literature.

This accumulation of various expressive forms neither initiated nor maintained an overall structure (pictorial, phonetically, grammatical or literary) as linguists believe. Literary Chinese continued to overwhelm and reconstruct its basic structure and reshape its characteristics, expand its boundaries, and culminate into unprecedented diversity by absorbing many non-literary and non–Chinese forms of expression. This history defies the very concept of literary language by incorporating non-verbal and post-literary (in the West, known as post-modern) expressions. Words, after being used, explored, and stretched for thousands of years, were no longer silent marks on the paper. They became alive; they could sing, dance, act, reach out; they could inspire or restrain creativity every time they were spoken or written; they could live behind closed eyes and haunt the mind.

This non-absolute and non-structural approach to linguistic history in terms of accidental and concrete interaction between literary language and non-literary expression challenges the basic presumptions of the "science of language." It illustrates when and how a literary language takes its form, as it is inspired by the languages of music, art, dance, theatrical and ritual gestures in specific places and times, and how it adopts or assimilates foreign literary expressions. It does not only construct an original view of Chinese, but also presents an important revision to linguistic history at large. Equipped with this new method, the history of many languages of the world could be seen and rewritten in completely different light.

Chapter Notes

Part I

1. Alster, 1976, 1985, 1988, 1997, 1990; Anderson, 1994, 1–83; Landels, 1999, 1–23, 110–129; Lu, 2000, 146; Pian, 1967; Picken, 1999, 83–125; M.L. West, 1993, 1994, 1999.
2. Yilii, vii, quoted by Wellesz, 1957, 90. I have made minor changes to the original translation. For more about ancient musical instruments, see Fernald, 1944; Goodrich, 1941; Han and Campbell, 1996; Karlgren, 1942; Moul, 1908; Picken, 1955, 1981, 1981–2000; Thrasher, 1993, 2000; Traynor and Kishibe, 1951; Wang Zichu, 2003, 2006; Wellesz, 1957, 90–93; Xiao, Yung, and Wong, 2001; Yang Mu, 1993.
3. Adlington, 2000; Dingle and Simeone, 2007; P. Evans, 1979; P. Griffiths, 1985a, 1995; Gulik, 1940, 1951; Jameux, 1991.
4. Boulez, 1971, 1986; Wellesz, 1957, 124–125; Dingle and Simeone, 2007; Griffiths, 1985, 1995, 3–20; Hill, 1995, 2005; Jameux, 1991; Koblyakov, 1993; Samuel, 1994.

Chapter 1

1. An, 1991; Harbottlen, 1999; Landels, 1999, 24–46; Liu, Zaisheng, 2004, 16; Zhang and Wang, 1998; Underhill, 1997.
2. Yang, Yinliu, 1981; Wu Ben, 1998, 1–2.
3. Gibson, 1937; Li, Chunyi, 1996; Liu, Xinhong, 2004; Picken, 1999; Wang Qinglie, 2007, 39–43; Zhao, Shigang, 1996, 54–58.
4. Creel, 1937, 99; Fang, Qidong, 1980; Li, Chunyi, 1964; 1994, 1996; Liu, Zaisheng, 2004, 32–36; Picken, 1999, 88–89; Qiu, Xiqui, 2000; Yang, Yinliu, 1981, Vol. 1; Wellesz, 1999, 88–90.
5. Lee and Shen, 1999; Yuan, Bingchang, 1986.
6. Creel, 1937, 99; Goodrich, 1941; Gulik, 1951; Lee and Shen, 1999; Moule, 1908; Traynor and Kishibe, 1951; Wellesz, 1999, 89–90; Yuan and Mao, 1986.
7. Fernald, 1944; Liu, Zaisheng, 2004, 48–49; Picken, 1955, 1981, 2000; Picken, 1999, 90–93.
8. Po Guo, *Mu tianzi chuan*, quoted in Liu, Zaisheng, 50–51; Zheng, Jiewen, 1992; Needham, 1988, 2: 53–54; Yu, Taishan, 2003, 2009.
9. Wang, Qinglie, 2007, 22–24; Huang, Houming, 2005; Guo, Dashun, 2005; Gao, Wei, 1989; Gibson, 1937; Lam, 1988; Wechsler, 1985; Yung, 1996.
10. *Shujing, Yushu Yihjyi*, 93; Picken, 1999, 100–101; Sachs, 1943, 137.
11. So, 2000.
12. Picken, 1999, 93–96.
13. Moule, 1901.
14. Picken, 1999, 102–104.
15. Liu, Zaisheng, 1989, 184–188; Sun, Mei, 1995, 24–66, 1996.

16. Lu, Buwei, 2000, 146; Picken, 1999, 94.
17. Lu, Buwei, 2000, 146–151.
18. Picken, 1999, 94–95; Lu, Buwei, 2000, 146–148.
19. Picken, 1999, 94–98.
20. Bernoviz, 1996; Huang, Xiangpeng, 2003; Huang, Xiangpeng, and Lam, 1992.
21. Bagley, 2004, 2008.
22. Pian, 1967, 1972, 1975; Lam, 1988.
23. Aguera-Arcas, 1975; Bernoviz, 1996; DeWoskin, 1982; Gulik, 1940; I Shou-Fan, 1977; Liang, Mingyue, 1972, 1973, 1980, 1984; Liebermann, 1987; Yung 1985.
24. Ye, 1986; Li, Changji, 1991; Li Ling, 1987; Sun Mei, 1996.
25. The translation is mine. From this point on, all the poetic translation is mine unless it is indicated otherwise.
26. Picken, 1999, 92–93.
27. Picken, 1999, 108.
28. Picken, 1999, 98.
29. V.C.K. Cheung, 2008, 2–4; Qian Mu, 1977, 90; Wang, Weizhen, 1988.
30. Yang, Yinliu, 1981, 114–116; Su and Xiao, 1982, 193–194; Wang, Weizhen, 6.
31. Cheung, 2008, 2–5; Qiu, Qiongsun,1989, 44–99; Sun and Xiao, 1982, 247–277; Wang, Weizhen, 114–115; Yang, Yinliu, 1981, 118.
32. Yang, Yinliu, 1986, 439; Zhang, Shibin, 1974, 75–76.
33. Ji, Liankang, 1986, 86–87; You, 236.
34. Bai, Juyi, as quoted in Yang, 1986, 326; Cheung, 2008, 7–8; Wang, Weizhen, 142; Yang, Yinliu, 1986, 326.
35. Cheung, 2008, 8–9; Wang, Weizhen, 143–145; Yang, Yinliu, 1955, 132–134; 1986, 326.
36. Cheung, 2008, 8; Wang, Weizhen, 144–146.
37. Pian, 1967; Picken, 1969b, 1999, 109–110.
38. Picken, 1999, 111–112.
39. Makarras, 1972, 1988; Moule, 1908, 146; Picken, 1999, 112; Riley, 1997; Shih, 1976; Sun, Mei, 1996.
40. Goldstein, 2007; Huang Jinpei, 1989; Makarras, 1971, 1972, 1988; Wichmann, 1990, 1991.
41. Gao, Fumin, and Zhou, Qin, 2006; Gao, Fumin, 2008; Li, Xiao, 2005; Liu, Bong-Ray M., 1976; Sun, Hongxia, 2006; Xia, Ye, 2006; Zhang, Geng, and Guo, Hancheng, 2006; Zheng, Lei, 2005; Zhou, Ruishen, 2008.
42. Bao, Chengjie, 2002; Cheng, Zhi, 2007; Hai, Zhen, 2003; Li, Siu Leung, 2006; Pian, Rulan Chao, 1967, 1972, 1975; Qi, Rushan, 2008; Shih, Wen-shan, 2000; Siu and Lovrick, 1007; Wang, Te-chen, 1979; Yan, Liang, 2003.
43. Bi, Goldlatt, and Lin, 2009; Ch'en, Shou-jen, 1991; Dujunco, 1994, 2003; Gao, Houyong, 1981; Huang, Dejun, 2010; Li, Ling, 1987; Sun, Mei, 1995; Wedde, 2008; Ye, Dong, 1983; Yung, 1989; Zhang, Geng and Guo, Hancheng, eds., 2006; Zhou, Yibai, 1975, 1979.
44. Dujunco, 1994, 2003; Ye, Dong, 1983.

Chapter 2

1. S. Allan, 2007; J.G. Anderson, 1943; Bolz, 1994, 6; Fairbank, 1992, 133–42; Loewe and Shaughnessy, 1999, 1–10, 124–231; Liu and Xiu, 2007; Norman, 1988, 58–59; Zeng, 1993, 1–10.
2. Boltz, 1994, 60–63, 1999; Chen, Mengjia, 1988; Dong, Zuobin, 1936, 1937, 2001a, 2001b; Tang, Lan, 28.
3. J.P. Allen, 1999; Bahrani, 2003; Campbell, 1989; Gardiner, 1973; S. Houston, 1989, 2004; Kettunen, H., and C. Helmke, 2004, 9–17; Schmandt-Besserat, 1992, 1996.
4. S. Allen, 2007; K.C. Chang, 1983; Chang, Xu, Lu, and Allen, 2005; Li, Liu, 2004; Underhill, 2002.
5. Boltz, 2003, 35–38; Postgate, Tao, Wang, and T. Wilkinson, 1995; Gao, Ming, 1982, 557–658.
6. Wenwu, 1983, 11: 21–30; Qiu, 2003, 30; Chang, Xu, Lu, and S. Allen, 2005.

7. Wenwu, 1989.

8. Li, Xueqin, 2003.

9. Gao, 1987, 36; Qiu, 2000, 30–32, *Xinhua Online*, 2007-05-18.

10. Wenwu, 1963, 306–7; Woon, 1987, 275–276.

11. Wenwu, 1963, 197, plate 141 and plates 167–171.

12. Boltz, 2003, 17; Qiu, 2000, 30–33; Tang, Lan, 1978; Woon, 1987, 17–22; Zeng, 11–20.

13. Liu, Bo, 1989; Kwan, 2005.

14. Guo, Moruo, 1972; Li, Xiaoding, 1965, 1977; Boltz, 1994, 1999; Gao, Ming, 1996; Guo, Moruo, 1972; Keightly, 1989; Li, Xueqin, 1985, 1987; Qiu, 1988, 163, 2000, 30; Wang, Ningsheng, 1981; Wang, Shuming, 1986; Yu, Xingwu, 1973, 1979.

15. Wang Ningshen, 1981; Zheng and Mu, 1988; Qiu, 2000, 29–39.

16. Qiu, 2000, 33; Wang, Shuming, 1986; Woon, 1987, 27; Wenwu, 1974.

17. Wang, Ningsheng, 1981, 33.

18. Yu, Xingwu, 1973, Tang, Lan, 1975, 72–73.

19. J.P. Allen, 1999; Boltz, 1994, 12; Daniels, 1996; Diakonoff, 1976; Gardiner, 1973; Glassner, 2003; Loprieno, 1995; Michalowski, 1980, 1987, 1993, 2000, 2006.

20. Wenwu, 1978; Li Xueqin, 1985; Qiu, 2000, 35–37.

21. Liu, Li, 2007; Feng, Shi, 1994.

22. Qiu, Xigui, 2000; Zhang, Guiguang, 2004; Li, Xiaoding, 1965; Liang, Donghan, 1959; Yang, Shuda, 2004, 2007; Yu, Shengwu, 1979; Dong, Zuobin, 2001; Li, Xiaoding, 1965; Zhang, Guiguang, 2004; Zhou, Fagao, 1974.

23. Boltz, 1994; Chen, Mengjia, 1988; Gao, Ming, 1996; Guo, Moruo, 1972, 1978–82; Keightley, 1978, 1989, 1999, 2000; Liu, Xiang, et al. 1996; Qiu, 2003; Thorp, 1981; Woon, 1987.

24. Fontenrose, 1978.

25. Boltz, 2003, 39–52; Dong, Zuobin, 1948, 1965, 2001; Li, Xiaoding, 1965; Qiu, 2000, 63–4; Yang, Shuda, 1933, 2004, 2007; Yu, Xingwu, 1979; Zhang, Guiguang, 2004.

26. Boltz, 1994, 60–61; Li, Xiaoding, 1965, 1977; Ramsy, 1987, 269; Woon, 1987; Yang, Shuda, 1933.

27. Boltz, 1994, 54; Chen, Mengjia, 1988; Dong, Zuobin, 1965; Fang, Shuxin, 1992; Jin, Xiangheng, 1993; Li, Xiaoding, 1965; Mair, 2001, 33–36; Rong, Gong, 2000; Qiu, Xigui, 2000, 29–67; Sun, Haibuo, 1934.

28. Mair, 2001, 37–42; Keightley, 1989; Zhao, Cheng, 1988.

29. Zhang, Gueiguang, 2004, 2–5; Boltz, 1994, 31–33; Zhao, Cheng, 1988.

30. Boltz, 1994, 33–35; Chang, 1983, 573–4; Chen Mengja, 1988; Cheung, 1983, 323–325; Chou Hung-hsiang, 1976; Keightley, 2000; Liang Donghan, 1959; Wang Hongyuan, 1993; Wang Yuxin, 2006; Woon, 1987; Xu Yahui, 2001; Yu Xingwu, 1979; Zhang Gueiguang, 2004, 3–5, 10–14.

31. Boltz, 1994, 12.

32. Chen, Zhaorong, 2003; Qui, Xigui, 2000.

33. Sun, Haibuo, 1934; Jin, Xiangheng, 1993; Rong, Gong, 2000; Fang, Shuxin, 1992; Li, Xiaoding, 1965; Dong, Zuobin, 1965.

34. Dong, Zuobin, 2001a, 2001b, 2001c; Yang, Shuda, 2004, 2007; Zhang, Guiguang, 2004, 87–98.

35. Liang, Donghan, 1959; Wang, Yuxin, 2006; Yu, Xingwu, 1979.

36. Qiu, 2000, 67; Zhang, Guiguang, 2004, 87–88.

37. Chan, Zhaorong, 2003; Qui, 2000, 60–70; Rawson, 1987; Rong, Gong, 1985; Shaughnessy, 1991; Wang, Hui, 2006; Zhou, Fagao, 1974.

38. Boltz, 1986, 1994; Keightley, 1996; You, Guoqing, 2001; Ramsey, 1987; Shaughnessy, 1991, 1997b; Tsien and Shaughnessy, 2004.

39. Qiu, 2000, 68–70; Chen, Zhaorong, 2003.

40. Qiú, 2000, 79–93; Zeng, 1993, 31–35.

41. Boltz, 1993; Coblin, 1978; Cook, 1996; Creamer, 1989; Ding Fubao, 1959; He, Jiuying, 1995; Lu, Zongda, 1981; Norman, 1988, 63–78; Serruys, 1984; Thern, 1966; Wang, Guowei, 1979; Xu, Shen, 1978, 1989, 2007; Zeng, 1993, 11–74; Zhao, Pingan, 1999; Zhu, Minshen, 1999.

42. Diringer, 1982; Qui, 2000, 80–94; Zeng, 1993, 54–58.
43. Chang and Miller, 1990; Fazzioli, 1987; Harrist, and Fong, 1999; Lai, 1973.
44. Ciyuan, 1986.
45. Boltz, 2003, 104–110; Wang, Li, 1981, 1: 157–166.
46. Wang, Li, 1981, 1: 162.
47. Hansen, 1993.
48. Karlgren, 1968: 1.
49. Boltz, 1994, 2003.
50. Boltz, 2003, 1994, 67–8, Ramsey, 1987, 136–137; Wieger, 1927, p. 14–15; T.L. Wu, 1990, 200; Luo, Zhenyu, 1958, p. 177; Woon, 1987, 12, 291; Li, Xiaoding, 1970, 6: 2005–13.
51. Norman, 1988; L. Wang, 1962: 1.151; S. Xu, 1963, 48–63; Woon, 1987, 147–8.
52. Ciyuan, 1707–1908; Defrancies, 1986, 116–130.
53. Ciyuan, 1984, 455–581.
54. Ciyuan, 1984, 1017, 1905, 2941.
55. Ciyuan, 1984, 2582–2587, 3595–3597.
56. Boltz, 1999, 115–116, 2003, 156–177.
57. Mair, 2001, 40–42.
58. This has been updated from J. Norman, 1988, 72.

Chapter 3

1. Fang Yuren, 1986, 1: 49.
2. Shen Yadan, 2007, 101; Li, Chunyi, 1994, 94–95.
3. Li, Chunyi, 1994, 94–95.
4. *Shi Jing*, 1993, 1–2.
5. Guo, Zhuping, 2002; Lin, Jiali, 2009; Liu, Xiang and D. Hawkes, 1959.
6. Wang, Kunwu, 1998, 155; Ge, Zhaoguang, 1999, 167; Shen, Yadan, 2007, 123–139.
7. Shen, Yadan, 2007, 181–185; Chen, Yuanfeng, 1999, 230–232; Liao, Xudong, 1995, 39–40; Wen, Yiduo, 1982, 1:279–280.
8. Liao, Yudong, 1995, 22–23; Qu, Yuan, 1979; Shen, Yadan, 2007, 187–191.
9. Goodman, 2006, 130–134.
10. J.R. Allen, 1992; Birrell, 1993, 2008; Cai, Zongqi, 1996; Goodman, 2006, 128–129; Guo, Maoqian, 1996; Han, Ning, 2009; Wang, Yunxi, 1996; Wu, Dashun, 2009; Wu, Dexin, 2006; Xiao, Difei, 1984; Zhang, Yu, 2009.
11. Gong, Kechang, 1997; Mair, 2001, 223–247.
12. Li, Tiandao, 2004; Li, Xiaozhong, 2000; Loewe, 1986, 170–171; Owen, 1974; Watson, 1993, 259–306.
13. Birrell, 1993a; Chen, Yingshi, 1984, 2002, 2003; Graham, 2008; Gulik, 1940, 1951, 1969; Liang, Mingyue, 1973, 1980, 1984; Lieberman, 1987; Thompson, 1998; Wu, Wenguang, 1990; Xu, Jian, 1982; Ye, Mingmei, 1991.
14. Goodman, 2006, 27–30.
15. Dai, Weihua, 2005; Xiao, Difei, 1984, 15–25; Liu, Dajie, 1997, 236–238; Shen, Yandan, 2007, 205–213; Wu, Xiaoping, 1998, 51–53; Xu, Fuguan, 2004, 23–24; Xu, Xueyi, 1998, 67; Zhu, Guangqian, 1982, 2: 185–186, 1984, 13.
16. Akehurst and Davis, 1995; Gasparov, 1996, 115–116; Ge, Xiaoyin, 2009; Goldin, 1983; Kelley, 1993.
17. Han, Chuanda, 1997; Ruan, Ji, 1989.
18. Cai, Zongqi, 2002; Liu, Xie, 1992; Meow, 2004, 59; Owen, 1992, 152–154.
19. Branner, 2006, 109–112.
20. Guo, Shaoyu, 1983, 2: 190–209; Wang, Liqi, 1983, 101–2; Xia, Chengtao, 1964; Zhan, Ying, 1963, 163–92.
21. Lin, Shuenfu, 1994, 6–8; Liu, Yaomin, 1982, 192–218; Shi, Yidui, 1985, 131–50.
22. Lin, Shuenfu, 1994, 8–9.
23. Ji, Yün, 1941, 154–56; Lin, Shuenfu, 1994, 9–10; Mather, 2003; Meow, 2004, 60–61.
24. Mou, 2003; Owen, 1996, 2006a, 2006b; Rouzer, 1993; Yang, Jingqing, 2007; Yang, Xiaoshan, 2003.

25. Mair, 2001, 276.
26. Yeh, 2008c, 2008d; J.Y. Liu, 1962; Mair, 2001, 275–278.
27. Ge, Jingchun, 2009; Mair, 2001, 295–298; Varsano, 2003.
28. Chou, 1995; McCraw, 1992; Watson, 2002; Yeh, Chia-ying, and Hightower, 1998; Yeh, Chia-ying, 2008b; D. Young, 2008.
29. Chou, 1995; Hung, 1952; McCrew, 1992; Owen, 1981; J.D. Schmidt, 2003; Watson, 1986, 2002.
30. Li, Shangyin, 1986, 1999; J.Y. Liu and S. Li, 1969; Liu, Xuekai, and Yu, Shucheng, 2004.
31. Liu, Xuekai, 2007; Rouzer, 1993; Yeh, 2008d; Zhu, Yian, 1996, 18.
32. Fong, 1987; Hu, Yunyi, 2007; P. Yu, 1994; Chang, Kangi-Sun, 1980; Yeh, 2007a, 2007b, 2007c.
33. P. Yu, 1994, x–xi; Wang, Li, 1979, 509; Wu, Xionghe, 1985, 279–297.
34. Shi, Yidui, 1985; P. Yu, 1994, 6–9, 15.
35. Owen, 1994, 61–63.
36. P. Yu, 1994, 71–106.

Chapter 4

1. S. Allan, 2007; Bagley, 2001; Barnhart, 1997, 19–20; Chang, Kwang Chih, 2005; Liu, Li, 2004; Liu and Xiu, 2007; Underhill, 2002.
2. Briessen, 1962, 192–193.
3. Acker, 1954–1974, 10–12; S. Bush, 1985, 18–21; M. Shaw, 1988; Watson, 1967.
4. Acker, 1954–1974, 2–4.
5. Acker, 10–11.
6. Rawson, 1992, 50–74; Wen, Wu, and Sun, Shuming, 2002; Sullivan, 1962, 1984, 13–38; Sun, Shuming, 2005; Thorp and Vinograd, 2001, 27–55; Wu, Hung, 1995, 18–27, 2006a, 2006b; A.F. Howard, 2006.
7. Barnhart, 1997, 15–138; Lee, 1962, 9–12; Rawson, 1992, 43–74; Thorp and Vinograd, 2001, 55–177; Wu, Hung, 1992, 53–76, 189–213.
8. Barnard, 1958, 1972, 1973; Cook, 2004; Rao Zongyi, 1985, 1987; Lawton, 1991; Li, Ling, 1985; Wu, Hung, 1997; Zeng, 1993.
9. Liu, 2007; Reyes-Valerio, C. 1993; Watson, 1967.
10. Wu, Hung, 2000, 77–83.
11. Wu, Hung, 2000, 84–5; 2003; Abe, 2002.
12. Barnhart, 1997, 26–34; Lee, 1994, 1961–64; Sullivan, 1984, 194–260.
13. Barnhart, 1997; Chen, Pao-chen, 1987.
14. Bush, 1985, 32–34; Sakanishi, 1939, 30–33.
15. Bush, 1985, 35.
16. Munsterberg, 1955, 14; Siren, 1933, plate 9, 1939, 30–31.
17. Barnhart, 1997, 118–133.
18. Cassetari, 1990; Sullivan, 1980, 1984; Barnhart, 2002; Wen, Fong, 1992; Wu, Hung, 1996.
19. Munsterberg, 1955, 19–30; Barnhart, 1997, 65–69; Karetzky, 1996.
20. Briessen, 2003; Chen, Brunelle, and Cortabarria, 2006; M.H. Fong, 1984.
21. Munakata, 1974; Clapp, 1991; W. Watson, 2003.
22. Bush, 145–148, 170–177; Sullivan, 1999; Barnhart, 2002.
23. Karetzky, 1996; Sakanishi, 1939, 79; Munsterberg, 1955, 34–36.
24. Bush, 1985, 213.
25. Munsterberg, 1955, 40.
26. Ebrey, 1999, 162–163.
27. Bush, 1985, 152.
28. Hearn, 2002; Sakanishi, 1935; Barnhart, 1997, 372–76.
29. Cahill, 1962, 4–5.
30. Calhill, 1962, 5.
31. Cahill, 1976, 3–6.
32. Cahill, 1976, 111–112.

33. Cahill, 1976, 90–91.
34. Cahill, 1976, 72–73; Wang, Tzi-cheng, 2001.
35. Cahill, 1976, 118.
36. Cahill, 1976, 119.
37. Wen C. Fong, 1992; Siran, 1974.
38. Cahill, 1976, 124–125.
39. Cahill, 1976, 121–122; Lee and Ho, 1968; Lee, 1994, 460–467.
40. Cahill, 1996, 8–15, 23–29.
41. R.E. Harrist, 1987; Fong, Wen, and M.K. Hearn, 1981–1982.
42. Lee, 1968; Sullivan, 1979; Fu Shen, 1977.

Chapter 5

1. *Shijing*, Ode 32.
2. *Shijing*, Ode 29.
3. *Shijing*, Ode 303.
4. Guo, Muoro, 1962, 18–20, 1996, 1–20; Zhang, Guiguang, 2004, 202–209.
5. Crump, 1996; He, Jin, 2001; Liu, Jianguo, 2004.
6. Huai, Nanzi, 7/2, S. Allan, 1997, 29–32.
7. Loewe, 1979, 50–52; S. Allan, 1981b, 1984a, 1997, 25–29; Birch and Fowler, 2000, 1–16.
8. Nivison, 1999; Shaughnessy, 1997a, 2006.
9. Keightley, 1978, 1989, 2000; Mair, 2001, 59–69; Shaughnessy, 69–100.
10. Menzi, 9/7a; S. Allan, 1997, 25.
11. S. Allan, 1997, 53–55; Chen, Mengjia, 1988, Hu, Houxuan, 1999.
12. *Shanhaijing*, 9/97a–b, 14/65a–b; S. Allan, 1991, 26–28.
13. S. Allan, 1997, 29–30; He, Jiejun, 2004; Ming, Zuoqiu, 1989.
14. Bagley, 1987, 2001; McDermott, 1999; Wechsler, 1985; Yung, Rawski, and Watson, 1996.
15. S. Allan, 1991, 33–34.
16. S. Allan, 1991, 33–37; Csikszentmihalyi, 2004.
17. Shijing, "Chang Fa," Ode 304.
18. S. Allan, 2007; Fairbank, 1992; Loewe and Shaughnessy, 1997, 1999, 2006; Liu and Xiu, 2007; Nivision, 1999, 2009.
19. Birch, 2000, 1–2.
20. Birch, 2000, 2–4; Carus, 1974.
21. Birrell, 1993; Burkert, 1983; Edmunds, 1990; Woodard, 2007; S. Allan, 1981a, 1981b, 1984a, 1984b, 1991.
22. Birch, 2000, 17–28.
23. Mair, 2001, 73–74.
24. *Dao de jing*, I; the translation is mine.
25. "Tian lun" in Xun Zi and Knoblock, 1988–1994; B. Watson, 2003; Graham, 1978, 1981, 1983; Watson, 1963, 78–93.
26. Ames, 1983b, 1989; Bodde, 1979; Jan Yunhua, 1977, 1980a, 1980b, 1983; Kohn, 2000; Kohn and Lafargue, 1998; Peerenboom, 1993, 27–30; Tu, 1979.
27. Henricks, 2000, 123–129; Ames and Hall, 2003, 225–231. The translation is mine.
28. Henricks, 2000, 20–132.
29. Peerenboom, 1993, 51–55.
30. Nielsen, 2003; Wei, 2005.
31. Maciocia, 1989, 1–6.
32. Needham, 1988, 2:41–42.
33. Graham, 2004; Ho, Peng Yoke, 1985, 11–12; Johnston, 2010; Needham, 1988, 2: 165–184; Porkert, 1974.
34. Ames and Hall, 2003; Lao, Zi and Roberts, Needham, 2: 262–276; Yi, Jing, "xici shang," 3b; Feng, Yulan, 1952–1953, 824–845; Wilhelm and Baynes, 1967; Ho, Peng Yoke, 1985, 10–12.
35. Needham, 1988, 2: 262–323.

36. Needham, 1988, 2: 257–267; Feng, Youlan, 1952–1953, 11–14.
37. Lloyd, 1971, 15–49.
38. Alioto, 1987, 44.
39. Lindberg, 1992, 35–9; Lloyd, 1971, 71–9; Plato, Republic, 530b–c, Timaeus, 28b–29a.
40. Dauben, 2007; Ho, Peng Yoke, 1985; Martzloff, 1996; Needham, 1988, 3: 93–110, 171–173; Pigott, 1999; Sun Xiaochun and Kistemaker, 1997; Wang, Zhongshu, 1982.
41. Ho, Peng Yoke, 1985, 3–4; Needham, 1988, 2: 15–17.
42. Liezi tianrui, zhuan 1.; Xunzi wangzhibian, zhuan 5 as quoted in Ho, Peng Yoke, 1985, 4. I have made changes in translation.
43. Zhu, Xi, 2001; Chan, Wing-tsit, 1967, 1–5; Ho, Peng Yoke, 1985, 5. I have made changes in translation.
44. Graham, 1961, 1990; Chan, Wing-tsit, 1967, 1987, 1989.
45. Wexler and Irvine, 2006.
46. Euclid, 1956, 2010; Dauben, 2007; Guo, Shuchun, 1997; Ho, Peng Yoke, 2007.
47. *Zhuzi quanshu, zhuan* 49, p. 1b; Adler, 1998, 1999; Wing-tsit Chan, 1963, 1967, 1986, 1989; Kim, 2000; T.A.Wilson, 1995; Tillman, 1992; Ho Peng Yoke, 1985, 5.
48. Le Blanc, 1985; E.M. Chen, 1989; Robinet, 1990; Zhang and Ryden, 2002.
49. Zhuzi quanshu, 49, 1a–5b as quoted in Ho, Peng Yoke, 1985, 5–6.
50. Zhuzi quanshu, 48 in Ho, Peng Yoke, 1985, 5.
51. Ho, Peng Yoke, 1985, 25; Zhang and Ryden, 2002.
52. Huainanzi, 2009, chapter 4; He Peng Yoke, 1985, 26–27. I have made changes in translation.
53. Ho, Peng Yoke, 1985, 25–27.

Chapter 6

1. Qu, Yuan, 1979, 2009; Hawkes, 1985.
2. Hawkes, 1985, 8.
3. Qu, Yuan, 2009.
4. Hawkes, 1985, 49–53.
5. Brewitt-Taylor, 2002; De Crespigny, 1990, 2010; Luo, Guanzhong, 2004.
6. Cao Cao, 1975.
7. Haun, Saussy; Chang, Kangi-Sun, 1999, 113–114; Rexroth and Ling, 1982, 52–53.
8. Jiang, Zuyi, 1991; Chang, Kangi-Sun, 1980; Murakami, 1976; Ono Naoto, 1998; Owen, 1994; Tang Guizhang, 1993; Yang, Haiming, 1987.
9. Chang, Kangi-Sun, 1980, 107–157; Hightower, 1981, 1982; Liu, J.Y., 1970, 1974; 53–99; Mair, 2001, 318; Own, 1994; B. Watson, 1986.
10. Note: The words "wrong" [cuÒ] and "can't" [mÒ] rhyme in Chinese.
11. Note: The words "wrong" [cuÒ] and "can't" [mÒ] rhyme in Chinese.
12. Leung, 1976, 1985; Liu, J.Y., 1970, 1974; Mair, 2001, 317–8; Tang and Pan, 1982; Zeng Daxing, 1990.
13. Landau, 1994, 1–16.

Chapter 7

1. Chen, Naiqian, 1962; Crump, 1983, 1993; Fong, 1987; D. Johnson, 1980; Schlepp, 1980, 2001; Shih, 1976; Sui, Shusen, 1964; Wang, Guowei, 1975.
2. Guan, Hanqing, 2004; Sui, Shusen, 1964; Yang, Zhaoying, 1997, 2007; Zhang, Kejiu, 1995, 1996.
3. See his "Of Myself" [zi shu], Sui, Shusen, 1964, 575.
4. Sui, Shusen, 1964, 575–592.
5. Sui, Shusen, 1964, 156, 180–181.
6. Sui, Shusen, 1964, 172–173.
7. Schlepp, 2001, 376–378.
8. Dolby, 2003; Sui, Shusen, 1964, 268–270, Schlepp, 2001, 378.
9. Sui, Shusen, 1964, 245, 284.

10. Sui, Shusen, 1964, 363–364.
11. Sui, Shusen, 1964, 437. The translation is mine. Ho, Kwai-cho, 1994.
12. Ye, 1977.
13. Dolby, 1976, 1978, 2008a; Guo, Yingde, 1997; Li, Xiusheng, 1996, 1997; Swatek, 2003; Tang, Xianzu, 2003; Xu, Fuzuo, 1988; Birch, 1980.
14. Ye, Lang, Fei, Zhenggang, and Wang, Tianyou, 2007, Chapter 29.
15. Goldstein, 2007, 3–4; Mackerras, 1972, 1997; Wichmann, 1991.
16. Ye Diaoyuan described the *pi-huang* tune in his Bamboo Branch Songs at *Hankou* [*Hankou zhuzhi ci*] in 1850. Wang, Di, 2003; Xu, Mingting, 1999.
17. Wichmann, 1991, 1–24; Xu, Chengbei, 1999, 2000, 2006; Mackerras, 1972.
18. Goldstein, 1999; Wang, Der-wei, 2003; Wichmann, 1991, 7–11, 177–224; Zhang, Yuci, 1959–1962.
19. Li, Ruru, 2010, 301–306; Mackerras, 1971, 1988, 123–126.
20. Li, Ruru, 2010, 55–82; Riley, 1997, 175–192.
21. Mei, Lanfang, 2000, Vol. I; Zhongguo Xijujia Xiehui, 1961.
22. Zhongguo Xijujia Xiehui, 1961; Wichmann, 1991, 29–52; Riley, 1997, 136–140.
23. Goldstein, 2007; Huang, Jinpei, 1989; Li, Ruru, 2010; Mackerras, 1976, 473–501; Scott, 1982; Wang, Li, Cao, Wang, and Mao, 2006; Wichmann, 1990, 1991.
24. Li and Cao, 2006; Mackerras, 1982; Goldstein, 2007, 17–54; Scott, 1957, 28–40, 1971; Wu, Mei, Huang, and Mei, 1981; Wichmann, 1991, 177–178.
25. Wichmann, 1991, 178–180.
26. Wichmann, 1991, 180–185.
27. Scott, 1957, 92–184; Wichmann, 1991, 25, 48–57.
28. Cai, Yi, 1989; Hu, Ji, 1957; Tang, Wenbiao, 1984; Wang, Guowei, 1984; Xu, Muyun, 2001.
29. Blackmore, 2000, xi–xii; Dolby, 1978, 1988b, 45–48; Cai, Yi, 1989; Ning, Xiyuan, 1988; A.C. Scott, 1957, 185–218; Tang, Wenbiao, 1984; Weiberg, 1963; Zhang, Chuanyin, 1990, 1993; Zhang, Yuci, 1960.
30. Aoki, Masaru, 1965, Vol. 1; Luo, Jintang, 1960; Riley, 1997; Shih, Chung-wen, 1976, 120–123; Wichmann, 1991.
31. Dolby, 1988b; Shih, Chung-wen, 1976, 123; Wang, Jie, 1959.
32. Dolby, 1988b, 49.
33. Grout, 2003, 401–402.
34. J. Hu, 1988; A.C. Scott, 1957; Beijing shi yishu yanjiusuo, 1999; Zhou, Yibai, 1953.
35. Riley, 1997, 84–88; P'an, 1995.
36. Sui, Shusen, 1964, 248; Chen, Naigan, 1962, 626.
37. Sui, Shusen, 1964, 248; Chen, Naigan, 1962, 626; Schlepp, 1980, 107–108.
38. Wichmann, 1991, 177–182.
39. Lynn, 383–390.

Chapter 8

1. Gu, 2009.

Bibliography

Abe, Fusajiro. 1930–1939. *Soraikan kinsho* [Chinese Painting in the Abe Collection]. 6 vols. Osaka.

Abondolo, D.M. 2001. *A Poetics Handbook: Verbal Art in the European Tradition.* London: Routledge.

Abraham, G. 1979. *The Concise Oxford History of Music.* London: Oxford University Press.

Acker, W.R.B., trans. 1954–1974. *Some T'ang and pre–T'ang Texts on Chinese Painting, Translated and Annotated.* 2 vols. Leiden: E.J. Brill.

Addiss, S. 1987. Music for the Seven-String Ch'in. *Tall Mountains and Flowing Waters: The Arts of Uragami Gyokudo.* 29–48. ed. S. Addiss. Honolulu: University of Hawaii Press.

Adler, J. 1998. Response and Responsibility: Chou Tun-I and Confucian Resources for Environmental Ethics. *Confucianism and Ecology: The Interpretation of Heaven, Earth, and Humans.* eds. M. Tucker and J. Berthrong. Cambridge: Harvard University Press.

_____. 1999. Chu Hsi's Use of the I Ching. *Sung Dynasty Uses of the I Ching.* ed. K. Smith. Princeton: Princeton University Press.

Adlington, R. 2000. *The Music of Harrison Birtwistle.* Cambridge, UK: Cambridge University Press.

Aguera-Arcas, J.B. 1975. A Study of Three Famous Compositions for the Chinese Long Zither. Master of arts thesis. Ann Arbor: Godard College, University Microfilms.

Akehurst, F.R.P., and J.M. Davis, eds. 1995. *A Handbook of the Troubadours.* Berkeley: University of California Press.

Albright, W.F. 1966. *The Proto-Sinaitic Inscriptions and Their Decipherment.* Cambridge, MA: Harvard University Press.

Aldwell, E., and C. Schachter. 1989. *Harmony and Voice Leading.* Orlando: Harcourt Brace Jovanovich.

Algeo, J. 1990. Semantic Change. *Research Guide on Language Change* (399–408). ed. E.C. Polomé. Berlin: Mouton de Gruyter.

Alioto, A.M. 1987. *A History of Western Science.* Englewood Cliffs, N.J.: Prentice-Hall.

Allan, J.R. 1992. *In the Voice of Others.* Ann Arbor: Michigan Monographs in Chinese Studies, Vol. 63.

Allan, S. 1972–3. The Identities of Taigong Wang in Zhou and Han Literature. *Monumenta Serica* 30: 57–99.

_____. 1981a. *The Heir and the Sage: Dynastic Legend in Early China.* San Francisco: Chinese Materials Center.

_____. 1981b. Sons of Suns: Myth and Totemism in Early China. *Bulletin of the School of Oriental and African Studies* 44 (2): 290–326.

_____. 1984a. Drought, Human Sacrifice and the Mandate of Heaven in a Lost Text from the Shang Shu. *Bulletin of the School of Oriental and African Studies* 47 (3): 523–39.

_____. 1984b. The Myth of the Xia Dynasty. *Journal of the Royal Asiatic Society* 2: 242–56.

_____. 1991. *The Shape of the Turtle: Myth, Art and Cosmos in Early China.* Albany: SUNY Press.

_____. 2007. Erlitou and the Formation of Chinese Civilization: Toward a New Paradigm. *The Journal of Asian Studies*, 66: 461–496.

_____, and Cohen, A.P., eds. 1980. *Legend, Lore and Religion in China: Essays in Honor of Wolfram Eberhard on His Seventieth Birthday*. San Francisco: Chinese Materials Center.

_____, Li Xueqin, and Qi Wenxin. 1985. *Oracle Bone Collections in Great Britain*. 2 vols. Beijing: Zhonghua Shuju.

Allen, J.P. 1999. *Middle Egyptian: An Introduction to the Language and Culture of Hieroglyphs*. Cambridge, UK: Cambridge University Press.

Alster, B. 1976. On the Earliest Sumerian Literary Tradition. *Journal of Cuneiform Studies* 28: 109–126.

_____. 1985. Sumerian Love Songs. *Revue d'Assyriologie et d'Archéologie Orientale* 79. 127–159.

_____. 1988. Sumerian Literary Texts in the National Museum, Copenhagen. *Acta Sumerologica* 10: 1–15.

_____. 1997. Sumerian Canonical Compositions. C. Individual Focus. 1. Proverbs. *The Context of Scripture, I: Canonical Compositions from the Biblical World*, 563–8. ed. W.W. Hallo. Leiden: Brill.

_____, and M.J. Geller. 1990. *Sumerian Literary Texts*. London: British Museum.

Ames, Roger T. 1983. *The Art of Rulership*. Honolulu: University of Hawaii Press.

_____. 1985. The Common Ground of Self-Cultivation in Classical Taoism and Confucianism. *Qing Hua Journal of Chinese Studies* 17 (1–2): 65–97.

_____. 1991. Meaning as Imaging: Prologomena to a Confucian Epistemology. *Culture and Modernity: East-West Philosophic Perspectives*, 227–274. ed. E. Deutsch. Honolulu: University of Hawaii Press.

_____. 1995. Emotions and the Actions of the Sage: Recommendations for an Orderly Heart in the Huainanzi. *Philosophy East and West*. 45 (4): 527–544.

An, Chin-huai. 1982. The Shang City at Cheng-chou and Related Problems. *Studies of Shang Archaeology*, 15–48. ed. K.C. Chang. Ithaca: Yale University Press.

An, Z. 1991. Radiocarbon Dating and the Prehistoric Archaeology of China. *World Archaeology*. 23: 193–200.

Anderson, B. 1983. *Imagined Communities*. London: Verso.

Anderson, J.G. 1943. *Researches into the Prehistory of the Chinese*. Stockholm: Museum of Far Eastern Antiquities.

Andersen, P. 1989. The Practice of Bugang. *Cahiers d'Extrême-Asie* 5 (5): 15–53.

Anderson, W.D. 1994. *Music and Musicians in Ancient Greece*. Ithaca, NY: Cornell University Press.

Aoki, Masaru. 1936. *Zhongguo jinshi xiqu shi* [History of Recent Chinese Drama]. trans. Wang Gulu. Shanghai: Shangwu.

Apel, W. 1953. *The Notation of Polyphonic Music, 900–1600*. Cambridge, MA: Harvard University Press.

Apfel, E., and C. Dahlhaus. 1974. *Studien zur Theorie und Geschichte der musikalischen Rhythmik und Metrik*. 2 vols. Munich: Dr. Emil Katzbichler.

Arnold, B.T. 2005. *Who Were the Babylonians?* Leiden: Brill.

Atlas, A.W. 1998. *Renaissance Music*. New York: W.W. Norton.

Auden, W.H. 1966. *Collected Shorter Poems 1927–1957*. London: Faber.

Auer, P., E. Couper-Kuhlen, and F. Muller. 1999. eds. *Language in Time: The Rhythm and Tempo of Spoken Interaction*. New York: Oxford University Press.

Austin, W.W. 1966. *Music in the Twentieth Century*. New York: Norton.

Aylmer, C. 1981. *Origins of the Chinese Script: An Introduction to Sinopalaeography*. London: East Asia Books.

Bahrani, Z. 2003. *The Graven Image: Representation in Babylonia and Assyria*. Philadelphia: University of Pennsylvania Press.

Bai, Qianshen. 2003. *Fu Shan's World: The Transformation of Chinese Calligraphy in the Seventeenth Century*. Cambridge, MA: Harvard University Asia Center.

Bailey, D. 1992. *Improvisation: Its Nature and Practice in Music*. London: British Library National Sound Archive.

Ban, Gu. 1962. *Han Shu* [Book of Han]. ed. Yan Shigu. Beijing: Zhonghua Shuju.

Bao, Chengjie. 2002. *Fascinating Stage Arts*. Beijing: Foreign Languages Press.
Barnard, N. 1958. A Preliminary Study of the Ch'u Silk Manuscript: A New Reconstruction of the Text. *Monumenta Serica* 17: 1–11.
_____. 1972. *Studies on the Ch'u Silk Manuscript*. Australian National University Monographs on Far Eastern History 4.
_____. 1973. *The Ch'u Silk Manuscript: Translation and Commentary*. Canberra: Australian National University Press.
_____. 1981. The Nature of the Ch'in "Reform of the Script" as Reflected in Archaeological Documents Excavated Under Conditions of Control. *Science in Traditional China: A Comparative Perspective*, 181–214. ed. J. Needham. Hong Kong: Chinese University Press.
Barnhart, R. 1970a. *Marriage of the Lord of the River: A Lost Landscape by Tung Yüan*. Ascona: Artibus Asiae Supplementu.
_____. 1970b. Survivals, Revivals, and the Classical Tradition of Chinese Figure Painting. *Proceedings of the International Symposium on Chinese Painting*, 143–210. Taipei.
_____. 1972a. Chinese Calligraphy: The Inner World of the Brush. *The Metropolitan Museum of Art Bulletin* 30 (5): 230–241.
_____. 1972b. *Wintry Forests, Old Trees: Some Landscape Themes in Chinese Painting*. New York: China House Gallery.
_____. 1983a. *Peach Blossom Spring: Garden and Flowers in Chinese Paintings*. New York: Metropolitan Museum of Art.
_____. 1983b. *Along the Border of Heaven: Sung and Yüan Painting from the C. C. Wang Family Collection*. New York: Metropolitan Museum of Art.
_____. 1993. *Painters of the Great Ming: The Imperial Court and the Zhe School*. Dallas: Dallas Museum of Art.
_____. 1994. *The Jade Studio: Masterpieces of Ming and Qing Painting and Calligraphy from the Wong Nan-p'ing Collection*. New Haven: Yale University Art Gallery.
_____, Wen C. Fong, and M.K. Hearn. 1996. *Mandate of Heaven: Emperors and Artists in China: Chinese Painting and Calligraphy from the Metropolitan Museum of Art*. New York: Metropolitan Museum of Art.
_____, L. Shaojun, J. Cahill, Wu Hung, Nie Chongzheng, eds. 1997. *Three Thousand Years of Chinese Painting*. New Haven: Yale University Press.
Barry, K. 1987. *Language, Music, and the Sign*. Cambridge, UK: Cambridge University Press.
Barzun, J. 1982. *Critical Questions on Music and Letters, Culture and Biography, 1940–1980*. ed. B. Friedland. Chicago: University of Chicago Press.
Baugh, A.C. 1959. *A History of the English Language*. London: Routledge and Kegan Paul.
Baxter, W.H. 1992. *A Handbook of Old Chinese Phonology*. Berlin: Mouton de Gruyter.
Bayly, A. 1970. *The Alliance of Music, Poetry, and Oratory*. New York: Garland.
Beare, W. 1957. *Latin Verse and European Song*. London, Methuen.
Beijing yisu yanjiu suo [Beijing Research Institute of Arts]. 1999. *Zhongguo jing ju shi* [A History of Chinese Peking Opera]. Beijing: Peking Opera Press.
Bent, I. 1995. *Music Analysis in the Nineteenth Century*. 2 vols. Cambridge, UK: Cambridge University Press.
Berlin, A. 1992. *The Dynamics of Biblical Parallelism*. Bloomington: Indiana University Press.
Bernoviz, N. 1996. The Chinese Diao: Modal Practice in Fifteenth Century Qin Music. Master of arts thesis (music), University of Pittsburgh.
Bi, Feiyu, H. Goldlatt, and S. Lichun Lin. 2009. *The Moon Opera*. Boston: Houghton Mifflin Harcourt.
Bickford, M. 1996. *Ink Plum: The Making of a Chinese Scholar-Painting Genre*. Cambridge, UK: Cambridge University Press.
Birch, C. 1980. *The Peony Pavilion*. Bloomington: Indiana University Press.
_____, and R. Fowler, eds. 2000. *Tales from China*. Oxford: Oxford University Press.
Birrell, A. 1993a. *Popular Songs and Ballads of Han China*. Honolulu: University of Hawaii Press.
_____. 1993b. *Chinese Mythology: An Introduction*. Baltimore: Johns Hopkins University Press.
_____. 1999. *The Classic of Mountains and Seas*. Harmondsworth: Penguin.
_____. 2001. Myth. *The Columbia History of Chinese Literature*, 58–69. ed. V. Mair. New York: Columbia University Press.

Blum, S. 1994. *Music-Cultures in Contact: Convergences and Collisions*. Basel: Gordon and Breach.
_____, ed. 1991. *Ethnomusicology and Modern Music History*. Urbana: University of Illinois Press.
Bokenkamp, S. 1997. *Early Daoist Scriptures, with a Contribution by Peter Nickerson*. Berkeley: University of California Press.
Bol, P., and K. Bol. 1992. *This Culture of Ours: Intellectual Transitions in Tang and Sung China*. Stanford: Stanford University Press.
Boltz, W.G. 1986. Early Chinese Writing. *World Archaeology* 17 (3): 420–436.
_____. 1993. Shu wen chieh tzu. *Early Chinese Texts: A Bibliographical Guide*, 429–442. ed. M. Loewe. Berkeley: University of California Press.
_____. 1994. *The Origin and Early Development of the Chinese Writing System*. New Haven: American Oriental Society.
_____. 1999. Language and Writing. *Cambridge History of China*, 74–123. eds. M. Loewe and E.L. Shaughnessy. Cambridge: UK: Cambridge University Press.
_____. 2000. *Monosyllabicity and the Origin of the Chinese Script*. Berlin: Max Planck Institute.
_____, and M.C. Shapiro. 1991. Studies in the Historical Phonology of Asian Languages. Philadelphia: J. Benjamins.
Boodberg, P.A. 1947. *Introduction to Classical Chinese*. Berkeley: University of California Press.
_____. 1947a. *UCJ: An Orthographic System of Notation and Transcription for Sino-Japanese*. Berkeley: University of California Press.
_____. 1940. "Ideography" or Iconolatry? *T'oung Pao* 35: 266–288.
_____. 1957. The Chinese Script: An Essay on Nomenclature (the First Hecaton). *Bulletin of the Institute of History and Philology*, Academia Sinica 39: 113–120.
Booth, M.W. 1981. *The Experience of Songs*. New Haven: Yale University Press.
Boretz, B. 1995. *Meta-Variations: Studies in the Foundations of Musical Thought*. Red Hook, NY: Open Space.
Boulez, P. 1971. *Boulez on Music Today*. Trans. S. Bradshaw and R.R. Bennett. Cambridge, MA: Harvard University Press.
_____. 1981. *Orientations: Collected Writings*. Ed. by J.J. Nattiez., trans. M. Cooper. Cambridge, MA: Harvard University Press.
_____. 1986. Oriental Music: A Lost Paradise? *Orientations* 421. London: Faber.
Bowman, W.D. 1998. *Philosophical Perspectives on Music*. New York: Oxford University Press.
Branner, D.P. 2000. *Problems in Comparative Chinese Dialectology: The Classification of Miin and Hakka Trends*. Berlin: Mouton de Gruyter.
_____. 2006. *The Chinese Rime Tables: Linguistic Philosophy and Historical-Comparative Phonology*. Philadelphia: J. Benjamins.
Brewitt-Taylor, C.H. 2002. *Romance of the Three Kingdoms*. North Clarendon, VT: Tuttle.
Briessen, F. van. 2003. *The Way of the Brush: Painting Techniques of China and Japan*. North Clarendon, VT: Tuttle.
Brinkman, D. and S. 2003. *Music from the Age of Shakespeare: A Cultural History*. Westport, CO: Greenwood.
Brogan, T.V.F. 1981. *English Verification 1570–1980*. Baltimore: Johns Hopkins University Press.
_____. 1989. *Verseform: A Comparative Bibliography*. Baltimore: Johns Hopkins University Press.
Bronson, B.H. 1969. *The Ballad as Song*. Berkeley: University of California Press.
Brown, J.R. 2001. *The Oxford Illustrated History of Theatre*. Oxford: Oxford University Press.
Bush, S. 1971. *The Chinese Literati on Painting: Su Shih (1037–1101) to Tung Ch'i-ch'ang (1555–1636)*. Cambridge, MA: Harvard University Press.
_____, and C.F. Murck. 1983. *Theories of the Arts in China*. Princeton: Princeton University Press.
_____, and Hsio-yen Shih, eds. 1985. *Early Chinese Texts on Painting*. Cambridge, MA: Harvard University Press.
Cahill, J. 1958. Ch'ien Hsüan and His Figure Paintings. *Archives of the Chinese Art Society of America* 12: 11–29.
_____. 1960. *Chinese Painting*. New York: Rizzoli.
_____. 1960. *Chinese Paintings, XI–XIV Centuries*. New York: Crown.
_____. 1961. *Chinese Album Leaves in the Freer Gallery of Art*. Washington, DC: Smithsonian Institution.

_____. 1971. *The Restless Landscape: Chinese Painting in the Late Ming Period.* Berkeley: University of California Press.

_____. 1976. *Hills Beyond a River: Chinese Painting of the Yu'an Dynasty, 1279–1368.* New York: Weatherhill.

_____. 1978. *Parting at the Shore: Chinese Painting of the Early and Middle Ming Dynasty, 1368–1580.* New York: Weatherhill.

_____. 1982a. *The Distant Mountains: Chinese Painting of the Late Ming Dynasty, 1570–1644.* New York: Weatherhill.

_____. 1982b. *The Compelling Image: Nature and Style in Seventeenth-Century Chinese Painting.* Cambridge, MA: Harvard University Press.

_____. 1988. *Three Alternative Histories of Chinese Painting.* Lawrence: University of Kansas Press.

_____. 1996. *The Lyric Journey: Poetic Painting in China and Japan.* Cambridge, MA: Harvard University Press.

Cai, Zhongde. 2003. *Yinyue zhidao de tanqiu: Lun Zhongguo yinyue meixue shi ji qita* [A Study on Chinese Musical Aesthetics and Others]. Shanghai: Shanghai Yinyue Chubanshe.

_____. 2004. *Zhongguo yinyue meixue shi* [A History of Chinese Musicology]. Beijing: Renmin Yinyue Chubanshe.

Cai, Zongqi. 1996. *The Matrix of Lyric Transformation: Poetic Modes and Self-Presentation in Early Chinese Pentasyllabic Poetry.* Ann Arbor: Center for Chinese Studies, University of Michigan.

_____, ed. 2002. *A Chinese Literary Mind: Culture, Creativity, and Rhetoric in Wenxin Diao-long.* Stanford: Stanford University Press.

Campbell, L. 1998. *Historical Linguistics: An Introduction.* Cambridge, MA: MIT Press.

_____, and M.C. Munztel. 1989. The Structural Consequences of Language Death. *Investigating Obsolescence: Studies in Language Contraction and Death,* 181–196. ed. N. Dorian. Cambridge, UK: Cambridge University Press.

Cao Cao. 1975. *Cao Cao shi wen xuan zhu* [Cao Cao's Poetry and Prose]. Ha er bin: Hei long Jiang Renmin Chubanshe.

Cao, Daoheng. 2000. *Yuefu shixuan.* Beijing: Renmin Wenxue Chubanshe.

Cao, Xu. 2002. *Gushi shijiu shou yu yuefu shi xuanping* [Studies of Nineteen Ancient Poems and Yuefu Poetry]. Shanghai: Guji Chubanshe.

Cassettari, S. 1990. *Chinese Landscape Painting Techniques.* North Ryde, Australia: Angus and Robertson.

Chan, A. 2004. Early Middle Chinese: Towards a New Paradigm. *T'oung Pao,* 90 (1/3): 122–162.

Chan, Sau Yan. 1986. *Improvisation of Cantonese Operatic Music.* University of Pittsburgh.

Chan, Wing-tsit. 1963. The Great Synthesis in Chu His. *A Source Book in Chinese Philosophy,* 605–63. Princeton: Princeton University Press.

_____. 1967. *Reflections on Things at Hand: The Neo-Confucian Anthology.* New York: Columbia University Press.

_____. 1986. *Chu Hsi and Neo-Confucianism.* Honolulu: Hawaii University Press.

_____. 1989 *Chu Hsi: New Studies.* Honolulu: Hawaii University Press.

Chang, Chung-ho, H.H. Frankel, Guoting Sun, and Kui Jiang, eds. *Two Chinese Treatises on Calligraphy.* New Haven: Yale University Press.

Chang, Kangi-Sun. *The Evolution of Chinese Tz'u Poetry: From Late T'ang to Northern Sung.* Princeton: Princeton University Press.

Chang, Kun. 1979. The Composite Nature of the Ch'ieh-yun. *Bulletin of the Institute of History and Philology* 50: 241–55.

Chang, Kwang-chih. 1980. *Shang Civilization.* New Haven: Yale University Press.

_____, ed. 1982. *Studies of Shang Archaeology: Selected Papers from the International Conference on Shang Civilization.* New Haven: Yale University Press.

_____. 1983. *Zhongguo Qing Tong Shi Dai* [Bronze Age China]. Beijing: Shenghuo, Dushu, Xinzhi Sanlian Shudian.

_____, Xu Pingfang, Lu Liancheng, and S. Allen. 2005. *The Formation of Chinese Civilization: An Archaeological Perspective.* New Haven: Yale University Press.

Chang, L. Mei-chih. 1992. A Prosodic Account of Tone, Stress, and Tone Sandhi in Chinese Languages. Ph.D. dissertation, University of Hawaii.

Chang, Leon Long-yien, and P. Miller. 1990. *Four Thousand Years of Chinese Calligraphy*. Chicago: University of Chicago Press.

Chang, Sun Kang-I. 1980. *The Evolution of Chinese Tz'u Poetry: From Late T'ang to Northern Song*. Princeton: Princeton University Press.

_____. 1986. *Six Dynasties Poetry*. Princeton: Princeton University Press.

_____. 1991. *The Late-Ming Poet Ch'en Tzu-lung: Crises of Love and Loyalism*. New Haven: Yale University Press.

_____, and S. Owen. 2010. *The Cambridge History of Chinese Literature*. Cambridge: Cambridge University Press.

Chao, Yuen Ren. 1928. *Xiandai Wuyu de yanjiu* [Studies in the Modern Wu Dialects]. Beijing: Qinghua University.

_____. 1930. A System of Tone Letters. *Le maître phonétique* 45: 24–27.

_____. 1940. A Note on an Early Logographic Theory of Chinese Writing. *Harvard Journal of Asiatic Studies* 5: 189–191.

_____. 1947. *Cantonese Primer*. Cambridge, MA: Harvard University Press.

_____. 1948. *Mandarin Primer*. Cambridge, MA: Harvard University Press.

_____. 1956. Formal and Semantic Discrepancies Between Different Levels of Chinese Structures. *Bulletin of the Institute of History and Philology* 28.1: 1–16.

_____. 1968b. *A Grammar of Spoken Chinese*. Berkeley: University of California Press.

_____. 1976. *Aspects of Chinese Sociolinguistics*. Stanford: Stanford University Press.

Chaves, J. 1985. The Expression of Self in the Kung-an School: Non-Romantic Individualism. *Expressions of Self in Chinese Literature*, 123–149. eds. Hegel and Hassney. New York: Columbia University Press.

Chen, C.-Y. 2001. *Tonal Evolution from Pre-Middle Chinese to Modern Pekinese: Three Tiers of Changes and Their Intricacies*. Berkeley: Project on Linguistic Analysis, University of California.

Chen, E.M. 1989. *The Tao Te Ching: A New Translation and Commentary*. New York: Paragon House.

Chen, H.-C., and Tzeng, O.J.L., eds. 1992. *Language Processing in Chinese*. Amsterdam: North-Holland and Elsevier.

Chen, Heqin. 1928. *Yutiwen yingyong zihui* [Character Used in Vernacular Literature]. Shanghai: Shangwu.

Chen, Jian. 2005. *Jiang dong yue fu* [Yuefu from East of the River]. Beijing: Beijing Chubanshe.

Chen, M. 2006. *Zhongyuan Guyue Shi Chutan* [A Preliminary Study of the Ancient Music in Center China]. Taibei: Yuexue Shuju.

Chen, M.Y. 1976. From Middle Chinese to Modern Peking. *Journal of Chinese Linguistics* 4: 113–277.

_____. 1979. Metrical Structure: Evidence from Chinese Poetry. *Linguistic Inquiry* 10: 371–420.

_____. 1980. The Primacy of Rhythm in Verse: A Linguistic Perspective. *Journal of Chinese Linguistics* 8:15–41.

_____. 1984. Unfolding Latent Principles of Literary Taste: Poetry as a Window onto Language. *Tsinghua Journal of Chinese Studies* 16: 203–240.

_____. 1986. The Paradox of Tianjin Tone Sandhi. *Proceedings of the Chicago Linguistic Society Meeting* 22: 98–114.

_____. 1987a. The Syntax of Xiamen Tone Sandhi. *Phonology Yearbook* 4: 109–150.

_____. 1991a. An Overview of Tone Sandhi Phenomena Across Chinese Dialects. *Languages and Dialects of China*, pp. 113–158. ed. W. Wang. Berkeley, CA: Journal of Chinese Linguistics.

Chen, Meie. 2006. *Zhongyuan guyue shi chutan* [A Preliminary History of Ancient Music in Central Plain of China]. Taibei: Lexue Shuju.

Chen, Mengjia. 1988. *Yinxu buci zongshu* [A General Description of the Oracle Bone Script]. Beijing: Zhonghua Shuju.

Chen, Minguan. 1982. *Jisuanji chuli Hanzi de liangzhong yunsuan he xingshi wenfa* [Two Operations and Formal Grammar of Chinese Character Processing by Computer]. *Yuyan Yanjiu* 1: 52–59.

Chen, Naiqian. 1962. *Yuan ren xiaoling ji* [A Collection of Yuan Xiaoling Poems]. Beijing: Zhonghua Shuju.

Chen, Pao-chen. 1987. *The Goddess of the Lo River: A Study of Early Chinese Narrative Hand-scrolls*. Ph.D. thesis, Princeton University.

Chen, Quanyiu. 2001. *XiZhou yuezhong de bianlie tantao* [A Study in the Organization of Musical Bells in Western Zhou]. *Zhongguo yinyue xue* 3: 29–42.

Chen, Shaorong. 2003. *Qinxi wenzi yanjiu: Cong Hanzishi de jiaodu kaocha* [Research on the Qín Lineage of Writing: An Examination from the Perspective of the History of Chinese Writing]. Taipei: Academia Sinica.

Ch'en, Shou-jen. 1991. *Improvisation in a Ritual Context: The Music of Cantonese Opera*. Hong Kong: Chinese University Press.

Chen, W., M. Brunelle, and B. Cortabarria. 2006. *The Fine Art of Chinese Brush Painting*. New York: Sterling.

Chen, Xiaomei. 2002. *Acting the Right Part*. Honolulu, University of Hawaii Press.

Chen, Yingshi. 1984. *Qinlu xue* [Study of Qin Temperament]. Shanghai: Conservatoire.

_____. 2002. *Yi zhong tixi, liang ge xitong*. [Musicology in China] 4.

_____. 2004. *Zhongguo yuelu xue tanwei: Chen Yingshi yin yue wen ji* [A Preliminary Study of Chinese Musical Temperament]. Shanghai: Shanghai Yinyue Xueyuan Chubanshe.

_____. 2005. *Dunhuang yuepu jieyi bianzheng* [Analysis of Musical Manuscript from Dunhuang]. Shanghai: Shanghai Yinyue Xueyuan Chubanshe.

_____, and Chen Lingqun. 2006. *Zhongguo yinyue jianshi* [A Brief History of Chinese Music]. Beijing: Gaodeng Jiaoyu Chubanshe.

Chen, Yuanfeng. 1999. *Yueguan wenhua yu wen xue: xian Qin shige shi de wenhua xunli* [The Culture and Literature of Yueguan]. Jinan: Shandong Jiaoyu Chubanshe.

Chen, Zhaorong. 2003. *Research on the Qín (Ch'in) Lineage of Writing: An Examination from the Perspective of the History of Chinese Writing*. Taibei: Academia Sinica.

Cheng, Yuanmin, Huang Xudong, Yi Hongshu, and Zha Kecheng, eds. 1995. *Zha fuxi, Qinxue wencui* [Collected Writings about the Qin]. Beijing: Meishu Xueyuan Chubanshe.

Cheng, Zhi. 2007. *Jingqiang yanjiu* [Studies of Singing in Peking Opera]. Tianjin: Guji Chubanshe.

Cheung, Kwong-yue. 1983. Recent Archaeological Evidence Relating to the Origin of Chinese Characters. *The Origins of Chinese Civilization*. In D.N. Keightley, ed., Berkeley: University of California Press.

Cheung, V.C.K. 2008. *Daqu*: The *Gesamtkunstwerk* of Ancient China. http://web.mit.edu/ckcheung/www/MusicalWritings_files/Daqu_webversion_Spring99.pdf

Chin, Annping. 2007. *The Authentic Confucius*. New York: Scribner.

Chmielewski, J. 1958. The Problem of Early Loan-Words in Chinese as Illustrated by the Word 'p'u-t'ao. *Rocsnik Orientalistczny* 22 (2): 7–45.

Cho, Gene Jinsiong. 2003. *The Discovery of Musical Equal Temperament in China and Europe in the Sixteenth Century*. Lewiston: Edwin Mellen Press.

Chou, E.S. 1995. *Reconsidering Tu Fu: Literary Greatness and Cultural Context*. Cambridge, UK: Cambridge University Press.

Chou, Hung-hsiang. 1976. *Oracle Bone Collections in the United States*. Berkeley: University of California Press.

Chou, J., and C. Brown. eds. 1985. *The Elegant Brush: Chinese Painting Under Qianlong Emperor*. Phoenix, AZ: Phoenix Art Museum.

Ciyuan [Origins of Words]. 1984. 4 vols. Beijing: Shangwu.

Clackson, J., and G. Horrocks. 2007. *The Blackwell History of the Latin Language*. Oxford: Blackwell.

Clapp, A. DeCoursey. 1991. *The Painting of T'ang Yin*. Chicago: University of Chicago Press.

Cleuziou, S. 1986. Tureng Tepe and Burnished Grey Ware: A Question of "Frontier"? *Oriens Antiquus* 25: 221–256.

Clinton-Baddeley, V.C. 1941. *Words for Music*. Cambridge, UK: Cambridge University Press.

Clunas, C. 1997. *Art in China*. Oxford: Oxford University Press.

Coblin, W.S. 1978. The Initials of Xu Shen's Language as Reflected in the Shuowen Duruo Glosses. *Journal of Chinese Linguistics* 6: 27–75.
_____. 2000. A Brief History of Mandarin. *Journal of the American Oriental Society* 120 (1): 537–52.
Cook, C.A. 2004. *Defining Chu: Image and Reality in Ancient China.* Honolulu: University of Hawaii Press.
Cook, N. 1990. *Music, Imagination, and Culture.* Oxford: Oxford University Press.
Cook, R.S. 1996. *The Etymology of Chinese Chén.* Berkeley: Department of Linguistics, University of California.
_____. 2006. *Classical Chinese Combinatorics: Derivation of the Book of Changes Hexagram Sequence = Zhou yi guaxu quanjie.* Berkeley: Sino-Tibetan Etymological Dictionary and Thesaurus Project.
Cook, V. 1988. *Chomsky's Universal Grammar: An Introduction.* Oxford: Basil Blackwell.
Cooper, G.B. 1998. *Mysterious Music: Rhythm and Free Verse.* Stanford: Stanford University Press.
Cooper, G.W., and L.B. Meyer. 1960. *The Rhythmic Structure of Music.* Chicago: University of Chicago Press.
Cooper, J.S., and G.M. Schwartz, eds. 1996. *The Study of the Ancient Near East in the Twenty-First Century: The William Foxwell Albright Centennial Conference.* Winona Lake, IN: Eisenbrauns.
Creamer, T.B.I. 1989. *Shuowen Jiezi* and Textual Criticism in China. *International Journal of Lexicography* 2 (3): 176–187.
Cropper, E., ed. 2009. *Dialogues in Art History, from Mesopotamian to Modern: Readings for a New Century.* Washington, DC: National Gallery of Art; New Haven: Yale University Press.
Cross, F.M. 1991. The Invention and Development of the Alphabet. *Origins of Writing,* 77–90. Lincoln: University of Nebraska Press.
Crossley-Holand, P.C. 1954. Chinese Music. *Grove's Dictionary of Music and Musicians.* ed. E. Blom, ii: 219–48. London.
Crump, J.I. 1980. *Chinese Theater in the Days of Kublai Khan.* Tucson: University of Arizona Press.
_____. 1983. *Song-Poems from Xanadu: Studies in Mongol-Dynasty Song-Poetry (San-ch'ü).* Ann Arbor: Center for Chinese Studies, University of Michigan.
_____. 1988. Book Review: Archaeology and Language. *Current Anthropology* 29: 437–468.
_____. 1992. When Specialists Collide: Archaeology and Indo-European Linguistics. *Antiquity* 66: 251–260.
_____. 1998. *Legends of the Warring States: Persuasions, Romances, and Stories from Chan-Kuo Tse.* Ann Arbor, MI: Center for Chinese Studies, University of Michigan.
Crump, J.I., trans. 1971. *Ballad of the Hidden Dragon (Liu Chih-yu'an chukung-tiao).* Oxford: Clarendon.
_____, trans. 1996. *Chan-kuo Ts'e.* Revised edition. Ann Arbor: University of Michigan Center for Chinese Studies.
Csikszentmihalyi, M. 2004. *Material Virtue: Ethics and the Body in Early China.* Boston: Brill.
Cui, Lingqin. 1987. *Jiao fang ji.* Shanghai: Guji Chubanshe.
Cullen, C. 1996. *Astronomy and Mathematics in Ancient China: The Zhou Bi Suan Jing.* Vol. 1. New York: Cambridge University Press.
Dahmer, von Manfred. 2003. *Qín: die klassische chinesische Griffbrettzither und ihre Musik in Geschichte, Geschichten und Gedichten* [Qin]. Uelzen: Medizinisch Literarische Verlagsgesellschaft.
Dai, Weihua. 2005. Lun wuyan shi de qiyuan [A Study of the Origins of Five Character Poems]. *Zhongguo shehui kexue* 6.
Dauben, J.W. 2007. Chinese Mathematics. *Mathematics of Egypt, Mesopotamia, China, India, and Islam: A Sourcebook,* 187–380. ed. V. J. Katz. Princeton: Princeton University Press.
Dawson, R.S., ed. *Ssu-ma, Chien. Historical Records: World's Classics.* Oxford: Oxford University Press.
Deady, K.W., and M.L. Dubois. 2004. *Ancient China.* Mankato, MN: Capstone Press.

De Crespigny, R. 1990. *Man from the Margin: Cao Cao and the Three Kingdoms.* Canberra: Australian National University.
_____. 2010. *Imperial Warlord: a Biography of Cao Cao, 155–220 AD.* Leiden: Brill.
DeFrancis, J. 1986. *The Chinese Language: Fact and Fantasy.* Honolulu: University of Hawaii Press.
_____. 1989. *Invisible Speech: the Diverse Oneness in Writing Systems.* Honolulu: University of Hawaii Press.
DeWoskin, K.J. 1982. *A Song for One or Two: Music and the Concept of Art in Early China.* Ann Arbor: Center for Chinese Studies, University of Michigan.
Deydier, C. 1980. *Chinese Bronzes.* New York: Rizzoli.
Diakonoff, I.M. 1976. Ancient Writing and Ancient Written Language: Pitfalls and Peculiarities in the Study of Sumerian. Assyriological Studies 20: 99–121.
Diehr, A. 2004. *Literatur und Musik im Mittelalter: eine Einführung.* Berlin: Erich Schmidt.
Ding, Fubao. 1959. *Shuowen Jiezi Gulin* [A Forest of Glosses on the Shuowen Jiezi]. 12 vols. Taipei: Shangwu.
Ding, Xixia. 2006. *Zhonggu changyong binglie shuangyinci de chengci he yanbian yanjiu* [Studies of Formation and Evolution of the Words of Double Syllables in Middle Chinese]. Beijing: Yuwen Chubanshe.
Dingle, C., and N. Simeone, eds. 2007. Olivier Messiaen: Music, Art and Literature. Aldershot: Ashgate.
Dixon, R.M.W. 1997. The Rise and Fall of Languages. Cambridge, UK: Cambridge University Press.
Dolby, W. 1976. *A History of Chinese Drama.* New York: Barnes and Noble.
_____, trans. 1978. *Eight Chinese Plays.* New York: Columbia University Press.
_____, trans. 2003. *Ma Chih-yuan's Complete san ch'u-aria Poems = Ma Zhì Yuan san qu qúan ji.* Edinburgh: Carreg.
_____. 2006. trans. *Gold-Producing Mansion = Yuan Wu Han-chen jin ge za ju ying wen ke ben: A Yuan Variety Play Drama by Wu Han-chen (13th–14th Century).* Edinburgh: Carreg.
_____, and Chenyu Liang. 2008a. Washing Silk: A Drama. Edinburgh: Carreg.
_____, and Shifu Wang. 2008b. *Westwing: China's Most Famous Drama.* Edinburgh: Carreg.
Dong, Meikan. 1999. *Zhongguo xiju jianshi* [A Short History of Chinese Theater]. Shanghai, Wenyi Chubanshe.
Dong, Tonghe. 1987. *Shanggu Yinyun Biaogao* [A Draft List of Ancient Chinese Prosody]. Beijing: Zhonghua Shuju.
Dong, Zuobin. 1936, *YinShang yinian* [Issues of Chronology of Shang and Yin]. Shanghai: Shangwu.
_____. 1937. *Jiagu nian biao* [Jiagu Chronology]. Shanghai: Shangwu.
_____. 1948a. *Yinxu wenzi: xiaotun 2* [Yin Shang Inscriptions]. Nanking: Zhongyang Yanjiuyuan Lishi Yanjiusuo.
_____. 1948b. *Xiaotun. Di 2 ben: Yinxu wenzi* [Inscriptions Xiaotun Vol. 2]. Nanjing: Zhongyang Yanjiuyuan Lishi Yanjiusuo.
_____. 1965. *Jiagu xue liushi nian* [Sixty years of Oracaology]. Taibei: Yiwen Yinshuguan.
_____. 2001a. *Yinlipu shisijuan.* [Yin Chronology]. Chengdu: University of Sichuan Press.
_____. 2001b. *Xuyin lipu* [Chronology of More Yin Inscriptions]. Chengdu: Sichuan University Press.
_____. 2001c. *Yinxu wenzi waibian* [More Yinxu Inscriptions]. Chengdu: Sichuan University Press.
Du, Yaxiong. 2004. *Zhongguo chuantong yueli jiaocheng* [A Textbook of Chinese Musical Theory]. Shanghai: Yinyue Chubanshe.
Duan, Anjie. 1927. *Pi pa lu* [A Story of Pi Pa]. Shanghai: Shangwu.
_____. 1987. *Yue fu za lu* [Collection of Yuefu]. Shanghai: Shangwu Chubanshe.
Duanmu, San. 1990a. A Formal Study of Syllable, Tone, Stress and Domain in Chinese Languages. Doctoral dissertation, Massachusetts Institute of Technology (MIT).
_____. 1990b. Tonal Patterns in Chinese Regulated Verses: Phonological Rules or Phonological Constraints? *MIT Working Papers in Linguistics* 12: Students' Conference in Linguistics 1990, 177–189.

_____. 1998. Wordhood in Chinese. *New Approaches to Chinese Word Formation: Morphology, Phonology and the Lexicon in Modern and Ancient Chinese.* ed. Jerome L. Packard, 135–196. Berlin: Mouton de Gruyter.

_____. 1999a. Metrical Structure and Tone: Evidence from Mandarin and Shanghai. *Journal of East Asian Linguistics* 8.1: 1–38.

_____. 1999b. Stress and the Development of Disyllabic Vocabulary in Chinese. *Diachronica* XVI: 1.1–35.

_____. 2000. *The Phonology of Standard Chinese.* Oxford, Oxford University Press.

_____. 2009. Syllable Structure and Limits of Variation. Oxford: Oxford University Press.

Dunhuang, Wenwu Yanjiusuo. 1959. *Dunhuang bi hua* [Dunhuang Murals]. Beijing: Wenwu Chubanshe.

Ebrey, P.B., ed. 1999. *The Cambridge Illustrated History of China.* Cambridge, UK: Cambridge University Press.

Edmunds, L. 1990. *Approaches to Greek Myth.* Baltimore, MD: Johns Hopkins University Press.

Edwards, R. 1976. *The Art of Wen Cheng-ming (1470–1559)* Ann Arbor: University Michigan Museum of Art.

Egan, C. 2000a. Reconsidering the Role of Folk Songs in Pre-T'ang Yueh-fu Development. *T'oung Pao* 86 1–3: 48–54.

_____. 2000b. Were Yueh-fu Ever Folk Songs? Reconsidering the Relevance of Oral Theory and Balladry Analogies. *Chinese Literature: Essays, Articles, Reviews* 22: 31–66.

Eichenbaum, P. 1996. *Arts of the Tang Court.* New York: Oxford University Press.

Elfenbein, J. 1987. A Periplus of the "Brahui Problem." *Studia Iranica* 6: 215–233.

Ellingson, T. 1986. Buddhist Musical Notations. *The Oral and Literate in Music.* Eds. Y. Tokumaru and O. Yamaguti. Tokyo.

Eoyang, E. 1973. The Solitary Boat: Images of Self in Chinese Nature Poetry. *Journal of Asian Studies* 32 (4): 593–621.

Euclid. 1956. trans. T.L. Heath. The Thirteen Books of Euclid's Elements. New York: Dover Publications.

_____. 2010. Euclid in Greek. Vol. 1, Book I. Cambridge, UK: Cambridge University Press.

Falkenhausen, L. von. 1993. *Suspended Music: Chime-Bells in the Culture of Bronze Age China.* Berkeley: University of California Press.

Fang, Shuxin. 1992. *Yinxu buci duandai yanjiu* [Studies of Oracle Inscriptions of Xin and Shang]. Taibei: Wenjin Chubanshe.

Fang, Yuren. *Shijing yuanshi* [The Origins of Shijing]. 2 vols. Beijing: Zhonghua Shuju.

Fazzioli, E., and R.H. Ko. 1987. *Chinese Calligraphy: From Pictograph to Ideogram: The History of 214 Essential Chinese/Japanese Characters.* New York: Abbeville Press.

Fei, Lingya. 2005. *Huaihe liuyu shijian taogu de yuanjiu* [Pre-History Claydrum in the Valley of the Huai River]. *Jiang-Han kaogu.* 2: 58.

Feng, Shengli. 2003. *A Prosodic Grammar of Chinese.* Lawrence: University of Kansas Press.

_____. 2005. *Hanyu yunlu yufa yanjiu* [Studies on Chinese Prosodic Grammar]. Beijing: Peking University Press.

Feng, Shi. 1994. *Shandong Dinggong Longshan shidai wenzi jiedu* [Reading and Analysis of the Writing of Longshan Period in Dinggong, Shandong Province]. *Kaogu* 1: 37–54.

Feng, Wenci. 2005. *Zhongguo yinyue shixue de huigu yu fansi* [Memorization and Re-Refection of the History of Chinese Music]. Shanghai: Shanghai Conservatory of Music Press.

Feng, Youlan. 1952–1953. *A History of Chinese Philosophy.* Trans. D. Bodde. Princeton: Princeton University Press.

Fenollosa, E. 1962. The Chinese Written Character as a Medium for Poetry. ed. Ezra Pound. *Prose Keys to Modern Poetry.* ed. K. Shapiro. New York: Harper and Row.

Fernald, H.E. 1944. Ancient Chinese Musical Instruments. *A Harp with a Thousand Strings, 395–440.* London: Hsiao Ch'ien.

Fong, G.S. 1987. *Wu Wenying and the Art of Southern Song ci Poetry.* Princeton: Princeton University Press.

Fong, M.H. 1984. Tang Tomb Murals Reviewed in the Light of Tang Texts on Painting. *Artibus Asiae* 45 (1): 35–72.

Fong, Wen C., et al. 1984. *Images of the Mind: Selections from the Edward L. Elliot Family and*

John B. *Elliot Collections of Chinese Calligraphy and Painting at the Art Museum, Princeton University.*
_____. and M.K. Hearn. 1981–1982. Silent Poetry: Chinese Paintings in Dougles Dillon Gallary. *The Metropolitan Museum of Art Bulletin.*
_____, and A. Murck, eds. 1991. *Words and Images: Chinese Poetry, Calligraphy, and Painting.* New York: Metropolitan Museum of Art.
_____. 1992. *Beyond Representation: Chinese Painting and Calligraphy, 8th–14th Century.* New York: Metropolitan Museum of Art.
_____, et al. 1996. *Possessing the Past: Treasures from The National Palace Museum, Taipei.* New York: Metropolitan Museum of Art.
_____. 2004. *Xinyin: Zhongguo shuhua fengge yu jiegou fenxi yanjiu* [Images of the Mind]. Trans. Li Weikun. Xian: Shaaxi Renmin Meishu Chubanshe.
Fontein, J., and M.L. Hickman. 1970. *Zen Painting and Calligraphy* Boston: Museum of Fine Art.
Fontenrose, J. 1978. *The Delphic Oracle: Its Responses and Operations.* Berkeley: University of California Press.
Fraser, G.S. 1970. *Metre, Rhyme and Free Verse.* London: Methuen.
Fu, Shen. 1977. *Traces of the Brush: Studies in Chinese Calligraphy.* New Haven: Yale University Press.
Fu, Sinian. 2004. *Shijing jiangyi* [Lectures on Shijing]. Beijing: Peking University Press.
Fu, Xinian, ed. 1988. *Zhongguo meishu quanji, Huihua pian 5: Yuandai huihua* [Complete Collection of Chinese Arts, Painting, Yuan Painting]. Beijing: Wenwu Chubanshe.
Fuller, M.A. 1990. The Road to East Slope: The Development of Su Shi's Poetic Voice. Stanford: Stanford University Press.
Furniss, I. 2008. *Music in Ancient China: An Archaeological and Art Historical Study of Strings, Winds, and Drums During the Eastern Zhou and Han Periods (770 BCE–220 CE).* Amherst, NY: Cambria Press.
Galliano, L. 2005. *Power, Beauty and Meaning: Eight Studies on Chinese Music.* European Foundation for Chinese Music Research, International Conference Firenze, L.S. Olschki.
Gao, Fumin. 2008. *Cha zi yan hong: Zhongguo Kun qu yi chan* [Kunqu Inheritance]. Ha'erbin: Heilongjiang Renmin Chubanshe.
_____, and Zhou Qin. 2006. *Zhongguo Kunqu luntan* [Studies of Kunqu]. Suzhou: Suzhou University Press.
Gao, Houyong. 1981. *Minzu qiye gailun* [An Introduction to Chinese Folk Instrumental Music]. Nanjing: Jiangsusheng Xinhua Shudian.
Gao, Ming. 1982. *Guowenzi leibian* [Collection of Chinese Words]. Beijing: Zhonghua Shuju.
_____. 1996. *Zhongguo guwenzi xue tonglun* [An Outline of Chinese Ancient Linguistics]. Beijing: Peking University Press.
Gao, Wei. 1989. Lunshen shidan de lizhi. *Qingzhu Su Bianqi kaogu Wushinian lunwenji,* 242. Beijing: Wenwu.
Gardiner, A.1973. *Egyptian Grammar: Being an Introduction to the Study of Hieroglyphs.* Oxford: Griffith Institute.
Gasparov, M.L. 1987. A Probability Model of Verse (English, Latin, French, Italian, Spanish, Portuguese). *Style,* 21/3: 332–58.
_____, G.S. Smith, M. Tarlinskaja, and L. Holford-Strevens. 1996. *A History of European Versification.* Oxford: Clarendon.
Gates, H.L., Jr., and K.A. Appiah. 1993. *Langston Hughes: Critical Perspectives Past and Present.* New York: Amistad.
Gatta, J. 2004. *Making Nature Sacred: Literature, Religion, and Environment in America from the Puritans to the Present.* Oxford: Oxford University Press.
Ge, Jingchun. 2009. *Li bai shi xuan* [Selected Poetry of Li Bai]. Beijing: Zhonghua Shuju.
Ge, Xiaoyin. 2009. An Investigation into the Stylistic Features and Principles of the Seven-Characters-a-Line Poetry in the Han and Wei Dynasties. *Frontiers of Literary Studies in China,* 3 (3): 400–454.
Ge, Zhaoguang. 1999. *Hanzi de mofang* [The Mystery of Chinese]. Shenyang: Liaoning Jiaoyu Chubanshe.

Gibson, E.H. 1937. Music and Musical Instruments of Shang. *Journal of the North China Branch of the Royal Asiatic Society* 68: 8–18.

Glassner, J. 2003. *The Invention of Cuneiform: Writing in Sumer.* Trans. Zainab Bahrani and Marc Van De Mieroop. Baltimore, Md.: Johns Hopkins University Press.

Goldsmith, J. 1990. *Autosegmental and Metrical Phonology.* Oxford: Blackwell.

Goldstein, J. 1999. Mei Lanfang and the Nationalization of Peking Opera, 1912–1930. *East Asian Cultures Critique* 7 (2): 377–420.

_____. 2007. *Drama Kings: Players and Publics in the Re-Creation of Peking Opera, 1870–1937.* Berkeley: University of California Press.

Gong, Kechang. 1997. *Studies on the Han fu.* Trans. D.R. Knechtges and S. Aque. New Haven: American Oriental Society.

Goodman, H.L. 2006. Tintinnabulations of Bells: Scoring-Prosody in Third-Century China and Its Relationship to Yueh-fu Party Music. *Journal of the American Oriental Society:* 126–138.

Goodrich, L.C. 1941. The Chinese Shêng and Western Musical Instruments. *China Magazine,* 17: 10–14.

Gowers, D., et al. 2002. *Chinese Jade from the Neolithic to the Qing.* Art Media Resources.

Graham, A.C. 1961. The Date and Composition of Liehtzyy. *Asia Major* 8: 139–198.

_____. 1978, *Later Mohist Logic, Ethics and Science.* Hong Kong: Chinese University Press.

_____. 1981. *Chuang-tzu: The Inner Chapters.* London: George Allen and Unwin.

_____. 1983. Taoist Spontaneity and the Dichotomy of "Is" and "Ought." *Experimental Essays on Chuang-tzu,* 3–23. ed.

V.H. Mair. Honolulu: University of Hawaii Press.

_____. 1986. *Yin-yang and the Nature of Correlative Thinking.* Singapore: Institute of East Asian Philosophies.

_____. 1986. *Studies in Chinese Philosophy and Philosophical Literature.* Singapore: Institute of East Asian Philosophies.

_____. 2004. *Later Mohist Logic, Ethics and Science.* Hong Kong: Chinese University Press.

_____, trans. 1990. *The Book of Lieh-tzŭ: A Classic of Tao.* New York: Columbia University Press.

Graham, W.T. 2008. *The Lament for the South' Yu Hsin's 'aiChiang-nan Fu.* Cambridge, UK: Cambridge University Press.

Griffiths, P. 1985a. *Olivier Messiaen and the Music of Time.* Ithaca: Cornell University Press.

_____. 1985b. *The String Quartet: A History.* New York: Thames and Hudson.

_____. 1995. *Modern Music and After: Directions Since 1945.* London: Oxford University Press.

Grimshaw, J. 1990. *Argument Structure.* Cambridge, MA: MIT Press.

Gu, Meilang. 2004. *Qinxue beiyao: shougao ben* [On Qinology]. 2 vols. Shanghai: Shanghai Yinyue Chubanshe.

Gu, Sharron. 2006. *The Boundaries of Meaning and the Formation of Law.* Montreal: McGill Queens University Press.

_____. 2009. *Law and Politics in Modern China.* Amherst, NY: Cambria Press.

Guan, Hanqing. 2004. *Selected Plays of Guan Hanqing.* ed. Wu Xiaoling. Beijing: Foreign Languages Press.

Guan, Xiechu. 1981. *Xi Zhou jinwen yufa yanjiu* [Studies of the Grammar of Bronze Inscription of Xi Zhou]. Beijing: Shangwu.

_____. 1994. *Zuozhuan jufa yanjiu* [A Study of the Grammar of Zuozhuan]. Hefei: Anhui Jiaoyu Chubanshe.

Guan, Yewei. 2006. *Tangdai yinyue shi* [A History of Tang Music]. Beijing, Zhongyang Minzu Daxue Chubansh.

Gulik, R.H. van. 1940. *The Lore of the Chinese Lute.* Tokyo: Charles Tuttle and Sophia.

_____. 1951. Brief Note on the Cheng, the Chinese Small Cither. *Tōyō Ongaku Kenkyū* 9: 10–25.

_____. 1958. *Chinese Pictorial Art as Viewed by the Connoisseur.* Rome: Istituto Italiano per il Medio ed Estremo Oriente.

_____. 1969. *Hsi K'ang and His Poetical Essay on the Lute.* Tokyo: Tuttle.

Guo, Dashun. 2005. *Huongshen wenhua* [Huongshen culture]. Beijing: Wenwu.

Guo, Maoqian. 2004. *Yuefu shiji* [Collection of Yuefu Poetry]. Beijing: Beijing Tushuguan Chubanshe.
Guo, Muoro. 1962. *Jia gu wen zi yan jiu* [Studies of Oracle Bone Inscription]. Beijing: Kexue Chubanshe.
_____. 1972. Zhongguo gudai wenzi de bianzheng fazhan. *Kǎogǔ* 3: 2–13.
_____. 1996. *Shi pi pan shu* [Ten Critical Essays]. Beijing: Dong Fang Chubanshe.
_____, and Hu Houxuan. 1978–1982. *Jiaguwen heji* [A Combined Collection of Oracle Bone Inscriptions]. Beijing: Zhonghua Shuju.
Guo, Ping. 2006. *Guqin congtan* [Studies of Guqin]. Jinan: Shandong Huabao Chubanshe.
Guo, Qingfan, ed. 1974. *Zhuangzi jishi* [Selection of Works of Zhuanzi and Commentaries]. Taipei: Heluo Tushu Chubanshe.
Guo, Shaoyu, ed. 1983. *Qing shihua xubian* [New Edition of Qing History]. Shanghai: Shanghai Guji Chubanshe.
Guo, Shuchun. 1997. *Zhongguo gudai shuxue* [Mathematics in Ancient China]. Beijing: Shangwu.
Guo, Yingde. 1997. *Ming Qing chuanqi conglu* [A General Collection of Chuanqi Scripts in Ming and Qing Dynasties]. Shijiazhong: Hebei Jiaoyu Chubanshe.
Guo, Zhuping, ed. 2002. *Chu ci*. Beijing: Zhongguo Shehui Kexue Chubanshe.
Guqin Qu Ji. 1983. [Collected Guqin Melodies]. 2 vols. Beijing, Conservatoire of Music.
Hai, Zhen. 2003. *Xiqu yinyue shi* [A History of Theatrical Music]. Beijing: Wenhua Yishu Chubanshe.
Hall, D. 1978. Process and Anarchy: A Taoist Vision of Creativity. *Philosophy East and West* 28 (3): 271–286.
_____. The Metaphysics of Anarchism. *Journal of Chinese Philosophy* 10 (1): 49–63.
_____. 1982. *The Uncertain Phoenix*. New York: Fordham University Press.
Han, Bangqi. 1965–70. *Yuelu juyao* [Music Scale: A Summary]. Taibei: Yiwen Yinshuguan.
Han, Chuanda. 1997. *Ruan Ji pingzhuan* [A Bibliography of Ruan Ji]. Beijing: Peking University Press.
Han, Kuo-huang, and P.S. Campbell. 1996. *The Lion's Roar: Chinese Luogu Percussion Ensembles*. Danbury, CT: World Music Press.
Han, Ning. ed. 2009. *Gu chui heng chui quci yanjiu* [Studies of Songs of Percussion and Wind Music and Their Lyrics]. Beijing: Beijing University Press.
Hanan, P. 1988. *Invention of Li Yu*. Cambridge, MA: Harvard University Press.
_____. 1996. *The Carnal Prayer Mat*. Honolulu: University of Hawaii Press.
_____. 1998. *Tower for the Summer Heat*. New York: Columbia University Press.
Handel, Z. 2009. *Old Chinese Medials and Their Sino-Tibetan Origins: A Comparative Study*. Taipei: Institute of Linguistics, Academic Sinica.
Hannas, W.C. 1997. *Asia's Orthographic Dilemma*. Honolulu: University of Hawaii Press.
Hansen, C. 1993. Chinese Ideographs and Western Ideas. *The Journal of Asian Studies* 52.2: 373–399.
Harbottlen, G., Zhang Juzhong, Wang Changsui, and Kong Zhaochen. 1999. *Nature* No. 785 998.
Harrist, R.E. 1987. Ch'ien Hsüan's Pear Blossoms: The Tradition of Flower Painting and Poetry from Sung to Yüan. *Metropolitan Museum Journal* 22: 53–70.
Harrist, R.E., and W. Fong. 1999. *The Embodied Image: Chinese Calligraphy from the John B. Elliott Collection*. Princeton: Princeton University Press.
Hashimoto, A.O. 1971. *Mandarin Syntactic Structures*. Princeton: Princeton University Press.
_____. 1972. *Studies in Yue Dialects I: Phonology of Cantonese*. Cambridge, UK: Cambridge University Press.
_____. 1986–7. Tonal Flip-Flop in Chinese Dialects. *Journal of Chinese Linguistics* 14: 161–183.
_____. 1987. Tone Sandhi Across Chinese Dialects. *The Wang Li Memorial Volumes* 445–474.
Hashimoto, M.J. 1978–9. *Phonology of Ancient Chinese*. 2 vols. Tokyo: Institute for the Study of Languages and Cultures of Asia and Africa.
Hasty, C.F. 1997. *Meter as Rhythm*. Oxford: Oxford University Press.
Hatch, C., and D.W. Bernstein. 1993. eds. *Music Theory and the Exploration of the Past*. Chicago: University of Chicago Press.
Hawkes, D., ed. and trans. 1985. *Ch'u Tz'u: Songs of the South*. Harmondsworth: Penguin.

He, Jiejun. 2004. *Ma wang dui han mu* Han Tomb at Ma Wang Dui]. Beijing: Wenwu.

He, Jin. 2001. *An Analysis of Zhan Guo Ce*. Beijing: Peking University Press.

He, Jiuying. 1995. *Zhongguo gudai yuyanxue shi* [A History of Ancient Chinese Linguistics]. Guangzhou: Guangdong Jiaoyu Chubanshe.

Hearn, M.K. 2002. *Cultivated Landscapes: Chinese Paintings from the Collection of Marie-Hélène and Guy Weill*. New York: Metropolitan Museum of Art, Yale University Press.

Hegel, R.E., and R.C. Hessney, eds. 1985. *Expressions of Self in Chinese Literature*. New York: Columbia University Press.

Henricks, R., trans. 2000. *Lao Tzu's [Laozi's] Tao Te Ching [Dao de jing]*. New York: Columbia University Press. A translation of Jingmenshi bowuguan [Museum of the City of Jingmen], *Guodian Chumu zhujian* [Bamboo Slips from a Chu Tomb at Guodian].

Hightower, J.R. 1981–2. The Songwriter Liu Yung. I and II. *Harvard Journal of Asiatic Studies*, 41 (2): 323–376; 42 (1): 5–66.

Ho, Kwai-cho. 1994. A Study of Zhang Yanghao (1270–1329) and His Sanqu. Ph.D. thesis, University of Hong Kong.

Ho, Peng Yoke. 1985. *Li, qi, and shu: An Introduction to Science and Civilization in China*. Hong Kong: Hong Kong University Press.

_____. 2003. *Chinese Mathematical Astrology: Reaching Out to the Stars*. New York: Routledge-Curzon.

_____. 2007. Eds. J.P.C. Moffett, and Sungwu Cho. 2007. *Explorations in Daoism: Medicine and Alchemy in Literature*. London: Routledge.

Ho, Wai-kam Ho. 1980. Aspects of Chinese Painting from 1100 to 1350. *Eight Dynasties of Chinese Painting: The Collections of the Nelson Gallery–Atkins Museum*, 25–34. Bloomington: Indiana University Press.

Hoch, J.E. 1990. The Byblos Syllabary: Bridging the Gap Between Egyptian Hieroglyphs and Semitic Alphabets. *Journal of the Society for the Study of Egyptian Antiquities* 20: 115–124.

Hock, H.H., and B.D. Joseph. 1996. *Language History, Language Change, and Language Relationship: An Introduction to Historical and Comparative Linguistics*. Mouton de Gruyter.

Hoffman, M. 2007. From Rebel to Rabbi: Reclaiming Jesus and the Making of Modern Jewish Culture. Stanford: Stanford University Press.

Houston, S.D. 1989. *Maya Glyphs*. Berkeley: University of California Press, Berkeley.

_____. 2004. *The First Writing: Script Invention as History and Process*. Cambridge, UK. Cambridge University Press.

Howard, A.F., Li Song, Wu Hung, and Yang Hong, eds. 2006a. *Chinese Sculpture*. New Haven: Yale University Press.

_____. 2006b. From the Han to the Southern Song. *Chinese Sculpture*, 107–256. New Haven: Yale University Press.

Hsu, Wen-ying. 1969. *Wuju quji: Huangdi Zhan Chiyou, Dayu Zhishui, Cailian Nü* [Music of Dance Theater]. Taibei: Zhengzhong Shuju.

_____. 1978. *The Ku-Ch'in*. Los Angeles: Wen Ying Studies.

Hung, W. 1952. *Tu Fu: China's Greatest Poet*. Cambridge, MA: Harvard University Press.

Hu, Houxuan, ed. 1999. *Jiaguwen heji shiwen* [Interpretations of the Combined Collection of Oracle Bone Inscriptions]. Beijing: Zhongguo Shehui Kexue Chubanshe.

Hu, Ji. 1957. *Sun Jin Zaju kao* [Textual Research on Zaju of Song and Jin Dynasties]. Beijing: Zhonghuu Shuju.

Hu, Taiyu. 2002. *Zhongshen zhi guo* [A Kingdom with Many Gods]. Bejing: Yanshe Chubanshe.

Hu, Yunyi. 2007. *Song ci xuan* [A Collection of Song Ci Poetry]. Shanghai: Gu Ji.

Huai Nan Zi. (Liu An) 2009. ed. Gu Qian. *Huai Nan Zi*. Beijing: Zhonghua Shuju.

Huang, Dejun. 2010. *Yue ju* [Yue Opera]. Shanghai: Wenyi Chubanshe.

Huang, Cuibo. 1998. *Tangdai guanzhong Fangyan Yinxi* [The Phonology of Central China Vernacular in Tang Dynasty]. Nanjing: Jangsu Guju.

Huang, Houming. 2005. Zhongguo shiyian yinyue wenhuaqu jin xiangguan Wunti chulun [Preliminary Study of the Geography of Pre-History Music Culture in China]. *Huaxia Gaogu* 2: 46–57.

Huang, Xiangpeng. 1986. Zhongguo chuantong yindao de shuxue Luoji guanxi wenti. *Zhongguo yinyue xue* 3: 11.

_____. 1993. *Suliu tanyuan: Zhongguo chuantong yinyue yanjiu* [Search the Origins: The Study of Chinese Traditional Music]. Beijing: Renmin Yinyue Chubanshe.

_____. 1999. *Zhongguo yinyue wenwu daxi* [Complete Collection of Chinese Music Relics: Hu Bei Province]. Zhengzhou: Daxiang Chubanshe.

_____. 2003. *Zhongguo chuan tong yin yue yi bai ba shi diao pu li ji* [A Collection of 180 Modes of Annotated Chinese Traditional Musical Scales]. Beijing: Renmin Yinyue Chubanshe.

_____, and J.S. Lam. 1992. Ancient Tunes Hidden in Modern Gongche Notation. *Yearbook for Traditional Music* 24: 8–13.

Hulst, H. van der, and N. Smith. 1988. Eds. *Autosegmental Studies on Pitch Accent*. Foris: Dordrecht.

_____, and K. Snider. 1993. eds. *The Phonology of Tone: the Representation of Tonal Register*. Berlin: Mouton de Gruyter.

Hung, T.T.N. 1987a. Syntactic and Semantic Aspects of Chinese Tone Sandhi. Ph.D. dissertation, University of California, San Diego.

_____. 1987b. Tianjin Tone Sandhi: Towards a Unified Approach. *Journal of Chinese Linguistics* 15: 274–305.

Huo, Ran. 1990. *Tangdai meixue sichao* [The Aesthetic Trends of Tang Dynasty]. Changchun: Changchun Chubanshe.

Hyman, L.M. 1975. Review of C. Cheng: A Synchronic Phonology of Mandarin Chinese. *Journal of Chinese Linguistics* 3: 88–99.

_____. 1977. ed. *Studies in Stress and Accent*. University of Southern California Press.

_____. 1978. Tone and/or Accent. *Elements of Tone, Stress and Intonation*, 1–20. ed. D. J. Napoli. Washington, DC: Georgetown University Press.

_____. 1979. A Reanalysis of Tonal Downstep. *Journal of African Languages and Linguistics* 1: 9–29.

_____. 1986. The Representation of Multiple Tone Heights. Bogers, Hulst and Mous, pp. 109–152.

_____. 1993. Register Tone and Tonal Geometry. *The Phonology of Tone: The Representation of Tonal Register*, 75–108. eds. Hulst and Snider. Berlin: Mouton de Gruyter.

_____. 2008. Word-Prosodic Typology. *Phonology* 23 (2): 225–258.

_____, and F. Katamba 1992. A New Approach to Tone in Luganda. Ms., University of California, Berkeley.

_____, F. Katamba, and L. Walusimbi. 1987. Luganda and the Strict Layer Hypothesis. *Phonology Yearbook* 4: 87–108.

_____, and Russell G. Schuh. 1974. Universals of Tone Rules. *Linguistic Inquiry* 5: 81–115.

I Shou-Fan, R. 1977. A Diachronic Study of the Ch'in Composition "Mei Hua San Nung." Master of arts thesis. Seattle: University of Washington.

Jakobson, R., and L.R. Waugh. 2002. *The Sound Shape of Language*. Berlin: Mouton de Gruyter.

_____, and M. Halle. 2002. *Fundamentals of Language*. Berlin: Mouton.

_____. 1987. *Language in Literature*. eds. K. Pomorska and S. Rudy. Cambridge, MA: Belknap Press.

Jan, Yunhua. 1977. The Silk Manuscripts on Taoism. *T'oung Pao* 63 (1): 65–84.

_____. 1980a. Tao Yuan or Tao: The Origin. *Journal of Chinese Philosophy* 7: 195–204.

_____. 1980b. Tao, Principle, and Law: The Three Key Concepts in the Yellow Emperor Taoism. *Journal of Chinese Philosophy* 7: 205–228.

_____. 1981. The Change of Images: The Yellow Emperor in Ancient Chinese Literature. *Journal of Oriental Studies* 19 (2): 117–137.

_____. 1983. Political Philosophy of the Shih Liu Ching Attributed to the Yellow Emperor Daoism. *Journal of Chinese Philosophy* 10: 205–228.

Ji, Liankang, ed. 1980. *Chuanqiu Zhanguo yinyue shiliao* [Documents of Music History of the Spring and Autumn and Waring States]. Shanghai: Wenyi Chubanshe.

_____. 1986. *Sui Tang Wudai Yinyue Shiliao* [The Record of Music History in Sui, Tang and Five Dynasties]. Shanghai: Shanghai Wenyi.

Ji, Yun. 1941. *Shenshi sisheng kao* [Shen Yue's Study of Four Tones]. Changsha: Shangwu.

Jiang, Kongyang. 1986. *XianQin yinyue meixue sixiang lungao.* Beijing: Renmin Wenxue Chubanshe.

Jiang, Wenye. 2008. *Kongzi de yue lun* [The Theory of Music by Confucius]. Shanghai: Huadong Shifan Daxue Chubanshe.

Jiang, Zuyi. 1991. *Zhongguo renmin wenxue shi* [The History of the Literature of Chinese People]. Shanghai: Shanghai Wenyi Chubanshe.

Jin, Dan. Xueliang Ma, and M. Bender. 2006. *Butterfly Mother: Miao (Hmong) Creation Epics from Guizhou, China.* Indianapolis, IN: Hackett.

Jin, Ningfen. 1992. *Nanju yanjiu bianqian* [Changes in Nanju Studies]. Tianjin: Tianjin Jiaoyu Chubanshe.

Jin, Qianqiu, ed. 1990. *QuanSongci zhongde yuewu ziliao* [The Record of Music and Dance in Complete Song Ci]. Beijing: Renmin Yinyue Chubanshe.

Jin, Xiangheng. 1993. *Xu jiaguwen bian* [Additional Collections of Oracle Bone Inscriptions]. Taibei: Yiwen Yinshuguan.

Jiu Tang Shu. Yinyue zhi [Old Book of Tang Music]. 1975. Chap. 28–31. ed. Liu Xu. Beijing: Zhonghua Shuju.

Johnson, D. 1980. *Yuan Music Dramas: Studies in Prosody and Structure and a Complete Catalogue of Northern Arias in the Dramatic Style.* Ann Arbor: Center for Chinese Studies, University of Michigan.

Johnston, I., trans. 2010. *The Mozi: A Complete Translation.* Hong Kong: Chinese University Press.

Jones, M.C. 2002. *Language Change: The Interplay of Internal, External, and Extra-Linguistic Factors.* Mouton de Gruyter.

Jorgens, E.B. 1982. *The Well-Tun'd Word.* Minneapolis: University of Minnesota Press.

Jullien, F. 2009. *The Great Image Has No Form, or on the Nonobject Through Painting.* trans. J.M. Todd. Chicago: University of Chicago Press.

Karetzky, P.E. 1996. *Arts of the Tang Court.* New York: Oxford University Press.

Karlgren, B. 1926. Philology and Ancient China. Cambridge, MA: Harvard University Press.

_____. 1935. *The Rimes in the Sung Section of the Shi King.* Goteborg: Elanders boktryckeri aktiebolag.

_____. 1936. On the Script of the Chou Dynasty. *Bulletin of the Museum of Far Eastern Antiquities* 8157–258.

_____. 1940. Grammata Serica: Script and Phonetics in Sino-Japanese. Stockholm. Reprinted from *Bulletin of the Museum of Far Eastern Antiquities* 12.

_____. 1949. *The Chinese Language.* New York: Ronald Press.

_____. 1954. *Compendium of Phonetics in Ancient and Archaic Chinese.* Stockholm: Museum of Far Eastern Antiquities.

_____. 1971. Sound and Symbol in Chinese. Hong Kong: Hong Kong University Press.

Katz, J.J. 1985. *The Philosophy of Linguistics.* Oxford: Oxford University Press.

Katz, V.J., and A. Imhausen, et al. 2007. *The Mathematics of Egypt, Mesopotamia, China, India, and Islam: A Sourcebook.* Princeton: Princeton University Press.

Kaufmann, W. 1967. "Ch'in Tablature," *Musical Notations of the Orient: Notational Systems of East, South and Central Asia*, Part III, Zither Tablatures, 267–296. Bloomington: Indiana University Press.

Keightley, D.N. 1978. Sources of Shang History: The Oracle-Bone Inscriptions of Bronze Age China. Berkeley: University of California Press.

_____. 1989. The Origins of Writing in China: Scripts and Cultural Contexts. *The Origins of Writing*, 171–202. ed. W.M. Senner. Lincoln: University of Nebraska Press.

_____. 1996. Art, Ancestors, and the Origins of Writing in China. *Representations*, Autumn, 56: 68–95.

_____. 1999. The Shang. *Cambridge History of Ancient China*, 232–291. eds. M. Loewe and E.L. Shaughnessy. Cambridge: Cambridge University Press.

_____. 2000. *The Ancestral Landscape: Time, Space, and Community in Late Shang China* (ca. 1200–1045 B.C.). Berkeley: University of California Press.

Kerr, R. 1991. Chinese Arts and Design. London: Victoria and Albert Museum.

Kim, J. 2003. *Out of the "Western Box": Towards a Multicultural Poetics in the Poetry of Ezra Pound and Charles Olson.* New York: Peter Lang.

Kim, Y.S. 2000. *The Natural Philosophy of Chu Hsi 1130–1200.* Philadelphia: American Philosophical Society.

Kime, M.W. 1969. Lyric and Song: Seventeenth-Century Musical Settings of John Donne's Poetry. Dissertation, University of Denver.

Kippen, J. 1988. The Tabla of Lucknow: A Cultural Analysis of a Musical Tradition. Cambridge, UK: Cambridge University Press.

Kirby-Smith, H.T. 1999. *The Celestial Twins: Poetry and Music Through the Ages.* Cambridge, MA: University of Massachusetts Press.

Kishibe, S. 2005. *Tōdai ongaku no rekishiteki kenkyū* [A Study on Tang Music]. Ōsaka: Izumi Shoin.

Knoblock, J. 1988–1994. *Xun-zi: A Translation and Study of the Complete Works.* Stanford: Stanford University Press.

_____, and J.K. Riegel, trans. 2000. *The Annals of Lu Buwei [Lu shi chunqiu]: A Complete Translation and Study.* Stanford: Stanford University Press.

Knoppers, G.N., and A. Hirsch. 2004. *Egypt, Israel, and the Ancient Mediterranean World: Studies in Honor of Donald B. Redford.* Leiden: Brill.

Kohn, L. 2000. *Daoism Handbook.* Boston: Brill.

_____, and M. Lafargue, eds. 1998. *Lao-Tzu and the Tao-Te-Ching.* Albany: SUNY Press.

Kramer, L. 1984. *Music and Poetry: The Nineteenth Century and After.* Berkeley: University of California Press.

Kri͡u͡kov, M.V. 2001. *The Language of Yin Inscriptions.* Chengdu: University of Sichuan Press.

Kwan, S. 2005. *Chinese Neolithic Pottery.* Hong Kong: Muwen Tang Fine Arts Publication.

Lachman, C.H., ed. 1989. *Evaluations of Sung Dynasty Painters of Renown: Liu Tao-chuns Sung-chao ming-hua ping.* Leiden: Brill.

Ladefoged, P., and I. Maddieson. 1996. *The Sounds of the World's Languages.* Oxford: Blackwell.

Laderman, Carol. 1993. *Taming the Wind of Desire.* Berkeley: University of California Press.

Lai, T.C. 1973. *Chinese Calligraphy: An Introduction.* Seattle: University of Washington Press.

Lam, J.S.C. 1988. *Creativity Within Bounds: State Sacrificial Songs from the Ming Dynasty (A.D. 1368–1644).* Ph.D. dissertation, Harvard University.

Lam, Lap. 2003. A Reconsideration of Liu Yong and His Vulgar Lyrics. *Journal of Song-Yuan Studies,* 33: 1–48.

Lan, Yusong. 2006. *Zhongguo Gudai Yinyue Shi* [A History of Music in Ancient China]. ed. Wu Daming. Beijing: Zhongyang Yinyue Xueyuan Chubanshe.

Landau, J. 1994. *Beyond Spring: Tz'u poems of the Sung Dynasty.* New York: Columbia University Press.

Landels, J.G. 1999. *Music in Ancient Greece and Rome.* NJ: Routledge.

Lao, Zi. 2001. *Dao de jing: The Book of the Way.* trans. M. Roberts. Berkeley: University of California Press.

Lau, F. 2008. Music in China: Experiencing Music, Expressing Culture. New York: Oxford University Press.

Laufer, B. 1962. *Chinese Pottery of the Han Dynasty.* Rutland, VT: Charles E. Tuttle.

Lawton, T. 1991. *New Perspectives on Chu Culture During the Eastern Zhou Period [Tung chou Ch'u wen hua t'ao lun hui].* Princeton: Princeton University Press.

Le Blanc, C., ed. trans. 1985. *Huai nan zi: Philosophical Synthesis in Early Han Thought: The Idea of Resonance (Kan-Ying).* Hong Kong: Hong Kong University Press.

Ledderose, L. 1979. *Mi Fu and the Classical Tradition of Chinese Calligraphy.* Princeton: Princeton University Press.

Lee, S.E. 1962. *Chinese Landscape Painting.* Cleveland: Cleveland Museum of Art.

_____. 1994. *A History of Far Eastern Art.* 5th ed. New York: Prentice Hall and Abrams.

_____, ed. 1998. *5000 Years: Innovation and Transformation in the Arts of China.* New York: Guggenheim Museum.

_____, and Ho Wai-kam. 1968. *China's Arts Under the Mogols: The Yuan Dynasty (1279–1368).* Cleveland: Museum of Arts.

Lee, Yuan-Yuan, and Shen, Sinyan. 1999. *Chinese Musical Instruments.* Chinese Music Society of North America Press.

Lee, Yun Kuen. 2002. Building the Chronology of Early Chinese History. *Asian Perspectives: The Journal of Archaeology for Asia and the Pacific* 41.

Legge, J., trans. 1971. *Shu ching: Book of History; A Modernized Edition of the Translations of James Legge.* Chicago: H. Regnery.

Leung, W. Lifang. 1985. *Liu Yong jiqi ci zhi yanjiu* [A Study of Liu Yong and His Ci Lyrics]. Hong Kong: Sanlian Shudian.

_____. 1976. Liu Yong and His Tz'u. Master of arts thesis, University of British Columbia.

Levin, S.R. 1971. The Conventions of Poetry. *Literary Style: A Symposium.* ed. S. Chatman. London: Oxford University Press.

Levis, J.H. 1936. *The Foundations of Chinese Musical Art.* Beiping: H. Vetch.

Lévy, A. 2000. *Chinese Literature, Ancient and Classical.* trans. W.H. Nienhauser. Bloomington: Indiana University Press.

Lewis, M.E. 2006. *The Flood Myths of Early China.* Albany: SUNY Press.

Li, Changji. 1991. *Zhongguo dudai sanqu shi* [A History of Ancient Chinese Melodies]. Shanghai: Huadong Shifan Press.

Li, Chunyi. 1958. *Zhongguo gudai yinyue shigao* [A Draft History of Music in Ancient China]. Beijing: Yinyue Chubanshe.

_____. 1994. *Xian Qin yinyue shi* [A pre–Qin History of Music]. Beijing: Renmin Yinyue Chubanshe.

_____. 1996. *Zhongguo Shanggu chutu Yueqi Zongshu* [A Summary of Ancient Music Instruments Unearthed in China]. Beijing: Wenwu.

_____. 2005. *Xian Qin Yinyue Shi* [A History of Pre-Qin Music]. Beijing: Renmin Yinyue Chubanshe.

Li, Guangdi. 1987. *Gu yue jing zhuan.* [The Ancient Yue Jing]. Shanghai: Shanghai Guji.

Li, Guotao. 2004. *Gudai Yueguan yu Gudai Xiju* [Ancient Music Office and Theater]. Guangzhou: Guangdong Gaojiao Chubanshe.

Li, Linfu. 1992. *Tang liu dian* [Six Codes of Tang]. Beijing: Zhonghua Shuju.

Li, Ling. 1985. *Changsha Zidanku Zhanguo Chu boshu yanjiu* [Studies of Changsha Zidanku Chu Boshu of Spring and Waring Period]. Beijing: Zhonghua Shuju.

_____. 1987. *Guangdong yinyue mantan* [A Detailed Discussion of Guangdong Music]. *Minzu Minjian Yinyue* 2: 29–33.

Li, Meiyan. 2003. *Qindao zhi Sixiang Jichu yu Meixue Jiazhi zhi Yanjiu: zi Xian Qin Liang Han qi Wei Jin Nan Bei Chao* [The Foundation and Aesthetics of Guqin Playing: From Pre-Qin, Two Han, Wei, Qin, to Nanbei Dynasties]. Gaoxiong: Liwen Wenhua Shiye Gufen Youxian Gongsi.

Li, Mingzhong. 2000. *Zhongguo Qinxue* [Chinese Qinology]. Vol. 1. Shanxi: Shanxi Society Science Magazine Association.

Li, Qingzhao. 2009. *Li Qingzhao shici xuan* [Selected Shi and Ci Poems of Li Qingzhao]. ed. Zhuge Yibing. Beijing: Zhonghua Shuju.

Li, Ruru. 2010. *The Soul of Beijing Opera: Theatrical Creativity and Continuity in the Changing World.* Hong Kong: Hong Kong University Press.

Li, Sui Leung. 2006. *Cross-Dressing in Chinese Opera.* Hong Kong: Hong Kong University Press.

Li, Tiandao. 2004. *Sima xiangru fu de meixue sixiang yu di yu wen hua xin tai* [Aesthetical Theory of Sima Xiangru's fu Literature and Its Cultural Form]. Beijing: Social Sciences Press.

Li, Xiangting. 1993. *Tangdai Guqin yanzou meixue ji yinyue sixiang yanjiu* [A Study of the Aesthetics and Musicology of Guqin in Tang Dynasty]. Taibei: Xing Zheng Yuan Wen Hua Jian She Wei Yuan Hui.

Li, Xiao. 2005. *Chinese Kunqu Opera.* San Francisco: Long River Press.

Li, Xiaobing. *Zhongguo xiju qiyuan* [The Origin of Chinese Theater]. Shanghai: Zhishi Chubanshe.

Li, Xiaoding. 1965. *Jiagu wenzi jishi* [Collection and Interpretation of the Characters of Oracle Inscription]. Taibei: Zhongyang Yanjiu Yuan Lishi Yuyan Yanjiusuo.

_____. 1977. *Hanzi shihua* [The Story of Chinese Writing]. Taibei: Lian Jing.

Li, Xiaozhong. 2000. *Sima xiangru ji jiaozhu* [Selected Writings Sima Xiangru and Analysis and Commentary]. Cheng Du: Bashu.

Li, Xiusheng. 1996. *Yuan zaju shi* [A History of Yuan Variety Theater]. Nanjing: Jiangsu Guji Chubanshe.

_____. 1997. *Guben xiqu jumu tiyao* [Outlines and Analyses of Old Opera Scripts]. Beijing: Wenhua Yishu Chubanshe.

Li, Xueqin. 1985. Kaogu faxian yu Zhongguo wenzi qiyuan [Archaeological Discoveries and the Origins of Chinese Writing]. *Zhōngguó wénhùa yánjiū jíkān* 2: 146–157. Shanghai: Fudan University Press.

_____. 1987. Lun xinchu dawenkou wenhua taoqi fuhao [On the Newly Discovered Dàwènkǒu Culture Pottery Inscriptions]. *Wénwù* 12: 75–80.

_____, G. Harbottle, Zhang Juzhong, and Wang Changsui. 2003. The Earliest Writing? Sign Use in the Seventh Millennium BC at Jiahu, Henan Province, China. *Antiquity* 77.

Li, Yuzheng. 1986. Qinzuo jinyin "yufu zhong." *Yueqi* 2.

Li, Zhizao. 1987. *Pangong liyueshu* [Collection of Court Music and Ritual]. Shanghai: Guji.

Li, Zuofeng. 2004. *Gudai hanyu yufa xue* [Grammology of Old Chinese]. Beijing: Shangwu.

Liang, Donghan. 1959. *Hanzi di jiegou jiqi liu bian.* [The Structure of Chinese Characters and Their Transformation]. Shanghai: Shanghai Jiaoyu Chubanshe.

Laing, E. The Development of Flower Depiction and the Origin of the Bird-and-Flower Genre in Chinese Art. *Bulletin of the Museum of Far Eastern Antiquities* 64 (1992): 180–223.

Lau, F. 2008. *Music in China: Experiencing Music, Expressing Culture.* New York: Oxford University Press.

_____, and Yayoi Uno Everett, eds. 2004. *Locating East Asia in Western Art Music.* Wesleyan University Press.

Liang, Ming-Yüeh. 1972. *The Chinese Ch'in: Its History and Music.* San Francisco, Chinese National Music Association, San Francisco Conservatory of Music.

_____. 1973. The Art of Yin-jou Techniques for the Seven-Stringed Zither. Ann Arbor, University Microfilms, Ph.D., University of California at Los Angeles.

_____. 1980. Ch'in. *New Groves Dictionary of Music and Musicians,* 6th ed. 3: 264–9. London: MacMillan.

_____. 1984. The Art of the Qin. *Music of the Billion,* 197–211.

Liao, Ben, and Liu Yanjun. 2000. *Zhongguo xiqu fazhan shi* [A History of the Evolution of Classical Chinese Dramas]. 4 vols. Taiyuan: Shanxi Jiaoyu Chubanshe.

Liao, Mingchun. 2001. *A Preliminary Study on the Newly-Unearthed Bamboo Inscriptions of the Chu Kingdom: An Investigation of the Materials from and About the Shangshu in the Guodian Chu Slips.* Taipei: Taiwan Guji.

Liao, Weiqing. 2006. *Zhonggu yuewu yanjiu* [Ancient Music and Dance]. Taibei: Li Ren.

Liao, Xudong. 1995. *Chuci yufa yan jiu* [A Study of the Grammar of Chuci]. Beijing: Yuwen Chubanshe.

Lieberman, F. 1983. *A Chinese Zither Tutor: The Mei-an Ch'in-p'u.* Trans. and commentary. Hong Kong: Hong Kong University Press.

_____. 1987. *The Chinese Long Zither Ch'in: A Study Based on the Mei-an Ch'in-p'u.* Ann Arbor: University Microfilms International.

Lightfoot, D. 1979. *Principles of Diachronic Syntax.* Cambridge, UK: Cambridge University Press.

_____. 1982. *The Language Lottery: Toward a Biology of Grammars.* Cambridge, MA: MIT Press.

_____. 1991. *How to Set Parameters: Arguments from Language Change.* Cambridge, MA: MIT Press.

Lin, Ci. 2006. *The Art of Chinese Painting.* Beijing: Wuzhou Chuanbo Chubanshe.

Lin, Jiali, ed. 2009. *Chu Ci with Comments and Interpretations.* Beijing: Zhonghua Shuju.

Lin, Shuenfu. 1978. *The Transformation of the Chinese Lyrical Tradition: Chiang K'uei and Southern Sung Tz'u Poetry.* Princeton: Princeton University Press.

_____. 1994. The Formation of a Distinct Generic Identity for Tz'u. *Voices of the Song Lyric in China,* 3–30. ed. P. Yu. Princeton: Princeton University Press.

Liu, Bo. 1989. *Qinghai caitao wenshi* [Designs on Painted Pottery from Qinghai]. Xining: Qinghai Renmin Chubanshe.

Liu, Dajie. 1997. *Zhongguo wenxue fazhan shi* [A History of Chinese Literature]. Tianjin: Baihua Wenyi Chubanshe.

Liu, J.Y. 1962. *The Art of Chinese Poetry*. Chicago: University of Chicago Press.
_____. 1968. *The Poetry of Li Shang-yin; Ninth-Century Baroque*. Chicago: University of Chicago Press.
_____. 1970. The Lyrics of Liu Yung. *Tamkang Review* 1 (2): 1–44.
_____. 1974. *Major Lyricists of the Northern Sung, A.D. 960–1126*. Princeton: Princeton University Press.
_____. 1975. *Chinese Theories of Literature*. Chicago: University of Chicago Press.
_____, and R.J. Lynn. 1988. Language — Paradox — Poetics: A Chinese Perspective. Princeton: Princeton University Press.
Liu, Jianguo. 2004. *Distinguishing and Correcting the Pre-Qin Forged Classics*. Xian: Shaanxi Renmin Chubanshe.
Liu, Li. 2004. The Chinese Neolithic: Trajectories to Early States. Cambridge, UK: Cambridge University Press.
_____, and H. Xiu. 2007. Rethinking Erlitou: Legend, History and Chinese Archaeology. *Antiquity* 81 (314): 886–901.
Liu, M. Bong-Ray. 1976. *Tradition and Change in Kunqu Opera*. Thesis, University of California, Los Angeles.
Liu, Nanzi. 1986a. *Nanqu xinzheng* [New Evidence of Nanqu]. Beijing: Zhonghua Shuju.
_____. 1986b. *Xiqu wenwu congkao* [A Collection of Studies of Xiqu Relics]. Beijing: Zhongguo Xiju Chubanshe.
Liu, Rueyu. 1990. *Zhongguo shixue* [Chinese Theory of Poetry]. Zhengzhou: Henan Renmin Chubanshe.
Liu, Shuiyun. 2005. *Ming Qing jiayue yanjiu* [A Study of Family Music in Ming and Qing Dynasties]. Shanghai: Guji Chubanshe.
Liu, Wu-chi, and I. Lo, eds. 1975. *Sunflower Splendor: Three Thousand Years of Chinese Poetry*. New York: Anchor Books.
Liu, Xiang, et al. 1996. *Shang Zhou guwenzi duben* [Reader of Shang-Zhou Ancient Characters]. Beijing: Yuwen.
Liu, Xiang, and D. Hawkes, trans. 1959. *Ch'u tz'u: The Songs of the South, an Ancient Chinese Anthology*. Oxford: Clarendon.
Liu, Xicheng. 1998. *Zhongguo yuanshi yishu* [Primitive Arts in China]. Shanghai: Wenyi Chubanshe.
Liu, Xie. 1992. *Wen xin diao long*. Guiyang: Guizhou Renmin Chubanshe.
Liu, Xinhong. 2004. Investigation and Study of Bian Nao of Shang Site. Master of arts thesis, Chinese Conservatory of Music.
Liu, Xu, et al. 2004. *Jiu Tang shu* [The Old Book of Tang]. Shanghai: Hanyu Dacidian Chubanshe.
Liu, Xuekai, and Yu Shucheng. 2004. *Li shangyin shige jijie* [Selected Poems of Li Shangyin and Interpretation]. Beijing: Zhonghua Shuju.
_____. 2007. *Wen Tingyun quanji jiaozhu* [Complete Works of Wen Tingyun and Commentary]. Beijing: Zhonghua Shuju.
Liu, Yaomin. 1982. *Ci yu yinyue* [Ci and Music]. Kunming: Yunnan Renmin Chubanshe.
Liu, Yongping. 1998. *The Origin of Chinese Law*. Oxford: Oxford University Press.
Liu, Zaisheng. 1989. *Zhongguo gudai yinyue shi jianshu* [A Summary of Ancient Chinese Music]. Beijing: Zhongguo Yinyue Chubanshe.
_____. 2003. *Zhongguo yinyue de lishi xingtai* [The Historic Shape of Chinese Music]. Shanghai: Shanghai Yinyue Xueyuan Chubanshe.
Liu, Z., et al. 2007. Influence of Taoism on the Invention of the Purple Pigment Used on the Qin Terra Cotta Warriors. *Journal of Archaeological Science* 34 (11): 1878–1883.
Lloyd, G.E.R. 1971. *Early Greek Science: Thales to Aristotle*. New York: Norton.
_____. 2002. *The Ambitions of Curiosity: Understanding the World in Ancient Greece and China*. Cambridge, UK: Cambridge University Press.
_____. 2004. *Ancient Worlds, Modern Reflections: Philosophical Perspectives on Greek and Chinese Science and Culture*. Oxford: Clarendon.
_____. 2006. *Ancient Worlds, Modern Reflections: Philosophical Perspectives on Greek and Chinese Science and Culture*. Oxford: Clarendon.

_____. 2007. *Cognitive Variations: Reflections on the Unity and Diversity of the Human Mind.* Oxford: Oxford University Press.

_____, and N. Sivin. 2002. *The Way and the Word: Science and Medicine in Early China and Greece.* New Haven: Yale University Press.

Loehr, M. 1980. *The Great Painters of China.* New York: Harper and Row.

Loewe, M. 1979. *Ways to Paradise: The Chinese Quest for Immortality.* London: George Allen and Unwin.

_____. 1986. *The Former Han Dynasty. The Cambridge History of China: Volume I: The Ch'in and Han Empires, 221 B.C.–A.D. 220,* 103–222. ed. D. Twitchett. Cambridge, UK: Cambridge University Press.

_____, and E.L. Shaughnessy, eds. 1999. The Cambridge History of Ancient China: From the Origins of Civilization to 221 B.C. Cambridge, UK: Cambridge University Press.

Loprieno, A. 1995. *Ancient Egyptian: A Linguistic Introduction.* Cambridge, UK: Cambridge University Press.

_____. 1996. *Ancient Egyptian Literature: History and Forms.* Leiden: Brill.

Lotz, J. 1960. Metric Typology. *Style in Language,* 135–40. ed. T. Sebeok. Cambridge, UK: Cambridge University Press.

Lowes, J.L. 1927. *The Road to Xanadu: A Study in the Ways of the Imagination.* Boston: Houghton Mifflin.

Lu, Buwei. 2000. *The Annals of Lu Buwei: A Complete Translation.* trans. J. Knoblock and J. Riegel. Stanford: Stanford University Press.

Lu, Ji. 1979. Yuanshi shizu shehui dao yindai de jizhong taoxun Tansuo woguo wushen yinjie de xingcheng. *Yinyue Luncong* 2.

Lu, Zongda. 1981. *Shuowen Jiezi tonglun* [A General Survey of *Shuowen Jiezi*]. Beijing: Beijing Press.

Lülü, Zhengyi, ed. 1968. *Qing Kangxi and Qianlong.* Taibei: Taiwan Shangwu Yinshuguan.

Luo, Guanzhong. 2004. *Three Kingdoms.* Beijing: Foreign Language Press.

Luo, Qin, ed. 2007. *Zhongguo yinyue shi yanjiu juan* [Studies on the History of Chinese Music]. Shanghai: Shanghai Conservatory of Music.

Lv, Weifen, and Yang Lian. 1995. eds. *Zhang ke jiu ji jiao zhu* [A Collection of Zhang Kejiu's Work with Commentaries]. Hang Zhou: Zhejiang Guji Chubanshe.

Lyall, C.J. 1918–24. *The Mufaḍḍaliyyāt: An Anthology of Ancient Arabian Odes.* 3 vols. Oxford: Clarendon.

Lynn, R.J. 2001. Mongol-Yuan Classical Verse (Shih). *The Columbia History of Chinese Literature,* 383–390. ed. V. Mair. New York: Columbia University Press.

Ma, Xueliang. 1999. *Minzu yuyan yanjiu wenji* [Studies of Ethnical Dialects]. Beijing: Zhongyang Minzu Xueyuan Chubanshe.

_____, and Dai Qingxia. 1993. Yi yuzhi yuyin bijiao yanjiu [Comparative Study of the Phonology of the Yi Language Branch]. *Minzu yuwen yanjiu wenji* [Collected Research Studies on Nationality Languages]. Beijing: Zhongyang Minzu Xueyuan Chubanshe.

Maciocia, G. 1989. *The Foundations of Chinese Medicine: A Comprehensive Text for Acupuncturists and Herbalists.* Edinburgh: Churchill Livingstone.

Mackerras, C. 1971. The Growth of the Chinese Regional Drama in the Ming and Ch'ing. *Journal of Oriental Studies* 9 (1): 58–91.

_____. 1972. *The Rise of Peking Opera 1770–1870.* Oxford: Oxford University Press.

_____. 1988. *Chinese Theater: From Its Origins to the Present Day.* Honolulu: University of Hawaii Press.

Maddieson, I. 1984. *Patterns of Sounds.* Cambridge, UK: Cambridge University Press.

_____, and P. Ladefoged. 1996. *The Sounds of the World's Languages.* Oxford: Blackwell.

Mair, V.H. 1983. *Tun-huang Popular Narratives.* Cambridge, UK: Cambridge University Press.

_____. 1986–87. Notes on the Maudgalyayana Legend in East Asia. *Monumenta Serica* 37: 83–93.

_____. 1989. *T'ang Transformation Texts.* Cambridge, MA: Harvard University Press.

_____. 1990. *Tao Te Ching: The Classic Book of Integrity and the Way, by Lao Tzu; An Entirely New Translation Based on the Recently Discovered Ma-Wang-Tui Manuscripts.* New York: Bantam Books.

_____. 2001. *The Columbia History of Chinese Literature.* New York: Columbia University Press.

Mao, Dun. 1962. Guanyu xiaoxuesheng xuehui pinyin zimu huisheng wenti [Concerning the Problem of Elementary School Children Losing Their Mastery of the Phonetic Alphabet]. *Wenzi Gaige* 62.

Martzloff, J. 1996. *A History of Chinese Mathematics.* New York: Springer.

Mascarelli, G., and R. Mascarelli. 2003. *The Ceramics of China: 5000 BC to 1900 AD.* Atglen, PA: Schiffer.

Mather, R.B., ed. 2003. *The Age of Eternal Brilliance: Three Lyric Poets of the Yung-ming Era (483–493).* 2 vols. Leiden: Brill.

McCarthy, J., and A. Prince 1986. *Prosodic Morphology.* Waltham: Brandeis University.

_____. 1993a. *Prosodic Morphology.* Rutgers University.

_____. 1993b. *Generalized Alignment.* Amherst: University of Massachusetts.

_____. 1994a. *Prosodic Morphology, Parts 1 and 2.* Utrecht: Prosodic Morphology Workshop.

_____. 1994b. Emergence of the Unmarked: Optimality in Prosodic Morphology. *North East Linguistics Society* 24: 333–379.

_____. 1995a. Prosodic Morphology. *The Handbook of Phonological Theory.* John A. Goldsmith, ed. Cambridge, MA, and Oxford, UK: Blackwell, 318–366.

_____. 1995b. *Faithfulness and Reduplicative Identity.* Amherst: University of Massachusetts.

McCawley, J. 1970. A Note on Tone in Tiv. *Studies in African Linguistics* 2: 257–270.

_____. 1993. *Everything That Linguists Have Always Wanted to Know About Logic but Were Ashamed to Ask.* Chicago: University of Chicago Press.

McCraw, D. 1992. *Du Fu's Laments from the South.* Honolulu: University of Hawaii Press.

McDermott, J.P. 1999. *State and Court Ritual in China.* Cambridge, UK: Cambridge University Press.

McNair, A. 1998. *The Upright Brush: Yan Zhenqing's Calligraphy and Song Literati Politics.* Honolulu: University of Hawaii Press.

McWhorter, J.H. 2002. *The Power of Babel: A Natural History of Language.* London: Heinemann.

Mei, Lanfang. 2000. *Mei lanfang quanji* [Complete Works of Mei Lanfang]. 8 vols. Shi Jia Zhuang: Hebei Jiaoyu Chubanshe.

Mei, Tsulin. 1970. Tones and Prosody in Middle Chinese and the Origin of the Rising Tone. *Harvard Journal of Asiatic Studies* 30: 86–110.

_____. 1977. Tones and Tone Sandhi in Sixteenth Century Mandarin. *Journal of Chinese Linguistics* 5: 237–260.

Meow, Hui Goh. 2004. Tonal Prosody in Three Poems by Wang Rong. *The Journal of the American Oriental Society.* 124: 59–75.

Miao, Jianhua. 2006. *Guqin meixue sixiang yanjiu* [Studies on the Aesthetic of Guqin]. Shanghai: Shanghai Yinyue Xueyuan Chubanshe.

Michalowski, P. 1980. Sumerian as an Ergative Language. *Journal of Cuneiform Studies* 32: 86–103.

_____. 1987. Language, Literature and Writing at Ebla. *Ebla: 1975–1985: Dieci anni di studi linguistici e Filologici,* 165–175. Ed. L. Cagni. Naples: Instituto Universitario Orientale.

_____. 1993. Tokenism. *American Anthropologist* 95: 996–99.

_____. 2000. The Life and Death of the Sumerian Language in Comparative Perspective. Ann Arbor: University of Michigan. http://www-personal.umich.edu/~piotrm/DIG LOS-1.htm.

_____. 2006. The Lives of the Sumerian Language. *Margins of Writing, Origins of Cultures,* 159–184. Chicago: Oriental Institute of the University of Chicago.

Minford, J., and J.S.M. Lau., eds. 2000. *Classical Chinese Literature.* New York: Columbia University Press.

Ming Shi. Yue 1 1974. eds. Zhang Tingyu, et al. 1516. Beijing: Zhonghua Shuju.

Ming, Zuoqiu, and B. Watson. 1989. *The Tso Chuan: Selections from China's Oldest Narrative History.* New York: Columbia University Press.

Minkova, D. 2003. *Alliteration and Sound Change in Early English.* Cambridge, UK: Cambridge University Press.

Mitani, Yoko. 1981. Some Melodic Features of Chinese Qin Music. *Music and Tradition: Essays* on *Asian and Other Music Presented to Lawrence Picken*, 123–142. eds. D. Widdess and R. Wolpert. Cambridge, UK: University Press.

Mou, Huaichuan. 2003. *Rediscovering Wen Tingyun: A Historical Key to a Poetic Labyrinth*. New York: State University of New York Press.

Moule, A.C. 1908. A List of the Musical and Other Sound Producing Instruments of the Chinese. *Journal of the North China Branch of the Royal Asiatic Society* 39: 1–160.

Moule, G.E. 1901. Notes on the Ting-chi, or Half-Yearly Sacrifice to Confucius. *Journal of the North China Branch of the Royal Asiatic Society* 33: 37–73.

Munakata, Kiyohiko. 1974. Ching Hao's "Pi-fa-chi": A Note on the Art of Brush. *Artibus Asiae*. Supplementum, 31: 1–56.

_____. 1991. *Sacred Mountains in Chinese Art*. Urbana: University of Illinois Press.

Munsterberg, H. 1955. *The Landscape Painting of China and Japan*. Rutland, VT: Charles S. Tuttle.

_____. 1986. *Symbolism in Ancient Chinese Art*. New York: Hacker.

Murakami, Tetsumi. 1976. *Sōshi kenkyū: Tō Godai hoku-sō hen* [Song Ci Studies: Tang, Five Dynasties and Northern Song]. Tokyo: Sobunsha.

Murck, A. 2002. *Poetry and Painting in Song China: The Subtle Art of Dissent*. Cambridge, MA: Harvard University Asia Center for the Harvard-Yenching Institute.

_____, and Wen Fong, eds. 1991. *Words and Images: Chinese Poetry, Calligraphy, and Painting*. New York: Metropolitan Museum of Art; Princeton: Princeton University Press.

Mutschler, F., and A. Mittag. 2008. *Conceiving the Empire: China and Rome Compared*. Oxford: Oxford University Press.

Nakata, Yujiro, and J. Hunter, eds. 1983. *Chinese Calligraphy: A History of the Art of China*. New York: Weatherhill.

Nan, Zhuo. 1988. *Jie gu lu*. Shanghai: Shanghai Guji Chubanshe.

Needham, J. 1988. *Science and Civilisation in China*. 4 vols. Cambridge, UK: Cambridge University Press.

Nettl, B. 1993. *The Study of Ethnomusicology*. Urbana: University of Illinois Press.

_____. 1993a. *Words and Song, Language and Music: An Enduring Issue in Ethnomusicology*. Wade, 1993, 107–119.

_____. 1998. *In the Course of Performance: Studies in the World of Musical Improvisation*. Chicago: University of Chicago Press.

_____. 2001. Improvisation. *New Grove Dictionary of Music and Musicians*. London: MacMillan.

Newnham, R. 1987. *About Chinese*. New York: Penguin Books.

Ng, On Cho, and Q.E. Wang, eds. 2005. *Mirroring the Past: The Writing and Use of History in Imperial China*. Honolulu: University of Hawaii Press.

Ng, So Kam. 1992. *Brushstrokes: Styles and Techniques of Chinese Painting*. San Francisco: Asian Art Museum of San Francisco.

Nie, Chongzheng, ed. 1999. *Qingdai gongting huihua: Gugong bowayuan cang wenwu zhenpin* [Qing Dynasty Court Paintings in the Palace Museum]. Shanghai: Kexue Jishu Chubanshe.

Nielsen, B. 2003. *A Companion to Yi Jing Numerology and Cosmology: Chinese Studies of Images and Numbers from Han (202 BCE–220 CE) to Song (960–1279 CE)* London: Routledge-Curzon.

Niles, J.D. 1983. *Beowulf: The Poem and Its Tradition*. Cambridge, MA: Harvard University Press.

Nivison, D.S. 1999. *The Key to the Chronology of the Three Dynasties: The "Modern Text" Bamboo Annals*. Philadelphia: University of Pennsylvania Press.

_____. 2009. *The Riddle of the Bamboo Annals*. Taipei: Airiti Press.

Norman, J. 1988. *Chinese*. New York: Cambridge University Press.

_____, and W. South Coblin. 1995. A New Approach to Chinese Historical Linguistics. *Journal of the American Oriental Society* 115: 576–84.

Noske, R. 1992. Moraic Versus Constituent Syllables. *Silbenphonologie des Deutschen*, 284–328. eds. P. Eisenberg, K.H. Ramers, and H. Vater. Tübingen: Narr.

_____. 1993. *A Theory of Syllabification and Segmental Alternation: With Studies on the Phonology of French, German, Tonkawa and Yawelmani*. Tübingen: Niemeyer.

Ouyang, Yuqian. 1980. *Tangdai wudao* [Tang Dance]. Shanghai: Wenyi Chubanshe.
Ouyang, Zhongshi, and Wen C. Fong. 2008. *Chinese Calligraphy (The Culture and Civilization of China)*. New Haven: Yale University Press.
Ouyang, Xiu, et al. 1987. *Xin Tang shu* [The New Book of Tang]. Shanghai: Shanghai Guji Chubanshe.
Owen, S. 1974. Hsieh Hui-lien's "Snow Fu": A Structural Study. *Journal of the American Oriental Society*, 94 (1):14–23.
_____. 1981. *The Great Age of Chinese Poetry: The High T'ang*. Cambridge, MA: Harvard University Press.
_____. 1985. *Traditional Chinese Poetry and Poetics: Omen of the World*. Madison: University of Wisconsin Press.
_____. 1986. *Remembrances: The Experience of the Past in Classical Chinese Literature*. Cambridge, Mass.: Harvard University Press.
_____. 1992. *Readings in Chinese Literary Thought*. Cambridge: MA: Harvard University Press.
_____. 1994. Meaning the Words: The Genuine as a Value in the Tradition of the Song Lyric. *Voices of the Song Lyric in China*, 30–69. ed. P. Yu. Berkeley: University of California Press.
_____. 1997. *An Anthology of Chinese Literature: Beginnings to 1911*. New York: Norton.
_____. 2006. The Late Tang: Chinese Poetry of the Mid-Ninth Century (827–860). Cambridge, Harvard University Press.
_____. 2006a. *The Making of Early Chinese Classical Poetry*. Cambridge, MA: Harvard University Press.
Packard, J.L. 2000. *The Morphology of Chinese: A Linguistic and Cognitive Approach*. New York: Cambridge University Press.
Parrish, C. 1958. *The Notation of Medieval Music*. London: Faber and Faber.
Parsons, J. 2004. *The Cambridge Companion to the Lied*. Cambridge, UK: Cambridge University Press.
Paterson, L.M. 1995. *The World of the Troubadours: Medieval Occitan Society, C. 1100–C. 1300*. Cambridge. UK: Cambridge University Press.
Peerenboom, R.P. 1993. *Law and Morality in Ancient China: The Silk Manuscripts of Huang-Lao*. Albany: SUNY Press.
Pei, Xuehai. 1996. *Gu shu xu zi ji shi* [A Collection of Empty Words in Ancient Chinese]. Shanghai: Shanghai Shudian.
Pian, Rulan Chao. 1967. *Song Dynasty Musical Sources and Their Interpretation*. Cambridge, MA: Harvard University Press.
_____. 1972. *Text Setting with the Shipyi Animated Aria*. Cambridge, MA: Harvard University.
_____. 1975. Aria Structural Patterns in the Peking Opera. In *Chinese and Japanese Music-Dramas*, 65–97. ed. J.I. Crump and W.P. Malm. Ann Arbor: University of Michigan, Center for Chinese Studies.
Picken, L.E.R. 1955. The Origin of the Short Lute. *Galpin Society Journal* 8: 32–42.
_____. 1969a. Tang Music and Musical Instruments. *T'oung Pao* 55: 74–122.
_____. 1969b. Review: Music and Musical Sources of the Song Dynasty. *Journal of the American Oriental Society* 89 (3): 600–621.
_____. 1981. *Music and Tradition: Essays on Asian and Other Musics Presented to Laurence Picken*. Cambridge, UK: Cambridge University Press.
_____. 1981. *Music from the Tang Court*. Trans. and eds. 7 vols. Oxford: Oxford University Press.
_____. 1999. *The Music of Far Eastern Asia. I. China. Ancient and Oriental Music*, 83–134. ed. E. Wellesz. Oxford: Oxford University Press.
_____. 2000. *Music from the Tang Court*. Cambridge, UK: Cambridge University Press.
Pierrehumbert, J. 1980. The Phonology and Phonetics of English Intonation. Ph. D. dissertation, Massachusetts Institute of Technology.
_____. 1990. Phonological and Phonetic Representations. *Journal of Phonetics* 18: 375–94.
_____, and M.E. Beckman. 1988. *Japanese Tone Structure*. Cambridge, MA: MIT Press.
Pigott, V.C. 1999. *The Archaeometallurgy of the Asian Old World*. Philadelphia: University of Pennsylvania Museum of Archaeology and Anthropology.
Porkert, M. 1974. *The Theoretical Foundations of Chinese Medicine: Systems of Correspondence*. Cambridge, MA: MIT Press.

Post, J.C. 2004. *Ethnomusicology: A Guide to Research*. New York: Routledge.

Pregadio, F. 2005. *Great Clarity: Daoism and Alchemy in Early Medieval China*. Stanford: Stanford University Press.

Preminger, A. and T.V.F. Brogan. 1993. eds. *The New Princeton Encyclopedia of Poetry and Poetics*. Princeton: Princeton University Press.

Pulleyblank, E.G. 1970. Notes on the hP'ags-pa Alphabet for Chinese. *W.B. Henning Memorial Volume*, 358–375. ed. M. Boyce and I. Gershevitch. London: Lund Humphries.

_____. 1970–71. Late Middle Chinese. *Asia Major* 15: 197–239, 16: 121–68.

_____. 1973. Some New Hypotheses Concerning Word Families in Chinese. *Journal of Chinese Linguistics* 1: 111–25.

_____. 1978. The Nature of the Middle Chinese Tones and Their Development to Early Mandarin. *Journal of Chinese Linguistics* 6: 173–203.

_____. 1984. *Middle Chinese: A Study in Historical Phonology*. Vancouver: University of British Columbia Press.

_____. 1991. *Lexicon of Reconstructed Pronunciation in Early Middle Chinese, Late Middle Chinese, and Early Mandarin*. Vancouver: University of British Columbia Press.

_____. 1994a. The Old Chinese Origin of Type A and B Syllables. *Journal of Chinese Linguistics* 22: 73–100.

_____. 1994b. Pharyngeal Glides and Zero Initials in Chinese. *Proceedings of the 3rd International Conference on Chinese Linguistics*, City Polytechnic of Hong Kong, July 14–16, 1994.

_____. 1995. European Studies on Chinese Phonology: The First Phase. Europe Studies China, 339–367. ed. M. Wilson and J. Cayley. London: Han-shan Tang Books.

_____. 1996. Prosody or Pharyngealization in Old Chinese? The Origin of the Distinction Between Type A and Type B Syllables. *Journal of American Oriental Society* 116 (1): 105–116.

_____. 1998. Qieyun and Yunjing: The Essential Foundation for Chinese Historical Linguistics. *Journal of the American Oriental Society* 118: 200–216.

_____. 1999. Chinese Traditional Phonology. *Asia Major* 3rd ser., 12: 101–37.

Qi, Chongtian. 1990. *On Calligraphy*. Beijing: Peking University Press.

_____. 1997. *Shu fa wen zi xue* [Calligraphy and Scripture]. Beijing: Beijing Yuyan Wenhua Daxue Chubanshe.

_____. 1997a. *Shengyun yuyuan zidian* [A Dictionary of Phonology and Etymology]. Chongqing: Chongqing Chubanshe.

Qi, Rushan. 2008. *Jingju zhi bianqian* [The Evolution of Peking Opera]. Shenyang: Liaoning Jiaoyu Chubanshe.

Qian, Mu. 1977. *Guo Shi Dagang* [An Outline of Chinese History]. Taipei: Guoli Bianyi Guan.

Qian, Nanyang. 1981. *Xiwen gailun* [A General Study of Playwrights]. Shanghai: Guji.

_____, ed. 1956. *Song Yuan xiwen jiyi* [Collected Texts of Song and Yuan Nanxi]. Shanghai: Gudian Wenxue.

_____, ed. 1979. *Yongle dadian xiwen sanzhong jiaozhu* [Three Collected and Annotated Xiqu Texts from the Great Collection of Yongle]. Beijing: Zhonghua Shuju.

Qian, Zhixi. 2000. *Han Wei yuefu de yinyue yu shi*. Zhengzhou: Daxiang Chubanshe.

Qiao, Jianzhong. 1999. *Zhongguo yinyue* [Chinese Music]. Beijing: Wenhua Yishu Chubanshe.

_____, ed. 2003. *Zhongguo chuantong minjian yishi yinyue yanjiu* [Studies of Traditional Ceremonial Music in China]. Kunming: Yunnan Renmin Chubanshe.

Qinqu Jicheng [Collection of Qin Music]. 1981. Beijing Guqin Research Associate, Institute of Music at the Academy of Arts and Literature, Chinese Ministry of Culture. Beijing: Zhonghua Shuju.

Qiu, Qiongsun. 1989. *Yanyue tanwei* [A Study of Yan Music]. Shanghai: Guji.

_____. 1999. *Lidai yuezhi luzhi jiaoshi*. [Music Scale and System of Measurement of Dynasties]. Beijing: Renmin Yinyue Chubanshe.

Qiu, Xigui. 1988. *Wenzixue gaiyao* [A Summary of Chinese Writing]. Beijing: Shang Wu.

_____. 1992a. *Guwenzi lunji* [Study of Chinese Writing]. Beijing: Zhonghua Shuju.

_____. 1998. A Talk About the Method of Empty Words in Bronze Inscription. *Gudai hanyu yanjiu* 1.

_____. 2000. *Chinese Writing*. Trans. G.L. Mattos and J. Norman. Berkeley: University of California Press.

_____. 2004. *Zhongguo chutu guwenxian shijiang* [Ten Lectures on Unearthed Inscriptions]. Shanghai: Fudan University Press.

Qu, Yuan. 1979. *Jiu ge* [Nine Songs]. ed. Wen Xiao. Beijing: Renmin Wenxue Chubanshe.

_____. 2009. *Chu Ci* [The Song of the South]. Beijing: Zhonghua Shuju.

Ramanna, R. 1993. *The Structure of Music in Raga and Western Systems.* Bombay: Bharatiya Vidya Bhavan.

Ramsey, S.R. 1987. *The Languages of China.* Princeton: Princeton University Press.

Rao Zongyi. 1985. *Chu boshu* [Chu Silk Text]. Beijing: Zhonghua Shuju.

_____. 1987. The Calligraphic Art of the Chu Silk Manuscript. *Orientations.* 18.9: 79–84.

Rawski, E.S, R.S. Watson, and B. Yung. eds. 1996. *Harmony and Counterpoint: Ritual Music in Chinese Context.* Stanford: Stanford University Press.

Rawson, J. 1980. *Ancient China: Art and Archaeology.* New York: Harper and Row.

_____. 1983. *The Chinese Bronzes of Yunnan.* London: Sidgwick and Jackson.

_____. 1984. *Chinese Ornament: The Lotus and the Dragon.* New York: Holmes and Meier.

_____. 1987. *Chinese Bronzes: Art and Ritual.* London: British Museum.

_____. 1990a. *Ancient Chinese and Ordos Bronzes.* Hong Kong: Oriental Ceramics Society of Hong Kong.

_____. 1990b. *Western Zhou Ritual Bronzes from the Arthur M. Sackler Collections.* Cambridge, MA: Harvard University Press.

_____. 1995. *Chinese Jade from the Neolithic to the Qing.* London: British Museum.

Rawson, J. ed. 1992. *The British Museum Book of Chinese Art.* London: British Museum Press.

Reichl, R., ed. 2000. *The Oral Epic: Performance and Music.* Berlin: VWB.

Ren, Bantang, ed. 1987. *Dunhuang geci zongbian* [Complete Collection of Duanhuang Lyrics]. Shanghai: Guji.

Ren, Jiyu, and Zhong Zhaopeng, eds. 1991. *Daozang tiyao* [A Conspectus of the Daoist Canon]. Beijing: Chinese Academy of Social Sciences.

Riley, J. 1997. *Chinese Theatre and the Actor in Performance.* Cambridge, UK: Cambridge University Press.

Robbins, R.H. 1968. ed. *Secular Lyrics of the 14th and 15th Centuries.* Oxford: Clarendon.

Roberts, I. 1993. *Verbs and Diachronic Syntax.* Dordrecht: Kluwer

Roberts, Michael. 1989. *The Jeweled Style: Poetry and Poetics in Late Antiquity.* Ithaca: Cornell University Press.

Robinet, I. 1990. The Place and Meaning of the Notion of Taiji in Taoist Sources Prior to the Ming Dynasty. *History of Religions* 23 (4): 373–411.

Rogers, H., and S.E. Lee. 1988. *Masterworks of Ming and Qing Painting from the Forbidden City.* Lansdale, PA: International Arts Council.

Rong, Geng. 1985. *Jin wen bian* [A Collection of Bronze Inscriptions]. eds. Zhang Zhenlin and Ma Guoquan. Beijing: Zhonghua Shuju.

_____. 2000. *Yinqi buci: fushi wenji wenbian.* [Oracles of Yin and Shang Dynasties]. Beijing: Beijing Tushuguan Chubanshe.

Rose, K. 1990. *Later Chinese Bronzes.* Oxford: Oxford University Press.

_____. 1991. Chinese Art and Design: Art Objects in Ritual and Daily Life. Woodstock, NY: Overlook Press.

_____. 2004. *Song Dynasty Ceramics.* London: V and A.

Rouzer, P.F. 1993. *Writing Another's Dream: The Poetry of Wen Tingyun.* Stanford: Stanford University Press.

Ruan, Ji. 1989. *Ruan Ji shiwen xuanji* [A Selection of Poetry and Prose of Ruan Ji]. Chengdu: Bashu Shushe.

Rumi, Jalāl al-Dīn M. 2001. *Rūmī, Poet and Mystic, 1207–1273: Selections from His Writings.* Trans. R.A. Nicholson. Isfahan: Ebrahim Sepahani.

Rychner, J. 1955. *La Chanson de Geste.* Geneva, Librairie E. Droz.

Sachs, C. 1924. Musik des Altertums. Breslau: F. Hirt.

_____. 1940. *The History of Musical Instruments.* New York: W.W. Norton.

_____. 1943. *The Rise of Music in the Ancient World.* New York: W.W. Norton

_____. 1952. *World History of the Dance.* New York: Seven Arts.

_____. 1953. *Rhythm and Tempo.* New York: W.W. Norton.

Sacks, D. 2004. *Letter Perfect: The Marvelous History of Our Alphabet from A to Z.* Broadway Books.

Safir, K. 1985. *Syntactic Chains.* Cambridge, UK: Cambridge University Press.

Sakanishi, S. 1935. *An Essay on Landscape Painting (Kuo Hsi).* London: J. Murray.

———. 1939. *The Spirit of the Brush.* London: J. Murray.

Santangelo, P. 2003. *Sentimental Education in Chinese History: An Interdisciplinary Textual Research on Ming and Qing.* Leiden: Brill.

Schlepp, W. 1980. San-ch'u: Its Technique and Imagery. Madison: University of Wisconsin Press.

———. 2001. Yüan San-Ch'ü. The Columbia History of Chinese Literature, 370–382. ed. V. Mair. New York: Columbia University Press.

Schmandt-Besserat, D. 1977. *An Archaic Recording System and the Origin of Writing.* Malibu: Undena Publications.

Schmidt, J.D. 2003. *Harmony Garden: The Life, Literary Criticism, and Poetry of Yuan Mei (1716–1798)* London: RoutledgeCurzon.

Scott, A.C. 1957. *The Classical Theatre of China.* New York: Barnes and Noble.

———. 1988. The Performance of Classical Theater. *Chinese Theater: From Its Origins to the Present Day,* 118–144. ed. C. Mackerras. Honolulu: University of Hawaii Press.

Scruton, R. 1999. *The Aesthetics of Music.* Oxford: Clarendon.

Seckel, D. 1993. The Rise of Portraiture in Chinese Art. *Artibus Asiae,* 53 1–2: 7–26.

———. 1997. *Das Portrat in Ostasien.* Heidelberg: Winter.

Sedley, D. 1998. *Lucretius and the Transformation of Greek Wisdom.* Cambridge, UK: Cambridge University Press.

Serruys, P. L-M. 1984. On the System of the Pu Shou in the Shuowen Chiehtzu. *Zhōngyāng yánjiùyuàn lìshǐ yǔyán yánjiùsuǒ jíkān* [Journal of the Institute of History and Philology, Academia Sinica]. 55 (4): 651–754.

Sethares, W.A. 2005. *Timbre, Spectrum, Scale.* London, Springer-Verlag.

Shankman, S., and S.W. Durrant, eds. 2002. *Early China/Ancient Greece: Thinking Through Comparisons.* Albany: SUNY Press.

Shaughnessy, E.L. 1991. *Sources of Western Zhou History: Inscribed Bronze Vessels.* Berkeley: University of California Press.

———. 1997a. *Before Confucius: Studies in the Creation of the Chinese Classics.* Albany: State University of New York Press.

———. 1997b. *New Sources of Early Chinese History: An Introduction to the Reading of Inscriptions and Manuscripts.* Berkeley: University of California.

———, trans. 1997c. *I Ching: The Classic of Changes.* New York: Ballantine Books.

———. 2006. *Rewriting Early Chinese Texts.* Albany: SUNY Press.

Shaw, M. 1988. Buddhist and Taoist Influences on Chinese Landscape Painting. *Journal of the History of Ideas,* 49 (2): 183–206.

Shen Dongsheng Institute of Cultural Relics and Archaeology. 1997. *Dawenkou xuji: Dawenkou yizhi dire, sanci fajue baogao* [Reports on the Second and Third Dig on the Site of Dawenkou]. Beijing: Kexue Chubanshe.

Shen, Jianshi. 1985. *Guangyun Shengxi* [A Dictionary of Chinese Phonology]. Beijing: Zhonghua Shuju.

Shen, Kang-shen. J.N. Crossley, A.W.C-Lun and Hui Liu. 1999. *The Nine Chapters on the Mathematical Art: Companion and Commentary.* New York: Oxford University Press.

Shen, Xiao-nan. 1990a. *The Prosody of Mandarin Chinese.* Berkeley: University of California Press.

———. 1990b. Tonal Coarticulation in Mandarin. *Journal of Phonetics* 18: 281–295.

———. 1992. On Tone Sandhi and Tonal Coarticulation. *Acta Linguistica Hafniensia.* 24: 131–152.

Shen, Yadan. 2007. *Jijing chiyin: Hanyu shige de minyue xingshi jiqi lishi bianqian* [Sound of Silence: Musical Form of Chinese Poetry, Its History and Evolution]. Shanghai: Renmin Chubanshe.

Shi Jing. 1993. Trans. Xu, Yuanchong. Changsha: Hunan Chubanshe.

Shi san jing zhu shu: fu jiao kan ji. 1980. ed. Ruan Yuan. 2 vols. Beijing: Zhonghua Shu Ju.

Shi, Yidui. 1985. *Ci yu yinyue guanxi yanjiu* [Studies of the Relationship Between Ci and Music]. Beijing: Zhongguo Shehui Kexue Chubanshe.

Shi, Zhijiang, ed. 1997. *Gu jin yue lu* [Collection of Music Ancient and Contemporary]. Chengdu: Sichuan Renmin Chubanshe.

Shih, Chung-wen. 1976. *The Golden Age of Chinese Drama: Yüan Tsa-chu*. Princeton: Princeton University Press.

Shih, Wen-shan. 2000. *Intercultural Theater: Two Beijing Opera Adaptations of Shakespeare*. Ph.D. thesis. University of Toronto.

Silbergeld, J. 1982. *Chinese Painting Style: Media, Methods, and Principles of Form*. Seattle: University of Washington Press.

Sinor, Denis. 1990. *The Cambridge History of Early Inner Asia*. Cambridge: Cambridge University Press.

Siren, O.O. 1927. *Chinese Paintings in American Collections*. London: B.T. Batsford.

_____. 1938. *Early Chinese Paintings from the Bahr Collection*. London: B.T. Batsford.

_____. 1956–1958. *Chinese Painting: Leading Masters and Principles*. 2 vols. London: Lund, Humphries.

_____, R. Fry, L. Binyon, B. Rackham, A.F. Kendrick, and W.W. Winkworth. 1935. *Chinese Art: An Introductory Handbook to Painting, Sculpture, Ceramics, Textiles, Bronzes and Minor Arts*. London: B.T. Batsford.

Siu, Wang-Ngai, and P. Lovrick. 1997. *Chinese Opera: Images and Stories*. Vancouver: University of British Columbia Press and University of Washington Press.

Smith, R.J. 1993. *Cosmology, Ontology, and Human Efficacy: Essays in Chinese Thought*. Honolulu: University of Hawaii Press.

So, J.F. 2000. *Music in the Age of Confucius*. Washington, DC: Smithsonian.

Solt, M.E. 1970. *Concrete Poetry: A World View*. Bloomington: Indiana University Press.

Song Shi. Lüli. 1977. eds. Tuo Tuo, et al., 1609–1617; 1920–22. Beijing: Zhonghua Shuju.

Song Shi. Yue 1. 1977. eds. Tuo Tuo, et al., 2949–2960. Beijing: Zhonghua Shuju.

Song Shi. Yue 2. 1977. eds. Tuo Tuo, et al., 2961–2970. Beijing: Zhonghua Shuju.

Song Shi. Yue 6. 1977. eds. Tuo Tuo, et al., 3055–3067. Beijing: Zhonghua Shuju.

Spiller, M.G.R. 1992. *The Development of the Sonnet: An Introduction*. London: Routledge.

Spining, C.M. 1975. *Ming Dynasty Handbooks for the Ch'in: An Examination of Tiao-i: 'Idea of the Mode.'* Master of arts thesis, Boston University.

Spring, M. *The Lute in Britain: A History of the Instrument and Its Music*. Oxford: Oxford University Press.

Stock, B. 1983. *The Implications of Literacy: Written Language and Models of Interpretation in the Eleventh and Twelfth Centuries*. Princeton: Princeton University Press.

_____. 1990. *Listening for the Text: On the Uses of the Past*. Baltimore: Johns Hopkins University Press.

Stockwell, R.P., and D. Minkova. 1997. Prosody. *A Beowulf Handbook*. Eds. R.E. Bjork and J.D. Niles. Lincoln: University of Nebraska Press.

Strassberg, R.E. 2002. *A Chinese Bestiary: Strange Creatures from the Guideways Through Mountains and Seas* [*Shan hai jing*]. Berkeley: University of California Press.

Stravinsky, I. 1970. *The Poetics of Music: In the Form of Six Lessons*. Cambridge, MA: Harvard University.

Su, Jinren, and Xiao Lianzi. 1982. eds. *Songshu Yuezhi Xiaozhu* [Book of Sung, Music with Commentaries]. Shandong: Qilu Shushe.

Su, Shi. 2006. *Dongpo yuefu* [Yuefu of Su Dongpo]. Beijing: Beijing Tushu Guan Chubanshe.

_____. 2009. *Su shi shici xuan* [Selected Shi and Ci Poems of Su Shi]. Beijing: Zhonghua Shuju.

Sui Shu. Lüli. 1973. eds. Wei Hui and Linghu Delai, 403. Beijing: Zhonghua Shuju.

Sui Shu. Yinyue. 1973. eds. Wei Hui and Linghu Delai, 373. Beijing: Zhonghua Shuju.

Sui, Shusen. ed. 1964. *Quan Yuan sanqu* [*The Complete Yuan Sanqu*]. 2 vols. Beijing: Wenshi Chubanshe.

Sullivan, M. 1962. *The Birth of Landscape Painting in China*. Berkeley: University of California Press.

_____. 1979. *Symbols of Eternity: The Art of Landscape Painting in China*. Stanford: Stanford University Press.

_____. 1980. *Chinese Landscape Painting: The Sui and T'ang Dynasties.* Berkeley: University of California Press.

_____. 1984. *The Arts of China.* Berkeley: University of California Press.

Sun, C. Chu-chin. 1995. *Pearl from the Dragon's Mouth: Evocation of Scene and Feeling in Chinese Poetry.* Ann Arbor: Center for Chinese Studies, University of Michigan.

Sun, Haibo. 1934. *Jia gu wen bian* [Collection of Oracle Inscriptions]. Beiping: Yanjing University.

Sun, Hongxia. 2006. *Min jian xi qu* [Folk Theater]. Beijing: Zhongguo Shehui Chubanshe.

Sun, Mei. 1995. Nanxi: The Earliest Form of Xiqu. Ph.D. dissertation, University of Hawaii.

_____. 1996. Performances of Nanxi. *Asian Theater Journal* 13 (2): 141–166.

Sun, Shangyong. 2007. *Yuefu wenxue wenxian yanjiu* [Studies of the Literature of Yuefu]. Beijing: Renmin Wenxue Chubanshe.

Sun, Shuming. 2005. *Ancient Sculpture.* Beijing: Foreign Language Press.

_____, and Wen Wu. *Ancient Sculpture.* Beijing: Foreign Language Press.

Sun, Xiaochun, and J. Kistemaker. 1997. *The Chinese Sky During the Han: Constellating Stars and Society.* Leiden: Brill.

Sun, Xuanling, and Dongsheng Liu, eds. 1990. *Zhongguo Gudai Gequ* [Ancient Chinese Songs]. Beijing: Renmin Yinyue Chubanshe.

_____. 1988. *Yuan Sanqu di Yinyue* [The Music of Yuan Drama]. Beijing: Wenhua Yishu Chubanshe.

Swatek, C. 2003. Peony Pavilion Onstage: Four Centuries in the Career of a Chinese Drama. Ann Arbor: University of Michigan Center for Chinese.

Tang, Guizhang, ed. 1993. *Cihua congbian* [Edited Collection of Ci Remarks]. 5 vols. Beijing: Zhonghua Shuju.

_____, and Pan Junzhao. 1982. Lun Liu Yong Ci [On Liu Yong's Ci Poems]. *Cixue yanjiu lunwen ji* [Collected Essays on Ci Studies]. Shanghai: Shanghai Guji Chubanshe.

Tang, Lan. 1975. *Guanyu Jiangxi Wucheng wenhua yizhi yu wenzi de chubu tiantiao.* [A Preliminary Investigation of the Script on the Ancient Cultural Remains at Wúchéng, Jiāngxī]. *Wénwù* 7 72–76.

_____. 1979. *Lun Da Wenkou wenhua zhongde taowenqi* [Study of the Clay Music Instruments in Da Wenkou Culture]. *Gugong Bowuyuan Yuankan.* 2: 1–16.

_____. 1981. *Gu wenzixue daolun* [An Introduction to Ancient Inscription]. Jinan: Qilu Shushe.

_____. 1986. *XiZhou qingtongqi mingwen fendai shizheng* [Historic Evidence of the Chronology of Bronze Inscriptions in Western Zhou]. Beijing: Zhonghua Shuju.

Tang, Wenbiao. 1984. *Zhongguo gudai xiju shi chugao* [A Draft History of Chinese Classical Theatre]. Taibei: Lianjing Chuban Shiye Gongsi.

Tang, Xianzu, and Zhang, Guangqian. 2003. *A Dream Under the Southern Bough.* Beijing: Foreign Languages Press.

Tang, Yue. 2003. *Zhongguo yinyue wudao* [Chinese Music and Dance]. Hefei: Anhui Jiaoyu Chubanshe.

Tenzer, M. 2006. *Analytical Studies in World Music.* Oxford: Oxford University Press.

Thern, K.L. 1966. *Postface of the Shuo wen chieh tzu, The First Comprehensive Chinese Dictionary.* Madison: University of Wisconsin Press.

Thompson, J. 1997. *Xi Sheng: Music Beyond Sound; The Silk-String Zither.* Hong Kong: Toadall Sound.

_____. 1997a. Rhythm in Shen Qi Mi Pu. *Asian Music,* 40–72.

_____. 1998. *Xi Sheng: Music Beyond Sound: Transcriptions of Music for the Chinese Silk-String Zither.* Hong Kong: Toadall Sound.

Thomson, W. 1999. *Tonality in Music: A General Theory.* San Marino, Everett Books.

Thorp, R.L. 1981. The Date of Tomb 5 at Yinxu, Anyang: A Review Article. *Artibus Asiae* 43 (3): 239–246.

_____, and R.E. Vinograd. 2001. *Chinese Art and Culture.* New York: Abrams.

Thrasher, A. 1993. Bianzou: Performance Variation Techniques in Jiangnan Sizhu. *Chime* 6: 4–21.

_____. 2000. *Chinese Musical Instruments.* New York: Oxford University Press.

_____. 2008. *Sizhu Instrumental Music of South China: Ethos, Theory and Practice.* Leiden: Brill.

Tillman, H. 1992. *Confucian Discourse and Chu Hsi's Ascendancy.* Honolulu: Hawaii University Press.

Ting, Pang-hsin. 1975. *Chinese Phonology of the Wei-Chin Period: Reconstruction of the Finals as Reflected in Poetry.* Seattle: University of Washington.

Traynor, L.M., and S. Kishibe. 1951. On the Four Unknown Pipes of the Shō (Mouth Organ) used in Ancient Japanese Court Music. *Tōyō Ongaku Kenkyū* 9: 22–53.

Tsao, Penyeh. 1989. *Taoist Ritual Music of the Yu-Lan Pen-Hui (Feeding the Hungry Ghosts Festival) in a Hong Kong Taoist Temple.* Hong Kong: Hai Feng.

_____. 1998. *Tradition and Change in the Performance of Chinese Music: A Special Issue of the Journal Musical Performance.* London: Routledge.

Tsien, Tsuen-hsuin, and E.L. Shaughnessy. 2004. *Written on Bamboo and Silk: The Beginnings of Chinese Books and Inscriptions.* Chicago: University of Chicago Press.

Tu, Weiming. 1976. *Centrality and Commonality: An Essay on Chung-Yung.* Honolulu: University of Hawaii Press.

_____. 1979. The "Thought of Huang-Lao": A Reflection of the Lao Tzu and Huang Ti Texts in the Silk Manuscript of Ma-wang-tui. *Journal of Asian Studies* 39 (1): 95–110.

Underhill, A. 1997. Current Issues in Chinese Neolithic Archaeology. *Journal of World Prehistory* 11: 103–160.

_____. 2002. *Craft Production and Social Change in Northern China.* New York: Kluwer Academic.

Uno, Naoto. 1998. *Liu Yong lungao: Ci de yuanliu yu chuangxin* [A Study on Liu Yong: The Origin of Ci and Its Innovation]. Trans. Zhang Haiou and Yang Zhaohong. Shanghai: Shanghai Guji Chubanshe.

Varsano, P.M. 2003. *Tracking the Banished Immortal: The Poetry of Li Bo and Its Critical Reception.* Honolulu: University of Hawai'i Press.

Vennemann, T. 1988. *Preference Laws for Syllable Structure and the Explanation of Sound Change: With Special Reference to German, Germanic, Italian, and Latin.* Berlin: Mouton de Gruyter.

Vervoorn, A. 1990. *Men of the Cliffs and Caves: The Development of the Chinese Eremitic Tradition to the End of the Han Dynasty.* Hong Kong: Chinese University Press.

Vinograd, R. 1992. *Boundaries of the Self: Chinese Portraits 1600–1900.* New York: Cambridge University Press.

Waley, A. 1937. *The Book of Songs.* New York: Houghton Mifflin.

_____. 1958. *An Introduction to the Study of Chinese Painting.* New York: Grove Press.

_____. 2005. *The Book of Songs.* London: Routledge.

_____. 2005a. *The Life and Times of Po-Chü-I.* London: Routledge.

Wan, Yi. 1982. *Qingdai gongting yinyue* [Qing Court Music]. *Gugong bowuyuan yuankan* 2: 8–18.

_____, and Huang Haidao. 1985. *Qingdai gongting yinyue* [Qing Court Music]. Beijing: Zijincheng Chubanshe.

Wang, Binglu. 2005. *Mei'an Qinpu* [Meian Qin Music]. Beijing, Zhonghua Shuju.

Wang, Chong. 1938. *Lun Heng Jiao shi.* ed. Huang Hui. Changsha: Shangwu.

Wang, Der-wei D. 2003. Impersonating China (in Essays and Articles). *Chinese Literature: Essays, Articles, Reviews* 25: 133–163.

Wang, Di. 1982. *Qin Ge* [Qin Songs]. Beijing: Wenhua Yishu Chubanshe.

Wang, Di. 2003. The Rhythm of the City: Everyday Chengdu in Nineteenth-Century Bamboo-Branch Poetry. *Late Imperial China* 24 (1): 33–78.

Wang, Guangqi. 1931. *A Study of Qin Tablature Transcription.* Beijing: Zhonghua Shuju.

_____. 1933. *Zhongguo Shiciqu zhi Qingzhong Lü* [System of Stress in Chinese Poetry and Drama]. Shanghai: Zhonghua Shuju.

_____. 1975. *Song Yuan xi qu kao* [A Study of Song and Yuan Musical Theater]. Tainan: Minmian Chubanshe.

_____. 1989. *Dongxi Yuezhi zhi Yanjiu* [A Study of Musical Systems of the East and West]. Shanghai: Shanghai Shuju.

_____. 2007. *Zhongguo yinyue shi* [History of Chinese Music]. Beijing, Tuanjie Chubanshe.

_____. 2009. *Wang guo wei wen xuan* [Selected Works of Wang Guowei]. ed. Lin Wen Guang. Cheng Du: Sichuan Wenyi Chubanshe.

Wang, Guowei. 1984. *Wang Guowei xiqu lunwenji* [A Collection of Xiqu Essays of Wang Guowei]. Beijing: Zhonguo Xiju Chubanshe.

Wang, Haoxian. 1992. *The Ch'in: Its Role in Chinese Music.* Master of arts thesis, Binghamton University.

Wang, Hongjun. 2007. *Zhong lü yan jiu* [A Study in Zhong Rhythm]. Shanghai: Shanghai Yinyue Chubanshe.

Wang, Hongyuan. 1993. *The Origins of Chinese Characters.* Beijing: Sinolingua.

Wang, Hui. 2006. *Shang and Zhou Bronze Inscriptions.* Beijing: Wenwu Chubanshe.

Wang, Jiaosheng. 1989. Complete Ci Poems by Li Qingzhao: A New Translation. *Sino-Platonic Papers* 13: 1–157.

Wang, Jinhui. 2003. *Cong jizhong shiti zhi bijiao kan wuyanti jueqi de birenxing* [The Necessity of the Emergence of Five-Character Verse from a Comparison of Several Poetic Forms]. *Shandong shifan dexue xuebao (renwen shihui kexue ban)* Vol. 3.

Wang, Jisi. 1981. *Yuan sanqu xuanzhu* [A Collection of Yuan Sanqu with Commentaries]. Beijing: Beijing Chubanshe.

_____. 2001. *Jin Yuan xiqu.* Beijing: Renwen Chubanshe.

_____. 2004. *Wang Jisi wen ji* [A Collection of Writings of Wang Jisi]. Guangzhou: Zhongshan University Press.

Wang, Kefen. 1984. *Zhongguo wudao shi* [A History of Chinese Dance]. Beijing: Wenhua Yishu Chubanshe.

_____. 2008. *Xiaoguan nishang: dunhuang yuewu* [Lute, Pipe and Dashing Address: Dunhuang Music and Dance]. Lanzhou: Gansu Jiaoyu Chubanshe.

Wang, Kunwu. 1996. *Sui Tang Wudai yuanyue zayan geci yuanjiu* [Studies in the Lyrics of Yanyue During Sui, Tang, and Five Dynasties]. Beijing: Zhonghua Shuju.

_____. 1998. *Zhongguo zaoqi yishu yu zongjiao* [The Early Arts and Religion of China]. Shanghai: Dongfang Chubanshe.

_____. 2002. *Hanwen fuojing zhongde yinyue shiliao* [The Documents]. Chengdu: Bashu Shushe.

Wang, Li. 1963. *Hanyu yinyun* [Phonology of Chinese]. Beijing, Zhonghua Shuju.

_____. 1979. *Huanyu shiyun xue* [Prosody of Chinese]. 1979. Beijing: Zhonghua Shuju.

_____. 1980. *Hanyu Shigao* [A History of Chinese Language]. Beijing, Zhonghua Shuju.

_____. 1981. *Gudai hanyu.* [The Ancient Chinese]. 4 vols. Beijing: Zhonghua Shuju.

_____. 1980. *Shijing yundu* [Shijing Prosody]. Shanghai: Guji.

_____. 1985. *Hanyu yuyin shi* [A History of Chinese Phonology]. Beijing: Zhongguo Shehui Kexue Chubanshe.

_____. 1992. *Qingday guyin xue* [Ancient Phonology of Qing]. Beijing: Zhonghua Shuju.

_____. 2003. *Wang Li cilu xue* [Wang Li's Prosody]. Taiyuan: Shenxi Remin.

Wang, Ningsheng. 1981. *Cong yanshi jishi dao wenzi faming* [From Primitive Record-Keeping to the Invention of Writing]. *Kǎogǔ Xuébào* 1: 42–59.

Wang, Pu. 1955. *Tang hui yao.* Beijing: Zhonghua Shuju.

Wang, Pu. 1991. *Tang hui yao.* Shanghai: Guji.

Wang, Qinglei. 2007. *Xi Zhou yuexuan zhidu de yinyue kaogu xue yanjiu* [Archeological Study of the Bell System in Western Zhou]. Beijing: Wenwu.

Wang, Shuming. 1986. *Tan lingyanhe yu dazhucun chutu de taozun wenzi* [A Discussion of the Pottery "Script" Excavated at Língyánghé and Dàzhūcūn]. *Qí Lǔ Kaogu congji.*

Wang, Te-chen. 1979. *Chinese Opera.* Taipei: Center for Public and Business Administration Education, National Chengchi University.

Wang, Tzi-Cheng. 2001. Wu Zhen's Poetic Inscriptions on Paintings. *Bulletin of the School of Oriental and African Studies* 64 (2): 208–239.

Wang, Wei. 1958. *Poems by Wang Wei.* trans. Chang, Yin-Nan, and L.C. Walmsley. Rutland, VT: C.E. Tuttle.

_____. 1991. *Laughing Lost in the Mountains: Poems of Wang Wei.* Trans. T. Barnstone, W. Barnstone, and Haixin Xu. Hanover, NH: University Press of New England.

Wang, Weizhen. 1988. *Han Tang daqu yanjiu* [A Study of Han and Tang Daqu]. Taipei: Xueyi.

Wang, Yinglin. 1987. *Yu hai* [Jade Sea]. Shanghai: Shanghai Guji.

Wang, Yunxi. 1996. *Yuefu shi shulun* [Studies and Commentaries on Yuefu Poetry]. Shanghai: Guji.

Wang, Yuxin. 2006. *Shang Zhou jiaguwen* [The Oracle Inscriptions of Shang and Zhou Dynasties]. Beijing: Wenwu Chubanshe.

Wang, Zhenzhong. 1998. *Zhongguo wenming qiyuan de bijiao yuanjiu.* Xian: Shaanxi Renming Chubanshe.

Wang, Zhongshu. 1982. *Han Civilization.* Trans. K.C. Chang, et al. New Haven: Yale University Press.

Wang, Zhuo. 1987. *Biji man zhi* [A Collection of Ci Criticism]. Shanghai: Shanghai Guji Chubanshe.

_____. 1991. *Bi ji man zhi* [Collection of Yuefu]. Beijing: Zhonghua Shuju.

Wang, Zichu. 2003. *Zhongguo yinyue kaoguxue* [The Archaeology of Chinese Music]. Fuzhou: Fujian Jiaoyu Chubanshe.

_____. 2006. *Chinese Musical Instruments.* Beijing: Ministry of Culture of the People's Republic of China.

Waters, G.F. 1985. *Three Elegies of Ch'u: An Introduction to the Traditional Interpretation of the Ch'u tz'u.* Madison: University of Wisconsin Press.

Watkins, G. 1988. *Soundings: Music in the Twentieth Century.* New York: Schirmer.

Watson, B. 1963. *Mo Zi: Basic Writings.* New York: Columbia University Press.

_____, ed. 1986. *Columbia Book of Chinese Poetry.* New York: Columbia University Press.

_____, trans. 1993. *Records of the Grand Historian, Han Dynasty.* New York: Columbia University Press.

_____, trans. 1994. *Selected Poems of Su Tung-p'o.* Fort Worden, WA: Copper Canyon Press.

_____, trans. 2002. *The Selected Poems of Du Fu.* New York: Columbia University Press.

_____, trans. 2003. *Xunzi: Basic Writings.* New York: Columbia University Press.

Watson, W. 1967. Pre-Han Figures of Acrobats (British Museum). *The Burlington Magazine,* 109 (772): 417–419.

_____. 1995. *The Arts of China to AD 900.* New Haven: Yale University Press.

_____. 2003. *The Arts of China 900–1620.* New Haven: Yale University Press.

Wechsler, H.J. 1985. *Offerings of Jade and Silk: Ritual and Symbol in the Legitimation of the Tang Dynasty.* New Haven: Yale University Press.

Webern, A. 1963. *The Path to the New Music.* ed. W. Reich, trans. L. Black. Bryn Mawr: Theodore Presser.

Wedde, I. 2008. *Chinese Opera.* Wellington, NZ: Victoria University Press.

Wei, J. Lee. 2005. *The Names of the Yi Jing Trigrams: An Inquiry into Their Linguistic Origins.* Philadelphia: University of Pennsylvania Press.

Wei, Jiangong. 1996. *Guyinxi yanjiu* [A Study of Ancient Phonological Systems]. Beijing: Zhonghua Shuju.

Wei, Zheng, et al. 1973. *Sui shu* [The Book of Sui]. Beijing: Zhonghua Shuju.

Wegman, H. 1985. *Christian Worship in East and West: A Study Guide to Liturgical History.* trans. G.W. Lathrop. New York: Pueblo.

Wellesz, E. ed. 1999. *New Oxford History of Music, Volume I: Ancient and Oriental Music.* Oxford: Oxford University Press.

Wen, Fong. 1984. *Images of the Mind: Selections from the Edward L. Elliott Family and John B. Elliott Collections of Chinese Calligraphy and Painting at the Art Museum.* Princeton: Art Museum, Princeton University.

_____. 1992. *Beyond Representation: Chinese Painting and Calligraphy, 8th–14th Century.* New York: Metropolitan Museum of Art; New Haven: Yale University Press.

Wen, Fong, Chin-Sung Chang, and M.K. Hearn. 2008. *Landscapes Clear and Radiant.* New York: Metropolitan Museum of Art; New Haven: Yale University Press.

Wen, Fong, and R. Rorex. 1974. *Eighteen Songs of a Nomad Flute: The Story of Lady Wen-Chi, a 14th Century Handscroll in the Met.* New York: Metropolitan Museum of Art.

Wen, Huaisha. 1956. *Qu Yuan Jiu Ge jinyi* [New Translations of Qu Yuan's Jiu Ge]. Shanghai: Gudian Wenxue.

Wénwù, ed. 1963. *The Institute of Archaeology, Academia Sinica and the Bànpō Museum.* Xī'ān Bànpō. Běijīng: Wenwu.

_____. 1983. *Gansu Qin'an Dadiwan yizhi 1979–1982 nian fajue de Zhuyao shouhuo.* [Report on the 1979–1982 Excavations of a Site at Dàdìwān in Qín'ān, Gānsù]. 11: 21–30.

_____. 1989. *Henan Wuyang Jiahu xinshiqi shidai yizhi di er dao liu ci fajue baogao*. [Report on the Excavation of the Neolithic Period Pits Nos. 2–6 at Jiǎhú in Wǔyáng, Hénán]. 1: 1–14.

West, M.L. 1993.*Greek Lyric Poetry*. Oxford: Oxford University Press.

_____. 1994. *Ancient Greek Music*. Oxford: Clarendon Press.

_____, ed. 1999. ed. *Greek Lyric Poetry: The Poems and Fragments of the Greek Iambic Elegiac and Melic Poets (Excluding Pindar and Bacchylides) Down to 450 B.C.* Oxford: Oxford University Press.

Wettstein, H. 2004. *The Magic Prism: An Essay in the Philosophy of Language*. New York, Oxford University Press.

Wexler, S., and A. Irvine. 2006. Aristotle on the Rule of Law. *Polis* (23) 1: 116–138

Wichmann, E. 1991. *Listening to Theater: The Aural Dimension of Beijing Opera*. Honolulu: University of Hawaii Press.

Wieger, L. 1927. *Chinese Characters: Their Origin, Etymology, History, Classification and Signification; A Thorough Study from Chinese Documents*. New York: Dover.

Wilhelm, R., and C.F. Baynes, trans. 1967. *The I Ching; or, Book of Changes*. Princeton: Princeton University Press.

Wilson, T.A. 1995. *Genealogy of the Way: The Construction and Uses of the Confucian Tradition in Late Imperial China*. Stanford: Stanford University Press.

Wimsatt, W.K. 1954. *One Relation of Rhyme to Reason: The Verbal Icon*. Lexington: University of Kentucky Press.

_____, and M.C. Beardsley. 1959. The Concept of Meter: An Exercise in Abstraction. *Publications of the Modern Language Association of America* 74: 585–98.

_____, ed. 1972. *Versification: Major Language Types*. New York: Modern Language Association.

Winn, J.A. 1981. *Unsuspected Eloquence: A History of the Relations Between Poetry and Music*. New Haven: Yale University Press.

Wolpert, R.F. 1975. Lute Music and Tablatures of the T'ang Period. Ph.D. thesis, University of Cambridge.

Woon, Wee Lee. 1987. *Chinese Writing: Its Origin and Evolution*. Hong Kong: University of East Asia.

Written symposium. 2008. Theory and typology of words. Mouton de Gruyter.

Wu, Ben, and Tsao, Penyeh. 1998. *Tradition and Change in the Performance of Chinese Music*, 1–20. Harwood Academic Publication.

Wu, Dashun. 2009. *Wei Jin NanBei chao yuefu geci yanjiu*. [*Studies in Yuefu Lyrics of Wei, Jin, Southern and Western Dynasties*]. Shanghai: Shanghai Guji Chubanshe.

Wu, Dexin. 2006. *Yuefu shi de lishi: miao du yue fu shi 100 shou* [A History of Yuefu: Reading 100 Yuefu Poems]. Chongqing: Chongqing Chubanshe.

Wu, Hou (Empress of China). 1995. *Yueshu yaolu* [An Outline of the Book of Music]. Shanghai: Guji.

Wu, Hung. 1992. *The Wu Liang Shrine: The Ideology of Early Chinese Pictorial Art*. Stanford: Stanford University Press.

_____. 1995. *Monumentality in Early Chinese Art and Architecture* Stanford: Stanford University Press.

_____. 1996a. *The Double Screen: Medium and Representation in Chinese Painting*. Chicago: University of Chicago Press.

_____. 1997. *Hung Wu, The Origins of Chinese Painting (Paleolithic Period to Tang Dynasty): Three Thousand Years of Chinese Painting*, 15–85. New Haven: Yale University Press.

_____. 2000. Mapping Early Taoist Art: The Visual Culture of Wudoumi Dao. *Taoism and Arts of China*, 77–94. eds. S. Little and S. Eichman. Berkeley: University of California Press.

_____. 2003. *Han Tang zhi jian de shi jue wen hua yu wu zhi wen hua*. Beijing: Wenwu.

_____, ed. 2004. *Body and Face in Chinese Visual Culture*. Cambridge, MA: Harvard University Press.

_____. 2006b. From Neolithic to the Han. *Chinese Sculpture*, 17–104. eds. A.F. Howard, Li Song, Wu Hung, and Yang Hong. New Haven: Yale University Press.

_____. 2010a. *The Art of Yellow Springs: Understanding Chinese Tombs*. Honolulu: University of Hawaii Press.

_____. 2010b. *Reinventing the Past: Archaism and Antiquarianism in Chinese Art and Visual Culture*. Chicago: University of Chicago Press.

_____, and K.R. Tsiang. 2005. *Body and Face in Chinese Visual Culture*. Cambridge, MA: Harvard University Press.

Wu, Jing. 2003. *Yuefu guti yaojie* [Commanderies of Issues of Yuefu], 37–77. Beijing: Beijing Tushuguan Chubanshe.

Wu, Jinglüe, and Wenguang. 2001. *Yushan Wushi Qinpu* [The Qin Music Repertoire of the Wu Family]. Beijing: Eastern Press.

Wu, Wenguang. 1990. *Wu Jinglue's Qin Music in Its Context*. Ph.D. dissertation, Wesleyan University.

Wu, Xionghe. 1985. *Tang Song ci tong lun* [Analysis of Tang/Song Ci]. Hangzhou: Zhejiang Guji.

Wu, Xiaoping. 1998. *Zhonggu wuyan shi yanjiu* [Studies of Chinese Poetry in Five Characters]. Nanjing: Jiangsu Guji.

Wu, Zhao. 2005. *Jueshi qingyin* [The Purest Music in the World]. Suzhou: Guwu Xuan Chubanshe.

Xia, Ye. 2006. *Yueshi qulun: Xia Ye yin yue wen ji* [Selected Writings of Musical Theater by Xia Ye]. Shanghai: Yinyue Xueyuan Chubanshe.

Xiang, Chu, ed. 2006. *Dunhuang bianwen xuanzhu* [A Collection of Dunhuang Studies]. Beijing: Zhonghua Shuju.

Xiang, Xi. 1987. *Shi Jing yuyan yanjiu* [Studies of the Language of Shi Jing]. Changdu: Renmin Chubanshe.

_____. 2002. *Shi jing yu wen lun ji* [A Collection of the Study of the Language of Shi Jing]. Chengdu: Sichuan Minzu Chubanshe.

Xiao, Difei. 1984. *Han Wei Liu chao yuefu wenxueshi* [A History of Yuefu Literature in Han, Wei, and Six Dynasties]. Beijing: Renmin Wenxue Chubanshe.

Xiao, Mei, B. Yung, and A. Wong. 2001. *The Musical Arts of Ancient China*. Hong Kong: Hong Kong University.

Xiao, Youmei. 1989. A Study of the History of Chinese Brass and String Orchestra Before the 17th Century. *Art of Music* 2–4.

Xiu, Hailin. 1997. *Zhongguo gudai yinyue jiaoyu* [Music Education in Ancient China]. Shanghai: Education Press.

_____. 2004. *Zhongguo gudai yinyue meixue* [Music Aesthetics in Ancient China]. Fuzhou: Fujian Jiaoyu Chubanshe.

_____, Sun Keqiang, and Zhao Weimin, eds. 2004a. *Song-Yuan yinyue wenxue yanjiu* [A Study on Music Literature of Song and Yuan Dynasties]. Kaifeng: Henan University Press.

Xu, Chaolong. 2002. Zhongguo gudai "Shenshu Chuanshuo" de Yuanliu [The Origin and Development of "Magic Tree Legend" in Ancient China]. *Fusang yu Ruomu: Riben Xuezhe dui Sanxingdui Wenming de Xin Renshi* [Fusang and Ruomu: A New Light from Japanese Scholars on Sanxingdui Civilization], 205–228. Chengdu: Bashu Shushe.

Xu, Chengbei. 1999. *Jingju yu zhongguo wenhua* [Peking Opera and Chinese Culture]. Beijing: Renmin Chubanshe.

_____. 2000. *Mei Lanfang bainian ji* [To the Centennial Anniversary of Mei Lanfang]. Beijing: Zhongguo Shehui Kexue.

_____. 2006. *Mei lanfang yishu tan* [The Art of Mei Lanfang]. Nanjing: Jiangsu Jiaoyu Chubanshe.

Xu, Fuguan. 1976. *Zhongguo yishu jingshen* [The Spirits of Chinese Arts]. Taipei: Xuesheng Chubanshe.

Xu, Fuming. 1981. *Yuanren zaju yishu* [The Art of Yuan Zaju]. Shanghai: Wenyi Chubanshe.

Xu, Fuzuo. 1988. *Hong li ji* [The Story of Hong Li]. ed. Yuan Yu-Ling. Beijing: Zhonghua Shuju.

Xu, Jian. 1982. *Qinshi Chubian* [A Draft History of Qin]. Beijing: Renmin Yinyue Chubanshe.

Xu, Jian, et al. 2004. *Chu xue ji* [Book of Initial Learning]. 2 vols. Beijing: Zhonghua Shuju.

Xu, Mingting. 1999. *Wu Han Zhuzhi Ci* [Poems of Bamboo Branch at Hankou]. Wuhan: Hubei Renmin Chubanshe.

Xu, Muyun. 1963. *Jingju Ziyun* [Word Rhythm in Peking Opera]. Shanghai, Xinhua Shudian.

_____. 2001. *Zhongguo xiju shi* [A History of Chinese Theatre]. Shanghai: Guji.

Xu, Shangying. 2005. *Dahuan ge Qinpu* [Dahuange Qin Handbook]. Beijing: Zhonghua Shuju.

Xu, Shen. 1987. *Shuo wen Jie zi—Jizhuan* [A Collection of Shuowen Jiezi]. ed. Xu Kai (Tang). Beijing: Zhonghua Shuju.

_____. 1989. *Shuo wen Jie zi—Fu jianzi* [Shuo wen Jie zi with Indices]. ed. Xu Xuan (Eastern Han). Hong Kong: Zhonghuo Shuju.

_____. 2007. *Shuo wen jie zi zhu* [The Commentary of Shuo wen jiezi]. ed. Yucai Duan. Nanjing: Fenghuang Chubanshe.

Xu, T. 1997. *On Language*. Changchun: Hebei Normal University Publishing.

Xu, Xueyi. 1998. *Shiyuan bianti* [Debate About the Origins of Poetry]. Beijing: Renmin Wenxue Chubanshe.

Xu, Yahui. 2001. *Yinxu jiaguwen: Zhongguo sanqian duonian guwenzi* [Yinxu Oracle Inscriptions: Three Thousand Years of Chinese Writing]. Taibei: Guoli Gugong Bowuyuan.

Xu, Yi, and Meng Huaping. 2003. Zhongguo liyue wenmeing zhiyuan-yi Shiqian yuewu yizun weili [The Origins of Chinese Ritual Music: Examples of Pre-History Music and Dance]. *Dongnan Wenhu* 7: 9.

Xu, Yuanchong, trans. 2004. *300 Gems of Classical Chinese Poetry*. Beijing: Peking University Press.

Yan, Liang. 2003. *A Primer of Beijing Opera*. Beijing: Foreign Languages Press.

Yang, Bojun. 1981. *Gu Han yu xu ci* [The Empty Words in Old Han Chinese]. Beijing: Zhaonghua Shuju.

Yang, Haiming. 1987. *Tang Song ci shi* [A History of the Ci in Tang and Song]. Nanjing: Jiangshu Guji Chubanshe.

Yang, Jingqing. 2007. *The Chan Interpretations of Wang Wei's Poetry: A Critical Review*. Hong Kong: Chinese University Press.

Yang, Mu. 1993. *Chinese Musical Instruments*. Canberra: Australian National University.

Yang, Shuda. 1933. *Gusheng yuntao lunji* [Studies of the Phonology of Ancient Chinese]. Beiping: Haowang.

_____. 2004. *Jiweiju xiaoxue shulin* [A Collection of Studies in Bronze Inscriptions]. Hong Kong: Mingshi Wenhua.

_____. 2007. *Jiweiju jinwen shuo* [Discussions About Bronze Inscriptions]. Changsha: Hunan Jiaoyu Chubanshe.

Yang, Xiangkui. 1997. ZongZhou shehui yu liyue wenming [Society and Its Ritual Music in Zhou]. Beijing: Renmin Chubanshe.

Yang, Xiaoshan. 2003. *Metamorphosis of the Private Sphere: Gardens and Objects in Tang-Song Poetry*. Cambridge: Harvard University Press.

Yang, Yinliu. 1955. *Zhongguo yinyue shigang* [An Outline of History of Music in China]. Beijing: Yinyue Chubanshe.

_____. 1981. *Zhongguo gudai yinyue shigao* [A Draft History of Traditional Chinese Music]. 2 vols. Beijing: Renmin Yinyue Chubanshe.

_____. 1986. Shuo Luan ji qita [About Luan and Other Issues]. *Yang Yinliu Yinyue Lunwen Xuanji*, 349–59. Shanghai: Shanghai Wenyi.

Yang, Zenglie. 1990–91. Lijiang Dongjing yinyue diaocha [Investigation of Lijiang's Dongjing Music]. *Lijiang Wenshi Ziliao* 9: 114–38; 10: 30–47.

Yang, Zhaoying (Yuan). 1997. *Chaoye xinsheng taiping yuefu* [The Ballads of the Pax Magnifica]. 9 vols. Jinan: Qi Lu Chubanshe.

_____, ed. 2007. *Yang chun bai xue* [The Snows of Shining Spring]. Shanghai: Shanghai Guji Chubanshe.

Yang, Zongji. 1996. Qinxue Congshu [Studies on Qin Music]. Beijing: Zhonghua Shuju.

Yao, Xuexian, and Long Jianguo. 1991. *Liu Yong ci xiang zhu ji ji ping* [Studies of Liu Yong's Ci]. Zhengzhou: Zhongzhou Guji.

Ye, Dong. 1983. *Chaozhou xianshiyue, Guangdong xiaoqu* [Types and Forms of Chinese Folk Instrumental Music]. Chap. 11, Minzu qiyue de ticai yu xingshi. Shanghai: Shanghai Wenyi Chubanshe.

Ye, Dongjie. 1986. *Dunhuang pipa qupu* [Pipa Music of Dunhuang]. Shanghai: Shanghai Wenyi Chubanshe.

Ye, Jiaying. 1997. *Han Wei Liuzhao shijiang lu* [A Collection of Lectures on Poetry of Han, Wei and Six Dynasties]. Shijia Zhuang: Hebei Jiaoyu Chubanshe.

Ye, Lang, Fei Zhengang, and Wang Tianyou. 2007. *Zhongguo wenhua daodu* [A History of Chinese Culture]. Beijing: Sanlian Shudian.

Ye, Liangfu. 1977. Principles of K'un Ch'u Singing. *Asian Music.* 8 (2): 4–25.

Ye, Mingchun. 2007. *Zhongguo gudai yinyue shenmeiguan yanjiu* [A Study of Musical Aesthetics in Ancient China]. Beijing: Renmin Yinyue Chubanshe.

Ye, Mingmai. 1991. *Gu qin yin yue yi shu* [The Music Art of Guqin]. Taibei: Taiwan Shangwu.

Yee, Chiang, and S.I. Hsiung. 1964. *The Chinese Eye: An Interpretation of Chinese Painting.* Bloomington: Indiana University Press.

Yeh, Chia-ying (Ye, Jiaying). 1994. Wang Kuo-wei's Song Lyrics in the Light of His Own Theories. *Voices of the Song Lyric in China*, 257–297. ed. P. Yu. Berkeley: University of California Press.

_____. 2007a. *Nan Song mingjia ci xuanjiang* [Selected Studies of Ci by Prominent Poets of Southern Song]. Beijing: Peking University Press.

_____. 2007b. *Bei Song mingjia ci xuanjiang* [Selected Studies of Ci by Prominent Poets of Northern Song]. Beijing: Peking University Press.

_____. 2007c. *Tang Song ci shiqi jiang* [Seventeen Lectures on Tang and Song Ci Poetry]. Beijing: Peking University Press.

_____. 2008a. *Ye Jiaying shuo Ruan Ji Yong huai shi* [Ye Jiaying's Study of Ruan Ji's Yong Huai Poetry]. Beijing: Zhonghua Shuju.

_____. 2008b. *Ye Jiaying shuo Du Fu shi* [Ye Jiaying's Talk About Poetry of Du Fu]. Beijing: Zhonghua Shuju.

_____. 2008c. *Ye Jiaying shuo chu sheng Tang shi* [Ye Jiaying's Lectures on Early Tang Poetry]. Beijing: Peking University Press.

_____. 2008d. *Ye Jiaying shuo zhong wan Tang shi* [Ye Jiaying's Lectures on Mid and Late Tang Poetry]. Beijing: Zhonghua Shuju.

_____, and J.R. Hightower. 1998. *Studies in Chinese Poetry.* Cambridge, MA: Harvard University Press.

Yi, Cai. 1989. *Zhongguo gu dian I qu xu ba hui bian* [A collection of Chinese classical musical theatre, with introduction]. Jinan: Qi Lu shushe.

Yi, Cunguo. 2003. *Zhongguo Guqin Yishu.* [The Arts of Chinese Guqin]. Beijing: Renmin Yinyue Chubanshe.

Yi, Ruan. 1981. *Huang you xin yue tu ji* [An Illustrated History of Chinese Musical Instruments]. 3 vols. Beijing: Shangwu.

Yin, Wei. 2001. *Qinshi yanyi* [A History of Guqin]. Yunnan: Renmin Chubanshe.

Yin, Falu, and Xu, Shuan. 1989. *Zhongguo wenhua shi* [A History of Chinese Culture]. Beijing: Peking University Press.

Ying, Youqin. 1997. *Illustrations of Chinese National Instrument.* Shanghai: Shanghai Music Publication.

Yip, M. 1980. The Tonal Phonology of Chinese. Ph.D. dissertation, Massachusetts Institute of Technology.

_____. 1989. Contour Tones. *Phonology Yearbook* 6: 149–174.

_____. 1990. The Phonology of Cantonese Loanwords: Evidence for Unmarked Settings for Prosodic Parameters. *New Directions in Chinese Linguistics.* ed. J. Packard. Dordrecht: Kluwer Academic.

_____. 1991. Prosodic Morphology of Four Chinese Dialects. *Journal of East Asian Linguistics* 1: 1–35.

You, Guoqing. 2001. *Gu gong Xi Zhou jin wen lu.* Taibei: Guoli Gugong Bowuyuan.

You, Yumiao. 1936. Han, Tang, Song De Daqu [Daqu in Han, Tang, and Song Dynasties]. *Wenxue Nianbao*, 235.

Yu, Feian. 1988. *Chinese Painting Colors: Studies on Their Preparation and Application in Traditional and Modern Times.* trans. J. Silbergeld and A. McNair. Seattle: University of Washington Press.

Yu, Pauline, ed. 1994. *Voices of the Song Lyric in China.* Berkeley: University of California Press.

_____. 1987. *The Reading of Imagery in the Chinese Poetic Tradition.* Princeton: Princeton University Press.

_____, ed. 2000. *Ways with Words: Writing About Reading Texts from Early China*. Berkeley: University of California Press.

Yu, Xingwu. 1973. Guanyu guwenzi yanjiu the ruogan wenti [Some Issues Pertaining to the Study of Ancient Chinese Writing]. *Wénwù* 2: 32–35.

_____. 1979. *Jiagu wenzi yilin* [A Collection of Translation of Jiaguwen]. Beijing: Zhonghua Shuju.

Yu, Siu Wah. 1996. The Meaning and Cultural Functions of Non-Chinese Music in the Eighteenth Century Manchu Court. Ph.D. dissertation, Harvard University.

Yu, Taishan. 2003. *Xiyu tongshi* [A Complete History of the Western Regions]. Zhengzhou: Zhongzhou Guji.

_____. 2009. *Zaoqi sichou zhilu wen xian yanjiu* [Studies of the Early Research on the History of Silk Road]. Shanghai: Shanghai Renmin Chubanshe.

Yuan, Bingchang, and Jizeng Mao. 1986. *Zhongguo shaoshu minzu yueqi zhi* [A History of Music of the Ethnic Minorities in China]. Beijing: Xinshijie Chubanshe.

Yuan Shi. Liyue. 1976. ed. Song Lian. Beijing: Zhonghua Shuju.

Yueshu [Treatise on Music]. Chen Yang. 1103. 200 juan. Siku Quanshu, ed.

Yue shu yaolu [Book of Music]. ed. Wu hou (The Empress of Tang). 1999. Shanghai: Guji.

Yung, B. 1989. *Cantonese Opera: Performance as Creative Process*. Cambridge, England: Cambridge University Press.

_____. 1985. Da Pu: The Recreative Process for the Music of the Seven-String Zither. *Music and Context: Essays in Honor of John Ward* 370–384. ed. A. Dhu Shapiro. Harvard University Press.

_____. 1989. *Cantonese Opera: Performance as Creative Process*. Cambridge, UK: Cambridge University Press.

_____. 1997. *Celestial Airs of Antiquity: Music of the Seven String Zither of China*. Madison: A–R Editions.

_____, E.S. Rawski, and R.S. Watson, eds. 1996. *Harmony and Counterpoint: Ritual Music in Chinese Context*. Stanford: Stanford University Press.

Yung, Sai-shing. 1987. Mu-yu Shu and the Cantonese Popular Singing Arts. *Gest Library Journal* 2, No. 1: 16–30.

Zeng, Daxing. 1990. *Liu Yong he tade ci* [Liu Yong and His Ci Poetry]. Guangzhou: Zhongshan University Press.

Zeng, Youhe. 1993. *A History of Chinese Calligraphy*. Hong Kong: Chinese University Press.

Zhang, Anzhi. 2002. *A History of Chinese Painting*. Beijing: Foreign Languages Press.

Zhang, Dainian, and E. Ryden. 2002. *Key Concepts in Chinese Philosophy*. Yale University Press.

Zhang, Geng, and Guo Hancheng, eds. 2006. *Zhongguo xiqu tongshi* [A General History of Chinese Theater]. Beijing: Zhongguo Xiju Chubanshe.

Zhang, Guiguang. 2004. *Guwen zi lunji* [Studies of Characters of Ancient Literature]. Beijing: Zhonghua Shuju.

Zhang, He. 1998. *Qinxue rumen* [Introduction to Qin Music]. Beijing: Zhonghua Shuju.

Zhang, Huaying. 2005. *Gu Qin* [Guqin]. Guizhou, Zhejiang Renmin Chubanshe.

Zhang, J., and Wang, X. 1998. Notes on the Recent Discovery of Ancient Cultivated Rice at Jiahu, Henan Province: A New Theory Concerning the Origin of Oryza Japonica in China. *Antiquity* 72: 897–901.

Zhang, Kejiu. 1995. *Zhang Kejiu ji jiao zhu* [Collection of Works of Zhang Kejiu with Commentary]. eds. Lv Weifen and Yang Lian. Hangzhou: Zhejiang Guji Chubanshe.

_____. 1996. *Zhang Kejiu xiao ling bai shou* [100 Short Poems of Zhang Kejiu]. eds. Du Nanbai and Li Xianfa. Beijing: Zhongguo Wenxue Chubanshe.

Zhang, Shibin. 1974. *Zhongguo yinyue shilun shugao* [A Preliminary Study of the Theory of Chinese Music and Poetry]. Hong Kong: Union Press.

Zhang, Yu. 2009. *Xinyufuci yanjiu* [New Studies of Yuefu]. Beijing: Beijing University Press.

Zhang, Yuci. 1959–1962. *Jingju Changqiang* [Singing in Peking Opera]. 2 vols. Beijing: Yinyue Chubanshe.

Zhang, Yujin. 2004. *Xi Zhou hanyu yufa yanjiu* [Studies of Chinese Grammar in Western Zhou Dynasty]. Beijing: Shangwu.

Zhang, Ziqian. 2005. *Cao man suo ji* [Diaries]. 10 v. Beijing: Zhonghua Shuju.

Zhao, Cheng. 1988. *Jiaguwen jianming cidian* [A Short Dictionary of Jiaguwen]. Beijing: Zhonghua Shuju.

Zhao, Jingshen. 1980. *Qulun chutan* [A Preliminary Study of the Theory of Xiqu]. Beijing: Wenyi Chubanshe.

Zhao, Pingan. 1999. *Shuowen Jiezi xiaozhuan yanjiu* [A Study of Small Seal of Shuowen Jiezi]. Nanning: Guangxi Jiaoyu Chubanshe.

Zhao, Shigang. 1996. *Zhongguo yinyue wenwu daxi, Henan* [Complete Collection of Chinese Music Relics, Henan]. Zhengzhou: Da Xiang Chubanshe.

Zheng, Hongchun, and Mu Haiting. 1988. Shenxi Xian Hualouzi Keshenzhuang erqi wenhua fajue [Excavation of the period — two ancient cultural remains at Hualouzi in Changan, Shaanxi], *Kaogu yu Wenwu* 5–6: 229–239.

Zheng, Jiewen. 1992. *Mu tianzi zhuan tongjie* [Commentaries of Biography of Zhou Emperor, Mu]. Jinan: Shandong Wenyi Chubanshe.

Zheng, Lei. 2005. *Kunqu*. Hangzhou: Zhejiang Renmin Chubanshe.

Zheng, Zhang, Shangfang. *Shanggu yinxi* [Phonetic System of Archaic Chinese]. Shanghai: Jiaoyu Chubanshe.

Zheng, Zuxiang. 1998. *Zhongguo gu dai yin yue shi xue gai lun* [The Historiography of Music in Ancient China]. Beijing, Renmin yinyue Chubanshe.

Zhirmunsky, V.M. 1966. *Introduction to Metrics: The Theory of Verse.* trans. C.F. Brown, eds. E. Stankiewicz and W.N. Vickery. The Hague: Mouton.

Zhongguo Xijujia Xiehui. 1961. *Mei Lanfang yanchu juben xuanji* [A Selection of Mei Lanfang's Performance's Script]. Beijing: Zhongguo Xiju Chubanshe.

Zhongguo xiqu yanjiu yuan [Chinese Opera Institute], ed. 1959. *Zhongguo gudian xiqu lunzhu Jicheng* [A Collection of Studies of Chinese Traditional Theater]. 10 vols. Beijing: Zhongguo Xiju Chubanshe.

Zhongguo xiqu yinyue jicheng. Beijing juan [A Collection of Scores of Chinese Music Theater: Book of Beijing]. 1992. Editorial Committee of Zhongguo xiqu yinyue jichange, ed. Beijing: Beijing Chubanshe.

Zhongguo yin yue wen wu da xi, Xinjiang juan [Archaeological Collection of Chinese Music: Book of Xinjiang]. 1996. eds. Zhou Changfu and Wen Zengyuan. Zhengzhou: Daxiang Chubanshe.

Zhongguo yin yue wen wu da xi, Henan juan [Archaeological Collection of Chinese Music: Book of Henan]. 1996. ed. Cui Yan. Zhengzhou: Daxiang Chubanshe.

Zhongguo yin yue wen wu da xi, Beijing juan [Archaeological Collection of Chinese Music: Beijing]. 1996. ed. Han Bing. Zhengzhou: Daxiang Chubanshe.

Zhongguo yin yue wen wu da xi, Shanghai, Jiangsu juan [Archaeological Collection of Chinese Music: Shanghai and Jiangsu]. 1996. ed. Wang Wei. Zhengzhou: Daxiang Chubanshe.

Zhongguo yin yue wen wu da xi, Shanxi juan [Archaeological Collection of Chinese Music, Shanxi]. 2000. eds. Xiang Yang and Tao Zhenggang. Zhengzhou: Daxiang Chubanshe.

Zhongguo yin yue wen wu da xi, Hubei juan [Archaeological Collection of Chinese Music: Hubei]. 2008. ed. Wang Zichu. Zhengzhou: Daxiang Chubanshe.

Zhongguo yin yue wen wu da xi, Hunan juan [Archaeological Collection of Chinese Music: Hunan]. 2006. eds. Gao Zhixi and Xiong Chuanxin. Zhengzhou: Daxiang Chubanshe.

Zhongguo yin yue wen wu da xi, Shaanxi juan [Archaeological Collection of Chinese Music: Shaanxi]. 1996. ed. Zhang Huanwu. Zhengzhou: Daxiang Chubanshe.

Zhongyang yinyue Minzu yinyue yanjiusuo xueyuan [Central Institute of Folk Music], ed. 1956. *Kunju chuida qupai* [Instrumental Melodies of Kunju]. Beijing: Yinyue Chubanshe.

Zhou, Fagao. 1974. *Jin wen gu lin* [Dictionary of Bronze Inscription]. 16 vols. Hong Kong: Chinese University Press.

Zhou Li Zhushu. *Shi San jing Zhu shu*. 1980. 1: 795

Zhou, Qingqing. 2003. *Zhongguo minjian yinyue gailun* [An Outline of Chinese Folk Music]. Beijing: Renmin Yinyue Chubanshe.

Zhou, Qingyun. 1914. *Qinshu Cunmu* [Catalogue of Qin Books]. 4 vols. China: Mengpo Shicangban.

_____. 1919. *Qin Shi Bu* [Qin History Supplement]. 5 vols. China: Mengpo Shicangban.

_____. 1919. *Qin Shi Xu* [Qin History Continuation]. China: Mengpo Shicangban.

Zhou, Ruishen. 2008. *Kunqu gudiao* [Ancient Melodies of Kunqu]. Beijing: Beijing Press.

Zhou, Shaoliang, ed. 1955. *Dunhuang bianwen huilu* [Collection of Dunhuang Lyrics]. Shanghai: Shanghai Chuban Gongsi.

Zhou, Shihui. 2009. *Qinqu geci yanjiu* [A Study of the Lyrics of Qin Music]. Beijing: Peking University Press.

Zhou, Yibai. 1975. *Zhongguo xiqu fazhan shi* [A History of the Development of Chinese Theater]. Taipei: Minmian Chubanshe.

_____. 1979. *Zhongguo xiqu fazhan shigang* [A Brief History of the Development of Chinese Theater]. Shanghai: Guji.

Zhou, Zian. 1722, 2000. Wuzhi Zhai Qinpu [Wuzhi Zhai Qin Music]. Beijing: Zhonghua Shuju.

Zhou, Zumo. 2000. *Wenzi yinyun xungu lunji* [Studies on the Practice of Word Pronunciations and Rhythms]. Beijing: Peking University Press

_____. 2001. *Zhou Zumo yuyanxue lunwen ji* [Zhou Zumo's Essays on Linguistics]. Beijing, Shangwu.

_____. 2004. *Zhou Zumo wenzi yinyun xungu jiangyi.* [Zhou Zumo's Lectures on Pronunciation, Rhythm, and Studies of Words]. Tianjin: Guji.

Zhu, Changwen. 2001. *Qin shi* [Qin History]. Haikou: Hainan Chubanshe.

Zhu, Fengjie. 1995. *Yugu Zhai Qinpu* [Yugu Zhai Qin Music]. Shanghai: Guji.

Zhu, Guangqian. 1982. *Zhu Guangqian mei xue wen ji* [Zhu Guangqian on Aesthetics]. 5 vols. Shanghai: Shanghai Wenyi Chubanshe.

_____. 1984. *Shi lun* [Analyze Poetry]. Beijing: Sanlian.

Zhu, Houjue. 2006. *Feng xuan xuan pin* [Qin Music]. Beijing: Zhongguo Shuju.

Zhu, Jiajin, and Ding Ruqin. 2007. *Qingdai neiting yanju shimo kao* [The Beginning and the End of Theater in the Qing Inner Court]. Beijing: Zhongguo Shudian.

Zhu, Minshen. 1999. *Shuowen Jiezi yu Zhongguo guwenzi xue* [*Shuowen Jiezi* and Chinese Ancient Linguistics]. Shanghai: Fudan University Press.

Zhu, Qianzhi. 1989. *Zhongguo yin yue wen xue shi* [A History of Chinese Literature on Music]. Shanghai: Shanghai Shudian.

Zhu, Quan, ed. 1425, 2001. *Shen qi mi pu* [Secret Scour of Magical Music]. Beijing: Zhongguo Shudian.

Zhu, Wenwei, and Lu Qichang. 1994. *Xian Qin yuezhong zhi yanjiu* [Studies of pre–Qin Music Bells]. Taibei: Nantian Shuju.

Zhu, Xi, ed. 2001. *Chuci jizhu* [A Collection of Chuci with Commentaries]. Shanghai: Guji Chubanshe.

Zhu, Yian. 1996. *Tangshi yu yinyue* [Tang Poetry and Music].Guilin: Lijiang Chubanshe.

Zhu, Zhiping. 2005. *Hanyu shuangyin fuheci shuxing yan jiu* [A Study of the Tendency of Double Syllable Combined Words in Chinese]. Beijing: Peking University Press.

Zou, Changlin. 2000. *Zhongguo li wenhua* [Ritual Culture of China]. Beijing: Shehui Kexue Wenxian Chubanshe.

Zufferey, N. 2003. *To the Origins of Confucianism: The "Ru" in Pre-Qin Times and During the Early Han Dynasty.* New York: Peter Lang.

Index